a1

The Beatles
and the Historians

*An Analysis of Writings
About the Fab Four*

ERIN TORKELSON WEBER

McFarland & Company, Inc., Publishers
Jefferson, North Carolina

Library of Congress Cataloguing-in-Publication Data

Names: Weber, Erin Torkelson.
Title: The Beatles and the historians : an analysis of
writings about the Fab Four / Erin Torkelson Weber.
Description: Jefferson, North Carolina : McFarland & Company,
2016. | Includes bibliographical references and index.
Identifiers: LCCN 2016011760 | ISBN 9781476662664
(softcover : acid free paper) ∞
Subjects: LCSH: Beatles—Historiography.
Classification: LCC ML421.B4 W4 2016 | DDC 782.42166092/2—dc23
LC record available at http://lccn.loc.gov/2016011760

British Library cataloguing data are available

ISBN (print) 978-1-4766-6266-4
ISBN (ebook) 978-1-4766-2470-9

Front cover: The Beatles, 1962 (Photofest)

Printed in the United States of America

McFarland & Company, Inc., Publishers
Box 611, Jefferson, North Carolina 28640
www.mcfarlandpub.com

For my parents, Ray and Liana,
and for my husband, Scott.

Acknowledgments

To Cheryl Golden, without whose guidance, encouragement and instruction this book would not have been written. For guiding me through every step, and introducing me to so many others who helped along the way.

To Michael Austin, for examining my first chapter, and for his information on publishing practices, recommendations, and suggestions.

To B. Lee Cooper, for reading and reviewing all the chapters, as well as his recommendations and guidance.

To Jeremy Rosell, my first reader.

To Del Torkelson, for his editing and suggestions.

To the friends who helped make this possible, including Jill, Chad, and Louise.

Table of Contents

Preface

The Beatles and the Historians provides a historian's analysis of the Beatles story from 1962 to the present day. The book employs historical methods and source analysis to explain the various narratives that have developed from the inception of the group and throughout Beatles' history. It tells the familiar story of the Beatles in an unprecedented way by applying the tools of legitimate history to one of the most popular phenomena of the twentieth century. Primary and secondary sources including movies, interviews and individual and group biographies are analyzed to determine their authenticity, credibility, and influence on Beatles history. Efforts by members of the group and the rock press to shape the historical narrative and the politics of the time are also discussed. The book explores three major themes: Beatles' history and its major debates; the use of historical methods to analyze the sources that have been used to write that history, and the historiography of the group: How their story has been told over time.

Hundreds of books have been written about the Beatles, widely regarded as one of the most important cultural icons of the 20th century, but few authors have applied credible source analysis to their research. Many Beatles books claim to be definitive histories, but almost all fail to meet the standards of legitimate history. Despite the large amount of both popular and academic Beatles scholarship, no previous works have evaluated the various narratives which emerged throughout Beatles history or applied historical methods or historiographical analysis to the subject. This book uses a historian's methodology to separate fact from mythology and provides in-text examples of source analysis, the application of historical methods, and the historiography of a popular, contemporary subject.

In addition to exploring the Beatles from a new perspective, this book offers a new way to look at historiography, which tends to concentrate on military or diplomatic topics, rather than cultural subjects. As a result historical methods analysis of popular media has not been as thoroughly examined. In contrast, this book concentrates on the popular press's role in crafting

1

narratives, and provides extensive analysis of numerous mass-media sources. More recent books on historiography such as John Lewis Gaddis's *The Landscape of History* have provided information on the traditional standards used in historiographical analysis, but this book differs by applying those standards directly to a specific, modern and very media-saturated topic.

This is not a history or biography of the Beatles, or an analysis of the band's music. Although some of the work's source analysis contains evaluations similar to those provided in Michael Brocken and Melissa Davis's invaluable *The Beatles Bibliography: A New Guide to the Literature* (the only major work in Beatles historiography which contains serious source analysis), this book is not, like Brocken and Davis's work, an annotated bibliography. While *The Beatles Bibliography* contains assessments of primary and secondary sources and, at times, offers conclusions regarding their overall credibility and accuracy, it does not apply historical methodology to the sources, place them in their respective narratives, or examine the arc of Beatles historiography as a whole. In contrast, the present work, *The Beatles and the Historians,* applies historical methods in-text to a topic of continuing popularity and growing academic importance.

This study blends the three subjects—the Beatles, historiography, and historical methods—by employing essential works on historical methods and historiography to examine the most influential sources concerning the Beatles. Works such as Gilbert Garraghan's *A Guide to Historical Method* and James D. Startt's *Historical Methods in Mass Communication* are used to evaluate the major sources. March Bloch's *The Historian's Craft* and John Lewis Gaddis's *The Landscape of History*, among others, provide guidance in evaluating the patterns of Beatles historiography. Determining which Beatles sources were influential enough to merit source analysis involved a number of factors, including how well the book sold, its critical reputation both when it was published and decades later, the amount of original research it contained, its role in shaping or diverging from the prevailing narrative, and its imprint on successive works. The most important works of every narrative are examined, such as *The Beatles: The Authorized Biography, Lennon Remembers, Shout!, Many Years from Now, Revolution in the Head, The Complete Beatles Recording Sessions,* and others.

These historical methods, historiography and Beatles sources are used to examine the four major narratives that make up Beatles historiography. Chapter One, "The Fab Four Narrative," covers the officially approved version of the Beatles story, which lasted from 1962 until 1970. Chapter Two discusses the *Lennon Remembers* narrative, which lasted from 1970 through 1980, rejected its predecessor's major narrative components and saw the emergence of Beatles historiography's two most contentious debates. Chapter Three, "The *Shout!* Narrative," explores how, in the wake of John Lennon's murder in December 1980, extremely influential yet methodologically flawed secondary works concretized a partisan, incomplete version of the Beatles story. Chapter Four, "The Lewisohn Narrative," examines how the emergence of previously unavailable primary sources, the essential quality of historical distance, and improved methodology resulted in a new Orthodoxy.

For Beatles fans, this book provides an original way to look at the band's story which, for more than 50 years, has become enmeshed in myth. For students of historical methods and historiography, the book offers an in-depth exploration of a previously unexplored but fascinating topic. By focusing on a modern subject, the work provides examples of how to apply source analysis not only to traditional sources such as government documents and diary entries, but also to the thousands of mass-media messages that shape and influence current historiography even as it unfolds.

Introduction

The Beatles and History

In the fifty years since the Beatles first conquered Britain, America and then the world, there have been hundreds of books and countless articles written about the band. Fierce, informed and sometimes partisan debates are waged by fans on various internet forums. Movies, documentaries and merchandise continue to find an eager audience. Their music and their mystique continue to sell. The world finds the Beatles endlessly fascinating.

This fascination extends beyond the band's songs, largely regarded as some of the most beloved and influential of the 20th century, to individual members of the Beatles and the group as a whole. Their story has been told countless times over the last five decades: In individual and group biographies, in magazines and movies, by journalists, musicologists and by the Beatles themselves. These works have produced popular but sometimes contradictory versions of Beatles history. In fifty years, four major and, in some cases, contradictory narratives have dominated Beatles historiography.

Historiography—the study of the way history has been and is written—is necessary to understanding any major historical event or cultural phenomenon, whether it is African American slavery in the antebellum South, the causes of World War I, or the Beatles, one of the great cultural icons of the 20th century. In fifty years, the Beatles have amassed one of the largest historiographies of any cultural subject, and certainly the largest of any musical group. It is time—past time—for these works to be examined using the same historical methods and standards that are applied to the letters of Winston Churchill, the slave narratives of the Works Progress Administration, or the letters of Cicero.

In some ways, the Beatles' story fits perfectly into the historiographical pattern. In others, it breaks new, more modern ground. The Beatles promoted an official story that, while leaving a powerful imprint, suffered from obvious bias and self-promotion, as all official versions do. This official narrative publicly and abruptly collapsed, leaving a vacuum. The version that followed depended heavily on primary sources but, like many early narratives, relied on incomplete information and was, in many cases, partisan and incorrect. Eventually secondary sources began to insert themselves into and direct the narrative, and while they claimed impartiality, many of them lacked historical distance, demonstrating noticeable biases and methodological errors. Once an adequate amount of time had passed, and previously unreleased, overlooked or unavailable primary sources became available, a new, more methodologically sound narrative emerged challenging the prevailing Orthodoxy that had dominated ever since the band's breakup.

Issues in Beatles Historiography

Each camp in Beatles historiography has accused the other of revisionism. Yet revisionism is a part of historiography, and simply because a narrative has been revised does not mean that the new, revised version is incorrect. In historiography, official narratives are inherently suspect and early narratives are always incomplete and often incorrect. Condemning later narratives simply because they did not come first excludes sources and perspectives essential to understanding the truth of the subject. Without revisionism and evolving and changing narratives, we would still teach students that slavery in the antebellum American South was a relatively benign institution that cost slave owners more than it profited them, or that sole responsibility for the outbreak of World War I should rest on Germany's shoulders.

Those who have read previous Beatles works will know that the majority of the books, articles, and other materials about the band have been written not by historians, but by journalists. There are some who may consider it unfair to judge journalists by historian's standards. But in a century or two, when people are still reading about the Beatles and studying their music, their artistry, their dynamic and their cultural impact, the historical methods employed in this book *now* are the same standards that will be used to judge the sources *then*.

Beatles historiography presents some unique challenges for anyone trained in the traditional historical method. What historian Marc Bloch regards as the most credible of primary sources—those intended for private use, rather than public consumption—are minimal in number. From 1962 on, the Beatles and those around them were involved in selling their own version of events. The documents and primary sources available, particularly those from the era around the group's breakup, display significant agendas.

Those rare documents not intended for public use that do exist are held in private collections, rather than government archives and are inaccessible to all but a very select few. However, the overall number of available primary and secondary sources number in the thousands.

Just as there is a glut of written source material, there is also no shortage of physical evidence, or relics. After the Beatles spent a night in a hotel, the very sheets they slept on were stripped from their beds, ripped into patches, and sold to eager fans as souvenirs, echoing the scramble for saintly relics in the Middle Ages. Those dirty sheets are just one example of the thousands of Beatles souvenirs that exist today, available anywhere from eBay to the British Museum. Some items have been lost, others stolen, but thousands remain.

Unlike in diplomatic or military history, in Beatles history there are no warring or even allied nations, viewing the same battle through vastly different eyes and attempting to sell victory or defeat to the general population. (There are, however, camps in Beatles historiography). The conventional primary sources of modern historical methods—the diplomatic cables, private correspondence and political speeches—are largely absent. Instead, we have perhaps the first major historiography primarily shaped by the popular media, rather than the government, the church or historians.

Many of the secondary works, written primarily by journalists, contain no citations, documentation or bibliographies. In Beatles studies, there are no peer reviewed academic journals; most book reviews were originally printed in popular periodicals. Numerous works incorporate facts into the narrative without citing sources, identifying the author of a quote, or separating authorial opinion from evidence. Some works in Beatles historiography could be best identified as historical fiction: compelling, dramatic and well written stories based on true events but which ultimately fail as credible accounts according to the historical method. Others invent dialogue and recount scenes that the writer never witnessed, or describe word for word the inner thoughts and feelings of the principle figures without identifying them as authorial speculation. Many fail to meet one of the fundamental requirements of legitimate history: "We have no right to make any assertion which cannot be verified."[1]

While the Beatles themselves consisted of four individuals: John Lennon, Paul McCartney, George Harrison, and Ringo Starr, the amount of attention each individual Beatle has received from writers has been unequal. Most of the books, articles, movies and other materials have focused on the group's major songwriters, Lennon and McCartney, to the detriment of a greater understanding of Harrison and Starr. This concentration on Lennon and

McCartney ensures there are many unexplored issues involving Harrison and Starr's roles in the Beatles, and prevents a greater knowledge of the group's overall dynamic. Because the majority of Beatles writing focuses on the key figures of Lennon and McCartney, this analysis of Beatles historiography also follows that pattern.

Many of the most influential sources in Beatles history were written without adequate historical distance, yet their story has been chronicled so extensively that historiographical analysis is necessary. It has been approximately sixty years since John Lennon met Paul McCartney at a church festival, fifty since the Beatles "invaded" and conquered America, forty-five since the band broke up and thirty-five since John Lennon's murder. Two Beatles, McCartney and Starr, are still alive, allowing for what John Lewis Gaddis described in *The Landscape of History* as the "nightmare that haunts historians," where the biographical subject returns "like Hamlet's ghost, to let us know what they think of what we've written."[2] At various points all four Beatles disputed secondary accounts of their lives, characters and work, to little avail.

Access to the major figures, including but not limited to Lennon, McCartney, Harrison and Starr, has been and is still highly coveted by those attempting to tell their story. Numerous writers have rewarded access to the key figures, usually provided in the form of interviews or access to private archives, with favorable and sympathetic portrayals in their work. Those figures which have refused biographer's interviews are often described in more negative terms.

Many "facts" were never verified. However, they were repeated in biography after biography and from narrative to narrative until they became accepted wisdom. Some of the primary sources suffer from credibility issues as well: the Beatles admitted to lying in interviews and inventing stories, not only to sell their records or particular agendas but also simply to distract themselves from the tedium of endless interviews and press conferences. During their careers all four Beatles used heavy drugs, including cocaine, LSD and heroin. How those drugs may have affected the accuracy of their statements, interviews and writings (the primary sources used by Beatles biographers) have never been fully discussed. Likewise, the impact of drugs on their behavior and the decisions they made, particularly during the band's breakup, has never been properly analyzed.

Numerous Beatles authors also apply a blatant moral double standard: absolving or omitting the character and musical flaws of their favorite Beatle while emphasizing or inventing those of the group's other members. While rendering moral judgment on historical figures is one that historians themselves disagree on—Bloch argues against it, Gaddis favors it—all agree that when such judgments are applied, they should be done impartially and apply equally to all figures. In sources and narratives across Beatles historiography, this essential fairness is lacking.

In addition, issues of authorial agenda and bias have never been properly addressed. Certain works that are widely viewed as biased still receive high critical regard. While some authors acknowledge the value of primary sources over secondary sources in their research, very few have analyzed either category of sources for credibility, agenda, or verification. Hearsay and unverified testimony is often misrepresented as fact. The purpose and agenda behind primary sources is rarely mentioned or analyzed when the material is recounted in secondary sources. Essentially, analyzing the credibility of primary and secondary sources is almost nonexistent.

Though the Beatles, their music and their story hold mass appeal for a large and diverse audience, their historiography has been dominated by a very narrow demographic of writers. Almost without exception, both the official version and later narratives were constructed by male British or American journalists. The majority of these are rock and roll, music or cultural journalists. A number of musicologists have also analyzed and evaluated the Beatles' work. Few of these writers are professional researchers, and almost all are either members of the Beatles' own generation or the generation immediately following.

There are valid reasons for portraying the group from this perspective. The Beatles themselves were all male, as were all the key members of their inner circle—Brian Epstein, George Martin, Mal Evans, and Neil Aspinall, among others. Their story is a patriarchal one, where the two most important females (prior to the arrivals of Yoko Ono and Linda Eastman) are Mary McCartney and Julia Lennon, most notable for the influence their early deaths had on each of their son's lives.[3] Journalists were able to gain access to the band or members of the inner circle on a far more regular basis than any other profession, and were privy to information that was largely unavailable to others.

But authoritative appreciation for the Beatles' music and their story is not and should not be restricted to male writers of a certain generation or particular profession. A diversity of authors, providing varying perspectives, is a strength that Beatles historiography sorely lacks. In addition, due to the generational issue, many Beatles writers find themselves unable to separate the personal from the professional, recounting vividly the first time they scoured the cover of *Sgt. Pepper* in the summer of 1967, or where they were when they first heard of the group's breakup, or Lennon's death. These memories add a valuable personal perspective to their work. However, the whole of Beatles historiography suffers because, so far, the personal perspective has been virtually the *only* perspective, and many of the premier secondary works of Beatles historiography lack adequate historical distance.

The Great Debates in Beatles Historiography

The great debate of modern historians—"Who is to blame for the outbreak of World War I?"—is a contentious and never ending argument waged by scholars in history journals, articles and books. The conflict between the official narrative—it was solely Germany's fault—and later narratives blaming Russia, France, imperialism, and the alliance system still provoke impassioned arguments from historians. This debate helps make World War I such a compelling subject, for both historians and historiographers.

Two major debates have been waged throughout Beatles historiography. Both emerged upon the death of the official narrative in 1970–1971; both are due to the bitter and public nature of the band's breakup. The first debate concerns the issue of genius, and who should get the label. The genius of the whole of the Beatles' work is never seriously doubted or disputed. It is the efforts by biographers to crown one particular individual within the group, usually Lennon or McCartney, as the sole or greater genius that provokes the fiercest arguments. Some authors go so far as to identify themselves as belonging to either a Lennon camp or a McCartney camp, slanting much of their work and choosing their evidence accordingly.

The other conflict concerns the group's dissolution. Much like the question surrounding the Great War, the debate revolves around blame: Who was responsible for the end of the world's most beloved band? Unsurprisingly, authorial agenda plays a significant role in the answer, with each camp attempting to blame the other.

Intertwined but unacknowledged between these two debates is the subjectivity of music, and the tenuous authority of writers, particularly those with no musical training, to bestow or withhold the title of genius on musicians. The credentials of those determining whether a particular song or album is genius or mediocre vary wildly across the spectrum of Beatles writing, yet this issue is never addressed. Musicologists such as Wilfrid Mellers or Ian MacDonald bring a more informed but still subjective ear to the endless evaluations of the Beatles' music, and disagree on the beauty and power of certain songs.

An example of this inconsistency is seen in the wildly diverse opinions on *Lady Madonna*, a single written by McCartney and released by the Beatles in 1968. In his 2008 biography of Lennon, author Philip Norman finds "Lady Madonna's" lyrical depth nonexistent, dismissing it as a song about "a sluttish earth mother's laddered tights,"[4] and Jonathan Gould finds it "powerful yet willfully inconsequential."[5] By contrast Mark Lewisohn, in *The Complete Beatles Recording Sessions*, describes it as "a terrific single, curiously overlooked today by those analyzing the group's output."[6] In 1995 musician and writer Mark Hertsgaard argued "Lady Madonna's" lyrics "express a sympathy and empathy for the harried, economically trying life of single mothers."[7] Beatles insider Tony Bramwell argues that the song was inspired by McCartney's mother, Mary, who died when the songwriter was 14. McCartney himself describes the song as "a tribute to the mother figure."[8]

Much of "Lady Madonna's" ultimate value appears to depend on the eye of the beholder, or, in this case, the ear of the listener. Yet the subjectivity of personal opinion is never addressed; neither are the authorial agendas of the writers. Historians have argued before over whether the title of genius is deserved: Was Ulysses S. Grant a strategic military genius, or a butcher? For decades the answer depended, in part, whether the historian asking the question lived north or south of the Mason-Dixon line. However, such debates have been based on quantifiable evidence: casualties, battle terrain, logistics, victories or losses. One of the greatest debates in Beatles historiography concerns the issue of genius: Was the greater genius Lennon, or McCartney? Or were they equal talents? One writer declares that the sole genius, inarguably, is Lennon. Another champions McCartney; neither questions their authority to unilaterally dispense the title.

The Historical Method, the Beatles and The Beatles and the Historians

The purpose behind this book and this introduction is not to condemn Beatles historiography, which has produced some essential and exhaustively researched accounts of an undeniably fascinating story. Instead, the goal is to discuss the differing narratives that have attempted to tell that story, why they emerged, and determine which narrative best employs historical methodology. Traditional methods of the historical method are used, including source criticism: When and where was the source produced? Who produced it? Does it retain its original integrity? Is the source credible? What was the author's agenda in writing it? How close in time was the source to the event? These standards are applied to both primary and secondary sources and discussed within the overall context of Beatles historiography.

Likewise, when there are contradictory sources, the typical procedure will be used: If all sources agree on an event, it will be considered proved. Eyewitness testimony that lacks verification from other, independent sources will be regarded as valuable but not unquestionable. However, eyewitness testimony will be granted more weight than secondhand accounts or hearsay. When two sources disagree and all means of assessment have been exhausted, the source which best accords with rational thinking will be considered the more accurate one. In determining the reliability of evidence, both primary and secondary sources will be evaluated by the same standards: evidence of bias, the possibility of forged or corrupted sources, and the influence of authorial agenda, among other rules. How the politics of the times affected the prevailing narratives is also discussed.

This book includes both historiographical and historical methods analysis, and much of the historical analysis is heavily influenced and guided by Marc Bloch's *The Historian's Craft*, Mark T. Gilderhus's work *History and Historians: A Historiographical Introduction*, James Startt's *Historical Methods in Mass Communication*, Gilbert J. Garraghan's *A Guide to Historical Method*, and John Lewis Gaddis' *How Historians Map the Past,* among others.

Those thousands of books about the Beatles have produced a fascinating, compelling story with contradictory narratives, and have created a body of work that merits historiographical analysis. My hope is that this study of the historiography of the Beatles will provide new insights not only into the group but also into those who have chronicled that story. It will also provide an accessible examination of historiography and historical methods by concentrating on a more modern and cultural topic, the Beatles, than is typical of most historiography studies. By the end, I hope you will agree with me that the historiography of the Beatles—how their story has been and is *still* being written—is as dramatic, controversial, and compelling as the Beatles story itself.[9]

CHAPTER ONE

The Fab Four Narrative

History has to do with beings who are, by nature, capable of pursuing conscious ends.
　　　　　　　　　　—Marc Bloch, *The Historian's Craft*

Separating Fact from Mythology

The story endured for decades. It began in Liverpool, a Northern English port city under attack by the German *Luftwaffe* in the fall of 1940. In it Mimi Smith, a young middle-class woman, dodged bombs amid the din of air raid sirens in order to reach the hospital and meet her newborn nephew John Winston Lennon. Smith—who raised her nephew—recounted the harrowing story to Hunter Davies, the official Beatles biographer, in 1966. Smith's account of her famous nephew's birth became part of the Beatles' legend. It was repeated in newspaper articles, biographies of Lennon's life, and the obituaries that followed his sudden, violent murder. This one dramatic story encapsulated two of the most important facts about the four men who became the Beatles: John Lennon, Paul McCartney, George Harrison and Ringo Starr were war babies, and they were born and raised in Liverpool, a port city in Northern England. That Lennon, who later in life became a peace advocate, was born during an air raid added one more piece to the Beatles' mythology.

There was no reason for Davies to question Smith's account of Lennon's birth. Liverpool, a strategically valuable port city, was one of the *Luftwaffe*'s primary targets during the Battle of Britain and endured repeated bombings after August 1940. Smith's credibility as an eyewitness was also excellent. She recounted the story in a direct interview with Davies, conducted for the purpose of the group's authorized biography, and had no obvious reason to lie. Davies accepted her testimony, and Smith's dramatic story of Lennon's birth became one of the first facts to which a reader was introduced to in any biography of the Beatles.[1]

Despite its prevalence, the legend was not true. Lennon's birth date— October 9, 1940—was well known, but it took decades until a single researcher went back through old wartime copies of the *Liverpool Echo*—the city's major newspaper—and discovered that the night of Lennon's birth had been quiet: there were no air raids or sirens as Julia Lennon was giving birth to her first child. Later biographers of Lennon and the Beatles acknowledged the existence of Smith's story and then dismissed it as inaccurate, moving on to recount more parts of the Beatles' myth, which contained many other unverified "facts." Few Beatles biographers grasped the essential lesson exemplified in Mimi Smith's fictitious account: in recounting history all evidence, including direct eyewitness testimony requires analysis and, if necassary, independent verification.

Preeminent Beatles scholar Mark Lewisohn acknowledged this fundamental requirement in his essential reference book, *The Beatles Live!* In the book's introduction, Lewisohn criticizes previous works that claimed to tell the band's history: "They almost all share in a fundamental lack of care in the accuracy department, and often show little or no 'research' beyond the borrowing of 'facts' from other incorrect books."[2] The band's producer, George Martin, declared that most studies about the group contained a great deal of "misinformed rubbish" that had nonetheless been "avidly devoured."[3] In his biography *A Day in the Life*, Beatles author Mark Hertsgaard identifies some major flaws of Beatles historiography.

> Many authors of Beatles books use technically factual evidence in misleading ways—for example, by quoting a source who supports the author's point of view while ignoring countervailing evidence, or by presenting one source's perspective on a given event or situation as the truth … when in fact it was just one person's opinion about it. Standards of proof have, in short, been appallingly low.[4]

Although many works on the Beatles claim to be definitive, accurate histories, very few demonstrate sound research methods. These methods, which historians such as Leopold Von Ranke and Marc Bloch have developed over centuries, are essential to producing legitimate, enduring historical writing. For decades, journalists accepted primary sources' testimony without properly examining it for agenda or accuracy, which allowed inaccurate information to be copied from book to book until it became accepted wisdom. Many of those "facts" introduced in the official narrative were never verified but recycled from biography to biography and narrative to narrative, influencing every successive version of the Beatles story. In his book *A Guide to Historical Method*, Gilbert J. Garraghan describes the consequences of failing to properly analyze evidence: "A person without proper criteria for evaluating the information that reaches him from the outside runs the risk of a thousand deceptions and errors."[5] Bloch, one of the most influential historians of the 20th century, emphasizes how a few errors produce more errors in order to justify themselves: "By its very nature, one fraud begets another."[6] Because so many works on the Beatles fail to apply historical methods they muddle history with myth by presenting verified facts, hearsay, unverified testimony, personal opinion and authorial speculation as equally credible. As a consequence of this, much of what has been regarded for decades as Beatles "history" is instead, by definition, myth, "an account of any kind which purports to be historical but is really fictitious, wholly or in part."[7]

The story of the Beatles—the 20th century's most popular and critically acclaimed rock and roll band—has become enmeshed in myth. At times deliberately engineered, the Beatles' mythology was an inextricable part of their historiography dating back to the very beginning of their fame. It started with the first interviews the group gave on the cusp of stardom in late 1962. From the date that 16-year-old John Lennon met 15-year-old Paul McCartney (a date now literally *chiseled in stone* on the wall of the building where the two officially first met) to the deaths of Lennon and Harrison, it has taken decades for Beatles writers and researchers to begin to separate the facts from the mythology.

These efforts to distinguish truth from legend are complicated for a number of reasons. The official mythology of the Beatles was both deliberately engineered and, like the band's music, almost universally popular. This powerful official mythology is the first major narrative in Beatles historiography. From 1962 until their public dissolution in 1970, the Beatles promoted a singular version of their story which consisted of three major themes. First, they depicted themselves as an indivisible unit of four best friends. Until 1969, band members dismissed any accounts of serious tensions. The message of unity, despite the widely varying personalities within the group, was emphasized in articles and interviews, biographies and movies. Second, during the official era, the group whitewashed certain aspects of its story and, especially during the early years, publicly and repeatedly dismissed the very real frustrations associated with their fans and unparalleled fame. During their touring years, all four members strove to present an acceptable, marketable image that suppressed the more negative aspects of their lives. The third major component of the Fab Four narrative was its promotion of the Lennon/McCartney songwriting partnership. Lennon and McCartney—as well as other members of the Beatles circle—emphasized the unprecedented collaborative nature of the partnership that produced most of the Beatles' greatest songs. The initial version presented Lennon and McCartney as a unit of equally talented, collaborative songwriters who worked together to create a catalog attributed to both men.

Lennon and McCartney's roles as the primary songwriters and dominant personalities resulted in another, longstanding impact on Beatles historiography. While both lead guitarist George Harrison and drummer Ringo Starr were very popular in the official narrative and were accorded varying degrees of respect as musicians and eventually as songwriters, the Fab Four version of the Beatles story, including press and biographical coverage, concentrated primarily on Lennon and McCartney. This tendency only increased in later narratives, inaccurately diminishing Harrison and Starr's contributions. As a result, very few works in Beatles historiography devote as much time, analysis, and research to Harrison and Starr as Lennon and McCartney. Starting with the official version and continuing into every successive narrative, the creative and personal relationship between Lennon and McCartney is the axis around which Beatles history revolves.

Whitewashing the Official Narrative: No Sex or Drugs, and Some Rock and Roll

The beloved, "moptop" image of the Fab Four narrative resulted from a number of factors and promoters. Each of the individual Beatles played a role in creating and sustaining it, as did their manager Brian Epstein and other members of the Beatles' inner circle. The worldwide press and popular opinion also contributed. For much of their existence as a functioning band, the Beatles were viewed as untouchable. The press withheld unpleasant, unapproved knowledge in exchange for access to the band and the perks provided by that access.[8] The public, for the most part, approved of the beloved official version and did not wish to see it contradicted.

> It was almost as if the media and the general public sought to turn their beloved "moptops" into pets. The result was a whitewash of epic proportions. Throughout the age of Beatlemania, the press never let slip a word about the Beatles' promiscuous sex lives, or their predilection for pills, marijuana and (later) LSD—despite the fact that these Fab peccadilloes were common knowledge among the journalists who followed them around the globe. Even when certain details of their checkered past did emerge in print ... it hardly mattered anymore; people were sure to find excuses for "their" Beatles, and forget all about the offending incident.[9]

Certain facts regarding the band or the individuals within the group were dismissed, ignored or overlooked. Knowledge of Epstein's homosexuality, Lennon's occasional acts of violence, several paternity claims filed against McCartney[10] or the Beatles' drug use—elements that contradicted the more sanitized, official version—were suppressed for years.

The two topics most commonly censored by the press were the Beatles' sexual promiscuity, particularly on tour, and their drug use. In 1970, four years after the group stopped touring, Lennon famously compared the band's sexual exploits to Fredrico Fellini's orgiastic movie *Satyricon*.[11] While other Beatles insiders have since declared that Lennon's description was somewhat exaggerated, the complete absence of any mention of sex in contemporaneous press accounts cannot be regarded as anything but an attempt to protect the Beatles' popular reputations and preserve the official narrative. In 1964, segments of the press were scandalized when McCartney and Starr vacationed together with their girlfriends: Epstein mentioned the associated furor in his book *A Cellarful of Noise*. The press storm prompted by this rather tame story, however, was one of the few Beatlemania era stories that hinted at the subject of sex. Until Lennon began his public relationship with Yoko Ono in 1968, "the group's public image remained impeccable."[12] Likewise, no one mentioned their increasing drug use, even as they progressed from speed to pot to LSD, cocaine and, in Lennon's case, heroin. Only in 1967, when McCartney publicly admitted to having used LSD, did the press broach the issue. Numerous other pieces of information were omitted or altered to fit the prevailing narrative. Epstein initially suppressed knowledge of the existence of Cynthia, Lennon's first wife, in order to ensure that all the Beatles appeared "available" to their female fans. Discussions about revealing Epstein's homosexuality in the group's official biography were rejected at the request of Epstein's mother after his death. Lennon's severe beating of Liverpool disc jockey Bob Wooler at McCartney's 21st birthday party in June 1963 was expertly spun by the group's press representative and Epstein and the press at the time quickly forgot it.

This whitewashing contributed to a triumphant commercial success; by the end of 1964 the Beatles were the world's most popular band, propelled primarily by their music but also in part by their fresh, charming and clever image. Michael Braun, who wrote the first book on the group, described the popular British perception of the group in 1964 as "four local lads with funny but acceptable haircuts" and described them as "clean, adorable, cheeky."[13] Ironically, part of their appeal was their candid view of the music business. The Beatles bluntly acknowledged that wealth was very important to them. They also criticized mainstream British acts for not being honest about their lives and rebelled against the manufactured image of most pop stars, mocking their claims that "so and so doesn't drink, doesn't smoke, doesn't go out late."[14]

The prevailing view of the Beatles as clean and lovable continued for years, faltering at only a few key points during the official narrative until their public breakup.

Deliberately constructing this image required cooperation from the press, which either chose not to reveal unapproved information or simply accepted the Beatles' version of the facts. Lewisohn acknowledged this weakness in Beatles history: "Reportage of the group's background and success began to go awry in the very early days of the Beatles fame, often—with reason—fuelled by the Beatles' or their aides themselves, and it has not stopped to his day."[15] This manipulation of facts in service of a commercial image is one that is not unique to the Beatles, but common practice within the music business. Every band that was a contemporary of the Beatles underwent a transformation. However, because of the importance, depth and endurance of Beatles historiography, these initial manipulations of the facts skewed the Beatles' depiction for decades. Once a piece of information became part of the accepted wisdom it proved very difficult to dislodge. One of the most remarkable aspects of the Beatles' mythology is how quickly and coherently it formed, obscuring history in the wake of fame and legend. By the end of 1964, when the Beatles had conquered Britain and America, the cheeky mop-top image already was cemented in the cultural consciousness. Parts of the image remained even as time passed and the Beatles attempted to distance themselves from the Fab Four personae. Band members' deliberate efforts to change the world's initial perception of them—through drug references, controversial political and religious statements, and musical experimentation—met with varying degrees of success. In September 1967, four months after the group released *Sgt. Pepper's Lonely Hearts Club Band*—an album intended to bury their Beatlemania image—*Time* magazine still applauded the band's "good humor" and "exemplary behavior."[16]

Establishing and maintaining this image and their popularity required the Beatles to repeatedly sugarcoat, omit, or lie in interviews. Lennon admitted as much in the group's official biography, published in 1968: "Our image was only a teeny part of us. It was created by the press and by us. It had to be wrong because you can't put over how you really are. Newspapers always get things wrong."[17] Throughout their touring years, the Beatles' press conferences included constant assurances that they did not mind their frantic touring schedule, lack of privacy, endless interviews or deafening fans' screams at concerts. In 1963, Harrison told reporters "We don't have a private life anymore ... we're public property now. Not that we mind ... you get accustomed to it."[18] These reassurances grew progressively more fictitious with every press conference. Privately, Harrison and Lennon despised touring well before the group stopped in 1966.[19] As their unprecedented fame grew, their feelings towards it and their fans became increasingly mixed.[20] According to Lennon's lifelong friend Pete Shotton, throughout much of the Beatles fame, Lennon "viewed his fans ... as little more than a mob of shrieking idiots."[21] During the 1990s, Harrison described their relationship with fans as "a very one-sided love affair."[22] Decades later Martin, who at times accompanied the group on tour, defended their increasingly wary response to their fans and fame. "Royalty are trained from birth to cope with that sort of thing; the Beatles were not. They can hardly be blamed for wanting to put up a barrier against the world."[23] Martin also rejected the official, more romanticized versions of the Beatles story. "Make no mistake about their lives then; there was little glamour in their goldfish bowl, and far too many demands were made on them."[24]

Beatles publicist Tony Barrow, who traveled with them on tour, describes the typical danger, claustrophobia and boredom; the endless poker sessions, bad food, and invasive and delusional fans.[25] Another insider, Nat Weiss, recalls McCartney vomiting over the stress of a concert whose postponement almost resulted in a fan riot: "He was throwing up with all this tension."[26] Despite this reality, only once during the official narrative did the band denounce a touring experience; harshly criticizing their treatment at the hands of authorities in the Philippines after their disastrous 1966 trip there led to the band being pummeled in the airport up to the minute they boarded the plane to leave. Even under the cloud of death threats the group faced after Lennon's famous "bigger than Jesus" interview stirred a firestorm of bad publicity and violent threats in the United States, the group continued to project an image of professional calm. While parts of their Authorized Biography acknowledge their claustrophobia—"Being rich and powerful and famous enough to open any door was pointless. They were trapped"[27]—it was only after the official narrative dissolved that most primary and secondary sources presented a markedly less idealized version of their lives. Many later accounts, including retrospective descriptions by the Beatles themselves, concur with the conclusion drawn by Hertsgaard: "That the four Beatles survived with their sanity intact is wonder enough."[28] According to Harrison the four men may not have sacrificed their sanity,[29] but they came close: "The people gave their money and they gave their screams, but the Beatles gave their nervous systems, which is a much more difficult thing to give."[30]

The contrast between what the Beatles said in interviews and press conferences and what they revealed in private serves as an excellent example of why private sources retain more credibility with historians than their public counterparts. That primary sources intended for private consumption are more credible than those intended for public use is a basic law of historical methods, supported by historians from Leopold Von Ranke to Gilbert Garraghan to Marc Bloch. The obvious agenda behind the Beatles contemporary public statements—to sell their records, achieve and maintain their popularity and sustain their official mythology—does not nullify all their statements in press conferences or interviews. However, the official agenda, (as well as later testimony following the group's breakup and official narrative's dissolution) that contradicted the clean, moptop version provide convincing evidence that the Beatles were willing to whitewash their story to an extent. This self-censorship came to an abrupt end following the band's split, when the Beatles as a whole and Lennon in particular decided to de-mythologize the official narrative, but it still left a considerable impact on the Fab Four version and on Beatles history as a whole.

The Fab Four

Group unity was another of the official narrative's core messages. While the depiction of the Fab Four as an indivisible unit of four devoted friends was deliberately encouraged, both contemporary and retrospective evidence largely support this element. Most sources indicate that the emphasis on unity as depicted in the Fab Four narrative was not whitewash nor a myth but merely an oversimplified truth. The official narrative emphasized the band's friendship while glossing over the more complex inter-personal relationships among its members. At the time, this simplification obscured some of the nuances of the group's internal dynamics. With all four members invested in selling themselves as a unit, it was not until after the Beatles breakup, when the image of unity was shattered, that the members extensively discussed their one-on-one relationships. Because of this, much of the testimony concerning the band's inter-personal relations is hindsight, provided by the Beatles themselves or those insiders who knew them well during their functioning years. As secondary, retrospective accounts rather than contemporary ones, they also are influenced by the post-facto disagreements among the Beatles, and particularly between Lennon and McCartney, that accompanied the band's split.

The Fab Four narrative sold the band's friendship in interviews, movies and press conferences as enthusiastically as it did their clean image, but most evidence indicates that their affection for each other was more genuine than manufactured. The longevity of their friendships prior to fame reinforces this. Harrison and McCartney were young friends, and Lennon and McCartney swiftly became very close friends after their July 1957 introduction. In every interview and press conference across England, America and the world, all four Beatles repeatedly emphasized their genuine friendship. In 1963, it was McCartney: "We've all been mates for quite a long time, so we don't get on each other's nerves as much as we could. We're quite friendly."[31] In 1964, Harrison reinforced the message. "Our individual characteristics ... balance against one another remarkably well. It is because our personalities work at different pressures that we get on so well together as a team."[32] In a 1966 press conference in Tokyo, Lennon downplayed any conflicts within the group: "We don't have many troubles with each other, you know. And any ones that we do we talk it over."[33]

Observers also acknowledged the Beatles famous insularity, which only intensified in proportion to their fame. Even as the band outgrew its moptop personae, the contemporary depiction of the four as indivisible best friends strengthened: "Their friendship is an extraordinarily intimate and empathetic bond."[34] A 1967 article described their connection to each other: "They still have that same bond of loyalty to each other that they have always had. They are still each other's best friends. If they are asked to do something as a group and any one of them doesn't want to take part, then the scheme is dropped."[35] Many post-breakup eyewitness accounts also emphasize the group's unity and insularity. Shotton witnessed the band during its private moments and later described their interaction: "There never was, and probably never will be, a group more self-contained or tightly knit than the Beatles were in those days; the way their talents and personalities harmonized was little short of miraculous. Until about 1968 I never witnessed, or even heard about, a single serious disagreement between them."[36] Even accepted Beatles insiders such as Epstein or Martin acknowledged the barrier that divided the four men from everyone else. Decades later, Martin described the almost tangible bond between the band mates. "It was a brotherhood. It was like a fort, really, with four corners, that was impregnable. Nobody got inside that fort once they were together, not even Brian Epstein, nor I ... they had an empathy and a kind of mind-reading business."[37]

Their contemporary actions reinforce their collective identity. It was very rare for a Beatle to attempt any new undertaking without the eventual participation of the other three. When one of them became a vegetarian, the other three quickly followed suit. After Harrison became interested in Hare Krishna and Transcendental Meditation, Lennon, McCartney and Starr also followed the belief for a time.[38] Collective identity was such a strong aspect of the band's story that when its members decided to explore their own separate interests after completion of their 1966 album *Revolver* (with Lennon filming a movie, McCartney working on a film score, Harrison traveling to India) the press panicked and declared the Beatles were breaking up. A few years later, after the band *had* broken up, Lennon confided to a friend that part of the reason for its dissolution was an urge among its members for separate identities.[39]

This Fab Four version, with its emphasis on unity, abridged the more complex interaction between the individual band members. Personal relationships among the Beatles varied in a way that the official narrative never explored. All sources indicate that Starr—the last to join the band—was the one Beatle with whom all the other members had the easiest friendship. Easygoing, funny, and unburdened by a large ego, Starr's relationships with all his fellow Beatles were less complicated than their relationships with each other. Starr initially roomed with McCartney on tour and, even in the midst of the Beatles breakup (which pitted McCartney against the other three) was outspoken about his affection for the other man. In an emotional moment during a 1971 interview Starr declared "I love Paul, you know. I really do."[40] Starr's relationship with Harrison was very close. Harrison had been the key figure pushing for Starr's entry into the band, earning Starr's gratitude: according to Lewisohn they shared "a viscerally close and fundamental bond."[41] Starr regarded Lennon as a very close friend, buying a house nearby so they would be neighbors. Lennon's view of Starr, in Shotton's words, was "straightforward," perceiving the drummer as a "good natured, uncomplicated lad."[42] Davies also emphasized their bond: "John was in many ways closer to Ringo than any of the other Beatles," arguing that was, in part, because "Ringo wasn't in any way a rival—whereas Paul was as a songwriter and George was as a guitarist."[43]

Harrison's relationships with Lennon and McCartney, and theirs with him, were influenced by Harrison's age and his exclusion from the Lennon/McCartney songwriting partnership. The youngest Beatle, Harrison was nine months younger than McCartney and approximately two years younger than Lennon. While this gap mattered less as time went on, it continued to impact the men's creative and personal relationships. According to Martin, it was a source of unresolved tension between Lennon and Harrison to the end.

> George was a few, crucially spotty years younger than John…. John was condescending toward George in those early days, and this was still apparent when I first met them all … some undercurrent between the two men may have remained to the very end: the only people who came to actual blows with one another on "Let It Be" were John and George.[44]

Lennon's first wife, Cynthia, agrees with Martin's assessment, but expands it to include McCartney's attitude towards Harrison, particularly during their teenaged years: "They tolerated [Harrison] because he was good, but they patronized and often ignored him when they were absorbed in something together."[45] As a teenager Harrison initially hero-worshipped the charismatic Lennon and keenly felt his exile from the Lennon/McCartney partnership. After the band's breakup and Lennon's death, Harrison publicly emphasized his spiritual connection with Lennon as the first Beatles to take LSD together.[46] Other sources, including an eyewitness account of a serious private argument between the two, indicate that Harrison continued to resent Lennon's refusal to consider him as an equal. According to Shotton, "John regarded George almost as a younger brother: he felt genuine affection for him, yet seemed incapable of taking him seriously. [George] remained, like Ringo, little more than an assistant, a second class Beatle." Journalist Ray Connolly's accounts of conversations with Lennon reinforce this secondary perception of Harrison in Lennon's mind. "'Paul and me were the Beatles,' he would emphasize to me privately. 'We wrote the songs.'"

Of all four Beatles, McCartney and Harrison knew each other the longest, and McCartney had lobbied for Lennon to accept the younger boy into the band. However, Harrison's relationship with McCartney was similarly fraught. The age gap between Harrison and McCartney was narrower (only nine months) but McCartney was a grade above Harrison at their school, the Liverpool Institute. Like Lennon, McCartney viewed the age gap as insurmountable and admittedly never outgrew the tendency to treat Harrison, at times condescendingly, like a younger brother. Harrison complained about this in a May 1970 interview, arguing that McCartney was incapable of accepting that he had changed.[47] Evidence indicates that, like Lennon, McCartney never viewed Harrison as a musical or songwriting equal.[48] McCartney, "the main musical force in the studio,"[49] often disregarded Harrison's suggestions concerning songs McCartney had written. Harrison criticized McCartney for this many times after the breakup, including in their collective version of Beatles history, *Anthology*: "Personally, I'd found that the last couple of albums … the freedom to play as a musician was being curtailed, mainly by Paul … he wasn't open to anybody else's suggestions. John was always much more open when it came to how to record one of his songs."[50]

In a 1966 interview Harrison stated that Lennon and McCartney welcomed his songwriting: "They gave me an awful lot of encouragement. Their reaction has been very good…. I think they welcome my ideas."[51] However, this quote now appears to be more of an effort by Harrison to support the official story than an accurate representation of the band's interaction in the studio.[52] After 1970 Harrison repeatedly complained in interviews that Lennon and McCartney (as well as Martin) refused to support him as a songwriter, and that McCartney in particular stifled him by criticizing his guitar work and refusing to listen to his ideas. Testimony from Beatles engineer Norman Smith, who witnessed the band's interaction during the creation of their 1965 album, *Rubber Soul*, reinforces this: "As far as Paul was concerned, George could do no right."[53] Connolly also supports this view. He recounts witnessing McCartney's behavior towards Harrison three years later during *Abbey Road*: "I watched George Harrison become increasingly irritated when his playing of a guitar solo for the medley kept failing to satisfy Paul's demands. The perfectionist McCartney could be a hard taskmaster."[54] Years later, in *The Beatles Anthology*, Starr also acknowledged McCartney's increasing tendency to instruct rather than ask: "It got a bit like, 'I wrote the song and I want it this way,' whereas before it was 'I wrote the song—give me what you can.'"[55]

The friendship between Lennon and McCartney is by far the most analyzed relationship between any two individual Beatles. This is attributable to the overall tendency of Beatles historiography to focus on the two men, the importance of their songwriting partnership, and the public nature of their disagreements during the breakup. During the official narrative, however, their connection as the Beatles primary songwriters was emphasized. Both Lennon and McCartney's public statements reinforced their friendship, partnership, and their respect for each other's work. Their wildly differing personalities were portrayed as complimentary opposites, with McCartney's optimism, perfectionism, easy sentimentality, charm and diplomacy counterbalanced by Lennon's cynicism, sarcastic wit, laziness, blunt honesty and aggression.

> Paul needs an audience, but John doesn't. John is very lazy, unlike Paul. Without Paul he would often give up.... Both Paul and John have natural musical talent and originality, but they both have it in different ways. Paul can produce easy, sweet music like "Michelle" and "Yesterday," while John's music is much bumpier and more aggressive, like "I Am the Walrus." In a way, it comes out of their personalities.[56]

According to numerous contemporaneous sources, including the group's authorized biography, this combination of Lennon and McCartney's personalities and talents yielded the creative fission that drove the Beatles to their greatest heights. Later versions of Beatles history argued that their opposing musical strengths and personality differences ensured that the two men were incompatible, but under the official narrative, they were depicted as complementary opposites.

Any major indications of jealousy or personal divisions between Lennon and McCartney were publicly rejected. In a 1967 interview, journalist Thomas

Thompson assured readers that there was no schism in the music world's most famous friendship: "On the subject of jealousy within the group, Paul was most emphatic: 'There isn't any. Jealousy doesn't exist.'"[57] As with Harrison's 1966 reassurance that Lennon and McCartney supported him as a songwriter, all other evidence indicates that McCartney's statement was a lie given to support the official narrative. Despite their genuine and mutual affection and respect, jealousy and competitiveness undeniably affected the Lennon/McCartney friendship and partnership. Because of this, they play a key role in Beatles history. A few months after Lennon's death, McCartney described Lennon in a private phone conversation with Davies as "insecure" and "crazy with jealousy at times."[58] Such comments could be viewed as colored by McCartney's bias and retroactively influenced by the breakup; however, many other legitimate sources also have described Lennon's tendencies towards insecurity and jealousy. Beatles insiders, including Cynthia Lennon, Yoko Ono, George Martin, Derek Taylor, Pete Shotton, Tony Bramwell, Hunter Davies and Ray Connolly all provide testimony describing Lennon as pervasively jealous and intensely insecure. In public Lennon commanded remarkable charisma—musician Delbert McClinton described him as "the most charismatic person I had ever met"[59]—and a confidence that sometimes bordered on aggressive, but he admitted to often feeling worthless. These traits have become widely accepted throughout Beatles historiography as important elements to understanding the motivations behind some of Lennon's words and actions.

Like Lennon, McCartney exuded confidence in public: unlike Lennon, all evidence indicates it was not a false front. McCartney's ego was sizable, particularly during the Beatles era. In early 1968, near the height of his hubris, even McCartney's deliberate attempts to sound humble failed rather spectacularly. "You see, I went through a big part of my life without realizing that I had any faults ... then about two years ago I said to myself 'Come on, Paul, you're not *that* great.'"[60] The reporter to whom McCartney admitted this to softened the statement by acknowledging the years of worship and daily adoration that all four men encountered.[61] Justified or not, various eyewitnesses reinforce the argument that McCartney's considerable ego helped fuel the tensions within the band. Numerous sources also argue that McCartney was a demanding perfectionist, occasionally incapable of accepting criticism or suggestions even from his fellow Beatles. Elements such as Lennon's insecurity and McCartney's ego are important—not to summarily condemn the characters of either man, which falls outside the historian's purpose—but to gain an essential understanding of why and how the Beatles story unfolded as it did.

As a teenager McCartney initially hero-worshipped the older and charismatic Lennon, but his admiration was never as overt as Harrison's. McCartney, whose remarkable natural musical talent surpassed Lennon's,[62] was determined to be viewed as an equal, despite the age difference and Lennon's status as the group's founder. "I idolized John ... as I matured and grew up, I started sharing in things with him. I got up to his level.... We grew to be equals. It made him insecure. He always was, really."[63] McCartney admired and sometimes envied Lennon's scathing wit, skill with lyrics, and brutally honest fortrightness. Even in the Beatles days, he never quite outgrew the desire for praise from his teenaged idol, in part because it came so rarely. "If ever you got a speck of it, a crumb of it, you were quite grateful."[64]

Post-breakup accounts from virtually all Beatles insiders, including Lennon and McCartney, reveal a far more complex relationship between the two men than the simplified one in the official narrative. Years later Martin objected to reducing it to merely a competitive partnership: "They were brothers, and like brothers they pissed each other off quite a lot ... but they did love each other and adored what the other did and had an incredible bond."[65] While both men repeatedly declared their affection for each other, their contrasting personalities and the competitive nature of their songwriting partnership gave their interactions an edge that was only publicly acknowledged after the group's dissolution. "John would often say cruel things to Paul and Paul would come back and say 'I'll show him what I can do,' and Paul could be equally cruel to John and John would come up with something. Despite the love they had for each other, they would still egg each other on in a funny kind of way."[66] According to Shotton, Lennon both admired and resented McCartney's strengths.

> Paul was the one Beatle who posed any challenge to John's authority and preeminence within the group.... Paul was the only one he considered more or less his equal. John particularly admired and respected—yet at the same time envied—Paul's independence, his self-discipline, and his all around musical facility: all qualities in which John felt relatively lacking.[67]

Linda McCartney, who witnessed the most volatile period within the Lennon-McCartney relationship, denounced as irresponsible the post-breakup efforts by the press to paint the two men as irreconcilable opposites: "They were more similar than they were different."[68]

No other relationship within the Beatles underwent such a dramatic revision after the dissolution of the official narrative. The bitterness they directed towards each other during the group's public breakup prompted a new appraisal. The first major biography of Lennon, Ray Coleman's *Lennon: The Definitive Biography*, denounced the relationship as a fraud: "At the root of it lay the fundamental truth which millions of Beatles fans still find unpalatable:

John and Paul never had much in common."[69] Numerous authors dismissed the friendship between the two men as mere myth manufactured to support the official narrative, similar to how the group's image was whitewashed. Martin, one of the most valuable and credible sources in Beatles historiography,[70] always maintained that their bond was unique, different even than the one either man shared with Harrison or Starr. "John Lennon and Paul McCartney in particular were extremely good friends; they loved each other, really … you could, though, almost touch the rivalry between them, it was so intense and so real, despite its overriding warmth."[71]

In the wake of the breakup, as the former Beatles launched verbal barbs and lawsuits at each other, various authors downplayed the Fab Four element. The narratives that emerged in the 1970s and 1980s emphasized the divisions between the members that the band's dissolution had exposed. By the 1990s and the release of *The Beatles Anthology*, many writers harkened back to the unity depicted in the original narrative while acknowledging the more complex interactions within the group glossed over by the Fab Four version. The remaining Beatles did so as well. In addition to complaints he made about Lennon and particularly McCartney throughout *Anthology* Harrison, long regarded as the Beatle who most resented the experience, described much of their fellowship in a positive light. "We laughed a lot. That's one thing we forgot about for a few years—laughing. When we went through all the lawsuits, it looked as if everything was bleak, but when I think back to before that, I remember we used to laugh all the time."[72]

Lennon/McCartney

After the band's split, the Lennon/McCartney songwriting partnership was dismissed as a myth. Writers in the 1970s and 1980s argued that the two men had almost always worked independently and regarded the Lennon/McCartney collaboration as, with a few remarkable exceptions, virtually nonexistent. Shortly after Lennon's death influential rock critic Robert Christgau described it as "fecund, if often theoretical."[73] In his 1972 work *Twilight of the Gods*, the first musicological evaluation of the Lennon/McCartney catalog, Wilfrid Mellers dismissed the idea of the partnership, repeating the accepted wisdom that almost all of their greatest work had been composed without any input from the other.[74] This strain of thought continued into the early 1990s. Ian MacDonald, in the first edition of his essential work *Revolution in the Head*, also described the dyad as more myth than reality: "For most of their career, their partnership was a fiction."[75]

The story of rock and roll's most revered duo began to crumble in 1969, with the publication of Connolly's article "The Day the Beatles Died." In it Connolly, a journalist and witness to the Beatles last months, declared "they haven't composed a song together for years."[76] This rejection of Lennon/ McCartney as a songwriting unit was expanded by Lennon in his famous and extremely influential 1970 *Rolling Stone* interview, later called *Lennon Remembers*. Connolly's article declared that the Lennon/McCartney song-writing partnership had fallen apart; in his interview, Lennon denied that it ever really existed. The musician argued that he and McCartney had stopped writing together as early as 1962,[77] and that they had, with a few early excep-tions, always done their best work separately.[78] After the breakup the image of the two songwriters working side by side to create a song, such as in the group's authorized biography, was regarded as mythologizing promoted by the official narrative.

The Fab Four version of the Beatles story emphasized the Lennon/ McCartney team for good reason: it was unprecedented in the history of pop music; a convention-defying partnership of songwriters in which each wrote both melody and lyrics. In a considerable break with precedent, writing credit and profits were both always divided evenly, regardless of who had written the majority of a song. "Historically, joint songwriter agreements enumerated splits of 90:10, 85:15, 80:20, 75:25, 67:33 and every other fiddly fraction down to 50:50, but John and Paul went halves all the way, closeness and ambition shared and matched."[79] This equal attribution initially made it difficult, par-ticularly during the official era, to determine with any certainty which man had written which part of any particular song. For the Beatles, the songs they released under the Lennon/McCartney name, however theoretical or factual the partnership, were extremely popular and immensely profitable. During much of the Fab Four era it was in the interest of everyone involved, from the songwriters themselves to Epstein, Martin and others to promote Lennon/McCartney as a unit within the band.

They began doing so as early as their first interview. "We write the songs between us … mainly its John and I. We've written over a hundred songs."[80] The early years of Beatlemania coincide with the most productive period in the Lennon/McCartney songwriting partnership, in which they wrote many of their songs, in Lennon's later words, "eyeball to eyeball."[81] Trapped together in hotels, touring buses and backstage rooms, their proximity helped drive their collaboration. Evidence indicates that the Lennon/McCartney song-writing partnership at that time was not a manufactured myth but an accurate representation of how most Beatles songs were created. This was also the same period—1963 and 1964—in which the press and the public were introduced to the band. The initial version of the Lennon/McCartney songwriting team provided in articles and interviews at the time stressed the partnership's equal nature. In a 1963 interview, Lennon explained how they collaborated: "Sometimes half the words are written by me and he'll finish them off. We got along a word each, practically."[82] Most post-breakup accounts of their songwriting as well as musicological analysis and eyewitness accounts support the accuracy of these statements with regard to this time period. After the group stopped touring in 1966, the level of direct songwriting collaboration decreased, but the initial perception of the Lennon/McCartney songwriting partnership as constant remained the prevailing view. "The Beatles were the Beatles, our great symbol of the communal, and even the simple notion that John and Paul wrote many of their songs separately scarcely creased our consciousness."[83]

Throughout the official narrative, both Lennon and McCartney also repeatedly emphasized their mutual respect and admiration. In interviews they stressed their equality as songwriters and their partner's contributions to their songs. Citing each other as among the composers they admired most[84] they publicly praised each other's writing even as they privately competed over whose song would be anointed the group's next single. This promotion of their partner's skills and the Lennon/McCartney dyad was undeniably part of the official agenda of how to market the Beatles. However, interviews from the Beatles period provide evidence that both men freely admitted that their collaboration waxed and waned, and that, while their partner always provided input on or editing of the other's songs, they did not always write as a team. In a 1966 press conference, McCartney acknowledged "we do them separately and we do them together."[85] In a 1968 *Tonight Show* appearance, Lennon explained that they wrote in "every combination of two people writing a song … but we obviously influence each other."[86] Only in December 1969, as the group was splintering and almost a year after the two had written together seriously,[87] does evidence indicate that their efforts to sell the Lennon/McCartney songwriting partnership—"You can't say Paul and I are writing separately these days. We do both"[88]—were false.

The Role of Film in the Official Narrative: A Hard Day's Night

The group's first movie, 1964's *A Hard Day's Night,* was never intended to serve as the definitive 1960s portrait of the band or its members. Its creators, screenwriter Alun Owen and director Richard Lester, wanted to create a superior movie to the formulaic "jukebox musicals" that Elvis continued to churn out. The Beatles wanted to make a movie because it was expected of pop stars at the time. The producers wanted the movie's tickets and soundtrack sold before (as everyone fully expected to happen) the Beatles' bubble burst. Filmed in six weeks, the film was a critical and popular success in both Britain and the United States, reinforcing the group's premier status as the world's most popular band.

A Hard Day's Night reached a larger and more international audience than any of the Beatles prior interviews or press conferences. The movie pretended to depict a few days in the life of the band on tour as the members dealt with McCartney's disruptive "grandfather," their fans obsessive adulation, manager's demands, lack of freedom and their crowning musical performance. As with other parts of the Fab Four narrative, *A Hard Day's Night* stresses the four's ultimate unity in the midst of madness. In his evaluation of the group's first two movies, Beatles author Kenneth Womack describes how the films "labor to maintain the mythology of the group's collective identity."[89] Director Richard Lester emphasized that this aspect of the movie—"how they protect each other, how they were loyal to each other, how they cushioned themselves against the realities of the outside world"—was drawn from real life, and not invented for the film.[90]

The movie's pseudo behind-the-scenes angle left the viewer with a false impression of authenticity and solidified the band's image as cheery, cheeky, acceptable chaps. Years later, all four men publicly criticized and rebelled against the image exemplified by *A Hard Day's Night*. For many Britons and particularly Americans, the film offered the first opportunity to distinguish between the members of the group, who previously had been viewed by many fans as interchangeable personalities underneath bafflingly long hair. Written by Owen after he spent a few days with the Beatles on tour, the script sought to assign each member of the group a distinctive identity. This aspect of the movie—defining each member of the Beatles by one or two key characteristics—had an enormous impact on how they were viewed both during their careers as Beatles and, to a certain extent, for the rest of their lives. Written and released in order to capitalize on what many believed to be, at the time, the Beatles fleeting fame, *A Hard Day's Night* unintentionally became one of the most influential, if not accurate, sources in the Fab Four narrative and in all of Beatles historiography.

Decades later, Lester acknowledged the stereotyping had been somewhat inaccurate but defended it as necessary: "We tried to delineate their personalities artificially ... it was important to create artificially that George was mean, that Paul was the cute one, that John was the cynic, and that Ringo was at the back and unloved."[91] The consequences of this stereotyping continued long after the film left theaters. In *Reading the Beatles*, Womack describes the movie's permanent impact on the public perception: "'A Hard Day's Night' concretized the Beatles individual images for the current generation and … generations to come. Henceforth, Lennon became known for his sarcastic intelligence; McCartney for his boyish charm and good looks; George Harrison for being 'the quiet one,' and Ringo Starr for his affable personality and good-natured humor."[92] After the movie, the public perception of each Beatle's identity was so influenced by how they were stereotyped in *A Hard Day's Night* that the press took to identifying them by their defining characteristic. Thus Lennon became the smart one, McCartney the cute one, Harrison the quiet one, and Starr the lucky one. Fifty years later, after the deaths of Lennon and Harrison and McCartney's knighthood, the press continued to use these monikers. The Beatle's second film, *Help!*, strengthened these clichés. "In *Help!* The Beatles' characterizations were so stereotyped that they became wooden cut out figures: the cute sexy one, the smart sarcastic one, the moody cheapskate and the one with the inferiority complex."[93] In 1969, Starr complained that almost all potential movie scripts submitted to the band were rejected because they copied the formula of *A Hard Day's Night*[94]: "John would be witty, Paul would be pretty, I would be shy, and George would be George…. People really have tried to typecast us. They think we're still little moptops and we're not."[95]

This stereotyping affected not only perceptions about their personalities; it impacted public and critical opinion of their intelligence and musical skills. Lennon was identified as the smart one, an image reinforced by his sharp wit as well as his authorship of two books of short fiction, *In His Own Write* and *A Spaniard in the Works*. The stereotyping was not as kind to Starr, who was portrayed as lovable but inferior, an image that proved impossible for him to shake. Starr confronted the issue in a 1981 interview, criticizing his persona as "the downtrodden dummy…. I've been caught in this trap for almost twenty years now…. People always latch onto the first image and refuse to let go."[96] According to both *A Hard Day's Night* and *Help!* McCartney's most important attribute was his pretty face, and the musician's appearance was later used to dismiss his talents. Decades later *Time* acknowledged how McCartney's looks undermined his reputation: "[Paul] was cute, coquettish— almost the girl of the group—so how could he be smart?"[97] After the band's split, the caricatured depictions provided in Beatles movies influenced how various biographers viewed them and their contributions to the music.

The impact that popular films have on the historiography of an event or an individual is immense, particularly if, as in the case of *A Hard Day's*

Night, it is the movie that introduces or familiarizes the public with the subject. At times, movies even can influence the course of history. In his famous essay "Hitler's Image of the United States," historian Gerhard Weinberg argues that the 1940 John Ford movie *The Grapes of Wrath*, an adaptation of John Steinbeck's Depression era-novel, may have played a role in Germany's decision to declare war on the United States in World War II. According to Weinberg, after viewing the movie, Hitler believed that the entire American West was dry, destitute and chaotic. *The Grapes of Wrath* depicted the United States as the very opposite of a rising industrial power, and this influenced Hitler's perception of America as a nation that posed little threat to Nazi Germany, helping lead to his December 1941 declaration of war on the country.[98] *A Hard Day's Night* and *Help!* did not contribute to any wars. However, the movies did guide and shape all successive Beatles history in a way that their creators never imagined or intended.

The Beatlemania Era Books: Love Me Do *and* A Cellarful of Noise

In addition to the exhaustive coverage the Beatles received in the popular press and the release of *A Hard Day's Night*, 1964 saw the publication of two books dealing with the group. *A Cellarful of Noise* , a brief autobiography of Epstein, was ghostwritten by Beatles insider Derek Taylor after extensive interviews with the group's manager. The book was short and concentrated more on Epstein's life and experiences than on the group itself. The pull of the Beatles was so strong, however, that it became a bestseller in Britain. Heavily edited, it omitted any mention of the Beatles' exploits on tour or Epstein's sexual orientation, although Epstein revealed the information to Taylor.[99] In the work Epstein emphasized his efforts to maintain stability in a band with such wildly differing personalities: "Balance, in a group as in life, is all."[100] As with other parts of the official narrative, *A Cellarful of Noise* stresses the collaborative nature of the Lennon/McCartney songwriting partnership and its unique structure. "Who writes the words and who the music? So people ask endlessly. The answer is that both write both."[101]

The most referenced and quoted parts are Epstein's descriptions of his personal relationships with each of the individual Beatles. His description of McCartney in particular contrasts with the singer's personae of the time as the "cute, charming" Beatle: "Paul is temperamental and moody and difficult to deal with ... he is a great one for not wishing to hear about things."[102] Epstein softens this criticism by praising McCartney's musical talents and loyalty to the group. Criticisms of Lennon—"sometimes he has been abominably rude to me"—are likewise balanced with descriptions of him as "a most exceptional man."[103] Harrison is identified as the Beatle most interested in money, a characterization reinforced throughout the official narrative: Starr is "uncomplicated."[104] *A Cellarful of Noise* was a sanctioned part of the band's story and claims "to put down an accurate account of the emergence of the Beatles" by Epstein.[105] But its significant omissions, its purpose in crafting the official narrative and the fact that it was actually authored by Taylor must be taken into account when determining its accuracy and credibility.

The popular impact of *A Cellarful of Noise* on Beatles historiography was initially less important than far more influential (if fictitious) accounts such as *A Hard Day's Night*. The same year as the movie's release, Penguin paperbacks published Michael Braun's *Love Me Do*. Braun, an American journalist in Britain, accompanied the group on some of its 1963 and 1964 tours and chronicled the members' lives. *Love Me Do* provides a direct, less censored account of the Beatles on tour than fans saw a few months later in *A Hard Day's Night* or would see again for years. These Beatles drank alcohol, used the word "fucking," and were openly pessimistic regarding their appeal to American audiences. "They've got their own groups. What are we going to give them that they don't already have?"[106] Braun declared "they don't care about projecting any sort of proper image,"[107] and parts of the book reinforce that. Their personalities are rougher than in many official era depictions: Braun recounts McCartney accusing a Catholic priest of hypocrisy over the Church's wealth; Harrison implores fans to "leave us alone"[108] and Lennon predicts that *A Hard Day's Night*, which had been filmed but not yet released, would be terrible.[109]

Braun's eyewitness account provides several quotations that are seen in virtually every Beatles biography, particularly Epstein's weary admission that, even in 1964, managing the group was taking its toll. "The Beatles, always the Beatles. They don't know it, but I cried tonight, I really did. They never noticed but I cried."[110] When describing the band's touring days, almost every Beatles writer uses Braun's account as a source, and its credibility is excellent. Written and published as the group was constructing its mythology, full of primary sources but not an authorized account, *Love Me Do* offers a candor that is rare among other primary sources of the time. Its timing is key: *Love Me Do* was written precisely when a few critics (most famously *The Times* William Mann) were beginning to take the Lennon/McCartney songwriting partnership seriously, but years before it became revered. Believing, as so many at the time did, that the band was a short-lived fad that would soon burn itself out, Braun was not awed either by its members or its music, which

he described as merely enjoyable. The agenda behind the book's publication—to sell cheap paperback copies about the Fab Four to teenage girls
before the bubble burst and fans moved on—reinforces its credibility. Unlike
many later books on the Beatles, Braun wrote *Love Me Do* without history,
narrative or mythology in mind.

"How Does a Beatle Live?"

By 1966, all four Beatles were rebelling against the cheery stereotypes
that had defined them since *A Hard Day's Night*. Their rapidly evolving music
had produced two successive albums, *Rubber Soul* and *Revolver*, which were
far more advanced lyrically and artistically than their early Beatlemania era
work. In press conferences and interviews the members ignored Epstein's
request to avoid controversial topics and openly discussed their opposition
to the Vietnam War and the segregation of African Americans. "Taxman,"
the first song on *Revolver*, was Harrison's scathing musical indictment of
England's tax laws. Their appearance also changed: they abandoned the mod
suits for more casual, hippie inspired wear and lost their uniform Beatles
haircuts. Privately, the group had also progressed from softer drugs, such as
marijuana, to harder drugs such as LSD.

During 1966 all four men gave extensive interviews to journalist Maureen Cleave, one of the very few women granted a major interview. Most
questions and interviews up to that point had focused on the Beatles lives on
tour, their music and their hair. Cleave concentrated on the Beatles' lives at
home, interviewing each of them separately. Her profiles provide valuable
contemporary evidence regarding their personalities, beliefs and ambitions
during what many regard as their artistic peak.

Discussion of the band as a fad had faded. Even those who did not
like the Beatles' music or personalities acknowledged their unique status,
something Cleave discussed in her article on Lennon: "The Beatles' fame is
beyond question." She emphasized the insularity of the group in their everyday lives—"The Beatles see only each other; they are better friends than
ever before"—and their detachment, particularly Lennon's, from real life.
Her profile of Starr conformed to the common picture, describing him as
"the least brilliant" and "the most ordinary" but also the most "'sensible,'"
"'mature'" and least "'complicated.'" Starr's marriage to his teenage sweetheart
Maureen and their family life were favorably described: "they are very happily
married." His relations with his fellow Beatles revealed the drummer's lingering uncertainty after his late entry into the group: "It took two years …

to get each other sorted out. But from then on I had the feeling there was four of us in it."[111]

Cleave's profile of Harrison begun by stating that the group's youngest member was overlooked and unappreciated. The "least well-known" Beatle," she described him as "strong-willed, uncompromising, delightful and original." In contrast to the early days of the official narrative, when all four Beatles had reassured the fans of their appreciation, Harrison expressed his frustration with fame: "I never asked to be famous.... I got more famous than I wanted to be." His skills as a songwriter were mentioned but not lavishly praised: "He wishes he could write fine songs as Lennon and McCartney do." The article reinforced the perception of Harrison as the Beatle most interested in business and what was happening to the millions of pounds the group was generating. Like Cleave's interviews with Lennon and McCartney, it also included Harrison's blunt opinion on a controversial topic. Harrison condemned the Vietnam War, two years before the Tet Offensive: "It's wrong. Anything to do with war is wrong."[112]

Cleave found Starr sensible and uncomplicated; Harrison was revealing if uncompromising once he had made up his mind. McCartney, in contrast, was a puzzle. According to her analysis neither his "sweet" looks nor his music provided a true picture of the man's character. Her portrayal of his personality extended beyond the rote description of merely "charming" that dominated the public perception. According to Cleave McCartney displayed "shriveling wit, a critical intelligence and enormous talent." Harrison had told Cleave that he had not deliberately pursued fame, but McCartney openly embraced it. Cleave acknowledged his geographic separation from the other Beatles as the only London-based member: "He is half-Beatle and half not." Immersed in a self-admitted "'self-improvement kick,'" as Cleave labeled it, McCartney made it clear he was determined to be viewed as more than the band's prettiest face and sweetest singer. McCartney peppered the interview with art and literature references, citing his fascination with *avant-garde* figures Stockhausen and Luciano Berio and his drive for radical artistic stimulation: "People are saying things and painting things and writing things and composing things that are great, and I must know what people are doing."[113] Decades later in his semi-autobiography, McCartney criticized what he viewed as the inaccurate portrayal of him in that period, possibly offering motivation for why he discussed his *avant-garde* art interests so extensively with Cleave: "At the time I was known as the cute Beatle, the ballad Beatle or whatever. I hate to think what I was known as. John was the cynical one, the wise Beatle, the intellectual. In fact at that time it was wildly in reverse."[114] In Starr's profile he had expressed affection for the United States, but McCartney was more critical, lamenting America's lack of a BBC and harshly condemning its history of racial discrimination, calling it "a lousy country where anyone black is a dirty nigger."[115]

Cleave's profile of Lennon is, with the possible exception of *Lennon Remembers*, the musician's most famous interview. As in the other three profiles, she offered her opinion of his personality in a quick sentence, describing him as "imperious, unpredictable, indolent, disorganised, childish, vague, charming and quick-witted." Much of Cleave's writing emphasized the man's laziness, and his intellectual restlessness. Harrison had criticized the Vietnam War and England's tax rates: McCartney had condemned America's racial discrimination. Lennon, who was reading about religion at the time, acknowledged Christianity's decline across post-war Europe: "Christianity will go…. It will vanish and shrink. I needn't argue about that; I'm right and I will be proved right. We're more popular than Jesus now; I don't know which will go first—rock 'n' roll or Christianity."[116] British readers ignored or agreed with Lennon's comments about religion when the original article appeared in March 1966; negative reaction was small. But when his statements (as well as McCartney's calling America "a lousy country") were re-printed immediately prior to the band's 1966 American tour in *Datebook*, an American teen magazine, a fierce backlash erupted. The American press called attention to Lennon's comments about religion and anti–Beatles protests spread. When the group arrived in America they faced death threats, radio boycotts, record burnings and protest marches from a small but vocal minority. The American press hounded Lennon about his statements. Away from the cameras, overwhelmed by the threats and the possibility they might have to cancel the entire American tour, the musician broke down in tears.[117] Some preachers denounced the group from their pulpits. It was the greatest blow to the Beatles' favorable image during the official narrative.

Because of the tumult it inadvertently caused, parts of Cleave's interview with Lennon are included in every biography of the group or Lennon. Its impact on the image of the Beatles—and on Lennon as a blunt man of honesty, uninterested in currying favor with the mainstream press—is undeniable. So is its influence on Beatles' history: it was after the hellish 1966 American tour that, frustrated with their treatment in the Philippines, sound quality at their concerts and the backlash over Lennon's comments, the band decided to quit touring. However, because so many Beatles works (understandably) concentrate on the fallout of Lennon's interview, Cleave's profiles of McCartney, Harrison and Starr are mentioned but rarely discussed in depth or quoted. This narrow focus on Lennon subverts the original intent of Cleave's interviews, which was to gain a greater understanding of all four Beatles. Omitting quotes from the other three interviews leaves their collective portrait less nuanced and perpetuates the tendency in Beatles historiography to devote the most ink to Lennon. It also magnifies Lennon's reputation as a man unafraid to make controversial statements while ignoring that both McCartney and Harrison also provided similarly outspoken, if overlooked, views in their conversations with Cleave.[118]

The Beatles' Authorized Biography

Officially authorized versions of history are by their nature incapable of providing the complete, unbiased story of an event or individual. Authorized accounts always trade a varying amount of impartiality in exchange for direct access. The degree to which the sanctioned work compromises impartiality varies wildly. Some—such as the "colored books" each major combatant published after World War I to justify their entries into and conduct during the war —are little more than propaganda, providing only the version approved by the historical subject or the government in power. Determining the truth from these versions of history is difficult, particularly when the government or biographical subject controls access to the archives. In these instances the primary figures' authorized accounts and the archival evidence they provide must, if at all possible, be verified by more independent sources or documents.

Verification from outside sources, and impartial historians, is critical in establishing the credibility and accuracy of a source and a narrative. During the 1920s, as the Great Powers debated in their history books over who was to blame for the Great War's carnage, American historians enjoyed an inherent level of impartiality that granted their findings more credibility in the eyes of the world. Unlike Germany, Russia, and France, the United States had not been involved in the pre-war build-up and its government provided no authorized version of its root causes afterwards. Because of this, in contrast to other nations' scholars, American historians had no political or subconscious motivation to blame their enemies or absolve their nation from causing the war. As a consequence, American historians' conclusions were highly valued and, in some instances, heavily courted by other nations.[119] Their independence granted their work a weight of authority.

The ultimate credibility of any authorized account depends on the answers to certain questions: How much independence was the author granted? Was the historian allowed to access *all* archives and sources, or only a particular selection? Did the author agree, explicitly or implicitly, to provide a more flattering account in exchange for access to a historical subject? What was the historian's personal relationship to the subject? Did the government or institution that authorized the history have a specific agenda? One of the key issues is the question of editorial control: Who had final say over the published version? Did the biographical subject demand the power to remove or add information from the biography over authorial objections? All official histories trade some degree of impartiality in exchange for valuable access. The historiographer's task is to ascertain the extent of that bias, and its influence on the work's accuracy.

The Beatles: The Authorized Biography (1968) written by British journalist Hunter Davies is, like all official histories, impacted by this conflict between impartiality and access. The accuracy of Davies' account has been the subject of sharp debate among Beatles writers and, at times, between individual Beatles. Lennon publicly dismissed the book as "bullshit"[120] in his 1970 de-mythologizing interview Lennon Remembers. According to biographer Bob Spitz, McCartney admitted that The Beatles was only 65 percent true.[121] Spitz argues that, according to McCartney, from the onset of their fame, all four Beatles agreed to provide "a version of the facts,"[122] including The Authorized Biography, that was not wholly accurate. Notorious Lennon biographer Albert Goldman scornfully dismissed The Beatles' credibility in a 1989 televised debate with Davies.[123] During the Lennon Remembers and Shout! narratives, which rejected the Fab Four version of the Beatles story, The Beatles: The Authorized Biography was regarded as tainted by association. Writers who used it as a source tended to select quotes and information that supported their particular theses and dismissed the rest as mythology or whitewashing.

Davies repeatedly has defended the work's accuracy, claiming that the omissions required by the Beatles (such as an acknowledgement of Epstein's homosexuality) were few.[124] He also argues that, while all four Beatles had to approve the final manuscript prior to publication, their requested changes were minimal. According to Davies, the most blatant example of authorized interference was the request by Lennon's Aunt Mimi to excise accounts of Lennon's mother's extramarital affairs, and the insertion of her statement "John was as happy as the day was long"[125] be added to the end of the chapter detailing Lennon's childhood.[126] This explicit authorized interference does not tell us, however, how much the Beatles agenda affected their behavior or statements as Davies chronicled them. While Davies' depiction indicates that the group openly accepted and behaved naturally around him, his purpose— to chronicle their lives and discuss their music in a serious biography, intended as a final written authority on the Beatles—must be taken into account. The extent to which the Beatles altered their behavior or testimony because of Davies' presence is unknowable, but that some level of alteration did occur is undeniable. The Heisenberg uncertainty principle, or concept that an observer's presence alters what is being observed—that the very act of measuring changes the measurement itself—spans disciplines from history to science.

Despite these flaws, Hunter Davies' *The Beatles: The Authorized Biography* is an invaluable and widely used source throughout Beatles historiography. With the exception of *Love Me Do*, it contains the most candid depiction of the group during the official era and is far more comprehensive. While it promotes every major element of the Fab Four narrative, every successive biography of the band or its members draws from Davies' work, sources and evidence.

However much impartiality Davies traded, and however much of a façade the Beatles presented in his presence, *The Beatles: The Authorized Biography* provides the most in-depth, eyewitness account of the group while it was still functioning. Davies began researching the book in 1966; after approaching McCartney and securing approval from Epstein, he interviewed family members and friends before shadowing the members themselves. The timing of Davies work is crucial: It was written at the height of the Beatles mystique, during their efforts to make the *Sgt. Pepper* album (a time when the Lennon/McCartney partnership was enjoying a creative peak). It is of crucial importance that the book was written prior to the entrance of Yoko Ono, Allen Klein, and Linda Eastman as key figures in the Beatles story. *The Authorized History* also secured interviews with immediate family members such as Harrison's mother, Louise, and McCartney's father, James, both of whom died within a decade of its publication. Consequently, later biographies are heavily reliant on Davies' interviews for testimony from these sources.

Davies pitched the biography to the group as a reference: rather than answering the same inane questions for the thousandth time, they could simply direct the interviewer to their biography. While this appealed to them, there were other agendas behind the Beatles cooperation. The band and its P.R. department had been shaping the narrative for years. The biography was a means for them to do so. It was also a tool for the Beatles to elevate the popular perception of them—to demonstrate that they had moved past the "I want to hold your hand" mop-tops, once and for all. This shared motivation among all members must be acknowledged as the Beatles' underlying agenda at the time the biography was researched and written. During the same time period in which Davies was shadowing the group, the Beatles were immersed in creating their 1967 album *Sgt. Pepper's Lonely Hearts Club Band*. Part of the motivation for the album, according to McCartney, was to make a conceptual break with their Fab Four personas:

> We were fed up with being the Beatles. We really hated that fucking four little mop-top boys approach. We were not boys, we were men. It was all gone, all that boy shit, all that screaming, we didn't want any more, plus, we'd now got turned on to pot and thought of ourselves as artists rather than just performers.[127]

At the same moment that they were determined to be viewed differently as artists, *The Beatles: The Authorized Biography* offered them a platform to do so.

As they had done in their interviews the year before with Cleave, the Beatles presented themselves as figures far different from the ones depicted in *A Hard Day's Night*. Harrison appeared as the most changed: his new devotion to Hare Krishna gave him a distinction his portrayals had previously lacked, and his frustration with the demands of being a Beatle was evident in his dismissal of the band as just another job. Years later, Davies described Harrison's mindset at the time, describing him as "obsessive"[128] over Hare Krishna and declaring "he hated, even then, the Beatles' days."[129] Davies' downplayed Harrison's growth as a songwriter, an element in the Beatles story that gained increasing importance in the band's waning years. "He looks at John and Paul as the composers and writers. He feels he has no need to bother when they are so good."[130] Starr's characterization changed the least, continuing the depiction of him as uncomplicated: "He is open and friendly, the sweetest of them all ... he is not self centered in any way." As with Harrison, the separation between Lennon and McCartney on one tier and Starr on another was explicit: "In the light of Paul and John's more obvious talents, he has kept himself even quieter than he is. But they rely on him a great deal."[131]

As part of the standard narrative, the biography continued the official pattern of downplaying the band's drug use and sexual exploits. It also provided information on Epstein's relations with various members of the band, reinforcing the previous impression made in *A Cellarful of Noise* that Epstein found McCartney the most difficult Beatle with whom to deal. "Brian always worried more about pleasing Paul. He could be upset by talking to Paul on the phone, but never any of the others."[132] Epstein died of a drug overdose in August 1967 while *The Authorized Biography* was being written. Davies' description of Epstein's depression and struggles during his final months was remarkably honest, given the book's proximity to Epstein's death: "he had become increasingly dependent on pills as his worries, real and imagined, took over and obsessed him ... he'd hardly been at his office for so many months and had rarely been up and out in daylight."[133] Views on Epstein's ability as manager have varied wildly over the decades, with some writers depicting Epstein as devastatingly naïve in contract negotiations and others praising his honesty and devotion to the band. In the immediate wake of Epstein's death, Davies chose to focus on the man's emotional ties to the group rather than his financial and business decisions: "His greatest pleasure was to be with them. He loved doing anything for them."[134]

The unity and insularity among all four Beatles was one of the work's major themes, with Davies acknowledging it on the authority of numerous primary sources: "They all belong to each other. Nobody, not even the wives, can break through it or even comprehend it."[135] Davies particularly emphasized Lennon's dependence on his band mates. "John most of all can't be without the other three for very long."[136] Lennon agreed: "We do need each other a lot."[137] Even Lennon's wife Cynthia concurred, but warned: "They seem to need you less than you need them."[138] Davies depiction of Lennon's home life and marriage was at times bleak, describing the musician as not talking to her or anyone for three days, watching television in silence, ignoring her and their young son, Julian. While numerous friends interviewed for the biography testified to Lennon's contentment at the time—"it's great that he's so happy"[139]—Davies ultimately provided a mixed description of Lennon's home life. Decades later in the introduction to later editions of *The Authorized Biography*, Davies explored the subject in greater and more negative detail. "John was always the hardest to talk to. I spent hours at his home in Weybridge in silence ... with Cyn, he could go on like that for weeks."[140] The only thing that broke him out of it, according to Davies, was contact with the other Beatles: "John's doziness at home left him when he came into the studio. Working with Paul seemed to make him more alive."[141]

The contrast between Davies depiction of Lennon's day-to-day existence and his account of McCartney's life could not have been starker. Unlike Harrison and Lennon, it was clear that McCartney relished his role as a Beatle. Decades later *Time* waxed poetic about this period of the musician's life: "He was at the height of his powers, creatively, physically and financially: a young genius getting richer and more famous every day; the fantasy of millions of women, he strode the world like a sun king."[142] His residence in London and his longstanding relationship with the beautiful, famous actress Jane Asher meant he was the most visible, culturally involved Beatle. While Lennon watched television in boredom, McCartney spent his days at art gallery openings and his nights in London's trendiest clubs. Delving into *avant-garde* music, art and the underground movement he was "the golden boy of the British counterculture."[143] In addition *The Beatles: The Authorized Biography* added another dimension to the prevailing image of McCartney as "the cute one," arguing that a fundamental change in the band's power structure had taken place and that he, and not Lennon, was in reality now the band's leader. "His way of making an effort has been especially vital to them since Brian Epstein died. Paul today makes most of the running ... in some ways Paul is the leader today, not John."[144]

This assessment by Davies diverged sharply from the official narrative's previous accounts of the group's hierarchy. From the very beginning of their fame, each member explained that, while the Beatles were a democracy, Lennon's personality, charisma and age made him the unofficial leader. McCartney explicitly identified Lennon as the leader in the group's first interview in November 1962, as well as in letters written before the band became famous. Numerous interviews and press conferences referred to Lennon as the "Chief Beatle," and Epstein's A Cellarful of Noise described Lennon as "the dominant figure in a group which is, virtually, without a leader."[145] Some of the most revealing parts of The Beatles: The Authorized Biography include Lennon describing his lifelong need for supremacy in any hierarchy, starting with his years as a schoolboy. "I was aggressive because I wanted to be popular. I wanted to be the leader.... I wanted everybody to do what I told them to do ... to let me be the boss."[146] Shotton concurred with Lennon's fundamental need to be in charge: "He had to be the leader at all times, either by fighting everyone or, if they were big, by undermining them by abuse or sarcasm."[147]

Lennon's preoccupation with being "number one" (even amid claims that the desire has diminished) is constant throughout The Beatles: The Authorized Biography. It flavors his discussion of his schoolboy experiences as well as his account of his first meeting with McCartney, providing one of the most revealing and famous quotes in all Beatles history: "I half thought to myself, 'He's as good as me.' I'd been kingpin up to then. Now, I thought 'If I take him on, what will happen?' It went through my head that I'd have to keep him in line if I let him join. But he was good, so he was worth having."[148] However, according to The Beatles, Lennon's overriding urge to dominate had softened to a point in which he did not openly object to McCartney's new status as the band's main authority. "[John] doesn't have to be number one, that's why he's so happy."[149]

What Davies did not explain in The Authorized Biography was that this change in Lennon's personality was prompted by his excessive use of LSD, which he began taking in large amounts in 1965. Where all eyewitness accounts agree that alcohol brought out Lennon's verbally aggressive and sometimes physically violent tendencies, LSD had the opposite effect, making him mellow and exacerbating his habitual laziness. Lennon's daily LSD diminished his songwriting output while McCartney, who only dabbled in the drug, surged ahead. This, coupled with a reduction in direct "eyeball to eyeball"[150] songwriting after the band ceased touring in 1966, had significant consequences on the structure of the Lennon/McCartney partnership. By 1967, while the two still competed over whose song would become the A-side single, "the reality was that McCartney could now turn out a song in a few hours, while Lennon needed weeks to come up with one."[151] By the time of *The Authorized Biography*'s publication, the combination of Epstein's death, McCartney's prolific songwriting, studio production, dogged work ethic, and Lennon's acid-induced complacency all resulted in a new publicly acknowledged fundamental restructuring of the Beatles hierarchy. Lennon evidently tolerated this in 1967; within a year he felt very differently.

The Beatles: The Authorized Biography not only chronicled the Beatles' story, it also helped shape their future. Lennon was fully aware that he had lost control not only of the group (Davies stated it in black and white in a book Lennon had to approve prior to publication) but also his supremacy within the Lennon/McCartney songwriting partnership. From the time they were teenagers collaborating on their first songs, songwriting output had ebbed and flowed between the two. One year McCartney would produce more songs, the next Lennon would write more. On their *A Hard Day's Night* album, Lennon's productivity exceeded McCartney's, something which the album's liner notes acknowledged: "John's is the dominant voice." Between March 1964 and November 1965 he produced three more coveted A-sides than McCartney. Now the pendulum had swung back in McCartney's favor: From April 1966 through November 1967, the same time period in which Davies was researching and writing, McCartney had four A-side singles to Lennon's one. (Determining which song was an A-side was done by majority vote among the Beatles and George Martin.) "By 1966, Lennon's insecurity was juxtaposed in time with McCartney's growing output ... what Lennon had worried about almost ten years earlier ... had materialized—McCartney, by way of his superior talents, was now leading the dyad and the group."[152] This power shift within the band, along with his unhappy marriage, the loss of a father figure in Epstein, and his excessive use of LSD sent Lennon spiraling into a depression. After Lennon stopped using LSD and returned from India in May 1968 disillusioned with the Maharishi and Transcendental Meditation, his ingrained urge to dominate re-asserted itself. By the time *The Beatles: The Authorized Biography* was published in 1968, the introduction of three of the most divisive figures in Beatles history—Yoko Ono, Linda Eastman, and, within a year, Allen Klein—seemed to render much of Davies' work obsolete.

Yoko Ono

Yoko Ono is the most divisive figure in Beatles history. Unfortunately, portrayals of her have tended to veer between two extremes. Ono often is depicted as a domineering egoist who pursued Lennon for his wealth and fame, manipulated him into a relationship, and ultimately destroyed the Beatles with her unreasonable expectations. Other narratives describe her as the love of Lennon's life; the daring artist who, unfairly rejected by Lennon's closest friends, spurred him to discover his true purpose and his political and artistic freedom outside the band's restrictive and commercial boundaries. Particularly in the early decades after the breakup, most writers approached Ono already clinging to one pole or the other. Consequently, few biographers attempted, let alone achieved, any impartial analysis of Ono's personality and artistry, her relationship with Lennon, or her impact on the band's dissolution.

This unbalanced view began with Ono's introduction into the Beatles story. Once her relationship with Lennon became public in summer 1968, the initial reaction of the popular press was at best bewildered and at worst racist. Both Lennon and Ono complained of persecution frequently over the years. Ono's Japanese ancestry, her profession as a female *avant-garde* artist, and the fact that both she and Lennon were married to and had children with other people when they began their relationship resulted in less than favorable coverage. In 1968, Connolly declared that press reaction to Ono depicted her as "either a joke or a hate figure or both."[153] Conversely, both during the breakup period and its aftermath, Ono received extremely complimentary portrayals from numerous counter-cultural and rock and roll magazines, particularly *Rolling Stone*, whose editor Jann Wenner she established a lifelong friendship with.

Later works in Beatles historiography also betray a profound schism and lack of impartiality in their analysis of Ono. Biographies by writers such as Goldman and Spitz as well as accounts from Bramwell describe Ono in unrelentingly negative terms, referring to her as "a malevolent omnivore"[154] and an "artist of mass destruction."[155] According to these writers Ono's motivations are always suspect, her art unappealing, her behavior uniformly selfish and manipulative, and the consequences of her actions—on both Lennon and the Beatles as a unit—are devastating. On the opposite side of the debate, biographers such as Philip Norman, Ray Coleman and rock and roll journalists Wenner and Robert Christgau have spent decades passionately promoting Ono as Lennon's personal savior and a true artistic visionary. In their interpretation, much of the criticism of Ono stems from prejudice: "Yoko presented an easy target for chauvinists, cynics and racists."[156] For the historian, such extreme portrayals from both sides display an obvious bias. "Balance and objectivity,"[157] two of history's core requirements as established by the father of modern history, Leopold Von Ranke, are conspicuously absent.

The first perspective's unremittingly negative portrayal of Ono turns her into a stereotype with no redeeming features whose effect on Lennon's life, art and personality is almost uniformly negative. On the opposite side of the divide, writers are so determined to celebrate Ono's artistic and personal partnership with Lennon that they excuse Ono's negative qualities and actions (such as her callous treatment of Julian, Lennon's son from his first marriage). Both sides reduce her portrayal to a caricature and both are occasionally guilty of ignoring or summarily dismissing primary sources that contradict their chosen view. As a consequence, both fail as legitimate history. "The writer of a historical narrative must deal with the contradiction. You cannot pretend the contradiction does not exist."[158]

While her apparent contribution to the breakup doubtless plays a role in this split perception, Ono's place as the most prominent female in Beatles historiography is also a factor. The Beatles story is dominated by males and their history has been written at every level, from primary sources to journalists to biographers, almost exclusively by men. The issue of gender difference between biographer and subject demands attention: It is widely acknowledged as a factor that impacts the interpretations of female historical figures. For centuries the story of Cleopatra, one of history's most powerful and wealthy females, was shaped and told exclusively by men, from her political and military rival Octavian to Plutarch to William Shakespeare. There is no doubt among historians that this exclusively male interpretation has somewhat obscured the truth of Egypt's last queen. In her discussion of history's perception of Cleopatra, Stacey Schiff addresses some of the ways in which masculine views on women influence their conclusions. Declaring "We remember her ... for the wrong reasons" Schiff details how Cleopatra's intelligence, political skill, wealth, and capable governance are overlooked because of her gender. She notes how the predominant view of Cleopatra is one of a "wanton temptress" that "elicited scorn and envy. Her story is constructed as much of male fear as of fantasy. Her power was immediately misrepresented because—for one man's historical purposes—she needed to have reduced another to abject slavery."[159] Cleopatra is history's most famous example of how male dominated narratives impact the depiction of females, but she is far from the only misrepresentation. The historiography of females from Catherine the Great and the Chinese Empress Cixi to artistic figures such as Sylvia Plath has been similarly affected.

In addition to gender, there are several other factors prompting the starkly unbalanced views of Ono, distorting the picture of her role in Beatles history. Lennon and Ono are at least partially responsible for this confusion. They provided the press with a version of their relationship that, at times, diverged from the facts. In the interest of constructing their own mythology, the two provided false accounts of the date of their first meeting and, reportedly, their first sexual encounter and obscured the truth of numerous other issues. Both also denied the claim that Ono pursued Lennon persistently for over a year prior to their public relationship[160] despite numerous eyewitness accounts to the contrary. (McCartney, Cynthia Lennon and Beatles insiders Shotton, Peter Brown and Bramwell all recount Ono's pursuit of Lennon.) Various authors now acknowledge how these early fictions have muddied the historical waters. "There are so many legends and counter-legends about Yoko Ono and John Lennon that it is hard to get to the truth, especially because the testimony of the principals—John and Yoko themselves—can't be taken at face value."[161]

Lennon, who had helped construct one less than completely accurate version of history with the Beatles (a mythology that, by 1969, he found stifling) and Ono deliberately romanticized and at times mythologized their story in order to "sell" it, and their art, to a skeptical and at times hostile world. The only real debate is to what extent. Lennon—an invaluable but hardly impartial primary source regarding his relationship with Ono—always passionately defended their relationship. He rejected any suggestion that she had negatively influenced his life, relationships with his fellow Beatles, or his work. On the contrary, Lennon argued numerous times that Ono's artistic influence liberated him from the restrictions imposed by the Beatles, just as she gave him the courage to leave his unsatisfying marriage. Publicly, he never failed to applaud her work as a musician: At times his praise veered on the edge of absurdity. In late 1970, during an attempt to promote their joint album *Plastic Ono Band*, Lennon described "Don't Worry Kyoko," a song on the album written and performed by Ono, as "important as anything we ever did … as the Stones or Townshend or ever did. It's one of the fucking best rock and roll records ever made."[162] Particularly during the breakup period, Lennon adopted the tactic of publicly defending his new artistic partner by criticizing the work he had done with McCartney in the Beatles. "Lennon was notorious for his revisionist exaggerations about the Beatles music."[163]

The central debate surrounding Ono concerns the extent of her culpability for the group's breakup. Ono's presence and participation in the studio undoubtedly increased tensions. What Beatles writers' debate is who was to blame. In numerous interviews, Lennon argued that McCartney and Harrison treated Ono terribly and clearly resented her presence, casting blame on their refusal to accept Ono into the group.[164] "Until the day he died.... John Lennon would gallantly insist that the problem had not been of Yoko's making and that the other three Beatles had behaved despicably towards her."[165] Ono states that she only joined Lennon everywhere, including the studio, at his insistence because he refused to be separated from her,[166] and later argued that she saw nothing unreasonable about her presence or participation. "But to me it was nothing for me to be sitting there. In fact, I think that there were moments that, I felt that, um, I was repressing my own creative instincts ... by just sitting there."[167] According to this version Lennon was forced into choosing between his three closest friends, or the love of his life, and chose Ono. *Rolling Stone* as well as Coleman, Norman and Christgau, who tend to favor Lennon and Ono's interpretation of events, support this version. "The other Beatles treated her shabbily and provocatively," Coleman asserts, claiming their response was motivated in part by "chauvinist pique."[168] In 1975 *Rolling Stone* declared "We know how the other Beatles stood in judgment like a jury" on Ono.[169] In his obituary for the musician, Christgau echoed Lennon in blaming McCartney, Harrison and Starr's refusal to accept Ono into the group as the reason for its dissolution.[170] In his 2008 biography of Lennon, Norman argues that Lennon's motivation in bringing Ono into the studio was "not to disrupt the old gang, but to augment it."[171]

The opposite side rejects the claim that the other Beatles' reaction to Ono's presence was unnecessarily provocative and maintains that their behavior was tolerable if not overly welcoming. At best, they argue that Lennon's attempt to integrate Ono into the band was unreasonable. "John took the Beatles' coolness toward Yoko as a personal affront, conveniently overlooking that it was he who was changing the rules on *them*."[172] The studio was, with only rare exceptions, off limits to spouses. The creative chemistry and power dynamics among the group's members were a delicate and intricate web, and the Beatles were no longer merely a teenaged band from which Lennon could add or subtract members at will but a worldwide phenomenon and multi-million dollar business.[173]

At worst, authors speculate that Lennon's insistence on bringing Ono into the studio was a deliberately provocative move. They argue it was as much a demonstration of Lennon's dominance over the other members, especially McCartney—"Yoko was a stick he could use to bash the back of his partner's head"[174]—as it was a sign of his passion for Ono. Beatles engineer Geoff Emerick, who witnessed countless recording sessions both before and after Ono, clearly identifies Lennon and Ono as instigating the conflict. Emerick describes the last recording session without Ono as "the last time all four

Beatles were really happy being together in the studio"[175] and complains about the atmosphere after her arrival, beginning with *The White Album* sessions. "There's no question that her presence at the sessions was disruptive. We all knew it, and on some level (John) must have known it too, but he didn't seem to care; bringing her into the sessions like that was almost an act of defiance."[176] Emerick as well as other eyewitness accounts and memoirs argue that Ono felt entitled to a place in the band: "She seemed to feel that she was part of the group now. In her mind, and in John's mind, she had become the fifth Beatle."[177] Bramwell, whose view of Ono is pervasively negative, states it bluntly: "She wouldn't accept that she wasn't a Beatle."[178]

The tension amid Ono's presence in the studio is one of the major reasons various Beatles writers blame her for causing or contributing to the group's breakup. Another is that—like her counterpart Linda Eastman—Ono also is blamed for weakening the emotional and artistic ties between Lennon and other members of the group, particularly McCartney. After Lennon brought Ono into the studio "McCartney felt judged, excluded, rejected."[179] Lennon acknowledged replacing McCartney with Ono as his partner in interviews and in songs. "I was feeling guilty because I was with Yoko and I was leaving Paul."[180]

As with the debate over Ono's artistic skills, her effect on Lennon's personality and her presence in the studio, there are wide divisions between those Beatles writers who argue whether replacing McCartney with Ono enhanced or diminished Lennon's work. The opinions on whether her artistic influence benefitted Lennon as much as he claimed are worlds apart. Some key Beatles writers applaud her impact. According to Coleman, her influence "had taken him into whole new areas."[181] After he met Ono, "John chose to renounce the role of pop star and revert to art ... the need to strike out, away from manufacturing music as he did with the Beatles, was central to John's growth."[182] These assessments echo Lennon's own statements: "She forced me to become *avant-garde* and take my clothes off when all I wanted was to become Tom Jones."[183] In one of the last interviews he ever gave, to *Playboy*, Lennon reinforced the message: "She's the teacher and I'm the pupil.... She's taught me everything I fucking know."[184] Norman, Coleman, Wenner and others use Lennon's statements to applaud Ono's influence on Lennon's songwriting and help him discover his true depth and honesty as an artist.

Other musicologists and journalists fiercely disagree. According to Connolly, the idea that Lennon only became a real artist after he broke from the Beatles and joined with Ono was "nonsense."[185] In *Revolution in the Head*, MacDonald described the impact of Ono's artistic influence on Lennon in more detailed and negative terms, declaring "The pair brought out the worst in each other."[186] MacDonald argues against "Ono's dangerously silly idea that 'art is all about the artist and no one else,'"[187] denounces Lennon and Ono's claim that 'all art is self-referential' as anti-social solipsism"[188] and declares that Lennon's scorn for the "novelist" songs McCartney preferred was "rooted in egoism," a "prejudice hardened into dogma by Yoko Ono."[189] Far from benefiting artistically from Ono's influence, MacDonald states that Lennon's later work suffers from McCartney's absence: "[Lennon] nevertheless remained too self-absorbed to admit that his post–Beatles music was missing anything, let alone that this absent element might perhaps be that friendly friction with his old colleague."[190]

Primary and secondary sources on both sides of the divide also argue whether the emotional distance Ono placed between Lennon and his band mates was a natural effect of the couple's passionate love affair and a sign of their growing maturity, or the result of Ono's deliberate attempt to separate Lennon from the other three Beatles. Again, Lennon absolved Ono of any blame. "We were naïve enough to let people come between us and that's what happened.... I don't mean Yoko. I mean businessmen."[191] Harrison disagreed, both at the time and decades later. "Maybe now if you talk to Yoko she may say she likes the Beatles or that she liked the Beatles. But she didn't really like us because she saw the Beatles as something that was between her and John. The vibe I picked up was that she was a wedge that was trying to drive itself deeper and deeper between him and us, and it actually worked."[192] Shotton, who described Ono as "the best thing that ever happened"[193] to Lennon because she had helped his friend out of a profound depression, agreed with Harrison: "Yoko's possessiveness and jealousy or insecurity ... proved to be such that she apparently couldn't bear to see John enjoying a close rapport with anyone other than herself."[194] Bramwell implies that Ono, who introduced Lennon to heroin, did so in a deliberate attempt to distance him from the other three Beatles: "Psychologically, it looked more and more like it might have been a power thing on Yoko's part to draw John in closer to her and farther away from other people."[195]

Using female manipulation to absolve or explain the motivations behind the actions of important male figures is common throughout history.[196] Octavian, Appian and Plutarch all employed such tactics in their depictions of Marc Antony's relationship with Cleopatra. It suited the chroniclers of Roman power—and in particular Octavian, Antony's former brother-in-law—to argue that Antony's actions were the result of his virtual enslavement by Cleopatra, rather than his own decisions. Unlike Cleopatra, however, Ono's role in history has not been recounted only by early critics or those with an agenda to portray her as a scheming woman. Some Beatles writers are fierce advocates of Ono's art and her relationship with Lennon. This stark division of opinion concerning Ono exists across much of the spectrum of Beatles history. It pits credible primary source against credible primary source and secondary source against secondary source, critical opinion against critical opinion and memoir against memoir. Unlike Cleopatra, whose story was only told after her death, Ono survived for decades after her most contentious part in the Beatles story, and used that time to influence views about Beatles history and her role in it. It is in her efforts to shape her historiography that Ono's resemblance to Cleopatra collapses. By promoting her version of events after the fact, her parallel historic figure is not the Egyptian queen but Octavian, whose survival ensured an enormous amount of influence on how history viewed his female rival.

While the gulf between the irreconcilable views of Ono has narrowed somewhat over the decades, with more current Beatles authors such as Doggett now attempting to portray her in a more objective light, the debate over Ono may never be fully resolved. Part of this is attributable to the subjective elements—personal opinions on artistry, questions of character and psychology—that surround the debates centering on Ono. Historical methods tells us, that in order to gain the most accurate picture possible, both the pro and anti-Ono sides need to curb their urge to summarily dismiss the opposing side's evidence while blindly endorsing their preferred view. Instead, they must demonstrate impartial source analysis of the various contradictory accounts surrounding Ono and then provide the most credible version of events. When source analysis fails to identify a version that is obviously superior in credibility, then the author must provide both versions, allowing the reader to choose. In *The Landscape of History*, John Lewis Gaddis discusses how to respond to two contradictory versions that appear evenly matched: "It is part of growing up to learn that there are competing versions of the truth, and that you yourself must choose which to embrace."[197] Garraghan, author of *A Guide to Historical Method* agrees with Gaddis, but adds a piece of advice: "When two sources disagree and there's no other means of evaluation, take the source which best accords with common sense."[198]

Linda Eastman

Linda Eastman's 1968 public entrance into the Beatles story initially was greeted just as negatively as Yoko Ono's. Like Ono, Eastman was perceived as a major cause of the group's dissolution. Both were accused of widening the personal, artistic and business divisions between Lennon and McCartney that contributed to the band's collapse: "In both cases the women severed their men from their friends and fellow Beatles."[199] Each was cast as a seductress who manipulated and controlled an important male. However, both fans and the press largely despised Eastman months before they began to assign blame for the Beatles split. *Life* magazine put it bluntly: "At the outset, everyone hated [Linda]."[200] Her primary crime was marrying McCartney. "Paul may have loved Linda but the fans didn't. And they made it immediately clear."[201] As McCartney's bride, Eastman ended his status as the last unmarried Beatle, provoking the ire of many female fans. "After years of fantasizing about McCartney," reported *The Guardian* in its coverage of the singer's March 1969 wedding, countless female fans wept over "having their fairy tale dreams of becoming Mrs. McCartney ... dashed." Newspapers described the scene outside the ceremony with hundreds of girls "moaning and weeping and making catty comments about the bride," amid an atmosphere similar to "a communal suicide pact."[202] Some of the most devoted female fans, otherwise known as "Apple Scruffs," were particularly vicious. The Scruffs, who kept a permanent vigil outside McCartney's house, verbally insulted Eastman in the presence of her six-year-old daughter whenever she went outside, reportedly scrawled "American cunt go home"[203] on the house's outside walls, and broke inside, stealing some of her photo negatives. (Eastman was a professional photographer). Decades later Linda McCartney described the behavior of some fans as "vile, really vile to me."[204]

After Ono, Eastman is the most prominent female in the Beatles story. Like Ono, her part has been chronicled almost exclusively by males. Just as Ono's Japanese ancestry influenced her media depiction, parts of the press regarded Eastman's Jewish and American roots as suspect, and referred to her as "A Jewish Princess."[205] The British press, fans and later biographers were not above taking cheap shots at Eastman's appearance. A common joke in the 1970s: "What do you call a dog with wings?" (which was a pun on the name of McCartney's second band, Wings), identified her as the punch line.[206] Beatles writers criticized her professional qualifications—"her ability as a photographer was not highly esteemed"[207]—her skill as a mother—"Heather (her daughter from her first marriage) learned to look after herself at an early age"[208]—and her sexual history—"Linda notched up approximately twenty lovers, most of whom were famous."[209] Despite its sexist connotations, "Groupie" was another epithet journalists and biographers attached to Eastman well into the 21st century. Throughout parts of Beatles historiography the sexual histories of Ono and Eastman (as well as other females) are used to judge the worthiness of their characters; few writers apply such judgment to the male Beatles, whose own sexual experiences numbered in the hundreds. Lennon, whose relationship

with Linda Eastman could be best described as mercurial,[210] in 1980 denounced
the way the press had treated both Ono and Eastman.

> She got the same kind of insults, hatred, absolute garbage thrown at her for no
> reason whatsoever other than she fell in love with Paul McCartney. They were
> insulting them on such a *personal level*—about the way they look and things
> like that, that they would never do to anybody, man or woman, in person.[211]

Eastman's portrayal also was impacted by her seemingly abrupt (and to
many, unwelcome) entrance into the Beatles story. For much of the Beatles
fame McCartney's significant romantic relationship was with the beautiful,
famous English actress Jane Asher. As one of the golden couples of swinging
London, they presented an ideal public image and were "the darlings of the
media."[212] Unlike the apathy in *The Authorized Biography* between Lennon
and his wife Cynthia, Davies depicted McCartney's relationship with Asher
as predominantly healthy and affectionate: "Jane and Paul make a very lovely
and loving couple. Everyone agrees on this."[213] The two abruptly ended their
engagement in summer 1968 and Asher, the inspiration for some of McCartney's greatest love songs, exited the group's story. The press, many fans, and
members of the Beatles circle regarded Eastman as an inferior replacement.
The perception of her unworthiness continued well into the 21st century:
"Linda seemed like no one's idea of an obsession-worthy muse, just some
random hippie-chick Paul liked."[214]

Many of those who accused Eastman of causing or contributing to the
group's breakup based their conclusions on two major arguments. The first
was that she had pushed McCartney to support her father Lee and brother
John, respected and successful New York entertainment lawyers, as the new
Beatles financial managers. Following the death of Epstein and the economic
chaos of Apple, the band's financial affairs were in disarray. McCartney suggested his new girlfriend's brother and father as the solution, but was over-
ruled by the other three, who chose the Rolling Stone's manager Allen Klein.
McCartney's refusal to join with the others and accept Klein as his manager
was attributed to being "too easily led" by Linda and her family.[215] Her influence and her family's self-promotion were identified as the key reasons behind
McCartney's refusal to accept Lennon, Harrison and Starr's choice of Klein,
which proved to be the insoluble division among the four.[216] Klein repeatedly
blamed the Eastman family in his 1971 interview with *Playboy*.[217] Lennon laid
part of the blame for McCartney's behavior on Eastman and her family in a
letter he wrote the McCartney's in 1971. Criticizing Eastman for being "Middle-Class," Lennon accused her family of causing the band's financial problems: "Of course the money is important to us ... especially after all the petty
shit that came from your insane family/in-laws," and hinted that he believed

McCartney's marriage (and, by extension, his business ties to the Eastmans) would be short lived. "*God help you out*, Paul—see you in two years—I reckon you'll be out then."[218]

After the band's dissolution both Lennon and numerous sources in the rock and roll press argued that the Eastman family wealth and background encouraged McCartney's bourgeois aspirations, conservative tendencies, and domesticity at a time when his musical partner, Lennon, was embracing the radical political left and the *avant-garde* art world with Ono. Under his wife and new in-law's' influence, they argued, McCartney became "conservative, domestic and boring"[219]; and this ideological split between the two, encouraged by their wives, widened the two men's existing divisions. Lennon reinforced this message in his extremely influential *Lennon Remembers* interview, which was published in 1971, weeks after McCartney announced he was suing the other three to dissolve the group. Labeling the Eastmans as "fucking stupid middle class pig(s),"[220] Lennon criticized McCartney for falling for the Eastmans "class snobbery": "Paul fell for that bullshit because he's got Picassos on the wall and because he's got some kind of East Coast shit. Form and not substance. And that's McCartney."[221]

Linda Eastman did promote her father and brother to McCartney. However, beyond the fact that she recommended them as a solution to Apple's financial struggles, there is no evidence directly supporting the claim that she demanded that McCartney choose her brother and father as the new financial managers for the Beatles. Nor is there any proving that she continued to demand he refuse to support Klein's appointment even as the managerial dispute led to increasingly hostile relationships between McCartney and the rest of the group. There *is* abundant evidence that Linda Eastman, as well as John and Lee Eastman, mistrusted and disliked Klein. But whether their aversion was motivated primarily by their personal self-interest or because of legitimate suspicions regarding Klein's financial dealings is debatable. There is no disputing that McCartney's life changed dramatically after he became a husband and father and, intentionally or not, his relationship with his new wife helped distance him from Lennon both personally and ideologically. McCartney admitted as much in a November 1969 interview: "We are individuals—all different. John married Yoko. I married Linda. We didn't marry the same girl."[222] Decades later in *Anthology*, Martin argued that Ono and Eastman contributed to the band's breakup because their entrance altered the emotional core at the heart of the group. "They [Ono and Eastman] were more important to John and Paul than John and Paul were to each other."[223]

Eastman and Ono are invariably compared with one another in the memoirs of various Beatles insiders and by the band's biographers. This is partly attributable to their roles as the two most prominent women in the Beatles story and the similar timing of their entrance into the group's life. It is associated with the pervasive pattern in Beatles historiography to compare every aspect of Lennon's life with McCartney's, and vice versa. Those Beatles writers who favor Ono are often more critical of Eastman, describing her as "simpering," or "flighty,"[224] criticizing her skills as a photographer (and in at least one 1970s work, as a mother) and comparing her personality, appearance and influence on McCartney unfavorably with Asher's.[225] On the opposite side of the spectrum, writers who openly dislike Ono often compare her unfavorably with Eastman. Bramwell, who knew both women, adopts this tactic in his account of his time with the group, *Magical Mystery Tours*. His description of Ono is resoundingly negative, deriding "Princess Yoko"[226] as "exceptionally jealous"[227] "pushy" "frightening" "imperious" and "a pain in the ass."[228] Conversely, his portrayal of Eastman is wholly complimentary. Bramwell describes her as "unpretentious" "down to earth" "polite" and "always pleasant."[229] Comparing the two would be "unfair," he argues, because "Linda was warm, funny, and talented,"[230] leaving readers to infer that Ono was none of those things.

The vitriol directed at Linda McCartney decreased as decades passed, although she received an overwhelming wave of negative press in the early 1970s when, at her husband's insistence, she joined his new band Wings. The theory that Ono helped instigate the band's split remains conventional wisdom: Well into the 21st century, some fans appear at McCartney's concerts wearing "Still Pissed at Yoko" shirts. In contrast, Eastman's role is now regarded as unintentional and secondary. Additionally, many of the female fans who initially despised Linda Eastman for becoming Linda McCartney later regarded her with a certain amount of affection and respect. This is likely a product of the McCartney's successful marriage, which lasted 29 years until Linda McCartney's 1998 death from breast cancer.

Allen Klein

Like Ono and Eastman, Allen Klein was a divisive figure from the moment he entered the Beatles story. While harsh views of Eastman, and, to a lesser extent, Ono have softened with time, Klein's reputation has only deteriorated. The last Beatles manager is now regarded as the final and major cause of the band's acrimonious break-up. Any accurate account of Klein's part in the Beatles story was complicated by clashing agendas, contradictory primary sources, financial self-interest, and open inter-Beatle warfare. In later years, the perception of Klein has been influenced by the post-breakup agendas of both sides of Beatles historiography, the emergence of new evidence highlighting Klein's questionable business practices, and the inevitable reality of judgments made in retrospect and with information that was contemporaneously unavailable to the players in Beatles history. Regardless of the depiction's accuracy, it has now become fashionable in the 21st century to regard Klein as the great villain—the "Monster of Rock"[231]—who brought about the Beatles' end. All the debates that revolved around Klein in the late 1960s and early 1970s are now considered resolved—and not in his favor.

Due to the predominantly negative perception of Klein in current Beatles historiography, in order to gain any accurate understanding of the man, his impact on the group and its breakup, it is essential to go back to contemporary, primary sources whenever possible. Decades after the collapse of the Beatles and years after Klein's death, there is an abundant amount of retrospective testimony—some of it from celebrities such as James Taylor and Paul McCartney to George Harrison and Peter Asher—condemning Klein. Later Beatles writers have the benefit of hindsight when it comes to Klein's financial and legal dealings (as well as his imprisonment in the late 1970s for tax evasion) but the players in Beatles history lacked this information at the time he entered the story. Armed with this abundance of anti–Klein evidence, some Beatles writers paint the man as such a villain (one biographer introduces him as "a tough little scorpion")[232] that they raise the significant question: *Why was Klein trusted and accepted into the Beatles' inner circle in the first place?* In presenting such a heavily retrospective view, these writers risk committing what Gaddis refers to as "the greatest of all historical errors: arrogantly judging our forebears in the light of modern knowledge perforce unknown to them."[233] In *You Never Give Me Your Money*, Doggett addresses the interpretive error caused by summarily casting Klein as the villain:

> Nobody in the Beatles milieu has received a more damning verdict from historians than Allen Klein. He was, one said, "a tough little scorpion"; for another, "fast-talking, dirty-mouthed ... sloppily dressed and grossly overweight"; again, "a short and fat, beady–eyed and greasily pompadoured." ... Yet we are asked to believe that three of the four Beatles found this "beady eyed" "grossly overweight" "scorpion" such an attractive figure that they were prepared to trust him with their futures. Clearly the Demon King didn't always exude the stench of sulfur.[234]

This dissonance is heightened by accounts which provide an opposing view. Numerous contemporaneous sources indicate that initially Klein's relationships with Lennon, Harrison and Starr were friendly and that they trusted him implicitly. In a 1971 interview journalist David Vetter declared that, during Klein's interactions with the three men, he displayed "charm and wit and tenderness."[235] In 1972 Derek Taylor defended Klein against accusations that he was motivated solely by greed: "He genuinely liked the Beatles from the first ... even Paul."[236] Decades later in *Anthology*, Starr still reminisced fondly about him: "I liked Allen. He was a lot of fun, and he knew the record business."[237]

Despite these sources, any active debates surrounding Klein's role in Beatles history have largely ceased over the decades as his portrayal has ossified. The first argument, beginning with Klein's introduction into the Beatles story in January 1969 and continuing for approximately the next four years, centers on whether he was the correct choice to succeed Epstein. On a more personal level (particularly for Lennon) the question was whether Klein merited guardianship over the Beatles' fortune and music. According to Lennon, Harrison, and Starr, the answer was a resounding yes. From 1969 until 1973, Lennon and Ono, and to a lesser extent Harrison and Starr, publicly and privately championed Klein as the best candidate. Klein, already suspect as an American taking control of a beloved British institution, defended his reputation in a 1969 interview: "It's been said I screw my clients. You find just one artist who'll say that. Not one ... it's not true. You can say I make a lot of money, or I'm a bastard.... But you can't say I screw my clients."[238] Both before and after the breakup three-fourths of the Beatles promoted Klein as their new manager and depicted McCartney's holdout as, at best, unreasonable and, at worst, selfish. In May 1970, Harrison identified McCartney's self-interest in preferring the Eastmans over Klein as the "only" reason for the recently announced breakup, arguing that the other man was "out-voted 3 to 1" and that while he, Lennon and Starr had the group's best interests in mind, McCartney did not: "We're not trying to do what's best for Paul and his in-laws, you know."[239]

The debate over whether Klein was the correct choice was waged in private, from Apple's boardrooms to Abbey Road to law offices in Manhattan, and in public, from the pages of the *New Musical Express* to the *London Times* to *Rolling Stone*. McCartney's 1971 legal victory, in which the court seemed to favor his position that Klein was an untrustworthy and divisive choice, settled neither the private nor public disagreement over the issue; it simply further entrenched each side and escalated the rhetoric. The debates about Klein's suitability only ended in 1973 after Lennon, Harrison and Starr refused to renew their contracts with Klein and then sued him. Armed with this *ex post facto* knowledge, very few post–1973 Beatles writers engage in any real examination of Klein's strengths and successes as manager.[240] In current Beatles historiography, there is scant debate over this once incredibly divisive issue that, at the official narrative's end, publicly pitted Lennon against McCartney and one version of Beatles history against another.

The evidence implicating Klein as unscrupulous is undeniable; however, not all of the facts were known to the players at the time. It must be noted that his reputation as a slippery but profitable businessman was well known throughout the rock and roll world before 1969: According to a 1974 interview with McCartney, that only enhanced Klein's appeal for Lennon: "John said, 'Anyone whose record is as bad as this can't be so bad,'" reasoning that McCartney described as "Lennonesque crap."[241] When he was introduced as the Beatles manager, Klein had already been under investigation in the United States for the Cameo-Parkway stock inflation scandal. In July 1970 the Rolling Stones refused to renew their contract with Klein, and in September the next year sued him for $29 million, a case which was settled out of court. In January 1971, immediately prior to the Beatles trial, he was convicted of ten counts of income tax fraud by the U.S. government. At the Beatles trial, Justice Terrence Stamp ruled that Klein had taken commissions in excess of what he was entitled. The most serious charge against Klein does not involve the Beatles but the Rolling Stones. As their co-manager in 1965, Klein persuaded the Stones to establish Nanker-Phelge, a tax shelter. Nanker-Phelge protected the band from Britain's astronomic tax rates, but did so by transferring the band's North American song catalog's publishing rights to Klein's ABKCO Company. The ultimate result of this was that Klein, and not the Stones, owned the rights to all the band's pre–1971 songs in the United States. (ABKCO retains the rights to this day: the Rolling Stones have always maintained that they did not understand that, in establishing Nanker-Phelge, they were signing away a fortune and permanently ceding their catalog's American publishing rights.) By 1969, as Klein was attempting to contact someone in the Beatles camp, Mick Jagger and the other Stones were already suspicious of their manager: They had hired a London law firm to do an independent appraisal of the band's finances, but chose not to inform the Beatles[242] they had done so.[243]

As with Ono and Eastman, the second major debate that revolves around Klein is his culpability regarding the band's breakup. No one questions *if* Klein contributed to the Beatles split and the bitter feelings that ensued; they merely speculate on the amount of damage he did and if his actions made the break irrevocable. In *The Complete Beatles Chronicle*, Lewisohn describes Klein's appointment as Beatles manager over McCartney's objections as nothing less than a schism that divided the group at its core. "Henceforth the Beatles were split into two opposing camps."[244] The reason for this view of Klein as the band's ultimate wedge is simple: The evidence implicating Klein with approaching the Beatles with a "divide and conquer" strategy, deliberately playing Lennon against McCartney and the Eastmans, is overwhelming: "Klein's version of personal management veils manipulation, turning three Beatles against one."[245]

Primary and secondary sources, both from those who did and did not initially favor Klein's appointment as manager, contemporaneous eyewitness accounts, legal testimony, private conversations and public interviews all reinforce this. Lennon acknowledged in *Lennon Remembers* that Klein deliberately courted him by emphasizing his belief in Lennon's preeminent place in the group. Klein did this by going through the Lennon/McCartney song catalog and identifying which lyrics Lennon had written, flattering the musician's insecure ego.[246] Klein's reason for adopting this approach is also widely accepted: With McCartney's ties to the Eastmans, whom the singer already had approached for help with the group's chaotic financial situation, Klein knew McCartney would never support his bid for Beatles manager. Klein had wanted and obsessed over the Beatles for years. He clearly regarded Lennon, who was, when the two met in January 1969, using heroin and angry that McCartney had become the *de facto* leader of the band, as his means to achieve this.

Klein's introduction into the Beatles story offers a fascinating example of how those who write history as it is unfolds can shape its outcome. Klein's cultivation of a personal connection with Lennon is regarded as one of the primary reasons for the singer's choice. From their very first meeting, Lennon was struck by how well Klein knew him: "He told me all that was happening with the Beatles, my relationship with Paul and George and Ringo. He knew every damn thing about us … and anybody that knew me that well, without ever having met me, had to be the guy that I could let look after me."[247] For Lennon, whose understanding of business was poor to nonexistent, this instinctive connection was a powerful indication that Klein was the right choice; in reality, it was a demonstration of how well Klein had done his research. "When wooing a new client, Klein would obtain and nearly memorize every item on the artist he could find, from press clips to contracts."[248] Klein pumped members of the Rolling Stones, who were friends and rivals of the Beatles, for information on the Fab Four and studied the group's interviews in an attempt to understand their personalities, situations and problems. Klein's access to Davies' *Authorized Biography* was of crucial importance. *The Beatles* was published in September 1968, months before Klein and Lennon had their face-to-face meeting. "Klein's reading of Hunter Davies biography had given him a glance of John's psychology."[249] Davies' work contained Lennon and Shotton's multiple descriptions of Lennon's ingrained need to be the alpha in any group, and Klein used that information as a key part of his pitch to Lennon. "When Klein met Lennon in January 1969, he pressed a different button: He stressed that there were four Beatles. Paul McCartney wasn't anybody's leader! Where did he get off, treating the others as if they were merely sidemen? It was just what John wanted to hear."[250]

Lennon and Ono were sold on Klein after their first meeting.[251] But Harrison and Starr were still potential clients for either Klein or the Eastmans. Klein promised both Harrison and Starr that he would make them wealthy enough to adopt a "fuck you, money"[252] attitude to business, and both signed with him. At another tumultuous meeting, Lennon and Klein goaded Lee Eastman into losing his temper, insulting Klein, and leaving.[253] Decades later in *Anthology*, Harrison argued that he chose Klein over Eastman because Klein, the self-made man, presented himself as a less class conscious, elitist option.[254] But the main reason, Harrison reasoned, was because of Lennon's influence. "I think I'll go with Klein because John's with him and he seemed to talk pretty straight … it was much easier if we went with him too."[255] This quote by Harrison is widely accepted as the motivation behind his choice, and is reinforced by statements Harrison made in a private argument with Lennon years later (which was witnessed by Lennon's girlfriend May Pang) where Harrison stated that he chose Klein out of deference to Lennon.[256]

However, any of Harrison's retrospective explanations must be evaluated in the light of later events, particularly his own exchange of lawsuits with Klein and the general consensus by the time *Anthology* appeared that Klein had been the incorrect choice. Lennon's vocal support for Klein *did* influence the other members: Starr also cited Lennon's influence as well as the class issue and the assumption that the Eastmans would be biased in favor of McCartney in his retrospective reasoning for why he chose Klein.[257] In *Powers of Two*, his analysis of the Lennon/McCartney dyad, Joshua Wolf Shenk describes Harrison and Starr's decision to follow Lennon as "pure primate politics,"[258] and argues that their willingness to follow Lennon's lead, along with McCartney's refusal, reveals a great deal about the structure of the Beatles hierarchy.

Dividing McCartney from the rest of the group was essential to Klein's strategy in becoming Beatles manager. It required having three Beatles—Lennon, Harrison and Starr—outvote another member three-to-one and ignore his veto, something unprecedented for any decision, which previously required unanimity.[259] Once Klein was appointed, the schism between McCartney and the other three over business matters only grew. Klein perceived the Eastmans (who had, in a forced compromise, been appointed as the Beatles attorneys) as threats looking over his financial shoulder. He delib-

erately portrayed himself to Lennon, Ono, Harrison and Starr as the Eastmans' working-class, blunt-spoken and self-made opposite. He mocked the
Eastmans in meetings by referring to them by their non-anglicized name,
which happened to be Epstein, and verbally insulted them. While he developed personal relationships with Lennon, Ono, Harrison and Starr, by his
own admission he failed to establish any sort of relationship with McCartney,[260] something about which he complained several times in his November
1971 *Playboy* interview.[261]

Klein's overall strategy was inherently precarious as well as divisive, in
that it necessitated sowing dissension between McCartney and the other
three. He did this by insulting McCartney's in-laws to their faces; flattering
Lennon's ego and using Apple's money to fund Ono's art shows,[262] overriding
or ignoring McCartney's protests and arguments about Klein's managerial
percentages and at times refusing to take the musician's calls even at the
office.[263] While McCartney's relationship with the Eastmans ensured that he
never would prefer Klein as his manager, both McCartney's 1971 trial testimony as well as outside, retrospective accounts argue that Klein's blustering,
aggressive approach significantly contributed to poor relations between the
two. Beatles engineer Glyn Johns witnessed one of Klein's confrontations
with McCartney in 1969. In his memoirs Johns recounts watching the musician attempt to defend himself "against Klein's attempts at bullying him into
submission," a scene Johns describes as "extremely unpleasant to witness."[264]
Lennon's relationship with McCartney was already tense. Both Lennon and
Harrison resented McCartney's increasing habit to record some of his songs
entirely on his own, without input from any of the other Beatles. Both also
chafed at McCartney's increasing tendency to instruct rather than request.
While serious tensions among all the band members pre-dated Klein's arrival,
McCartney argues that their new manager widened already existing divisions
and created new ones: "it became three to one and I was like the idiot in the
corner ... to Klein it looked like I was trying to screw the situation. He used
to call me the 'Reluctant Virgin.'"[265]

In addition, the Eastmans clearly regarded supporting McCartney as
more important than maintaining the group's unity. Both John and Lee Eastman insulted Klein in the presence of all four Beatles, a tactic which only
alienated them further from Lennon, Harrison and Starr. The Eastmans'
attempts to undermine Klein's authority to speak for McCartney contributed
to the band's failure to purchase the Lennon/McCartney song catalog, Northern Songs. In a pivotal series of business meetings in September 1969, John
Eastman argued that McCartney's voting power should equal that of the other
three. Starr rejected the idea, and accused them of working to divide the four

of them.[266] Eventually, McCartney stopped attending group meetings that included Klein, sending his lawyer in his stead and further alienating himself from the other three. Epstein had managed the Beatles successfully for years in large part because of his emphasis on maintaining balance in the group, but evidence indicates that both the Eastmans and Klein were less interested in balance than in advancing their own side.

Although Klein's divide and conquer strategy required exploiting and maintaining divisions between McCartney and the others there is every reason to believe that he never intended for those divisions to become irresolvable. Even as virtually every work in Beatles historiography argues that Klein fostered an enormous amount of animosity and that his actions helped spur the band's demise, no one argues that he *intended* to destroy the Beatles. Such a move, after all, would have gone against Klein's own financial self-interest and managerial reputation. At the same time, it must be acknowledged that Klein's poor relations with McCartney (the Beatle who had written or co-written their most commercially successful songs) also undermined Klein's self-interest.[267] When faced with such instances, Gaddis reminds readers that the application of common sense does not always provide a clearer version of the truth: "History is filled with examples of people making irrational rather than rational choices on the basis of inaccurate rather than accurate information."[268]

The End of the Fab Four Narrative

By the end of 1968 and the beginning of 1969, the cracks in the official narrative were becoming visible to the press and the public. The three major elements promoted in the Fab Four version—whitewashing the Beatles reputations, the unity of the band, and the Lennon/McCartney songwriting partnership—were being contradicted by a constant flood of new information. Some listeners heard the splintering within the group on the *White Album*, released in November 1968. During the album's recording, tensions were so bad that members at times recorded in different studios, with Starr actually briefly leaving the group, and the divisiveness showed in the music. During the recording of their subsequent "Get Back" project in early 1969, the London press reported that relations had gotten so tense that Lennon and Harrison engaged in a physical fight. Harrison denied it, but in *Summer of Love* Martin said that the two men came to blows, leading to Harrison walking out. In interviews McCartney, Lennon and Harrison all acknowledged the tensions created by Klein's appointment as Beatles manager. "Paul and I have a

difference of opinion on how things should be run.... Mainly we disagree on
the Klein bit," Lennon admitted.[269] Starr also publicly discussed the disagreements among the band members: "You know there's that old saying, you'll
always hurt the ones you love. And we all love each other and we all know
that. But we still sort of hurt each other occasionally."[270] As 1969 went on,
media speculation continued to grow that the Beatles were splitting, and
interviews with Starr in January and Lennon in December reinforced the
perception.

The Beatles image, which had remained mostly favorable in the mainstream press, also endured increasing attack. Many fans vocally disliked Ono
and Eastman and regarded Lennon's honeymoon Bed-In as bizarre. In October 1968, Lennon was arrested for drug possession; in March 1969, it was
Harrison's turn. Lennon's relationship with Ono and their public peace campaign made them objects of ridicule and scorn on both sides of the Atlantic
even as it endeared the couple to the underground and rock and roll press,
which shared their political views. The couple's first joint album, *Two Virgins*,
released in November 1968, included a highly controversial nude cover photo,
leading to public questions regarding Lennon and Ono's sanity. Meanwhile
McCartney vanished from the halls of Apple. The musician refused almost
all interviews for a year, leading to intense worldwide speculation that he
was dead. At the same time Lennon and Ono's media exposure increased as
they continued to promote their peace campaign and artistic partnership.
Lennon sent his Member of the British Empire award, which all four Beatles
had accepted in 1965, back to Buckingham Palace in a political protest.
Lennon's actions in particular seemed deliberately provocative. "1969 was a
year in which John seemed, in his own whimsical way, to be doing his level
best to destroy the myth of the Beatles."[271]

No one in their immediate circle publicly declared the death of the
Lennon/McCartney songwriting partnership, but some reviewers and listeners heard it in the music, and Lennon's new artistic collaboration with Ono
was clearly his priority, as the two of them released a flurry of albums and
singles together. Connolly, who chronicled the group's last years, declared
the end of Lennon/McCartney in his November 1969 article "The Day the
Beatles Died." "It is a common fiction that Lennon and McCartney still work
together ... but they haven't composed a song together for years." While Connolly acknowledged the tensions throughout the group, he identified the key
schism as existing between its two core members. "What is more serious is
the clash between John and Paul.... When they fight they can go on for hours,
neither side giving an inch."[272] In December 1969, Alan Smith's account of
the partnership was even more pessimistic, depicting the two men as oppos-

ing forces openly pitted against one another. In the interview Lennon discussed his unhappiness with the restrictions being in the Beatles placed on his music, declaring he no longer wanted to have his number of songs restricted due to the presence of McCartney and Harrison's songs. Contradicting the previous message of unity, including some of his own previous statements which minimized any accounts of conflict within the group, Lennon argued that stories of their disagreements were nothing new: "It's no news that we argue." For those fans looking for reassurance that the four men would overcome their differences, Lennon offered no guarantees: "The Beatles split up? It just depends on how much we all want to record together. I don't know if I want to record together again. I go off and on about it. I really do."[273]

What Lennon did not mention was that the Beatles had broken up four months earlier, and that he had ended it. At a September 1969 meeting the group's founder announced that he wanted a "divorce," and after that admission revealed his insecurity and frustration, placing the blame for them on McCartney's shoulders. Retrospective testimony from numerous sources, including accounts by Lennon's assistant Anthony Fawcett, McCartney, and Lennon himself chronicle the list of grievances: McCartney had dominated studio production, written too many songs and come up with too many ideas. According to Lennon his partner had become *too* productive, and used the *Magical Mystery Tour* album as an example: "I didn't write any of that except 'Walrus.' I'd accept it and you'd already have five or six songs."[274] While acknowledging his own notably lesser interest in studio production—"When we get into the studio, I don't care how we do it"[275]—he also criticized McCartney's tendency to direct how Beatles song were produced. As a private confession rather than a public interview, Lennon's criticisms provide the most credible piece of evidence to explain some of Lennon's motivations for his declaration of divorce. They do not nullify Lennon's later public statements about why he ended the band. However, as a private conversation, they do lack the obvious agenda of his later interviews.

Both Klein and McCartney urged Lennon to keep his decision to leave quiet, as the Beatles were in the midst of negotiating several business deals that would fall apart if the news went public. For months after, all four Beatles' public statements maintained the skeleton of the mythology they had helped create in 1962. Privately McCartney, Harrison and Starr speculated among themselves whether Lennon, who was prone to making bold judgments and then swiftly reversing himself, would change his mind. Lennon's public interviews seemed to offer hope, but privately there was no hint that he wanted the Beatles to continue.

After months of uncertainty which were marked by increasing hostility between himself and his fellow band-mates over Klein, McCartney broke the silence and ended the official narrative. In the press release to his April 1970 solo album *McCartney*, the musician revealed that the Beatles were not planning a new album or single, that what relationship he had with Klein was acrimonious and non-existent, and that he had not missed the other Beatles while working on his self-made album. What made headlines across the globe, however, was his announcement that he was taking a "break" from the group. Arguing that his first solo album was both "a rest" and "the start of a solo career," McCartney acknowledged that he was unsure whether his break was "temporary or permanent." His other statements revealed that, even if the band's splintering was temporary, his creative schism with Lennon was not. When asked "Do you foresee a time when Lennon-McCartney becomes an active songwriting partnership again," McCartney's response was a blunt "No."[276]

The *McCartney* press release rejected crucial aspects of the official narrative, in particular the Lennon/McCartney songwriting partnership and any remaining illusion of unity. However, at no point did McCartney mention that Lennon already had left the group. He never explicitly stated either in the press release or in an earlier phone conversation with Lennon that he would never work with the other Beatles again. But the story's momentum was overwhelming: "Around the world, virtually all other news items were relegated to second place in the morning newspapers, the evening newspapers, the radio and television bulletins"[277]; and its impact, historic. *The Daily Mirror* headline for April 10 read "Paul Quits the Beatles!" and the news went around the world, even reaching behind the Iron Curtain. Millions of fans responded to the story with grief, some of them weeping in public; the same response they had to the news of Lennon's murder 10 years later. *Time* described the reaction in its April 1970 coverage of the event: "From Liverpool to Piccadilly, the cries of anguish rent the air: The Beatles are dead!"[278] At the time, CBS news described the Beatles breakup as "an event so momentous that historians may one day view it as a landmark in the decline of the British Empire."[279] Decades later, *The Guardian* argued it was even more important than that.

In *The Landscape of History*, Gaddis cautions against simplifying the causes of historic events by identifying one or two obvious catalysts. Such an approach not only obscures history but often overlooks essential information. "Causes always have antecedents. We may rank their relative significance, but we'd think it irresponsible to seek or isolate—or 'tease out'—single causes for complex events."[280] After April 1970 the first debates on one of the most contentious subjects in Beatles historiography—who to blame for the Beatles' breakup—emerged. Even as most hoped for reconciliation, journalists and fans quickly assigned blame: directing it alternately at Ono or Klein, Eastman and her family, or McCartney. Since McCartney made the announcement much of the public blame fell on him. Yet identifying McCartney (or any individual) as the sole cause simply because he announced the split is a prime example of a common error in interpreting evidence: focusing so intently on what Gaddis describes as the "efficient" cause of an event that the underlying reasons *behind* the efficient cause are ignored.

Consequences of historic importance may result directly from efficient causes, but efficient causes by themselves, while factually accurate, ultimately offer an incomplete picture. Additional information, including identifying the "formal" and "final" causes, is necessary in order to gain any accurate understanding of an event's origin. Gaddis uses the assassination of Abraham Lincoln as his example. Why did Lincoln die? According to the efficient cause, Lincoln died because John Wilkes Booth put a bullet in his brain. While completely true, such an answer satisfies no one, because it ignores the key question of why Booth shot Lincoln. Gaddis then identifies the formal cause: Booth killed Lincoln because he hated him. But like the efficient cause, the formal cause leaves an underlying question: Why did Booth hate Lincoln? The final cause is then identified: Booth hated Lincoln because Booth supported the Confederacy and believed Lincoln's death would avenge its loss.[281]

Like Lincoln's death, the story of the Beatles breakup offers a way to view efficient, formal, and final causes. The efficient cause behind the Beatles breakup is McCartney's April 1970 public announcement that he was taking a break from the group, which publicly dissolved the official narrative and infuriated Lennon who, if he did want to take back his earlier declaration of divorce, could no longer do so without losing face. Any list of the formal causes behind McCartney's announcement must include Lennon's own September 1969 departure. While some initially blamed McCartney for the breakup simply because he made the announcement, most Beatles writers and fans have spent the last 40 years debating the extent to which the split was attributable to the final causes such as Klein, Ono, the Eastmans, Lennon's insecurity, McCartney's ego, drug use, musical differences, and Harrison's refusal to continue to conform to the traditional Beatles hierarchy.

McCartney's April 1970 announcement signified the end of the now battered official narrative in place since 1962. For months after the shock of the *McCartney* press release, no new narrative emerged to take its place; leaving a vacuum where one of the most powerful mythologies of the decade once existed. The Fab Four version of the Beatles story had now been exposed and implicitly or explicitly rejected by the band's own members, but with millions hopeful that the schism was temporary, it maintained a lingering influence until December of 1970 when new events and sources altered the direction of Beatles historiography.

From 1962 until 1970 the Beatles and their circle promoted and shaped music's most popular mythology. They willfully obscured aspects of the truth, creating a story which was embraced by millions of fans across the globe. Later versions of Beatles history—particularly the *Lennon Remembers* and *Shout!* narratives which dominated the group's historiography in the 1970s and 1980s—denounced the myth-making of the official narrative, and dismissed its three core elements as fiction. But the enduring influence of the first version of the Beatles story on their historiography is inarguable. It was under the auspices of the official narrative that the group became a global phenomenon, created its most famous music, and produced much of the core primary material and sources, including interviews and biographies, which Beatles writers and journalists mined for evidence for decades. It cemented, for better or worse, the public perception of the primary roles and characteristics of each individual Beatle; something which became crucial as their story splintered into different members' opposing versions. Just as importantly, it influenced every later narrative in Beatles history, in particular its direct successor the *Lennon Remembers* version. Following the wake of the Fab Four version, *Lennon Remembers* emerged during the group's breakup to offer a view of the Beatles story that was in direct opposition to its predecessor.

CHAPTER TWO

The *Lennon Remembers* Narrative

> It is much easier to accept with complacency an illusion ... which
> gratifies the interest of the moment.
>   —Marc Bloch, *The Historian's Craft*

The Dissolution of the Official Narrative

By December 1970, real life events meant that the official version of the Beatles story, which had been promoted and sold for eight years, now appeared idealized and obsolete. The press release that accompanied Paul McCartney's April 1970 solo album *McCartney*, in which he announced his intention to take "a rest"[1] from The Beatles, was viewed as the announcement of the group's breakup. Media speculation regarding the band's dissolution had intensified throughout 1969 and early 1970, but McCartney's April announcement still shocked and angered millions. His departure was the most important official contradiction of the Fab Four narrative, publicly revealing the deep divisions within the band and the Lennon/McCartney partnership. However, far more extreme revisions quickly followed. In the span of a year, from December 1970 through the end of 1971, both Lennon and McCartney destroyed the story they had spent the last eight years telling. The contentious and public nature of the Beatles' breakup had a massive impact on how the band's story was told in the years after its dissolution, and in the decades following.

Prior to 1969 all four Beatles always had presented a united front in public. Aspects of the Fab Four narrative had been manufactured, mythologized and whitewashed, but it had been the *singular* version. After the once unified band split into factions, markedly different versions of the band's "true" story emerged, most powerfully from the ex-Beatles themselves. It was during this time that the two major debates in Beatles historiography appeared. The first was the question of whether Lennon or McCartney deserved the title of genius and the most credit for the Beatles' musical brilliance. The second concerned their rupture: Who was to blame for the group's breakup? Both questions revolved around the Lennon/McCartney axis that, even with the dissolution of the official narrative, continued to dominate the Beatles' story. The decade following the band's dissolution saw Beatles history divide into two camps, with Lennon's initial version of events establishing itself as the new Orthodoxy. This schism exerted enormous influence across Beatles historiography, flavoring retrospective eyewitness testimony, authorial interpretation and musicological analysis.

The *McCartney* press release and resultant press reaction had publicly broken up the world's favorite band. From April to December of 1970, the public anxiously read newspapers and magazines discussing why the Beatles had split and what hopes there were for reconciliation. Both Ono and McCartney were blamed: where the popular perception identified Ono, the rock and roll press regarded the breakup as a consequence of McCartney's actions, in particular his refusal to support Allen Klein as the new Beatles manager. Although it was Lennon who had privately ended the group in September 1969, no one outside the Beatles' inner circle was aware of that at the time. In the initial days following the April 1970 announcement, Lennon did not correct this false impression. "Lennon sat back and allowed McCartney to become the focus of the world's anger."[2] McCartney's popular and professional reputations declined in the wake of the press release as anger grew at his perceived role in instigating the breakup; this helped influence critical reaction to his work for years. "McCartney was instantly vilified. His solo album and its follow-up, *Ram*, were viciously panned by critics, who only began to soften their stance with the arrival of Wings's *Band on the Run* in 1973."[3]

Among those determined to punish McCartney for his perceived transgression was Jann Wenner, editor of the fledgling American rock and roll newsmagazine *Rolling Stone*. Wenner pressured both his music editor and his reviewer to change their favorable review of the *McCartney* album. According to Greil Marcus, *Rolling Stone*'s music editor, he and Langdon Winner, the album's reviewer, regarded McCartney's solo effort as "wonderful" and wrote a favorable review that they were pressured to change. "Wenner saw the piece and said, 'We can't run it this way—he's just reviewing it as if it's a nice little record. It's not a nice little record; it's a statement and it's taking place in a context that we know: Its one person breaking up the band.'"[4] Wenner spent three hours pressuring Marcus, who then pressured Winner until both agreed and re-wrote the positive view of *McCartney,* changing it to a negative one. Wenner's actions regarding the *McCartney* album established a pattern of partisanship that continued for years. Both during the Beatles' breakup period and in the decades following, *Rolling Stone,* under the leadership of Wenner, almost unvaryingly sided with Lennon (and later Ono) in any dispute involving McCartney. Because this was occurring at a time when the number of influential rock and roll magazines could be counted on one hand, the fact that the most powerful music magazine in America actively supported Lennon's side in the Lennon-McCartney split had longstanding consequences on the popular perception of each man and their music.

While the *McCartney* press release had revealed to the world that the Beatles were no longer the indivisible unit of the official narrative, all four remained legally bound together, financially and musically, under a contract they had signed in 1967. For McCartney, the contract trapped him in an impossible relationship with Klein. McCartney had never wanted Klein as Beatles manager, did not trust him, and believed Klein was exerting too much control over his music. Outvoted three to one, McCartney had been legally bound by partnership law to accept Klein, but had distanced himself from his new manager and his fellow Beatles by increasingly relying on Lee and John Eastman, his new father and brother-in-law, regarding financial and legal matters. Relations between the Eastmans and Klein had almost immediately descended into bitter feuding, with both sides accusing the other of manipulation and mismanagement.

Lennon's September 1969 departure had privately ended the Beatles, but McCartney's membership in the now unofficially defunct band ensured that, even though the Beatles now existed only on paper, he remained under Klein's management. In the months following his *McCartney* press release the musician alternately pleaded and demanded with both Lennon and Harrison to dissolve the contract, which was the only way for McCartney to escape Klein's management. Both Lennon and Harrison demurred, citing the substantial tax penalties such a move would incur. McCartney persisted on the advice from the Eastmans, renowned New York attorneys with experience in music publishing, who were anxious for their new in-law and star client to extract himself financially from Klein. For McCartney, a meeting with Harrison in New York in November 1970 was the final straw. When he made another request to be released from the contract, Harrison replied: "You'll stay on the fucking label. Hare Krishna."[5] It should be noted that McCartney's version of Harrison's response is the only account we have: Harrison never discussed it, and while there is documentation to prove that the meeting took place, there is no way of verifying exactly what was said.[6]

Because Klein had not been a party to the 1967 contract, legally extracting himself from Klein's management required McCartney to sue Lennon, Harrison and Starr. On December 31, 1970, the media reported that McCartney was suing his fellow Beatles in order to permanently dissolve the group. The *McCartney* press release already had dented his popularity and reputation. The lawsuit intensified the widespread perception of him as the instigator. "McCartney, already regarded as the protagonist in the breakup of the Beatles, was now suing his three closest friends."[7]

Lennon Remembers

In January 1971, only a few weeks after the lawsuit was announced, *Rolling Stone* published the defining interview of the Beatles' breakup and one of the most important documents in the band's history. On December 8, 1970, Lennon gave one of the most extensive, powerful and influential interviews of his life to Wenner. Initially intended to promote his new album *Plastic Ono Band*, Lennon's interview descended into a diatribe against the official mythology, denouncing all three elements of the Fab Four narrative: the band's whitewashed image, their unity, and the Lennon/McCartney partnership. He rejected much of the band's catalog, dismissing almost all his previous Beatles' music as dishonest.[8] Lennon condemned the whitewashing of the Fab Four narrative, revealing the band's sexual exploits on tour, their strained interpersonal relations, drug use and Epstein's homosexuality. He attacked virtually everyone with whom he had worked during his time with the group, including producer George Martin, publicist Derek Taylor, and faithful assistant Neil Aspinall, accusing them of trying to steal credit for the Beatles' genius.

Both Lennon and Ono, who also participated in the interview, lobbied fiercely in favor of Klein, portraying him as a working class champion, savior of the Beatles' finances and victim of the Eastmans' snobbery.[9] Spurred by leading questions from Wenner (an admittedly novice journalist at this point)[10] Lennon denounced the importance of his artistic and personal relationship with McCartney, using rhetoric that *The Beatles Bibliography* later described as "toxic, yet infantile."[11] Falsely declaring that the two had stopped writing together as early as 1962,[12] Lennon argued that McCartney had conspired to turn he and Harrison into "sidemen" and had seized control of the group following Epstein's death only to lead them in circles.[13] Lennon attacked both McCartney and Harrison for what he regarded as their sexist refusal to welcome Ono into the studio as an equal and fervently proclaimed his own genius.[14] Contemptuously dismissing the largely favorable image of the band that had dominated in the press, Lennon declared that the Beatles "were the biggest bastards on earth,"[15] and argued that the others' refusal to accept Ono had driven the couple into taking heroin: "We took H because of what the Beatles and their pals were doing to us."[16]

It was an unprecedented interview, and its impact on Beatles historiography at the time was nothing short of seismic. The rock and roll press, and *Rolling Stone* in particular, embraced Lennon's new narrative. *Rolling Stone's* position as "the most important intermediary between the counterculture and the corporations"[17] made it particularly credible in the eyes of the underground, New Left, and rock and roll presses. The magazine's circulation at the time was approximately 250,000, meaning that a quarter of a million readers read their first, unforgettable version of the Beatles breakup from *Lennon Remembers* (as the resultant book collecting the interviews was titled). The abrupt dissolution of the official narrative resulting from the April 1970 *McCartney* press release had created a vacuum which *Lennon Remembers* dramatically filled. The raw, harsh denunciation of the Beatles mythology by the band's founder provided a powerful new version that was celebrated for its honesty and willingness to de-mythologize the Beatles' story. Objective assessments of the interview's credibility and accuracy were initially non-existent. "As he quickly carved out the role of 'arbiter of truth' among the four in the new era, his words were given virtually complete credence and taken at face value, reprinted for years later as 'The Gospel According to John.'"[18] Thirty years after its initial publication and well after contradictory sources had proven that many of Lennon's statements were exaggerated, unfair or incorrect, Wenner, with the support of Ono, continued to anoint *Lennon Remembers* as nothing less than the truth:

> The publication of these interviews was the first time that any of the Beatles, let alone the man who had founded the group and was their leader, stepped outside that protected, beloved fairy tale and told the truth about the sugar coated mythology of the Beatles and Paul McCartney's characterization of the breakup.[19]

The *Lennon Remembers* interview established a new narrative that was built on the rejection of its predecessor, the Fab Four narrative. Where the official version had whitewashed their image, promoted the band members unity and depicted an equal Lennon/McCartney songwriting partnership, these elements were now dismissed as illusory. According to the new narrative, Lennon was the Beatles' sole artistic genius, McCartney was little more than a conventional, commercial tunesmith with a pretty face, and Harrison and Starr were relegated to the fringes. Where the official narrative, particularly in the early years, publicly thanked fans for their support, they now were depicted as persecutors.[20] Under the *Lennon Remembers* version, the Lennon/McCartney core was split. The group's two chief songwriters were no longer collaborators and competitors but antagonists.[21] Lennon was lauded as an experimental, radical, politically active, artistic and *avant-garde* thinker, unfairly stifled by the more conservative, middle class McCartney. One of the new narrative's essential elements was the extent to which it dramatically downplayed the importance of and collaboration that had existed in the Lennon/McCartney partnership. By incorrectly claiming that Lennon and McCartney had stopped writing together very early on in their careers, significant contributions and edits that each man had made to the other's work went unacknowledged. Also, this version laid most, if not all, of the blame for the breakup at McCartney's door for his egotistical, controlling personality, domination in the studio, his chauvinistic criticism of Ono, his "pop" musical preferences and his selfish refusal to support Klein as Beatles manager.

This was the version of events that established itself as the prevailing Orthodoxy in the rock and roll press of the early 1970s and continued to influence how the Beatles' story was told for decades. "The *Rolling Stone* interview stood as [Lennon's] testament for the next decade at least, defining his attitude toward his fellow Beatles long after he had mellowed in his view."[22] Lennon's partisan interview served as the founding document of the new narrative, with serious implications for how the Beatles' story was viewed for years. Its unbalanced interpretation, providing only one side of the argument, had longstanding consequences. "Whenever judgment leans to one side we cannot help distorting and twisting the narrative in this direction."[23]

Lennon Remembers quickly established itself as one of the most important and widely used pieces of evidence in all of Beatles historiography: *The Beatles Bibliography* described it decades later as "a seminal piece of source material for Beatles researchers."[24] There are almost no works in Beatles' historiography written after its publication that do not include some information, analysis, or quotations from *Lennon Remembers*. This is partially attributable to the interview's undeniable value as a primary source spoken directly by Lennon, one of the key figures, during one of the most critical periods of Beatles history. Its primacy, both to Lennon and the breakup, reinforce its value as a piece of historical evidence, and one that Beatles' historians should use, although with reservations. Another reason for the interview's universal popularity is its exhaustive and comprehensive nature: the entire transcript of the interview is approximately 150 pages, far larger than the typical print interview. *Lennon Remembers* covers topics ranging from Lennon's childhood to his personal and professional relationship with Epstein to his thoughts on Chairman Mao, Charles Manson, Mick Jagger and Bob Dylan. In addition, there are no equivalently revealing interviews from McCartney, Harrison, or Starr that approach the visceral power of *Lennon Remembers*. Decades later, a reporter for *The Guardian* described the Lennon revealed in the interview: "Self-engrossed, witty, malicious, foolish, someone who is always ready to be disabused and abused ... a confused figure waging several wars at once and taking no prisoners."[25] The closest thing to a personal rebuttal of the *Lennon Remembers* interview is McCartney's 1997 semi-autobiography *Many Years from Now*. This gap of more than two decades allowed Lennon's story to cement its place as the preeminent version in the 1970s.

There is no denying that the *Lennon Remembers* interview is essential to understanding Beatles history. But there is also no denying that its overall credibility is questionable for a number of reasons, including its sole reliance on Lennon's eyewitness testimony. In *The Historian's Craft*, Bloch cautions against blindly accepting testimony from any source, however reputable: "There are no witnesses whose statements are equally reliable on all subjects and under all circumstances."[26] Surprisingly, given its ubiquitous presence in Beatles history, few Beatles' writers have addressed the interview's inherent weaknesses, and those who have only began to do so within the last 20 years. One author who does is Doggett, who evaluates the credibility of *Lennon Remembers* in *You Never Give Me Your Money*; another is Hertsgaard, who labeled the famous *Rolling Stone* interview as "a fascinating document" whose "claims must be evaluated with care and skepticism."[27] Eventually some writers acknowledged its numerous factual errors, including Lennon's declaration that he and McCartney stopped writing together as early as 1962, and his argument that he had written at least half of McCartney's song "Eleanor Rigby."[28] However, virtually all of the works that use the interview fail to analyze its overall credibility as a source, and a large number of heavily influential secondary sources initially unquestioningly accepted Lennon's statements and/or failed to place them in context.[29] Many authors, particularly those writing in the 1970s and 1980s, also failed to distinguish that the sentiments and criticisms Lennon expressed in *Lennon Remembers* were ones specific to that particular time, rather than to the entirety of his experience with his fellow Beatles.[30]

According to historical methods, three major factors call into question *Lennon Remembers* as a truthful, definitive account of the Beatles' functioning years and breakup. The first is that, while the interview was renowned for its stark honesty and efforts to de-mythologize the band's story, it was a source originally intended for public consumption, rather than private use.[31] Its pur-

pose was to "sell" Lennon's version of the Beatles and their breakup, not necessarily to provide the most truthful account of the individuals in the group
or of its demise. Those authors that choose to ignore Lennon's motivations
for or the circumstances surrounding the interview demonstrate poor source
analysis.[32] Unquestioningly regarding it as "history as well as revelation,"[33] as
Wenner, Coleman and other Beatles' writers have done, requires ignoring
Lennon's agendas for giving the interview. These include his promotion of
his artistic partnership with Ono, selling his new album, advocating for Klein,
and fiercely denouncing the idea that his genius had been aided by anyone
else, especially McCartney.[34]

Any accurate understanding of Beatles history requires that *Lennon
Remembers* cannot and should not be accepted as evidence without considering what motivated Lennon at the time he gave the interview. In *The Historian's Craft*, Bloch discusses an instance similar to Lennon's, in which Jean
Marbot, French hero of the Napoleonic Wars, wrote in his famous *Memoirs*
a stirring account of his own bravery and valor. Although his *Memoirs* became
famous, Marbot's account of his bravest deed, crossing the flooded Rhine to
rescue some prisoners of war, was contradicted by all other evidence. Bloch's
conclusion is illustrative of how to choose between such contrasting evidence.
"On one side, we have the *Memoirs*; on the other, a whole batch of documents
which belie them. We must now decide between these conflicting witnesses.
Which alternative will be judged the most likely.... Surely no one will hesitate.
The *Memoirs* have lied again."[35] This does not mean that the entirety of the
Marbot's Memoirs or Lennon's interview can be dismissed as historical evidence. It *does* mean that their inconsistencies should be confronted and their
agendas and errors acknowledged by the writers who use them as sources.

A second factor affecting the accuracy of the statements given in *Lennon
Remembers* is Lennon's state of mind when he made them. Although Lennon
claimed he gave the interview fresh from conquering his heroin and methadone
addictions, there is evidence to suggest that Lennon was still using heroin (and
possibly cocaine) when he sat down with Wenner.[36] The paranoia resulting
from such an addiction is only one of the ways the drug may have affected his
testimony, understanding and interpretation of the facts.

Even if Lennon was sober at the time of the interview, heroin and other
heavy drugs undoubtedly influenced his account of the band's final years.
Both Lennon and Ono began taking heroin very early in their relationship.
All evidence suggests that they spent much of 1968 and 1969 (key years in
the Beatles' breakup) under the drug's influence. In 1970 the two became
addicted to methadone, and went through withdrawal before engaging in
primal scream therapy. How much heroin, cocaine and methadone impacted

Lennon's behavior and statements during this period is impossible to calculate with certainty, but should be taken into account. In determining the credibility of eyewitness sources, Bloch emphasized how the "condition of the observer" impacts their observations: describing "fatigue, emotion, or the degree of attention" among the "circumstances that impair the accuracy of the perception."[37] Simply put, Lennon and Ono's heavy drug use from 1968 through 1970 diminishes their credibility as eyewitnesses during the period in question. We can only speculate how much the drug use by Lennon and the other band members contributed to the acrimony of the group's dissolution.

The third major factor that diminishes the credibility of *Lennon Remembers* is that Lennon himself later attempted multiple times to disavow and dismiss, in both public and private, the interview's significance. Martin, one of the major objects of criticism in *Lennon Remembers*, described one such instance. When Martin reportedly confronted Lennon about the "many unfair and untrue things" he had said the musician dismissed them: "'Why did you say all those things? It wasn't very nice.' He said, 'Oh, I was just stoned out of my head.' Unfortunately, that has become history now: it's accepted as the Bible."[38] Pang, Lennon's girlfriend, recounts a similar instance when Glyn Johns, another target, confronted Lennon about it. According to Pang, Lennon had forgotten what he had said and was "embarrassed" when Johns reminded him. Lennon then repudiated the importance of his statements. "'I was just lettin' off steam. That interview was just a lot of anger.' Glyn stared.... he had never expected that John would not remember what he had said ... like everyone else, he believed everything the public John said and took him very seriously."[39]

Lennon publicly downplayed the interview's importance several times in 1974 and 1975,[40] disavowing it during a radio broadcast with Harrison. Harrison criticized Wenner for publishing the interview as a book and refusing to acknowledge that Lennon now "disagreed with what he'd said" in *Lennon Remembers*, condemning the *Rolling Stone* editor for continuing to promote statements which "John said he no longer agreed with himself on." Lennon concurred, describing his words as a thoughtless reflex rather than an accurate portrait, making it clear he did not intend the interview to serve as his timeless manifesto. "If you accidentally bang your head and you shout, 'Ow!'—that's the end of it ... it doesn't go on for the next five years, right?"[41] In a 1980 interview with *Playboy*, Lennon also admitted that he had lied about certain things, particularly his collaboration with McCartney, in *Lennon Remembers*: "Yeah, I was lying. It was when I felt resentful, so I felt that we did everything apart. But, actually, a lot of the songs we did eyeball to eyeball."[42] In the same interview, Lennon later repeated the disclaimer when asked about his previous statements regarding his partnership with McCartney: "I said that, but I was lying."[43]

However, by the time Lennon began to modify and retract his statements, *Lennon Remembers* already had achieved a kind of scriptural status among some Beatles' fans. Part of this was due to Wenner's insistence on publishing the interview as a book over Lennon's strong, repeated objections.[44] Publishing *Lennon Remembers* as a book granted it a level of authority beyond that of the hundreds of previously existing Beatles' magazine interviews. Wenner's continuing dismissal of any suggestions that the interview is anything less than absolute truth is unsurprising. *Lennon Remembers* was a powerful journalistic coup for what was, in 1970, a magazine that only had been publishing for three years and owed much of its stature to its coverage of Lennon.[45] "Lennon's nude photograph with Ono in 1968 and the interviews he granted Cott in 1969 and Wenner in 1970 helped sustain the magazine's credibility."[46] It was the interview that made *Rolling Stone* famous and a legitimate force in the press. "No other *Rolling Stone* interview would carry such resonance."[47] Wenner dismissed Lennon's later efforts to downplay the interview. "Regardless of his subsequent changes in specific ideas and views, it still holds as *the* statement about the end of the Beatles."[48] Acknowledging its status as anything less than authoritative undermines what is widely regarded as *Rolling Stone*'s greatest and most enduring act of journalism. Whether or not Wenner regarded *Lennon Remembers* as the true story of the Beatles' breakup, it remains in the magazine's best interest to promote it that way.

As recently as 2000, Wenner argues in the book's new edition that the interview provides "*the* statement about the end of the Beatles."[49] This assessment is methodologically flawed for a number of reasons: It requires unquestioning acceptance of statements Lennon himself later rejected and admitted were lies, overlooks the viewpoints of McCartney, Harrison and Starr and ignores a wealth of contradictory evidence. In his essay "The Beatles for Sale and for Keeps," John Kimsey emphasizes how *Rolling Stone*'s partisan approach to the Beatles undermines its impartiality as a secondary source on the group and on its two core members in particular: "Wenner hitched his magazine's wagon to the Lennon-Ono star in 1971."[50] *The Beatles Bibliography* agrees, expressing disbelief at how "Twenty years after Lennon's death, Jann Wenner was still peddling the absurd and self-aggrandizing myth that Lennon was the heart and soul of the Beatles and McCartney the pop sugarcoating."[51] Ultimately, Wenner's dismissal of the questions surrounding the accuracy of *Lennon Remembers* displays a serious lack of objectivity.

The contrast between Lennon's efforts to distance himself from the interview and Wenner's continuing efforts to promote it offer a very contemporary example of how media agendas influence which sources acquire popularity and influence with the press. In his book *Historical Methods in Mass Communication,* James Startt provides some of the questions every historian or discerning reader should ask when analyzing evidence from mass media:

> The record of the mass media … is one of the richest of historical sources, and it deserves the serious attention of historians. In regard to the sources, "How are they organized? What type of influence did the editor have, and why? Who produced it, and how and why? What type of influence did it have, and why? Was it known equally for all its contents? Were there restraints placed upon its opinion, and did that opinion conform to some outside interest?"[52]

It also provides historians and others with an intriguing question: How credible is any source's *ex post facto* disavowal of previous statements, such as Lennon's attempts regarding *Lennon Remembers?* According to standard historical methods, there are reasons to believe that both Lennon's original version *and* his later self-revision provide the most credible version of events.

On one hand, the chronological immediacy of *Lennon Remembers* grants it a strong measure of validity regarding Lennon's views on the breakup. Lennon only downplayed *Lennon Remembers* once the most contentious intra-band legal and financial disputes had been settled, and it was in his own interest to adopt a less aggressive public tone. On the other hand, by applying Bloch's methodology concerning how the condition of the eyewitness affects testimony, Lennon's emotional state at the time he gave the interview (especially his anger and drug use) raises questions concerning its overall credibility. Once the immediate bitterness of the situation had passed and Lennon's anger and heavy drug use were no longer a factor, he offered a more accurate and impartial eyewitness account.

Such issues as the source's primacy and the emotional context in which the account was delivered emphasize how difficult it can be determining the overall validity of a source. In the case of *Lennon Remembers,* the question regarding the interview's ultimate credibility is heightened because of the undeniable influence it had on how the Beatles' story was told for decades. "Despite its frequent exaggerations, false claims, misremembered history, and prickly outbursts, this Lennon sit … became a central part of rock lore."[53] As a primary source, *Lennon Remembers* cannot be dismissed. But neither should it be blindly accepted as truth by writers who use it to shape the direction of Beatles history. "From the moment when we are no longer resigned to purely and simply recording the words of our witnesses, from the moment we decide to force them to speak, cross-examination becomes more necessary than ever."[54]

Lennon Remembers provides perhaps the most striking example of one of Beatles historiography's major weaknesses: a failure to apply basic source analysis, particularly to information provided by a primary source. Unfortunately, for far too long, various Beatles writers tended to accept interviews and statements by the primary figures involved without properly analyzing the agenda behind them. Some writers accepted and relayed interview material without using separate, independent sources or documentation to verify their claims. There are also numerous examples of this lack of source analysis in the initial, Fab Four narrative. However, the Fab Four narrative was a single version, while the post-breakup narratives consisted of competing and sometimes contradictory accounts. The failure of many writers to apply source analysis to interviews during the breakup period oversimplified Beatles' history such that the narrative was shaped less by facts and more by which side spoke the loudest and gave the most interviews.

The Rock and Roll Press Chooses Sides

McCartney's lawsuit and *Lennon Remembers* permanently and publicly divided the once unified Beatles story into two separate and conflicting versions. During the breakup, McCartney adopted a largely defensive tone with the press. With the exception of a particularly memorable exchange of letters with Lennon in Britain's *Melody Maker* magazine, he chose not to provoke his former partner, largely confining his reactions to some of Lennon's more extreme statements. Decades later, Connolly discussed the contrast. "No matter how much John publicly criticized Paul, in none of my interviews with Paul did he ever criticize John."[55] According to later statements by McCartney, this was a deliberate choice prompted in part by fear of Lennon's notoriously sharp wit and take-no-prisoners approach. Lennon and Ono, on the other hand, launched a press campaign that immediately began to revise the original, Fab Four version of Beatles history.

Both the popular and the rock and roll press covered the Beatles' breakup extensively. The dissolution of the world's most popular band made headlines across the globe from the prestigious, established London *Times* to the countercultural *Village Voice*. A contrast quickly emerged in the coverage. The smaller, independent and more radical underground press, which was closely linked with the rock press, supported Lennon and Ono's peace movement and at times criticized them for being insufficiently radical. The popular press in Britain and America, such as the major newspapers or magazines, reported on Lennon and Ono's "happenings" with disbelief, amusement or contempt.

In his book *Come Together*, Jon Wiener discusses the reaction of the mainstream press:

> Particularly in the London Press, John and Yoko received a torrent of abuse. "This must rank as the most self-indulgent demonstration of all time," one columnist wrote. Another commented that "John seems to have come perilously close to having gone off his rocker.... London's *Daily Mail* anointed Lennon 'Clown of the Year.'"[56]

In contrast the rock press, which supported Lennon's political activism, largely adhered to Lennon's version of the Beatles' story during the 1970s. In his essay "The Solo Years," Michael Frontani discusses how the countercultural press, the New Left and *Rolling Stone* "found common cause with John Lennon, while McCartney was demonized as a commercial hack for his refusal to say anything of consequence."[57]

Lennon Remembers offered the countercultural rock and roll press a compelling, simple version of the Beatles' breakup that, coincidentally or not, conformed to the political climate of the time. Lennon used the interview, as well as others, to discuss his devotion to political causes favored by the underground press and the New Left, which dominated much of the rock and roll press. At the same time, Lennon criticized his fellow Beatles for not following his lead in strident political activism. Lennon had lost credibility with much of the New Left when his 1968 song "Revolution" had expressed ambivalence toward, if not outright rejection of, violent revolution. "The underground press ate the Beatles alive after Revolution."[58] In *Lennon Remembers* Lennon reversed himself, declaring that he and Ono were now in for the revolution that so many anticipated was imminent.

Establishing themselves as leaders of the *avant-garde* art world and supporters of the radical left, both Lennon and Ono initially portrayed themselves equally as the heroes *and* victims of the Beatles' story. McCartney and his in-laws the Eastmans, were, in the language of the time "straights"[59]: conventional, commercial and, most critically for the politics of the time, members of the establishment.[60] McCartney's unquestioned commercial popularity both during and after the Beatles only reinforced this image,[61] as "rock and its ideology of anti-commercialism" viewed selling records as "selling out."[62] Where McCartney's musical tastes were far more catholic, encompassing music hall to rock to brass bands, in *Lennon Remembers* his former partner denounced all music except those rock songs that met his own personal requirements of honesty and authenticity.[63] In 1971, Lennon was promoting rock as *the* driving artistic and political force of the era, a stance which appealed to rock and roll's authorities. For a countercultural rock and roll press that was one of the primary voices fighting the cultural wars of the

1960s, the either/or choice between Lennon and McCartney was simple. Political, cultural, practical and stylistic reasons drove the rock press overwhelmingly into Lennon's camp, which set the tone for how the Beatles' story was told in the 1970s. Their depiction of the breakup and the general dismissal of the Lennon/McCartney songwriting partnership influenced the views of millions: The politics of the rock press became, in C. Vann Woodward's terms, "'the public's'[64] business."[65] This initial reporting influenced the perception of both men for decades; thirty years after *Lennon Remembers*, MacDonald still criticized rock critics for their "shallow media bias"[66] regarding McCartney.

In evaluating historiography, analysis always must account for the politics of the time period in which a piece of history is produced. Understanding the political environment in which the historical events occurred, as well as when they were recorded and interpreted, is one of any historian's fundamental responsibilities. History provides countless examples of political agendas influencing accounts of historic events and elevating or demeaning historic figures in order to promote contemporaneous political goals. In the biography *The Man Who Saved the Union*, historian H.W. Brands argues that American Civil War General and later President Ulysses S. Grant's reputation was unfairly attacked and Grant's legacy seriously diminished for politically motivated reasons. According to Brands, at the time of his death Grant's place in the American pantheon of heroes was indisputable, second only to the revered figures of George Washington and Abraham Lincoln. Within a generation, however, Grant was widely viewed as a drunk, corrupt politician, and a butcher of a General rather than the strategic military genius who had helped the Union win the American Civil War. This abrupt about-face was the result of former Confederates and Southerners who viewed the American Civil War as one unfairly and unjustly waged against the South. The "Lost Cause" narrative of the post–Bellum South focused their blame on Grant for the North's "war of aggression," publishing editorials and histories and erecting monuments that depicted Grant as a butcher. The adage that "history is written by the victors" was reversed: It was the defeated South that controlled the Civil War narratives to the extent that, according to Woodward, "Northern history books accepted the Southern view."[67] The political climate of the post–Civil War South, as well as the apathy towards the subject in the North, allowed this negative caricature of Grant to prevail for decades.

Just as the political agenda of the post-bellum South had an enormous impact on Grant's declining historical reputation, the charged political climate at the time of the Beatles split significantly shaped how the rock press of the time depicted the Beatles story. According to Frontani, perceptions in the rock press that held McCartney responsible for the Beatles' split, disdained his mainstream popularity, accepted Lennon's pronouncement of his own genius and chafed at McCartney's refusal to promote rock's "anti-establishment world view" resulted in the "the most hostile reception of any ex-Beatle."[68] He also argues that the severe generational split at the time played a role. In the early 1970s, McCartney's inter-generational appeal and more catholic musical tastes were regarded by the younger generation as a betrayal: "The apathy, even hostility, with which McCartney's early solo work was received by *Rolling Stone* was part of a process of defining the achievements and legacy of the youth culture that emerged in the 1960's."[69]

Articles in the rock press of the early 1970s buttress Frontani's assessment. In a 1971 *Village Voice* article, Paul Levinson criticized Christgau, his fellow journalist and music critic, for his politically motivated criticisms of McCartney: "I would like to comment to those (including Christgau) who seem so aggrieved of Paul McCartney's apolitical character…. Paul is apolitical, granted, but at least he's attempting to find fresh musical expressions."[70] Christgau previously had chided Lennon and criticized his lyrics as insufficiently radical and revolutionary. Now Christgau, who took the "lead in developing the self consciousness of the New Left and the counterculture about music and politics,"[71] turned his scorn on McCartney. That two of the most influential elements of the American rock press—the "Dean of American Rock Critics" as well as *Rolling Stone*—avidly supported Lennon continued to influence critical reception to Lennon's work, as well as McCartney's, for decades.

Lennon's very vocal and genuine support of political causes, particularly the peace movement and feminism, made him a great champion of the New Left. It elevated him, in the eyes of millions of members of his generation, to a level far beyond that of a rock star to that of a statesman or visionary. "A five hour talk between John Lennon and Richard Nixon would be more significant than any Geneva Summit Conference between the U.S. and Russia."[72] Lennon's deeply personal and political lyrics as well as his political activism were something behind which the rock and roll press could rally, as they promoted rock and roll as an artistic and political force. "Taking popular music seriously, as something 'more' than mere entertainment or distraction, has been a crucial feature of rock culture since its emergence."[73] By contrast McCartney's "story songs," emphasis on melody, and tendencies to celebrate domesticity, whimsy and romantic love were viewed as commercial and bourgeoisie, in no small part because his music sold so well.

Another important revision that accompanied the collapse of the official narrative was Harrison's increased stature as a songwriter. "George Harrison strode into 1971 as the most successful solo Beatle."[74] Harrison always had been regarded, both by the press and in the Beatles, as occupying an important but still lesser tier than Lennon and McCartney. With *The White Album*, however, Harrison began to produce songs that many considered equal to some of Lennon and McCartney's best compositions. This became even more evident on the last album the group recorded, *Abbey Road*, which contained two masterpieces by Harrison: "Here Comes the Sun" and "Something."

Lennon and McCartney were used to writing as a pair: Their creative processes both seemed to require an "other" in order to fully realize a song's potential. Even when they wrote independently each acknowledged the other's imprint on his work. "I wouldn't write like I write now if it weren't for Paul, and he wouldn't write like he does now if it weren't for me,"[75] declared Lennon in 1969, even as their partnership was dissolving. Once that collaboration collapsed, an intrinsic element of their songwriting that previously had been supplied by the other was lacking. Harrison, on the other hand, had wanted but never had a collaborator, and was used to composing alone. In November 1970, he released his first post–Beatles album, *All Things Must Pass*, a critically acclaimed masterpiece that widely outsold both Lennon's *Plastic Ono Band* and *McCartney*. Immediately, rock critics began to argue that Harrison's talents as a songwriter had been suppressed by the Lennon/McCartney partnership that had dominated Beatles' albums and that Harrison had proven himself the artistic equal of his two former band mates.

Harrison, stereotyped in *A Hard Day's Night* as the quiet, cheap, grumpy Beatle, seemed to flourish outside of the group's restrictions. In the breakup Harrison sided with Lennon and Klein, blaming McCartney's refusal to support him as a musician. "The conflict musically for me was Paul."[76] Harrison also identified McCartney's behavior as a primary cause of tension within the group.[77] However, Harrison tended to avoid the type of absolutist statements that came easily to Lennon and remained largely on the sidelines of the Lennon/McCartney press wars. His devotion to Hare Krishna granted him an image of spiritual awareness that both Lennon and McCartney seemed to lack. Harrison also conceived and masterminded the first major charity rock concert in August 1971, the Concert for Bangladesh, which elevated his reputation from rock star to humanitarian and produced hundreds of thousands of dollars for the impoverished nation. However, a few years later Harrison's musical reputation was dented by the critical and popular failure of his "Dark Horse" tour and by a plagiarism lawsuit regarding his biggest solo hit, "My Sweet Lord." Despite containing some excellent work, none of Harrison's later albums managed to reach the critical and financial peak he achieved with *All Things Must Pass* and discussion of Harrison as Lennon or

McCartney's musical equal faded. "George found that much of his respect had somehow been whittled away."[78]

The Beatles Trial

Throughout the 1960s the Beatles and their first manager, Brian Epstein, all stated numerous times that they regarded membership in the world's most famous band as a choice, not a prison sentence. If any one of the Fab Four wanted to leave, Epstein argued in *A Cellarful of Noise*, they were free to go: "I would not hold the Beatles ... to contractual formalities if I learned they didn't want to stay. There is no room in our relationships for contract slavery."[79] In press conferences, the Beatles affirmed that a member who was contractually bound but wanted to leave would not be forced to remain in the group. Lennon and McCartney declared they would let Harrison depart if he wanted to. Harrison agreed: "If I wanted to leave then they wouldn't try and stop me—or they wouldn't sue me I don't think."[80] Such statements reinforced one of the core messages of the official narrative, that the bond between the four men was more about music and friendship than finances and contractual obligations. In 1971 the naive belief that a Beatle could legally and financially extract himself from the other three, and do so with their blessings, was proven false.

On the last day of 1970, the public learned that McCartney was suing Lennon, Harrison, and Starr in order to dissolve the contract that legally bound the four men together as Beatles. In February 1971, in order to keep McCartney under contract, the three men found themselves attempting to convince High Court Justice Terrance Stamp that there were no irresolvable conflicts that prevented the Beatles from working together. For McCartney, who bore the burden of proof, his case rested not only on questions regarding Klein's financial management of Apple and reputation but also on proving that the Beatles were fundamentally broken beyond repair. The defense argued in favor of Klein's management and also maintained that any tensions in the band were temporary and ultimately could be solved. The only insoluble problem, according to the Fab Three, was McCartney's refusal to accept Klein as his manager.

Lennon, Harrison and Starr all gave written testimony to that effect and applauded Klein's financial and management decisions. Starr praised McCartney as the "greatest bass player in the world"[81] but criticized him for insisting on always getting his own way.[82] Harrison's omitted the existence of any other conflicts within the group besides those caused by McCartney. He failed to mention his own frustrations at the presence of Ono in the studio. He also declared that any tensions over McCartney's dominating role, or refusal to accept Harrison as an equal talent, were resolved after their recorded disagreement[83] during the *Let It Be* sessions.[84] Klein's court testimony defended his managerial decisions and argued the Beatles still could make music together, but his written appraisal of the band's state of affairs omitted the crucial fact that Lennon had quit in September 1969.

Lennon, pivoting away from the *Lennon Remembers* interview of only a few months earlier, also argued that while McCartney was acting "selfishly" and "unreasonably,"[85] any personal or musical disagreements between them could be overcome. In stark contrast to Lennon's statements to *Rolling Stone* that there was "not a chance"[86] of the Beatles recording together again, Lennon declared that the group still could perform as a functioning unit once McCartney simply bowed to majority rule and accepted Klein. The testimony of all four Beatles, which quickly became public, made a lasting impression on the public perception of the group's artistry and its inner workings. As with *Lennon Remembers*, parts of trial testimony were used by Beatles' writers for decades to explain the group's working relationship as well as its dissolution, but few authors addressed the very real agendas, contradictions or omissions that the testimony contained.

There were no irresolvable conflicts within the Beatles; and while Lennon, Harrison, and Starr wanted to save the band, McCartney wanted to end it. This was the initial version of the breakup that seared into the public consciousness. It was reported in the press and reinforced by the testimony of Lennon, Harrison and Starr at the trial. While unbalanced and at times inaccurate, its status as the founding Orthodoxy took decades to dislodge. At the time, McCartney's distrust of Klein was widely viewed as unreasonable— reporters described it as "irrational"[87]—while Lennon, Harrison and Starr's reluctance to being managed by McCartney's in-laws, the Eastmans, was perfectly understandable. With the powerful combination of the *McCartney* press release, the lawsuit, *Lennon Remembers* and then the trial, the media pushed the perception of McCartney as the villain and the other three as his victims. Connolly acknowledged how damaged McCartney's reputation had become in a 1972 article, declaring that "most of the press reports since the Beatles' breakup have looked bad"[88] for him.

Much of the trial hinged on the character of Klein, his suitability as manager, and whether he had been unfairly imposed on McCartney by the other three Beatles. The verdict regarding the controversial Beatles' manager "was a damning conclusion."[89] Justice Stamp declared that "confidence was gone" in Apple's business affairs; Klein's testimony was "untrue" and "dishon-

est" in parts, and he had taken commission to which he was not entitled.[90]
Stamp also ruled in McCartney's favor regarding the Beatles' dissolution.
Stamp noted that Lennon, Harrison and Starr had entered into contracts with
Klein which directly affected McCartney but whose existence McCartney
was unaware of. He judged that Apple and the Beatles partnership had "committed a grave breach of its duties" by "increasing ABKCO's commission …
without the plaintiff's knowledge and consent."[91] Ultimately, Stamp ruled that
forcing McCartney to remain locked into such a partnership would be
"unjust," and declared "It is not reasonable to expect the plaintiff to submit
to ABKCO's continued management."[92] However, Stamp's ruling in favor of
McCartney initially helped little in the court of public opinion, because his
victory spelled the end of the Beatles. "McCartney had unequivocally won
the first crucial round in the Beatles' legal battle, even if he now found himself
hated by the press, the fans[93] and the other band members."[94]

Klein, unable to personally defend himself at the trial, went on a press
offensive, which included granting an extensive November 1971 interview to
Playboy. Klein used the interview to promote the key points of the *Lennon
Remembers* version of events. He identifies McCartney as the instigator—"If
anybody broke up the Beatles, it was him"[95]—and does not mention Lennon's
September 1969 departure. He downplays the intimacy of the men's friendship, blaming McCartney's behavior for any distance—"Every time [John]
let his guard down McCartney hurt him"—and pronounces Lennon's
supremacy in the Lennon/McCartney partnership: "John had written most
of the stuff."[96] Klein repeatedly reassures readers of Lennon, Harrison and
Starr's personal and professional happiness and their eagerness to credit him
for it.[97] As Lennon and Ono had done in *Lennon Remembers*, Klein portrays
himself as a champion of artists, unfairly maligned by record companies, the
Eastmans, and the British press.[98]

In attempting to identify McCartney and his in-laws as the driving force
behind the breakup, the interview contains numerous crucial omissions and
claims later discovered to be false. Klein blames either Epstein's inexperience[99]
or the Eastmans' interference for every business failure that occurred under
his regime. He claims that his efforts to purchase Northern Songs, the company which owned the Lennon/McCartney song catalog, were sabotaged
when the Eastmans verbally insulted the bankers working on the deal.[100]
However, Lennon later revealed that *he* and not the Eastmans provoked the
bankers, telling the men "I'm not going to be fucked around by men in suits
sitting on their fat arses."[101] As Lennon had done in his *Rolling Stone* interview,
Klein described the pivotal 1969 meeting where Lee Eastman verbally insulted
him; he did this in an effort to portray Eastman as volatile and unstable and

therefore unfit to manage the Beatles. However, also like Lennon, he omits the key point that he and Lennon provoked Eastman's outburst by repeatedly insulting him. While Klein condemns McCartney's unreasonable and selfish behavior throughout the interview, the ultimate villains are the Eastmans, who were misleading and manipulating their new in-law and star client. Despite this, the interview offered hope of reconciliation, reassuring readers numerous times that, despite his actions, the three ex-Beatles still loved McCartney.[102] Reunion, however, was impossible until McCartney learned to "think for himself,"[103] and, presumably, extract himself from the Eastmans' clutches.

Klein repeated many of the same arguments in interviews with Peter McCabe. He attributed their loss at the trial not to legitimate questions regarding his financial dealings but to his "anti-establishment"[104] status, buttressing his and Lennon's reputations as rock and roll rebels. Reinforcing the message that the major disagreement lay with the Eastmans, he reassured everyone he would be happy to accept McCartney back and speculated that it would take two years for the other man to see the error of his ways. Some of Lennon's statements at the time also painted the Eastmans as the primary forces manipulating McCartney and preventing reunification. "Allen Klein would love it if Paul would come back. I want him to come out of it too, you know. He will one day. I give him five years, I've said that. In five years, he'll wake up."[105]

These interviews by Klein and Lennon, as well as similar comments from Ono, reinforced the *Lennon Remembers* narrative which blamed McCartney's unreasonable distrust of Klein and support for the Eastmans as the primary cause of the split. Like Lennon's *Rolling Stone* interview, their credibility is compromised by their purpose as public sources, Klein's obvious agenda at the time he gave them, and their numerous inaccuracies and omissions.

The Clash of Contradicting Narratives

After the trial, the division between McCartney and the Eastmans on one side and Lennon, Ono, Harrison, Starr and Klein on the other only seemed to widen, in no small part because their feud made for good press and sold papers . The publicly lopsided nature of the division among the Beatles, three against one, was a powerful argument against McCartney in the eyes of the public. The verdict to legally dissolve the Beatles went in McCartney's favor, but numerous other legal issues remained unresolved. Meanwhile both sides continued to champion their own particular version of the Beatles' story. "Now that the Beatles had broken up, their history was already being re-written."[106]

In his infamous *Rolling Stone* interview, Lennon had described McCartney as "A good P.R. man, Paul ... he's about the best in the world, probably."[107] As both camps waged a war of words against each other, Lennon pinpointed McCartney's skill in press relations while at the same time emphasizing his own stark, unfiltered and more credible honesty.[108] These frequent descriptions of McCartney's role as a P.R. man had the impact of devaluing what statements he did make concerning the breakup as placating, misleading or manipulative.

There was a considerable amount of truth to Lennon's portrayal of McCartney as the group's P.R. man. During the band's peak era, McCartney was the Beatle most willing to engage with the press and give interviews. McCartney acknowledged this in 1968: "That's my job ... chatting up the press and all that."[109] Accounts from Beatles insiders such as Tony Barrow, Alistair Taylor, Tony Bramwell and others testify to McCartney's willingness to play the public relations game super-stardom required. However, by the time of the *McCartney* press release and *Lennon Remembers*, any description of McCartney as a great P.R. man was woefully outdated and incorrect. The numbers indicate that, by then, the title rightfully belonged to Lennon. Lennon and Ono established themselves in London and later New York and were readily available to the press. But McCartney retreated with his new family to one of the most remote areas of Scotland and refused virtually all interview requests for more than a year. From 1969 through the end of 1971, during the crucial breakup years when the battle over the Beatles' story was raging, Lennon and Ono gave more than a dozen major interviews, including the extensive *Lennon Remembers* and "St. Regis" interviews, over 55 radio interviews, and appeared on the *Dick Cavett* show multiple times. Klein also provided extensive interviews to *Playboy* and McCabe. According to Barry Miles, author of McCartney's semi-autobiography, Lennon and Ono also gave dozens of smaller interviews, at one point doing as many as ten a day.[110] Granting such access paid off: Decades later, Kimsey described Lennon and Ono's version of events as "ubiquitous in the media."[111]

In contrast, McCartney gave approximately ten interviews during the same time period.[112] Three barely mentioned the Beatles at all. One discussed Jimi Hendrix's death, another McCartney's new marriage; a third reassured everyone that he was not, contrary to the worldwide rumor caused by his public silence, dead. Rather than launching a convincing press campaign, McCartney's strategy during much of this period was a billowing public silence, interrupted only by terse legal statements and short, defensive justifications. Decades later Connolly acknowledged McCartney's P.R. failures beginning with the *McCartney* press release: "He slipped up."[113] This silence allowed Lennon, Ono and Klein to shape the story of the Beatles' breakup even as it unfolded. Their version invariably cast McCartney in the role of the instigator as well as, ironically, a matchless manipulator of the press. It was a label that Beatles historiography continued to apply, somewhat unfairly, to McCartney for decades: in his 2008 biography *John Lennon: The Life*, Norman refers to McCartney several times as a "tireless P.R. man."[114]

This identification of McCartney as a slick P.R. man also contrasted sharply with Lennon, who strove to reinforce his image as the unreserved, impassioned truth teller with the guts to de-mythologize the official narrative. It took years before any major work on Beatles history acknowledged Lennon's own impressive and successful manipulation of the press, particularly during the band's split. Lennon's skill was the opposite of McCartney's obfuscating charm. Where McCartney withheld private and particularly unpleasant information from the press—"people know enough of my insecurities and my weaknesses, and they blast me left, right and center with it. I don't want to give them any more"[115]—Lennon divulged everything, however embarrassing, shocking, or contradictory. This allowed him, according to Pang, to "create an illusion of startling intimacy" with journalists while at the same time using "his bluntness as a way of keeping people at a distance."[116] It was an assessment that others close to Lennon echoed. The musician was prone to absolutist statements in both his private and public life. This made him a riveting interview subject, granting him an image of "a man of devastating truth and honesty"[117] but at times casts doubt on the accuracy of his testimony. MacDonald acknowledges this: "Trying to judge Lennon's outlook from his own words is an exercise complicated by an emotional instability which could tip him into wild exaggerations."[118] Journalists who knew Lennon well, such as Connolly, dismissed Lennon's exaggerated statements out of hand. So did Pang. "John's most influential interviews, interviews which people took as gospel truth, were for John occasions to blow off steam and then to forget what he had said."[119] Other journalists accepted and repeated some of Lennon's wilder claims without question, allowing them to become an accepted part of numerous Beatles' narratives.

McCartney's first major interview in more than a year came in April 1971, following his victory in court. It seemed designed in every way as a polar opposite of Lennon's *Rolling Stone* interview. Talking to the mainstream press in a relatively short article and adopting a reasonable tone, McCartney emphasized that his problem was with Klein, and no one else. "It's not the other three…. I don't think there is bad blood, not from my side anyway. So it's a business thing. It's Allen Klein."[120] In public, McCartney was dismissive of *Lennon Remembers*, declaring "I think he blows it with that sort of thing."[121] With its casual tone and refusal to reveal any starkly personal information, McCartney's interview with *Life* set the template for his relationship with the press well into the next decade. His later biographers noted (and chafed at) McCartney's reserve: "In complete contrast to the soul-baring extravaganzas that had become the norm for John Lennon interviews, Paul McCartney gave away nothing of himself whatsoever. Reading an interview with him became a frustrating experience."[122]

The omissions resulting from McCartney's refusal to reveal personal information are considerable. Nowhere in the article with *Life* does McCartney hint that his former songwriting partner's criticisms of him in *Lennon Remembers* had stung deeply; McCartney did not admit this until 1974, when relations between himself and Lennon had warmed considerably. Likewise, McCartney fails to mention that he had fallen into a deep depression following the *McCartney* press release and ensuing split.[123]

Although it can be viewed as the deliberate opposite of *Lennon Remembers*, McCartney's interview with *Life* shares certain commonalities with its counterpart. Like *Lennon Remembers*, it was a source designed for public use, used to sell McCartney's side of the story, and any quotes from it must be used with that understanding. McCartney also omitted personal facts, including any account of his depression. This was information which, at the time, would have offered a different view of his motivations: decades later McCartney depicted the lawsuit as the only way for him to re-gain control of his life and emerge from his severe depression.[124] The interview also publicly introduced one of the enduring themes of McCartney's version of the Beatles story: minimizing any tensions and hostilities that existed between him and the other band members. McCartney's first public attempt to dispute the solidifying *Lennon Remembers* narrative found some popular support, as evidenced by the fact that McCartney's solo work sold very well and he enjoyed considerable mainstream popularity. However, it failed to shift the narrative in the rock and roll press, which derided his *Life* interview as "perfectly calculated to preserve Paul's image of a decent, considerable nice guy. It was widely regarded in New York's more informed rock circles as perhaps the finest specimen of public-relations oriented garbage ever to spill onto the pages of a glossy."[125]

McCartney's attempts to publicly dismiss tensions became far more difficult after a public exchange of letters between McCartney and Lennon in the pages of *Melody Maker*, Britain's premier music magazine, in November and December 1971. Adopting the defensive tone that became his hallmark in

almost all subsequent interviews, McCartney responded to what he viewed
as attacks by the press and Lennon: "Everyone thinks I'm the aggressor but
I'm not, you know. I just want out."[126] After criticizing Klein and defending
the Eastmans, he naively declared that the situation would resolve itself if all
four ex-Beatles met alone and signed a piece of paper to legally and financially
dissolve their obligations to one another.[127] Lennon's response, printed in the
next month's issue, escalated the rhetoric and again identified McCartney as
the instigator. "If you're not the aggressor (as you claim) who the hell took
us to court and shat all over us in public? … have you ever thought you might
possibly be wrong about something? Your conceit about us and Klein is
incredible…. You must know we're right about Eastman![128] Lennon and
McCartney's public exchange in *Melody Maker* offers an example of how conscious each side was of promoting its own particular version of the splintered
Beatles' narrative.

"How Do You Sleep?"

The press was not the only public weapon available to each side. On his
second solo album, *Ram*, McCartney included a few critiques aimed at
Lennon in his song "Too Many People." In "Too Many People," McCartney
criticized Lennon for throwing away his greatest achievement by leaving the
Beatles and establishing himself as an underground political figure prosely-
tizing to others. McCartney also ensured that there was a picture of a pair of
copulating beetles on the album, presumably a message to his former band
mates. "Too Many People" was subtle but provocative: Lennon's response was
pointed and disproportionate. He countered publicly with "How Do You
Sleep," a song that reduced McCartney to his famous looks and agreed with
the worldwide rumor that the other man was dead. Lennon used the song to
attack McCartney's character, marriage and musical reputation. "On 'How
Do You Sleep' John stated that Paul had no talent."[129] The song denigrated
McCartney as a writer, declared that his only contribution to the Beatles was
"Yesterday," and referred to the other man's work as inferior. It also accused
McCartney of being controlled by his wife Linda, a jibe that, given Lennon's
relationship with Ono, reviewers noted the hypocrisy of.[130] In a demonstration
of Lennon's mercurial personality, he placed the song on his *Imagine* album,
whose title song was an anthem for peace.

Even *Rolling Stone*, Lennon's greatest media champion, balked at "How
Do You Sleep?," describing "John's character assassination of Paul McCartney"
as "horrifying and indefensible," as well as "unjust."[131] Perhaps stung by the

criticism, Lennon quickly dismissed the song's importance. "It's not serious. Like, if Paul was really, really hurt by it.... I'll explain it to him.... If he really thinks it's serious."[132] The day *Imagine* was released, Lennon described "How Do You Sleep?" as "an outburst. Things are still the same between us. He was and still is my closest friend, except for Yoko."[133] As with *Lennon Remembers*, he seemed almost surprised that so many people had taken "How Do You Sleep?" seriously, saying "If I can't have a fight with my best friend, I don't know who I can fight with."[134] By 1974, exasperated with answering questions about the song, Lennon argued that it was ultimately a private matter, declaring "I'm entitled to call [Paul] what I want to, and vice versa. It's in our family, but if somebody else calls him names I won't take it. It's our own business."[135]

Despite Lennon's labeling it a private matter, decades after the breakup, Beatles' writers still discussed Lennon's motivations behind writing, recording, and releasing "How Do You Sleep?"[136] One reason was because Lennon himself never offered a definitive answer: In December 1971 Lennon and Ono defended it as an appropriate response to *Ram* and rebuked fans requesting an end to the public hostilities, with Ono identifying Lennon as the victim: "Please stop attacking John for 'How Do You Sleep.'"[137] In a May 1972 conversation with Connolly, Lennon argued that he had written the song to "encourage Paul by writing and saying things that I thought would spur him on," and declared that his statements had been "misunderstood."[138] In a 1973 interview Lennon declared that he had really written the song about himself,[139] and a year later told reporters he intended to re-write it,[140] but in his 1980 *Playboy* interview, Lennon attributed it to sibling rivalry: "I used my resentment against Paul to write a song.... I don't really go around with those thoughts in my head all the time."[141]

At the time of the song's release, Christgau viewed it as retaliation for McCartney's provocations, describing it as "the kind of public act committed by a lover who wants to make sure he will never return in momentary weakness to the one who has rejected him so cruelly."[142] *Rolling Stone* argued it was prompted in part by "the traditional bohemian contempt for the bourgeoisie,"[143] reinforcing the common belief that much of the hostility between the two men was attributable to class differences. In *You Never Give Me Your Money* Doggett argues that "How Do You Sleep?" reveals the extent to which McCartney had become an authority figure for Lennon while agreeing that Lennon wrote the song about his own psyche and not McCartney's.[144] McCartney's 1997 semi-autobiography *Many Years from Now* continues McCartney's efforts to downplay the hostility between himself and Lennon: it mitigates Lennon's participation by citing eyewitness accounts arguing that at least half of the song's lyrics were written by Ono and Klein.[145]

Although "How Do You Sleep?" makes harsh statements concerning McCartney's character and musicianship, the song is a poor piece of evidence for many of the same reasons as *Lennon Remembers*. Like *Lennon Remembers*, the accuracy of "How Do You Sleep?" is compromised by Lennon's admitted anger at the time he wrote it and his later attempts to dismiss its importance. The song's value as a source in Beatles' history concerns what it reveals about Lennon's psychology and the Lennon/McCartney relationship at the time it was recorded, and not as the definitive statement on Lennon's perception of McCartney. Decades later, Connolly acknowledged how Lennon's statements helped damage McCartney's reputation but dismissed much of their claim to accuracy: "Those digs told us more about John than Paul."[146]

However, while Lennon somewhat disavowed the song's importance, there is no way of quantifying the impact "How Do You Sleep?" had on McCartney's reputation. Its appearance on Lennon's best-selling solo album, *Imagine*, left millions of record listeners convinced that Lennon regarded his old partner's musical talents with utter contempt. That the first album McCartney released after "How Do You Sleep?" was *Wild Life*, which received abysmal reviews, did not help his declining critical reputation and seemed to reinforce Lennon's musical criticisms of his former partner.

For those members of the public looking for any sign of public reconciliation between Lennon and McCartney, let alone a Beatles reunion, the prospects seemed bleak. The year that began with the publication of *Lennon Remembers* had been followed by the band's legal dissolution. The ensuing feud had led to "Too Many People" and "How Do You Sleep?" and ended with the bitter exchange of letters in *Melody Maker* in November and December of 1971. Interestingly, relations between Lennon and McCartney had been improving slowly in private even as they continued to spar in public. The two had been corresponding, and in December, Lennon sent McCartney a postcard declaring "War is over if you want it," along with what he mistakenly believed to be a bootlegged copy of the Beatles' failed audition at Decca from 1962.[147] The public and private relationship between the two former partners waxed and waned throughout the 1970s, but the events of 1971 influenced public perception of the two for years after relations had improved.

Apple to the Core

The Lennons' accessibility to the press continued to pay dividends even after the court had officially ruled in favor of McCartney. In 1972, Peter McCabe's *Apple to the Core*, the first book to attempt an in-depth examination of the business reasons behind the group's breakup, appeared. The book contained interviews with such figures as Yoko Ono, Allen Klein, John Eastman, Neil Aspinall and Derek Taylor at a time when memories were still fresh, emotions were still raw, and breakup-era agendas were still influencing testimony. More importantly, *Apple to the Core* was written and published more than a year before Lennon, Harrison and Starr all left Klein's management and then sued him. As such it provides the last major impartial portrayal of Klein before he emerged as a convenient scapegoat for both camps.

As an account of the Beatles' financial and legal issues, *Apple to the Core* relies too heavily on agenda-laden eyewitness testimony and interviews. This incidentally favors Lennon and Ono's version of events, as McCartney refused to be interviewed.[148] While all three ex-Beatles as well as Ono and Klein spoke to McCabe, McCartney's version of events is presented by his brother-in-law John Eastman. This is notable, as interviews with the Eastman family in Beatles historiography are very rare. However, it also weakens McCartney's side as Eastman only addresses business and financial issues, rather than personal ones, and spends his time sparring with Klein. Throughout the book both Eastman and Klein accuse the other of sabotage, deception, withholding vital business and legal documents and instigating the conflict that led to the Beatles' split. *Apple to the Core* was the first source to present one of the most severe accusations of subterfuge against McCartney: According to Klein, the Eastmans had encouraged McCartney to purchase additional shares of Northern Songs, the company which owned the Lennon/McCartney catalog, and in which he and Lennon had been equal shareholders. Klein presented McCartney's purchase of the extra shares as proof of his duplicity and the Eastmans' desire to undermine his management and gain control of the Beatles financial empire. McCabe fails to provide documentation to verify or disprove either side's claims,[149] but ultimately views the Eastmans as the aggressors: "Since 1969 they had loomed at Klein's shoulder: their hostility toward him knew no bounds."[150]

Apple to the Core argues that the breakup was caused by financial and business disagreements that stemmed from the Beatles' utopian business dream and tax shelter, Apple Corps. The core disagreement, according to McCabe, was McCartney's refusal to accept Klein as Beatles' manager, which was motivated by McCartney's middle class aspirations, difficult personality and musical ego.[151] The class issue, which Lennon had also identified in *Lennon Remembers*, is particularly emphasized: "The break between John and Paul is fairly easy to explain. Paul was getting more and more into this upper-middle class syndrome ... and John was getting further and further out."[152] McCabe's work reinforced the Orthodoxy originating in *Lennon*

Remembers and reiterated in Klein's *Playboy* interview that McCartney's class-conscious support of the Eastmans, prompted in part by his wife Linda, caused the split. It seriously downplayed any other tensions within the band, including those caused by Lennon's insistence in bringing Ono into the studio.

Unfortunately, McCabe's work also contains some more blatant examples of the sexual double standard common in many Beatles' works. *Apple to the Core* ignores the individual Beatles' extensive sexual histories, but described Linda McCartney as "an empress among groupies" whose "bed was always open," was "in and out of all sorts of different beds" and a "legend backstage."[153] McCabe's harsh emphasis on Linda McCartney's sexual history prior to her marriage (a history that was practically infinitesimal compared to any of the male Beatles, who received no such criticism or commentary) while disappointing, is not uncommon. The depiction of Linda McCartney in *Apple to the Core* is part of a larger trend by numerous male Beatles' writers that applies sexual double standards, patronizing language, objectification or body shaming (at one point McCabe mocks Linda McCartney's weight)[154] when describing females.

The Conflicting Testimony over "Eleanor Rigby"

After the breakup, the question of authorship—determining whether Lennon or McCartney wrote a particular lyric or melody—became one of the most popular sources of speculation in the rock press and among fans. Having publicly severed the Lennon/McCartney partnership, both men gave interviews in the early 1970s that laid claim to their share of the Beatles catalog. Most of Lennon's testimony regarding song authorship agrees with McCartney's accounts, and vice versa. This is a key point because, with the exception of the professional evaluations of musicologists and occasional testimony from various Beatles insiders who witnessed songwriting sessions, there is no other authoritative source on who wrote what in the partnership. McCartney emphasized this in his semi-autobiography. "It was only me that sat in those hotel rooms, in his house in the attic … seeing him not being able to write a song, and having me help; seeing me not being able to write a song and him help me."[155] For historians, the private nature of the Lennon/McCartney songwriting partnership means that, when testimony about authorship conflicts, it is a clash between equally credible primary sources that are also often the *only* sources.

Those few arguments that do exist usually are waged over lesser proportions of songwriting credit and are difficult to settle authoritatively. One of the rare songs in which *primary* authorship is disputed is "Eleanor Rigby," which appeared on their 1966 album, *Revolver*. In 1970, as the press war between the two was heating up, both men claimed to have written the majority of "Eleanor Rigby," one of the rare instances in which their testimony regarding songwriting credits directly clashed. In *Lennon Remembers*, Lennon claimed to have written "a good half of the lyrics or more" of "Eleanor Rigby."[156] In 1971, the most contentious year of the Beatles breakup, Lennon publicly stated in *Melody Maker* that he had written at least 50 percent of "Eleanor Rigby,"[157] and in *Hit Parader* the next year increased his claim to 70 percent of the lyrics.[158] During his famous 1980 *Playboy* interview Lennon declared that, while McCartney had come up with the original concept, he and not McCartney had written 70 percent of the song.[159] McCartney, as well as Martin, publicly disputed Lennon's claims. In his semi-autobiography *Many Years from Now*, McCartney reversed Lennon's apportioning of the credits and claimed 80 percent of "Eleanor Rigby,"[160] but Lennon's repeated declarations of authorship cast the writer's identity under official dispute.

This argument over one of the Beatles most critically acclaimed songs provides an excellent opportunity to analyze contradictory sources, decide which evidence is most credible, and determine the truth. In this case, analyzing eyewitness credibility and agenda does not help, as both Lennon and McCartney are equally valid eyewitnesses regarding their songwriting process. In the early 1970s, when the conflict over "Eleanor Rigby's" authorship arose, both men also had their own agendas for claiming the lion's share of credit for a song that already was regarded as one of the Beatles' greatest masterpieces. With both Lennon and McCartney as equally valid sources, separate pieces of evidence must determine the author of "Eleanor Rigby."

In the debate over "Eleanor Rigby," the balance of evidence overwhelmingly supports McCartney's claim of authorship. However, that a larger number of sources support McCartney does not by itself necessarily vindicate his claim. According to both Garraghan and Bloch, when comparing contrasting accounts, the fact that one account is backed by more sources does not necessarily render that version correct. Histories often involve testimony copied from previous accounts, which nullifies the borrowed, or copied testimony, and reduces the number of valid sources. "To unmask an imitation is to reduce two of more witnesses to only one."[161] It is only because there do not appear to be any imitations in the eyewitness testimony that McCartney's claim gains the additional credibility conferred by a larger number of supporting sources.

In ascertaining historical truth, the independence and credibility of the sources is as important as the amount. As with the quantity, the quality of evidence decidedly favors McCartney. The only piece of evidence backing Lennon's claim to authorship is his own testimony, but there is a significant amount of both circumstantial and direct evidence to support McCartney. That McCartney sang "Eleanor Rigby" on *Revolver* in 1966 is itself circumstantial evidence in his favor, since the Beatles' customary formula almost always made the song's primary author its lead singer. The song's theme—a story about a lonely spinster—also reflects McCartney's lyrical style more than Lennon's. "McCartney tended to write about other people; Lennon was more inclined to write about himself."[162] While such circumstantial evidence does not prove McCartney's claim, it supports it, and—if the only eyewitness testimonies regarding the song's authorship were Lennon and McCartney's conflicting accounts—such evidence would tilt the argument in McCartney's favor.[163]

However, in addition to this evidence, there is eyewitness testimony from at least four separate and independent sources, all of whom support McCartney's claim to authorship. Martin, universally regarded as an extremely credible source, has always identified "Eleanor Rigby" as McCartney's song.[164] In an interview poet William Burroughs, a friend of McCartney's, recounts witnessing McCartney attempting to write lyrics that fit the song's already-written melody. Pop singer Donovan also describes a similar, separate instance in which he witnessed McCartney working on the song.[165] While Donovan and Burroughs' testimony does not necessarily disprove Lennon's claim that McCartney brought him the first verse which Lennon then completed, it does provide independent evidence that McCartney was working on the song, corroboration which Lennon's account lacks. However, Lennon's friend, Pete Shotton, provides the most important evidence regarding the dispute. Shotton was present at Lennon's house when McCartney introduced the melody and some of the lyrics of "Eleanor Rigby" into a writing session with the other Beatles. According to Shotton, while he, Harrison and Starr all added ideas or lines to McCartney's song, Lennon's contribution to "Eleanor Rigby" was "virtually nil."[166] That Shotton, whose lifelong friendship with Lennon would indicate bias in *favor* of his friend, dismissed Lennon's claims to have written most of the song is an extremely powerful piece of evidence. The amount of testimony, the credibility of the witnesses, and the independence of the sources leave no doubt: "Eleanor Rigby" is primarily McCartney's song. The question for Beatles historians to ask is not—"Who wrote most of 'Eleanor Rigby,'"—but rather—"'Why did Lennon repeatedly claim credit for it?'"

Shotton attributed Lennon's erroneous claims to his friend's "extremely erratic"[167] memory, but separate evidence suggests at least three more reasons.

In the same interview in which he claimed to have written 70 percent of "Eleanor Rigby," Lennon also said he was "insulted and hurt"[168] when McCartney refused to ask him directly for help with finishing the last part of the song's lyrics, instead tossing them out to a group of people that happened to include Lennon. In his book *Long and Winding Roads*, Beatles author Kenneth Womack speculates that it was Lennon's anger at McCartney's cavalier treatment of their songwriting partnership that may have prompted Lennon's false claims of authorship.[169] This speculation is credible because of Lennon's well known tendency to allow his emotions, particularly anger, to exaggerate his testimony.

"Eleanor Rigby's" status as one of the Beatles greatest songs also may have played a role. From the moment millions of listeners first heard it on *Revolver*, "Eleanor Rigby" was considered a lyrical and musical masterpiece, a song unprecedented in the history of pop music.

> Much was made of the poetic quality of the lyric ... the critic Karl Miller included a transcription of "Eleanor Rigby" in his 1968 anthology, *Writing in England Today*. The poet Thomas Gunn, writing in *The Listener*, compared the lyric favorably to an Auden ballad.... In 1967, Allen Ginsberg made a point of playing the song during an audience with Ezra Pound ... "I don't think there's ever been a better song written," the lyricist Jerry Lieber would say of "Eleanor Rigby," and George Melly, hearing it for the first time, felt that "pop had come of age."[170]

"Eleanor Rigby's" critical acclaim may have motivated Lennon's attempts to portray himself as its author, particularly in the midst of the breakup-era debate over whether he or McCartney was the greater genius. During this same period, Lennon also reportedly declared in a private phone conversation with Connolly that he had written "about 80 percent of the lyrics" under the Lennon/McCartney name. Connolly summarily dismissed the untrue claim because of Lennon's tendency to be "prone to hyperbole at his most temperate times."[171] Status as the acknowledged author of "Eleanor Rigby" would have strongly reinforced either man's claim to genius.

A third possible reason theoretically can be traced back to Klein. During their first meeting Klein curried favor with Lennon in part by distinguishing his lyrics from McCartney's.[172] Whether Klein intentionally misinformed Lennon in order to flatter him or genuinely believed Lennon had written material actually by McCartney is unknown. However, Klein revealed in his 1971 *Playboy* interview that *he* was the one who had initially "reminded" Lennon of his authorship of "Eleanor Rigby": "John wrote 60 or 70% of the lyric on 'Eleanor Rigby.' He just didn't remember until I sat him down and had him sort through it all."[173]

It appears that in his efforts to become Beatles manager and gain Lennon's approval, Klein may have convinced the songwriter that he had written lyrics actually by McCartney. If true, the theory has implications for Beatles history that expand beyond the issue of the authorship of "Eleanor Rigby." If Lennon's false belief that he had written McCartney's song stemmed from Klein's reminders' of who wrote what, Klein's ability to convince Lennon he had written 70 percent of a song to which he had, in fact, contributed very little is a telling indication of Klein's power to convince Lennon of falsities. In turn, this aspect of Klein's relationship with Lennon may offer revealing insight into some of the musician's actions during the dissolution.

The Credibility of George Martin

In his book on *Historical Methods in Mass Communication*, historian James Startt provides some of the questions essential to source analysis, which historians use to determine the credibility of an eyewitness. "How near was this person to the event in time and space? How available was evidence to this person? How competent was this person to understand the event, including training, experience, class and cultural differences?"[174] According to these standards, no eyewitness source has more credibility than Beatles' producer George Martin regarding the group's work and creative process in the studio. Individual Beatles accounts' are invaluable but inherently biased, as the testimony of each tends to promote his own version of history. As a musician and producer who knew the Beatles well, Martin's musical and lyrical analysis is certainly more qualified than that of the many journalists, with far less musical training, who have provided their own versions.[175] Also, in contrast to the Beatles and most members of their inner circle, Martin's avoidance of recreational drugs means mind-altering substances did not influence his eyewitness accounts.

Besides the obviously biased McCartney, Martin is the most important primary source which publicly disputed many of Lennon's statements both during and after the *Lennon Remembers* era. Martin is viewed as an invaluable source on the Beatles' music, relationship dynamic, songwriting and breakup. The reasons for his credibility as an eyewitness are numerous. Martin worked with the Beatles on an almost daily basis for a period of eight years. He also socialized with them outside of the studio and accompanied them on some of their tours. He was well-acquainted with key members of their inner circle, including Brian Epstein, Neil Aspinall, Cynthia Lennon, Yoko Ono, and Linda McCartney. As their musical producer, Martin had a unique view of their overall dynamic, including Harrison and Starr's roles and contributions. As a participant in the creation of every album, Martin observed the collaborative and competitive nature of the Lennon/McCartney songwriting partnership and, like their friendship, witnessed it at some of its best and worst times.

Although Martin's testimony lacks the obvious reasons for bias, in the post-breakup era, associated with Lennon's or McCartney's statements, several issues could impact the value of his later accounts. Martin was stung by Lennon's criticism of him in *Lennon Remembers*, as well as a later exchange of letters in *Melody Maker* in 1971, in which Lennon devalued Martin's contributions and disputed his version of events. Although Lennon later dismissed some of his statements, Martin found them hard to forgive. Though Martin was very fond of Lennon, he was closer personally and musically to McCartney, and McCartney was the only ex-Beatle Martin produced again and frequently socialized with after the band's split. Their friendship strengthened over the decades: in a 2005 interview, McCartney described Martin as "one of the most important men in my life,"[176] alongside his father, brother and fellow Beatles. During the 1970s McCartney was more willing than Lennon to publicly acknowledge Martin's role in creating Beatles' music, describing the producer's contribution as "quite a big one, actually"[177]; it is reasonable to assume that Martin preferred McCartney's favorable appraisal over Lennon's more dismissive one. Parts of Martin's 1979 work *All You Need Is Ears*, particularly his defense of music written for commercial purposes,[178] can be read as a response to some of Lennon's statements in *Lennon Remembers*. For these reasons, Martin's memoirs and post-breakup interviews can be viewed as somewhat biased in favor of McCartney, although there is no factual evidence to prove this, and his affection for Lennon is evident throughout both of his books, numerous interviews, and *The Beatles Anthology*.

Martin is a credible source, in part, because his testimony shows he is capable of laying aside his own ego. "He is not one to blow his own trumpet."[179] In both of his books and countless interviews, Martin frankly acknowledged his important but still lesser role in crafting the Beatles' music. "There is no doubt in my mind that the main talent of that whole era came from Paul and John. George, Ringo and myself were subsidiary talents. We were not five equal people artistically: two were very strong and the other three were also rans."[180] Because of this acknowledgement of his lesser role, Martin does not have an obvious agenda to promote. Almost all secondary sources in Beatles historiography, from biographies to newspaper articles to documentaries, regard Martin as an invaluable and extremely credible source. His portrayal in Beatles historiography is almost universally complimentary.

Martin's version of the Beatles' story has remained consistent for the past fifty years. In every decade and throughout every narrative, Martin has maintained that Lennon and McCartney "were equal talents who collaborated but, more importantly, who competed."[181] In his 1979 book *All You Need Is Ears*, Martin dismissed the prevailing Orthodoxy of Lennon as the sole genius, describing Lennon and McCartney both as "two tunesmiths of genius."[182] In the 1980s, when numerous biographies, including Norman's extremely influential *Shout!* and Goldman's controversial *The Lives of John Lennon*, argued that Lennon and McCartney possessed incompatible personalities and were never close friends, Martin strongly disagreed. "They really loved each other very much, and they still—you know, even up until the very last moment … there was a great love between those two men … they respected each other, in spite of the words that they said in public."[183] Throughout every decade, Martin continued to argue that the true genius behind the Beatles' music was not Lennon *or* McCartney but rather the combination of and competition between two equally brilliant talents. "Yes, I think [Paul's] a genius. I'm happy to go into print on that. John, too."[184]

Another important voice that clashed with the prevailing *Lennon Remembers* narrative was Wilfrid Meller's *Twilight of the Gods*. Published in 1973, Meller's work was the first comprehensive examination of most of Lennon and McCartney's catalog by an academically trained musician. A professor of music at the University of York, Mellers avoided making moral or political judgments of either man and instead focused solely on discussing the music they had written. Repeating the accepted wisdom of the time, Mellers stated early in his work that Lennon and McCartney stopped writing together in the first few years of their partnership.[185] Consequently, Mellers identified songs that been the work of both men as solely the creation of either Lennon or McCartney. This unintentionally reinforced the lie, begun by Lennon in *Lennon Remembers*, that almost all of the men's music had been written without any input from the other. Whereas the rock press tended to focus on the artistic significance of deeply personal lyrics, Mellers expanded the view by also extensively discussing melody. In *Twilight of the Gods*, Mellers acknowledged McCartney's "non-personal narrative" lyrical style as opposed to Lennon's "introvert" approach but did not proclaim the superiority of one method over the other.[186] His musical evaluation of the Lennon/McCartney partnership ultimately provided a considerably more balanced analysis than was common at the time. "Even in separation and mutual hostility they still need one another as impetus to their finest work."[187]

Allen Klein: From "Human" to "Demon King"

The portrayal of Allen Klein throughout Beatles historiography is both fascinating and frustratingly incomplete. There is no doubt that Klein played a significant role in helping cause the Beatles' breakup, yet how significant a role remains unclear. Once Lennon, Harrison and Starr dismissed Klein as their manager and exchanged lawsuits with him, he became a convenient scapegoat for both sides of the Lennon/McCartney divide. During the breakup period Klein's portrayal in the press largely balanced between negative and positive depictions. Even after the trial, as manager of three of the four former Beatles, Klein wielded a great deal of power in the music industry. When reporters questioned Klein's reputation and business practices Lennon, Harrison and Starr all publicly defended his management and methods: Lennon, in particular, regarded criticism of Klein as snobbish. Most portrayals of Klein written at this time are roughly balanced. In numerous accounts, including Klein's 1971 *Playboy* interview and *Apple to the Core,* the writers acknowledge Klein's litigious past and questionable reputation. But they also emphasize his strong work ethic, lack of pretension, rags-to-riches story, forceful personality and deeply personal relationships with his clients.[188]

This balanced portrayal of Klein ended dramatically in March 1973, once the three former Beatles refused to renew his managerial contract and then sued him. Unfortunately, the reason Lennon, Harrison and Starr broke with Klein has never been resolved thoroughly. This is partly because most Beatles books do not devote the same meticulous analysis to the period following the band's breakup as they do to their earlier years. Another reason may be that for Lennon, Ono, Harrison and Starr, dismissing Klein after years of supporting him was tantamount to admitting that one of the major aspects of their version of the breakup—that Klein had been the correct choice to succeed Epstein—was incorrect. None of the Beatles who had picked Klein were particularly eager to admit to the world that their choice was a mistake. This, along with legal issues that emerged after they exchanged lawsuits with their former manager, may be the reason Lennon, Harrison, Starr and Ono had so little to say on the subject, and why so little evidence exists to explain their motivations.

At the time they initially downplayed their decision not to retain Klein's managerial services after years of praising him. Lennon's public criticisms of his former manager were uncharacteristically mild: referring to Klein as a "naughty," "greedy" boy, who failed "to do what he said he'd do, which was manage our affairs," and arguing that he split with Klein because the man "did little to rectify the mess" at Apple.[189] By March 1973, when he chose not to renew Klein's contract, Lennon had spent the last four years championing Klein to the press, particularly as a more human alternative to the automaton Eastman family.[190] Publicly attacking Klein meant tacitly admitting that McCartney (whose refusal to accept Klein as his manager had been cast by Lennon as a moral flaw, motivated by class snobbery and selfishness) had been correct. This was something Lennon eventually grudgingly admitted. "Let's say possibly Paul's suspicions were right."[191]

Beatles' authors have attributed the reasons for the split between Klein and the Fab Three to a number of causes. Norman argues that it was Klein's support of Harrison's stance, refusing Ono the chance to perform at the Concert for Bangladesh, which prompted Lennon to support the break.[192] In *The Lives of John Lennon*, Goldman identifies Ono as the instigator; angered at Klein's post-concert criticism of her performance at the One to One concert, she demanded the split with Klein.[193] Author Fred Goodman argues that the three ex-Beatles were frustrated with Klein's inability to reach a financial settlement with the Eastmans.[194] Doggett's *You Never Give Me Your Money* offers a very different interpretation. In addition to public questions concerning Klein's handling of the proceeds from Harrison's Concert for Bangladesh, they wanted to reunite with McCartney, an impossibility as long as they remained under contract to Klein.[195]

After he officially lost his place as the manager of any ex-Beatles, Klein's portrayal changed from roughly balanced to almost universally negative. By March 1974, *Crawdaddy* was noting Klein's suspicious ownership of the Rolling Stones' catalog and speculating about the damage he had done to his other high-profile band: "It is easy to conjecture about the little empire he might have been carving out for himself amid the chaos of the Beatles' finances."[196] Taylor, who had defended Klein in *Apple to the Core*, later described him as the "Demon King" in the Beatles' narrative.[197] Doggett declared "nobody in the Beatles milieu has received a more damning verdict from historians than Allen Klein."[198] As previously noted, there are several reasons for this. As the years passed, information regarding Klein's questionable business practices (particularly the Nanker-Phelge incident) became more widely known. Klein's imprisonment in the late 1970s for tax evasion also did little to buttress his reputation. Neither did the fact that both the Beatles and the Rolling Stones had rejected him, and that those relationships publicly ended in litigation and acrimony. Lennon, Ono, Harrison and Starr's lawsuit against Klein also tacitly vindicated McCartney's assessment of him as an untrustworthy and unfit manager. This meant that McCartney's preference for his in-laws, the Eastmans, over Klein no longer appeared so unreasonable to the public or to Beatles historians.

Of equal importance was that, with Klein exiled, it now benefited *both* sides in Beatles historiography to cast him as the villain. By blaming Klein, McCartney was able to downplay the breakup-era conflicts with his fellow Beatles. Klein's fall from grace reinforced McCartney's attempts to cast the disagreement as one primarily between himself and Klein rather than between himself and his friends. In later decades, McCartney portrayed the situation in very black and white terms, at times inflating the financial menace Klein posed, transforming his lawsuit into a quasi-fictitious all or nothing scenario: "I just saw it as 'I'm saving our fortune, or this guy's going to run away with it.'"[199] On the other side, Beatles writers who favored Lennon's version could overlook Lennon's own significant role in the dissolution if they emphasized Klein as the "Demon King." These writers focused on Klein's manipulations of Lennon from the very beginning of their relationship. "Klein played a clever game,"[200] Norman assures readers in *John Lennon: The Life*, reinforced by a statement from Ono: "Allen was very clever. He knew all of John's songs. He just kept on quoting lyrics. He'd memorized them all. And that got John."[201]

The Post-1971 Beatles

The depiction of the Beatles' story in 1971 cast a long shadow on how their history was written for decades. This is partly because of the public conflict among the band members, particularly Lennon and McCartney. Any efforts to reconcile, such as letters or phone calls, usually were conducted privately and therefore largely unknown at the time. Public disagreements, however, made the international news. In his biography of Lennon, Tim Riley argues that both men deliberately maintained a public but somewhat misleading distance: "To prevent runaway rumors and preserve their hard-fought integrity as solo figures, Lennon and McCartney visited far more often and more warmly throughout the seventies than they let on to the press."[202] Most of the publicly available evidence during the early 1970s indicated the two were locked in a permanent, bitter dispute aggravated by incompatible personalities. In early 1972, however, Lennon and McCartney met and declared a truce, agreeing to stop sniping at one another in the press and in their songs. Accounts such as those from Gus Van Synoc, a guitarist on Lennon's Elephant's Memory sessions, were overlooked or underutilized for decades. Synoc declared that the Lennon/McCartney feud "gets blown way out of proportion.... It was nothing for John to take a call from Paul and talk to him for 90 minutes while we took a break ... and they were not fighting or arguing ... and you would swear they were best friends."[203]

By August 1972, relations had improved to the point where Lennon, "nervous and insecure" about appearing on stage again, contacted McCartney and asked him to participate in Lennon and Ono's One to One concert in New York.[204] McCartney declined due to Klein's participation in organizing the event.[205] Four years later, in a possible retaliatory gesture, Lennon ignored McCartney's invitation to come to his 1976 Wings over America concert in New York.

After the 1972 truce, the amount of information and vitriol coming from Lennon and McCartney decreased. Deliberate efforts by both sides to frame and rewrite Beatles history tapered off. McCartney was preoccupied with his young family, which now included three daughters, and his new band Wings. Lennon also had other matters on which to concentrate. His political campaigning had made him a target of the Nixon administration, which tapped his phone and tried to deport him from the United States. In June 1972, Lennon released his third post–Beatles album, *Some Time in New York City*, a serious critical and popular failure. His relationship with Klein deteriorated throughout 1972 and 1973. So did his marriage to Ono; Lennon engaged in at least one affair, and there is unverified testimony arguing Ono did the same.[206] By October 1973 the couple separated, with Lennon and his assistant and girlfriend, May Pang, leaving for Los Angeles, evidently with Ono's blessing. The "Lost Weekend" separation between Lennon and Ono lasted 18 months, although, according to Pang, her affair with Lennon continued until 1978, years after Lennon returned to Ono. Lennon was not the only Beatle facing marital troubles: both Harrison and Starr also had separated from their wives. All three men also struggled with addictions: Lennon and Starr primarily with alcohol, and Harrison with cocaine. Meanwhile McCartney was arrested several times for marijuana possession.

It is interesting to note that many of Lennon's public statements softening or denying the *Lennon Remembers* version of events corresponded with or immediately followed his 18-month separation from Ono. While Lennon's public statements regarding his reconciliation with McCartney could be viewed as a way of appealing to both sides of the now divided Beatles fan base,[207] retrospective testimony reinforces the idea that, by 1973–74, the pair's breakup era bitterness had receded. According to musician Alice Cooper, Lennon's friend and companion during this time period, the man reacted violently to any outside criticism of McCartney. "If anybody said anything bad about Paul—he'd take a swing at you and say 'You can't talk about Paul like that.' Paul was his best buddy."[208] By 1975, Lennon was retreating from his political activism of the early 1970s, arguing that it had only happened because Jerry Rubin and Abbie Hoffman "greeted me off the plane and the next minute I'm involved, you know."[209] Lennon also brushed off his *Lennon Remembers* denunciations of some of his Beatles work.

All four former Beatles faced constant media questions regarding the possibility of a Beatles' reunion. In his first major interview with *Rolling Stone* in January 1974, McCartney left the door open now that Klein was no longer in the picture. He also gloated, declaring "of course I loved that" when asked about Lennon, Harrison and Starr suing Klein and accusing their former manager of mismanagement. For the first time, McCartney publicly admitted that he had been hurt by *Lennon Remembers* but added that, while he had never confronted Lennon about it, he was sure the other man no longer agreed with what he had said in his famous interview. McCartney also acknowledged his inability to accept criticism—"I don't like criticism whatsoever"[210]—one of the main complaints that the other Beatles had lobbed at him privately before the breakup and publicly during it. The interview contained one of the few public instances in which McCartney revealed that he and the other Beatles resented the accolades that Martin had received, especially in reviews that they believed granted Martin undue credit for *their* work. With both Lennon and McCartney's public statements reassuring fans that the old animosity had passed (in 1974 Lennon gave an interview to *Crawdaddy* which he quipped should be titled "Lennon Forgets")[211] and with the impediment of Klein removed, speculation regarding a formal Beatles reunion[212] increased to a fever pitch. In late 1974, several independent sources confirm Lennon was planning to join and perhaps write with McCartney, who was recording with Wings in New Orleans. Instead Lennon reunited with Ono. The two had a son, Sean, in late 1975 and Lennon retreated from the public eye. Lennon would not release any new material for five years, until *Double Fantasy*, his dual album with Ono in 1980.

At the same time, McCartney relished the spotlight. His 1973 album *Band on the Run* was a massive critical and financial success which helped restore his reputation with rock critics. Even Lennon praised it: "*Band on the Run* is a great album."[213] In 1976, McCartney and Wings launched an extremely successful world tour, leading to more interviews and questions about the Beatles. That McCartney's 1976 tour was such a triumph may have been too much for Lennon, "whose insecurity was almost instinctive."[214] Lennon had not toured since his time with the Beatles or released an album of new material since 1974. In April 1976, Lennon rebuked McCartney for visiting his New York apartment without calling first. Stung by the criticism, McCartney left and, according to most accounts, the two never saw each other again, although they did speak on the phone. In his memoir John Green, Lennon's tarot reader, argued that Lennon did not want to see McCartney because he did not want his old partner to know he was experiencing severe writer's block.[215] In his biography of Lennon, Norman interprets it as a demonstration of Lennon's determination to avoid distractions and be a responsible father to his second son, Sean.[216] Tom Doyle, author of *Man on the Run*, a biography of McCartney's life during the 1970s, offers a more cynical view:

> There was likely some jealousy at play on Lennon's part—the previous day had seen *Wings at the Speed of Sound* rise to the top of the U.S. Album Chart in the first of a seven-week run; he had recently read that Paul, due to Wings' newfound earning power, was worth 25 million and moaned to Yoko that he would never earn that kind of money.[217]

Lennon's relationship with Harrison was also strained following the end of his "Lost Weekend." During the breakup and especially after Lennon's death, Harrison publicly emphasized his closeness to Lennon and downplayed any divisions between them, choosing to focus on the spiritual connection the two had made as the first Beatles to take LSD together.[218] However, there is evidence of serious pre-existing disagreements between the two. In some of the last interviews he gave before his death, Lennon criticized Harrison for not mentioning him enough in his autobiography, *I Me Mine*.[219] In a 1976 fan created questionnaire supposedly filled out by Lennon, he described McCartney as "extraordinary" but Harrison as "lost."[220] The most vivid account of disagreement between the two came from Pang. She described a fierce argument when Harrison confronted Lennon over the latter's refusal to appear on stage with him during his 1974 appearance in New York:

> "Where were you when I needed you! … I did everything you said. But you weren't there"… George said that repeatedly in the past, he had sung what John wanted him to sing, said what John wanted him to say. Because John wanted it, George had gone along with the decision to go with Allen Klein. In the nearly four years since, John had virtually ignored him, a fact that pained George deeply.[221]

Neither Lennon nor Harrison ever confirmed the confrontation, and, as Pang's account of the argument is the only one we have, it qualifies as unverified testimony rather than fact. After Lennon's murder, Harrison emphasized his connection to Lennon, the idol he had hero worshipped from his earliest days in the band. However, according to numerous statements by McCartney, Harrison and Lennon had not reconciled their differences at the time of Lennon's death.[222]

The Death of John Lennon

After giving a spate of new interviews during his "Lost Weekend" and a few following his reconciliation with Ono, Lennon remained publicly silent for several years. When he reemerged, it was to promote his new album with Ono, *Double Fantasy.* During the breakup era, particularly 1971, Lennon's version of Beatles history was combative and dismissive. "It was as though having made the decision, he couldn't smash his Beatles' persona quickly or outrageously enough."[223] After his 1972 truce with McCartney, Lennon revised his views and retreated from some of his prior claims, including many of those he had made in *Lennon Remembers.* In his efforts to promote his new album, Lennon fell somewhere between the middle of both extremes.

Lennon's return to public life after years of silence made headlines, and his major interviews from 1980 received considerably more attention than the smaller ones he had done during his "Lost Weekend" in which had adopted a more generous tone towards his ex-band mates. Lennon's 1980 interviews had more of an enduring impact on public perception, particularly because they were followed so quickly by Lennon's murder and received so much attention as his last public words. The most famous of the musician's 1980 interviews, with *Playboy* magazine, was for sale at newsstands on the night of his murder.

The agenda behind Lennon's last interviews in 1980 was in some ways identical to his previous agenda in 1970 and 1971: to promote his new album and his artistic partnership with Ono, and to construct a new popular persona for himself. In *Lennon Remembers* he had cast himself as a revolutionary fighting against the musical and political establishment; now he was a contented househusband and father to his youngest son, Sean. The difference in his music was stark. Initial reviews for *Double Fantasy* were mixed, as some rock critics criticized Lennon for abandoning the overtly political and deeply personal lyrics that he had embraced in the early 1970s in favor of the topics that McCartney had been writing about for years.[224]

Like *Lennon Remembers,* Lennon's 1980 interview with *Playboy* offered a compelling narrative that projected the image Lennon wanted at the time and exerted considerable popular influence but was less than accurate in certain areas. In an effort to demonstrate his creative independence from his old partner, Lennon denied listening to McCartney's work—"I don't follow Wings, you know. I don't give a shit what Wings is doing"—an assertion later contradicted by one of Lennon's notes to his personal assistant, published years later, asking him to buy the new Wings album.[225] He displayed a considerable amount of revisionism, describing his political activism of the late '60s and early '70s as something he "dabbled" in, "more out of guilt than anything."[226] In *Lennon Remembers,* Lennon had declared that Harrison and McCartney's treatment of Ono had been a major source of conflict leading to the band's breakup, and had driven both he and Ono into using heroin.

Ten years later, Lennon declared that the other Beatles had treated Ono quite well in the studio. Ono agreed: "None of them were nasty to me."[227] Lennon denied having any interest in reuniting to write with McCartney, a statement that his producer on *Double Fantasy*, Jack Douglas, publicly disputed years later. "He was looking to get like, hooked up with Paul before Paul went to Japan, to do some writing."[228]

More importantly, at the urging of interviewer David Sheff, Lennon went through a large number of Beatles' songs and identified the primary author. This was something both Lennon and McCartney had done to a lesser extent in previous interviews. The *Playboy* interview was far more extensive, covering a greater amount of the Beatles' catalog and in more detail. As Lennon's last major statement on the songwriting credits, his analysis had a significant impact on Beatles' historiography and the enduring perception of the Lennon/McCartney songwriting partnership. Lennon's testimony has proven an invaluable source for Beatles' historians and provides a necessary check, preventing McCartney from providing the only in-depth song by song attribution of the Beatles' songwriting credits. However, Lennon's analysis was not entirely accurate; he claimed credit for two songs he had not written and, according to McCartney, failed to give his partner credit for certain contributions he had made to some of Lennon's work.[229]

Frontani argues that the credit's emphasis on lyrics oversimplified the music's origins, "further obscuring the contributions and talents of the individual Beatles' to their success, particularly McCartney's production and arranging prowess."[230] Lennon also publicly revealed his frustration that McCartney's songwriting output had exceeded his, particularly during and after 1967. Eleven years earlier, Lennon had privately criticized his partner for this; in the same meeting where he announced he wanted a divorce, the musician blamed McCartney for dominating the band's later albums by writing too many songs and controlling their production in the studio. In 1980 Lennon acknowledged that his jealousy of McCartney's urban lifestyle, bachelorhood and productivity during the *Sgt. Pepper's* period provoked his later resentful statements regarding the album.[231]

Decades later, under the Lewisohn narrative, these statements attained considerable significance in the eyes of many Beatles writers. Doggett, Jonathan Gould, and Mikal Gilmore, among others, argued that Lennon's resentment over McCartney's productivity and jealousy over his partner's more adventurous lifestyle may have provoked Lennon's insecurity and motivated some of his breakup-era actions. Because Lennon's 1980 public statements are reinforced by accounts of his 1969 private disagreement with McCartney, this strengthens their credibility.

On the subject of his old band, Lennon pivoted away from his *Lennon Remembers* opinions, something he stressed in repeated interviews. "You ask me about the Beatles, I'll tell you what I feel about them…. I love those guys, I love the Beatles, I'm proud of the music."[232] The rivalry between Lennon and McCartney which had produced many of the Beatles' greatest songs and some of the group's deepest divisions was still evident in Lennon's interviews, as it was in McCartney's, over ten years after the group had broken up. "I admire a lot of what Paul's done since we split up, I think a lot of it's shit. What do they want from me? So maybe it was sibling rivalry then."[233] Lennon further distanced himself from *Lennon Remembers* by acknowledging of the importance of his friendship and partnership with McCartney. Journalist Robert Hilburn expressed surprise at how Lennon now "spoke with affection about the Beatles days and how much he still looked forward to seeing Paul." When asked about the "sarcastic barbs" and "stinging lyrics" Lennon had directed at McCartney years earlier, the musician dismissed his previous statements. "'Aw, don't believe all that,' he said smiling. 'Paul is like a brother. We've gotten way past all that.'"[234] While Lennon denied any desire to reunite, in his last few weeks, he gave several interviews referring to Ono and McCartney as the two great artistic partners of his life. "Throughout my career, I've selected to work with … two people. Paul McCartney and Yoko Ono … the only initial move I ever made was bringing Paul McCartney into the group. And the second person who interested me that much as an artist and somebody I could work with was Yoko Ono."[235] On the day of his death, Lennon repeated the statement, declaring that, while he had worked with many different musicians over the years, he had only chosen McCartney and Ono as true partners.[236]

Lennon's murder on the night of December 8, 1980, by an obsessed fan stunned the world. The musician was returning from the studio when Mark David Chapman, who had traveled from Hawaii with the intention of murdering Lennon, shot him at the front of the Dakota, the apartment building where Lennon and Ono lived. The murderer offered different motivations for his crime over the years. These included mental illness and a desire for fame. Chapman also accused Lennon of hypocrisy. Lennon's status as a target of the Nixon administration encouraged some to speculate that the assassin had been politically motivated or even sponsored by the U.S. Government. However, the evidence to support this claim is extremely tenuous, based heavily on hearsay and anonymous sources.

Lennon's death was a tragedy for his family, friends, and for millions of people around the world. Lewisohn described it seven years later as "one of the most senseless events of the 20th century," a stunning loss which invoked "worldwide grief on an almost unparalleled scale."[237] Flags flew at half staff. Radio stations blanketed the airwaves with Beatles songs and Lennon's solo albums. People wept in public and gathered outside the Dakota to pay tribute. Several fans committed suicide. Vigils were held in cities across the globe. The public shock and mourning over his murder and all his death symbolized powerfully impacted how Lennon's image was shaped in the coming decades. Even the manner of his death contributed to the perception of Lennon as a man who had been far more than a rock star, or even one of the iconic figures of the 1960s. Christgau equated him with Martin Luther King, Jr., and the Kennedy brothers, the great political martyrs of the modern era. "Lennon's death was unprecedented ... he was assassinated, a fate heretofore reserved for kings, politicians, and captains of industry."[238] The political climate of the moment contributed to Lennon's lionization: for many, Lennon symbolized the sixties. Coupled with the new incoming Republican administration, Lennon's death signified the real end the decade. "It was as if all the turmoil from Lennon's era rushed back to fill the countercultural void created by November's election of Ronald Reagan as President."[239]

In the wake of Lennon's death, it was very difficult for journalists to attempt impartiality when chronicling his life and work. Emotions at the time were very strong, including among those who were telling the story as it unfolded and consequently helped shape it for posterity. Philip Norman, a journalist at the *Sunday Times*, later described typing up his obituary for Lennon with tears in his eyes.[240] *Rolling Stone*'s Wenner ensured that the original "balanced but hardly worshipful"[241] review of *Double Fantasy* was favorably re-written, and all the parts of the magazine's most recent unprinted interview with Lennon, where the musician had denounced Wenner, were confiscated. In his uncensored history of *Rolling Stone*, Robert Draper describes the press climate in the aftermath of Lennon's death. "This was not a time for objectivity. This was a time for remembering, for praising, for grieving and for begging forgiveness of the dead."[242]

Heavy emotion, combined with a desire to honor the dead and the immediacy of the moment created an image of Lennon that, while well accepted, was ultimately less than honest, accurate or complete. As *The Beatles Bibliography* exhaustively catalogs, countless newspapers and magazines printed less-than-accurate retrospectives and memorial issues. The facts of Lennon's life and his various roles—as a musician, songwriter, father, husband, friend and political activist—were quickly subordinated to the creation of the myth that surrounded the murdered man. Connolly acknowledged the disparity between the man he had known and the one remembered by the press: "You could already smell the dubious whiff of incense at the public canonization of a newly martyred saint."[243] The popular perception of Ono, too, shifted. Lennon's murder transformed Ono, for the first time, into a sympathetic figure and "won her an unprecedented level of public support."[244]

The impact Lennon's murder had on Beatles historiography is immense and, at the same time, unquantifiable. It not only elevated Lennon's reputation as a musician and a human being, it consequently affected those of the other three surviving members of the Beatles. Writers and journalists began to grant Lennon more than his share of credit for the band's unique genius. Almost immediately perception grew of, in Connolly's words, "John Lennon the myth, Lennon the martyr, Lennon the super genius, Lennon the real talent behind the Beatles, Lennon the man who saw through everything, Lennon the *avant-garde* artist and Lennon the gentle, peace loving guy who prayed for the world."[245] In praising Lennon many journalists relied heavily on interviews, such as *Lennon Remembers*, in which Lennon had pursued his own agendas and failed to verify the claims he made in them. Unsurprisingly it was McCartney whose reputation was the most affected by this new narrative that mythologized Lennon, although Harrison and Starr were also impacted. "Lennon's stature was elevated following his death, and his accomplishments and influence amplified often, perhaps unavoidably, at McCartney's expense.... For some, [Lennon] had become a kind of secular saint, increasingly above reproach."[246] In some instances, this shift occurred because of the tendency of many in the press to take Lennon and Ono's statements as truth without subjecting them to examination or verification. In others, it was a deliberate comparison between the martyred Lennon and the still living McCartney that inevitably cast McCartney as the opposition and Lennon's inferior. Decades later journalists acknowledged this: "After Lennon's death many writers seemed to feel that the best way to praise [Lennon's] achievement was to disparage McCartney," an approach that rock journalist Anthony DeCurtis later described as "both stupid and unfair."[247]

Some of those who eulogized Lennon seemingly could not do so without denigrating McCartney, Harrison and Starr or devaluing their contributions to the Beatles. "He [Lennon] stood for a mixture of tough minded realism ... wit and intellect. Paul on the other hand was a pretty boy."[248] The most famous example of this came from the *Village Voice*'s Christgau, one of America's most powerful rock critics. In a piece shortly following Lennon's death, Christgau referred to the three remaining Beatles as "hacks" and blamed their refusal to accept Ono into the band for the breakup.[249] He also repeated a number of misconceptions about Lennon that, while widely accepted, were untrue. This included praising Lennon, the only middle-class born Beatle, as a "working-class" hero and declaring that Lennon had always been the only artistic, *avant-garde* Beatle because "the others just didn't have the stuff."[250] His obituary of Lennon implied that the wrong Beatle had been killed. "Why is it always Bobby Kennedy or John Lennon? Why isn't it Richard Nixon or Paul McCartney?"[251]

It is impossible to know how differently Beatles' history would be written today had Lennon not been murdered. The impact of a sudden, unexpected event—such as Lennon's assassination—on the formation of historical narratives is one that historian C. Vann Woodward addresses in his essay "On Believing What One Reads: The Dangers of Popular Revisionism":

> Contemporaneously with sudden transitions ... there has taken place among public figures—and among some intellectuals as well—a hurried turning of coats, a lot of hasty conversions and quick changes of allegiances. Isolationists turned into interventionists, radicals into reactionaries.... Russophobes into Russophiles and back into Russophobes.[252]

Sudden, unexpected transitions or events—in Woodward's example, the abrupt switch in the American view of the Soviet Union from enemy to ally following Nazi Germany's invasion of the U.S.S.R. in June 22, 1940—cause seismic shifts in historical narratives. While the predominant narrative following Lennon's murder was not an abrupt reversal of the one preceding it, there's no doubt that Lennon's tragic death shaped every successive narrative. "In the weeks and months to come, the hagiography of John Lennon went into overdrive, spurred by the grief of his widow and the efforts of the press to satisfy and capitalize on the feelings of millions of broken hearted Beatles fans around the world."[253]

The popular desire to celebrate a figure of Lennon's stature following their death is common, natural and understandable. However, the celebration of Lennon's life and work had the effect of inaccurately minimizing the contributions of his fellow Beatles. For a historian, the immediate response to Lennon's death by many Beatles' writers emphasizes how essential historical distance, "the growing clarity that comes with the passage of time,"[254] is to accurate understanding and impartial analysis of the facts. Caught up in the emotion of the moment, it was very difficult, if not impossible, for some writers to employ the detachment and distance required in order to produce an accurate accounting of the Beatles' story. That certain facts went undiscovered or were ignored following Lennon's death, while not uncommon in history, had enduring consequences for Beatles historiography. The official Fab Four narrative which had controlled the Beatles' story in the 1960s and the *Lennon Remembers* narrative of the 1970s had also overlooked contradictory facts, but following Lennon's murder there was now an emotional motivation on the part of some writers to do so. The omission of those facts from the historical narrative, the enduring influence of Lennon's own words in *Lennon Remembers*, and the combination of strong emotion following Lennon's death all helped establish a new, third major narrative in Beatles history that dominated the band's historiography after December 1980.

CHAPTER THREE

The *Shout!* Narrative

The error was in considering the hypothesis as given at the outset.
—Marc Bloch, *The Historian's Craft*

The First Post-Breakup Biography

The period after Lennon's assassination in 1980 saw a new influx of secondary works devoted to the Beatles, marking a powerful structural shift in who told the band's story. First during the Fab Four narrative and later during the *Lennon Remembers* narrative, information had originated from the Beatles themselves or from members of their inner circle such as George Martin. While obviously influenced by their personal biases and agendas, they were versions largely structured, mythologized and sold by the four people at the center of the hurricane. Their value as primary sources was unquestionable, and so was their influence on the Beatles story.

Lennon's death marks the moment in Beatles historiography when the origins of the narratives changed. Before, they were crafted mainly by primary sources, particularly interviews and, during the Fab Four narrative, the authorized biography. Now secondary works produced by journalists and biographers emerged, shaping the band's story with their own interpretations. This transition from primary to secondary sources gained momentum as decades passed and numerous works, especially group and individual biographies, gained popular influence. This shift, which occurs over time with any topic of historical importance, is a significant marker in any subject's historiography. While acknowledging the inevitability of transitioning from primary to secondary sources, Gaddis discusses the perils of such an approach:

> With the passage of time, our representations become reality in the sense that they compete with, insinuate themselves into, and eventually replace altogether the firsthand memories people have of the events through which they've lived … we make the past legible, but in doing so we lock it up in a prison from which there's neither escape nor ransom nor appeal.[1]

With secondary sources now playing the dominant role in the historiography of the band and its individuals, narrative control became concentrated in the hands of journalists. Many of these reporters were overly influenced by the time period in which they wrote and demonstrated few of the essential requirements necessary for legitimate and enduring history. In the climate following Lennon's tragic death, few of the more important works attempted objectivity, "the most important and most difficult"[2] of requirements; all lacked adequate historical distance, and none distinguished between the proven facts, or outside of an event, from the more subjective inside *thoughts* of those at the event.[3]

The most important of these, and one of the most influential secondary works in all Beatles historiography, is Philip Norman's biography of the group, *Shout! The True Story of the Beatles*. Written in the late 1970s and published in March 1981, the book was received with considerable popular and critical acclaim: *The New York Times* declared it "thrilling" and "nothing less than the definitive biography."[4] Due in part to its inadvertently tragic timing, appearing a few short months after Lennon's murder, Norman's biography exerted an enormous impact on how readers, popular culture, and the press viewed the Beatles' characters, personalities, and talents. Its first edition sold more than 125,000 copies and was a financial and critical success.[5] Slightly revised editions were issued in 2002 and 2005, largely to critical acclaim. The work and its author wielded considerable influence on perception of the group for decades.

Relying heavily on interviews and eyewitness accounts and written in an evocative, novelistic style, *Shout!* is in many ways a master work. The book places the band in the political and cultural context of the 1950s and 1960s, discussing events such as the birth of rock and roll and the Profrumo affair. It also establishes an outline for the band's story—beginning with the birth of Lennon and ending with the breakup—which numerous other Beatles biographers copied. *Shout!* elevated rock and roll to the subject of serious biography and anointed its author, a journalist for Britain's prestigious *Sunday Times*, as the premier authority on the Beatles. In addition to *Shout!*, Norman also wrote obituaries for Lennon and later Harrison and participated in a number of interviews and documentaries discussing the group's dynamics, personalities and music. Norman's influence on popular Beatles historiography was immense. Part of this was attributable to his perceived independence: unlike Hunter Davies, author of the *The Beatles: The Authorized Biography*, Norman had no official attachment to the group. In the book's introduction, Norman emphasized how his work differed from previous accounts by revealing the truth, rather than merely repeating the legend.[6] *Shout!* was packaged and sold as a legitimate, definitive biography—its subtitle was "The True Story of the Beatles"—and was received as history by more than 100,000 readers. Decades after its first appearance, numerous journalists and other Beatles' writers still were declaring *Shout!* "by far the best" or "the definitive" biography of the group.[7] It was the first major biography of the band published since Davies' work in 1968; the first to include information on the Beatles' dissolution and Lennon's death, and the first written after the Lennon/ McCartney schism.

More than 10 years had passed since the publication of Davies' biography, and the Beatles story had changed dramatically from 1968 to 1981. *The Beatles: The Authorized Biography* was now a time capsule that did not mention *The White Album* or Yoko Ono, *Let It Be*, Linda Eastman or Allen Klein. The official Fab Four narrative, of which Davies' work had been a part, had collapsed in 1970, followed by the *Lennon Remembers* narrative. The *Lennon Remembers* narrative and the Lennon/McCartney press wars of the early 1970s exerted considerable influence on Norman's work. While most of *Shout!* was researched and written prior to Lennon's death, the assassination prompted new interest in the Beatles and created an audience eager to see a favorable portrayal of Lennon.

In the mid to late 1970s, Lennon retreated from many of the harsher declarations he had made in his 1970 de-mythologizing interview *Lennon Remembers*, dismissing both publicly and privately what some viewed as his timeless manifesto. In its coverage of Lennon's death, *Time* noted that "Lennon had taken pains lately to redefine details of his collaboration with Paul and to make sure credit was distributed accurately."[8] This overstated the case somewhat: Lennon still claimed, a few weeks before his death, to have written 70 percent of "Eleanor Rigby"[9] and accused McCartney of "subconscious sabotage"[10] of Lennon's truly great songs. Yet once the immediate bitterness of the breakup was past, he moved away from his more extreme statements and allowed a more equitable and factually accurate version of the Lennon/McCartney songwriting partnership to emerge.

Shout! failed to take this softening into account. It reverted the Beatles and the Lennon/McCartney partnership back to the caricatured portrayals of *Lennon Remembers*, depicting Lennon as the *avant-garde* hero, McCartney as the conventional villain and displaying what *The Beatles Bibliography* later described as an "almost slavish devotion to Yoko."[11] This may be because much of *Shout!* was written before Lennon's spate of interviews in 1980 in which he offered a warmer, albeit still mildly critical, view of McCartney and the Beatles than he had in 1970–71. Regardless of the reason for Norman's negative stereotyping, not only did *Shout!* clearly portray McCartney as

Lennon's creative inferior, it also presented him as conniving, conventional, egotistical, shallow and manipulative: a Machiavelli with a gift for melody. In contrast, Lennon was depicted as a great artist: revolutionary, daring, assertive, *avant-garde* and the unquestioned dominant creative force behind the Beatles. Any evaluation of the other members was perfunctory: Virtually every depiction of Harrison, either as a person or a musician, in *Shout!'s* 400 plus pages was negative. Starr merited few mentions and little more than token analysis or research. Decades later, a journalist summed up perhaps the largest weakness with Norman's approach: "He doesn't seem to cherish the Beatles very much, does he?"[12]

Despite its strengths, critical praise, and undeniable influence, *Shout!* is a flawed work of history for three reasons: inadequate historical distance, lack of documentation, and deliberate authorial bias. These weaknesses continued to erode its overall value and credibility as more research was done, sources became available, and impartial analysis was applied. Written only 11 years after the breakup, during the members numerous intramural disagreements, *Shout!* is heavily influenced by the negative portrayals that emerged from the personal conflicts among the ex-band mates. Like all secondary works written too soon after an historical event, it is a work that is clearly a product of its time, so that, as time passed, its value and credibility decreased.

Shout's chronological proximity to Lennon's death and the Beatles' breakup means it suffers from a lack of historical distance, "the quality that, more than any other, distinguishes academic rigor from popular memory or everyday journalism."[13] Simply put, Norman's work was written too soon after the events had occurred to achieve the necessary detachment and objectivity history requires. In his book *On Historical Distance,* Mark Saber Phillips discusses how essential the quality of distance is to an accurate historical understanding: "As the years pass … we come to see events more accurately, reduce them to their proper proportion, and observe their consequences with greater detachment."[14] At the time, *Shout!'s* proximity to key events had the effect of reinforcing its status as the prevailing Orthodoxy. By the standards of history, however, *Shout!'s* immediacy undermines its credibility as a definitive account. In the years following its publication, a significant number of primary and secondary sources emerged, including interviews, eyewitness accounts, memoirs, documents and transcripts. The timing of its publication prevented *Shout!* from including these sources, a weakness that limits its accuracy and, over time, undermines its factual credibility.

Although Norman interviewed scores of sources, including Aspinall and Martin, a wealth of primary sources eluded him. This included all four Bea-

tles, who refused to be interviewed; a standard rejection that nonetheless
irritated Norman to the point that he discussed it in the prologue to the 1981
edition. Norman then argued that their absence enhanced the book's overall
value, stating "the true story must seek a perspective far wider than theirs."[15]
It was a comment remarkably similar to one made by the great French historian Pierre Renouvin, when he explained why none of the initial histories
of the Great War incorporated testimonials from the individual soldier in
the trenches: "The evidence of soldiers … can rarely give information on
their conduct of operations, since their field of vision was too narrow."[16] Later
histories of World War I included the perspective of the average soldier and
later works on the Beatles contained more of their input, but in the first wave
of scholarship on both the Great War and the Fab Four, the views of those
in the trenches or on the stage were largely absent.

In the foreword to the original edition, Norman explained that he had
decided to approach *Shout!* as "a reporter and a novelist,"[17] and the strengths
and weaknesses of that decision are evident in the work. "A glorious example
of how to write about music,"[18] Norman's prose is descriptive, vivid and dramatic. Two of the most tragic figures in Beatles history receive more of Norman's attention than either Harrison or Starr: Brian Epstein, the band's
manager who died of an accidental drug overdose at 34, and Stuart Sutcliffe,
a friend of Lennon's from art school who died young. Norman's preference
for tragic figures—Sutcliffe, Epstein, and Lennon—enhances *Shout!*'s drama,
but skews the narrative: such a novelistic approach heightens the story's
drama and conflict, as when Norman hypothesizes on tenuous evidence, provided by an anonymous source, that Epstein was murdered.[19] Norman's
strengths, especially his writing style, are well displayed in his novelistic
approach. But they also severely weakened *Shout!*'s ultimate credibility as a
legitimate history: *The Beatles Bibliography* later criticized it for "using consummate journalistic and literary skills rather than historical research and
study."[20]

The second factor lessening *Shout!*'s overall credibility is its lack of documentation. Because he wrote as a journalist and a novelist, rather than an
historian, Norman failed to document his sources, list his interviewees, or
provide a bibliography. He did, however, rely on many of Davies' sources and
had full access to his predecessor's notes. While failure to cite sources was
the rule rather than the exception in Beatles writing at the time, and few
other concurrent Beatles works contained bibliographies, this failure to document undermines its enduring validity. Though Norman was not a historian,
his work was sold as *the* definitive biography of the Beatles and an accurate
recounting of their history, exacerbating the work's lack of a bibliography. In

The Historian's Craft, Bloch discusses the necessity of documentation, declaring that "every historical book worthy of the name ought to have a chapter explaining their research struggles and documentation."[21] With no footnotes, citations or even a bibliography, *Shout!* fails to qualify.

The flaws resulting from this lack of documentation are considerable. First, it offers no list of the number or names of the interviewees. Second, the text's lack of citations makes it nearly impossible to separate Norman's editorial comments (of which there are many) from information provided by sources. This makes it difficult to identify a quotation or fact's origin. Such omissions provide Norman a free hand to insert his personal opinions into Beatles history and frequently pass them off as the thoughts of the major figures. Examples include Norman's declaration that Lennon considered all McCartney's work on *The White Album* "cloyingly sweet and bland,"[22] McCartney found Lennon's "unmelodious and provocative,"[23] and that McCartney initially pursued Linda Eastman, his future wife, because of his "ever present social ambition."[24] By speaking for the subjects of his biography, Norman inserts himself extensively into the narrative. In numerous editions of *Shout!* as well as his later work, Norman fails at one of the major requirements of legitimate biography:

> A biographer has got to see things through another person's perceptions—to take over another mind, so to speak. You've got to subdue your own distinctiveness in order to do this; otherwise your biography will reflect what's inside your head rather than that of your subject.[25]

This exclusion of valuable sources and failure to document available ones undermines *Shout's* accuracy. In the 20 years following its publication, numerous documents and records became available, including the invaluable reference works by Lewisohn such as *The Complete Beatles Recording Sessions* and *The Complete Beatles Chronicle*. The primary sources Lewisohn cataloged in *The Complete Beatles Recording Sessions* in particular contradicted Norman's stereotypical portrayal of Lennon as the group's sole genius and innovator in the studio. *Shout!'s* absence of citations, as well as crucial sources, ensures that its value as a legitimate Beatles biography would have diminished as time passed and the group became the focus of more academic scholarship.

But even more damaging to the book's ultimate value is the author's evident and admitted bias. When discussing the issue of bias in history, distinguishing between deliberate and incidental bias is key. All historians agree that producing a totally impartial work of history is an impossible ideal. Elements beyond authorial control, from their genders and nationalities to the very language in which they think and write, influences their work. In *Historical Methods in Mass Communication*: Startt lists some of the factors that invariably factor into any historian's conclusions:

> Like journalists, historians are products of their own social environments. They can never completely escape the conditions that shaped and continue to shape them. They all have emotions, persuasions, and ethical standards.... Religion, nationality, geography, class awareness, gender, race, ideology, education, occupation, knowledge and experience give definition to human perceptions.[26]

Every author who has recounted history, from Tacitus to Macaulay to Shirer, has been affected by inherent biases beyond their ability to excise. Historians acknowledge the influence of these elements on how history is written and account for them when weighing a work's credibility.

There is a wide gulf, however, between unintentional bias resulting from inherent environmental factors and deliberate bias in pursuit of an author's particular agenda. Intentional bias by the author of a biography or history invariably taints it, calling into question the work's methodology, analysis and conclusions. "Partisanship," as Garraghan reminds us in *A Guide to Historical Method* "and good history do not mix."[27] Those works that demonstrate minimal bias are ultimately those with conclusions that retain their value and credibility. After World War I, the government of each major combatant published its own documents and analysis, known as the "colored" books, in order to justify their actions both leading up to and during the war. No historiography of World War I would be complete without these colored books. However, despite their value, Britain's Blue book and Germany's White book are inherently suspect sources due to their biases and function as propaganda. Because of this, no historian views any one of them as the definitive story of the First World War. When evaluated by historical standards, it is staggering that *Shout!* was able to achieve and maintain such an elevated and influential reputation while its writing, research, and analysis demonstrated a profound bias.

When historians demonstrate obvious bias, it usually tends to be along national, ethnic, religious or ideological lines. As a biography of a British pop band that had nothing to do with war, diplomacy or religion, *Shout!* is immune to these problems. Instead, *Shout!* demonstrates how unrestrained personal preference leads to authorial bias, and how authorial bias in turn impacts methodology and interpretation. The control of the Beatles story was fractured with the group's breakup and the professional division of its primary songwriting partnership. After the breakup, Lennon and McCartney became rivals, each promoting his own, somewhat incompatible, versions of the Beatles' story. In the great Lennon/McCartney schism that divided Beatles historiography, Norman clearly planted his flag in the Lennon camp. *Shout!* fails to meet, or even *attempt* to meet, the basic requirements of "detached and unbiased judgment."[28] When promoting the book in a 1981 TV interview, Norman declared that "John Lennon was three-quarters of the Beatles."[29] It is clear that hypothesis preceded Norman's research and writing on *Shout!*. As a piece of history, the work demonstrates what happens when researchers ignore Gaddis's caution in choosing which evidence to use: "It's all too easy to find what you're looking for when you've already decided ahead of time what it is."[30] Many of the work's greatest flaws result from the author's personal preferences and preconceived hypotheses.

Nominally a biography of the Beatles, the vast majority of *Shout!* concentrates on Lennon's life as an artist and an individual. Of the remaining Beatles, McCartney receives most of Norman's attention, mainly to serve as Lennon's foil; Harrison and Starr are virtually ignored. The sheer amount of attention devoted to Lennon is itself sufficient evidence of authorial bias. Lennon is introduced on the first page of the biography and his childhood thoroughly depicted: Harrison is not mentioned until page 50 and Starr does not appear until page 68 of a 400 page book. Norman later retreated from his assertion that Lennon was 75 percent of the Beatles, but Lennon's story consumes 75 percent of *Shout!*.

The biography was not the only platform the author used to promote his Lennon-dominated view of the group. Norman's disdain for McCartney and Harrison and his lack of interest in Starr continued to influence his other public statements about the band. Soon after publishing *Shout!*, Norman wrote a doggerel in the *Sunday Times* addressed to McCartney, calling facetiously for the musician's early death: "Oh deified Scouse/with unmusical spouse/for the clichés you load/may they bury you soon/to an anodyne tune/in the middlemost middle of the road."[31]

His 2001 obituary of Harrison was less charitable. Published days after Harrison's death from cancer, Norman continued to portray his own personal opinion as universal fact, inserting himself into the Beatles' narrative as much as possible. Declaring that "Harrison was never the world's greatest guitarist," Norman described George as a "miserable git," and as "essential to the Beatles as Paul McCartney's great cow eyes." Ignoring the numerous testimonies to Harrison's generosity, humor and musical skill, Norman declared that "George was born bitter," argued that descriptions of the architect of the Concert for Bangladesh as "a great humanitarian" were "a little strong," and referenced Harrison's affairs with prostitutes and Maureen Starkey, Starr's first wife. At the end, Norman denounced the "extraordinarily overblown tributes" dedicated to Harrison.[32]

While the author never admitted his bias against Harrison, Norman eventually acknowledged his dislike of McCartney, although his statements on his pro–Lennon/anti–McCartney bias proved defensive and contradictory. In the foreword to his 2005 revised edition of *Shout!*, Norman admitted the bias and acknowledged that his portrayal of McCartney in the original edition of the book was "wrong" to a certain extent:

> Others felt that my judgments of Paul McCartney were too harsh, perhaps even motivated by personal dislike. In the Beatles subculture, one inevitably finds oneself tagged either as a "John" person or a "Paul" person. I cannot pretend to be other than the former. Just the same, it was wrong of me—though it won me my initial access to Yoko, to say as I did on an American TV news program, that "John was three-quarters of the Beatles." I would not question McCartney's huge talent or deny that ... he was far nicer than he ever needed to be.[33]

However, a few years later Norman dismissed the "widespread (and untrue) perception that I am anti–Paul."[34] By 2012, when Norman decided to write a biography of McCartney, he claimed in an interview to have completely changed his views on the man. When *The Guardian*'s John Harris argued that *Shout!* depicted McCartney as "controlling, egotistical, and superficial," Norman admitted that his version of the musician was "harsh," but justified it by explaining his personal dislike of McCartney's music and public personae during the late 1970s at the time he was writing *Shout!*. After Norman began research for his 2008 biography of Lennon (for which McCartney allowed Norman to interview him via e-mail) the author said his interpretation of the man had shifted: "I started to get the point of him, and began to realize why John would have wanted this person around." Norman's discovery that McCartney was paying for Aspinall's cancer treatment also contributed: "That ... was more than enough to change my view."[35] In a separate interview with the *New York Times*, the author of *Shout!* again admitted his bias: "Yes, I was accused of being anti–Paul in *Shout!* and I did feel afterward I'd been unfair to him. I tried to make amends in the Lennon biography."[36] Norman's claim that he allowed his distaste for McCartney's late 1970's music and public persona to influence his portrayal of McCartney's life and music in the 1960s is a textbook example of what Gaddis refers to as "uprooting the past." As one manifestation of bias, "uprooting the past" occurs "when someone seeks to marginalize or even eliminate something he or she doesn't like in the present by rewriting history in such a way as to accomplish that end."[37]

Norman statements demonstrate he had no interest in following Bloch's recommendation of "laying aside his ego"[38] in any of his works on the Beatles. Instead, his ego and personal opinions on Lennon and McCartney determined his approach from the outset, predetermining his conclusions and weakening the value of his work. Startt strongly warns against this flaw in historical writing: "Interpretation should not be predetermined. The good historian does not set out with a theory and marshal facts to it … as facts are gathered to find the truth, they may lead to a theory, but theory never should be used to determine facts."[39] A work written to conform to a pre-determined theory often omits evidence and refuses to include contradictory sources. This refusal has the effect of eliminating valuable dissenting evidence from the narrative and results in a narrow and simplistic version of history. Regardless of subject, any work that determines the thesis before analyzing and gathering the evidence produces an incomplete and flawed conclusion.

Choosing a favorite Beatle is not an inherently fatal flaw. In *The Landscape of History*, Gaddis discusses the inevitability of personal opinion on history, and acknowledges that it does not automatically negate an author's work: "Personal preferences need not represent gross bigotry."[40] More, favoritism was an undeniable element of the group's story and fueled its popularity: fans had been picking their favorite Beatle since the group's Cavern Club days. Norman's argument that Beatles' authorities were divided into "John" people and "Paul" people was somewhat simplistic and self-serving but also partially accurate. What Norman failed to explain was why he believed his preference for Lennon, both as an artist and as an individual, necessitated producing a work that ignored contradictory sources, applied moral judgments unevenly, and elevated Lennon's reputation at the expense of the other Beatles.

Gaddis discusses the methodological flaws that invariably flow from deliberate authorial bias. "Personal preferences … may lead to value judgments in the narratives and affect the evaluation of the facts. Another problem resides in the historian's practice of choosing specific facts for inclusion … the chances of skewing the story in one way or another are enhanced even more."[41] Later Beatles writers, such as Spitz in his work *The Beatles: The Biography* and Doggett in *You Never Give Me Your Money* managed to produce largely impartial works while still harboring a personal preference for a particular Beatle. Norman simply did not even attempt such impartiality, and his bias extends throughout all of *Shout!*, influencing his selection of evidence, interpretations and conclusions.

Shout! therefore served as the origin of numerous misconceptions which persisted for decades as accepted wisdom in Beatles historiography. In the 1981 edition, Norman stated that McCartney wanted to expel Sutcliffe from the band in order to take his place as the group's bass player.[42] This was presented multiple times as a fact, and used as evidence of McCartney's manipulative personality. Norman provided no evidence to support the claim: it was wholly a matter of the author's interpretation. By the time of the book's re-edition, McCartney, Harrison and Starr had all publicly disputed the story of McCartney's "maneuvering" to get the bass. Instead, all three men argued that McCartney was forced into the position of bass player when Sutcliffe quit the band and both Lennon and Harrison refused the role.[43] Norman ignored their accounts, and the original story went unrevised in later editions.

This bias affects his analysis of the Beatles catalog as well, where Norman's personal opinions clearly conformed to the views Lennon argued in *Lennon Remembers* that the only great music was real, honest, highly personal and starkly revealing.[44] His minimal analysis of Beatles music was one of the few areas in which Norman attempted real revision in later editions, devoting more pages to discussing various albums and songs. *Shout!*'s author is one among numerous journalists and biographers with minimal to non-existent musical education or training to pass judgment on Beatles songs, anointing an individual or song "genius" or "masterpiece" status according to no basis stronger than personal opinion. Particularly during the *Shout!* narrative, writers untrained in music focused on lyrical analysis and ignored crucial components such as melody, instrumentation, countermelody, harmony and production. According to Startt, part of the process of internal criticism of primary and secondary sources—evaluating their credibility and value—involves determining the level of the author's expertise: "The interpretation of the experienced observer is more beneficial than the novice."[45] By applying this expertise standard to Beatles historiography, we can conclude that biographers who have trained in music or who have received musical educations provide more informed and therefore credible interpretations of the band's catalog than those without such training.

Perhaps the most striking evidence of Norman's partisanship is found in his starkly uneven application of moral judgments of the people in and around the group. Applying moral judgment to historical figures is a topic on which some of history's most pre-eminent authorities disagree. Bloch argued strongly against it. "History demands an understanding interpretation," wrote the historian in hiding in Nazi-controlled France. "Are we so sure of ourselves and of our age as to divide the company of our forefathers into the just and the damned?"[46] Gaddis, while taking into account Bloch's arguments, reached a different conclusion.

> There is one thing, though, that biographers—and historians generally—can't escape: it's to make moral judgments ... no work of history of which I'm aware has ever been written without making some kind of statement—explicitly or implicitly, consciously or subconsciously—about where its subjects lie along the

ubiquitous spectrum that separates the admirable from the abhorrent. The issue for historians then is not whether we should make moral judgments, but how we can do so responsibly.[47]

By any measure, *Shout!* fails this basic test of responsibility. Instead the author downplays or omits the failings of his favorite, Lennon, while emphasizing the flaws of the others. Throughout *Shout!* almost every action attempted by McCartney draws the author's scorn. McCartney's use of French in the song "Michelle" was "a plain act of social climbing."[48] His purchase of a house, after three years of living in London with his girlfriend's family, was "the result of minute social calculation."[49] Described alternately as "imperious" and "petulant," "pretty-faced Paul" was a "prima donna" who demanded to be "worshipped."[50] Similarly negative judgments were applied to Harrison, who was depicted as an annoying tag-along and mediocre musician who developed an absurd obsession with Hare Krishna.[51]

Such moral judgments are noticeably absent in Norman's depictions of Lennon and Ono. In the original edition, Lennon's severe beating of Liverpool DJ Bob Wooler at McCartney's 21st birthday party receives so little attention that Wooler is not even identified by name[52]; Ono's role in introducing Lennon to heroin is not mentioned. Where, in later editions, Norman criticizes Harrison's extra-marital affairs, Lennon and Ono's are not judged.[53] Most notably, Lennon's treatment of his first wife, Cynthia, and the neglect and abandonment of his son Julian, behavior which even Norman described in a 2008 interview as "unforgivable,"[54] is relayed by the author with no judgment at all. Considering that Norman felt qualified to judge McCartney's actions and motives in purchasing a house and the validity of Harrison's lifelong spiritual quest, he should have also considered himself capable of applying such moral standards to Lennon's assault on Wooler and the damage Lennon did to his first wife and elder son. But Norman offers no such moral assessment of either Lennon or Ono's actions.

As with *Lennon Remembers*, the *Shout!* narrative, which identified Lennon as the group's sole genius, required ignoring contradictory sources. Among those sources available to Norman at the time was the eyewitness testimony of one of the most highly regarded individuals in the Beatles' story, George Martin. While Norman interviewed Martin and, in the book, praised him as a peerless producer,[55] he chose to ignore Martin's own words from his 1979 work, *All You Need Is Ears* in which Martin repeatedly depicts Lennon and McCartney as equal talents.[56]

Given his admitted dislike of McCartney, Norman's conclusions on the two great debates in Beatles history were unsurprising. While Norman acknowledged Martin's assertion that McCartney was the most natural musician, he clearly saw Lennon as McCartney's artistic superior. He was as effusive in his praise of Lennon's work as he was critical of McCartney's and Harrison's[57]; and *Shout!* did little to contest the *Lennon Remembers* version of the breakup.

While *Shout!* largely has been regarded as biased by many Beatles' readers for decades, it was not until 2008, when Norman published his second major work of Beatles history, *John Lennon: The Life*, that the popular press acknowledged his anti–McCartney and pro–Lennon bias. Oddly, such acknowledgement often went hand in hand with praise for *Shout!*, as if such pervasive partisanship had a negligible impact on the work's overall value. Few of Norman's fellow journalists seemed bothered that the definitive biography of the Beatles was admittedly unfair to McCartney, marginalized Harrison, virtually ignored Starr and provided little insight on the band's music.

There is no disputing the work's legacy: *Shout!* left an enduring but flawed imprint on Beatles historiography. Its focus on Lennon diminished the contributions McCartney, Harrison and Starr all made to the Beatles' music, a pattern that only began to change after the publication of *The Complete Beatles Recording Sessions* years later. Its harsh condemnation of McCartney's character encouraged the perception of him, originating during the breakup era, as shallow, egotistical and manipulative. In addition, Norman's lack of interest in Harrison and Starr minimized their essential roles and prevented a more accurate picture of the band's personal and working relationship. For more than a decade following the publication of *Shout!* many other works in Beatles historiography also followed this pattern. *The Beatles Anthology* book, released in 2000, is the first major post–*Shout!* group biography in which Harrison and Starr receive equal coverage with Lennon and McCartney.

In many ways, *Shout!* borrowed heavily from the *Lennon Remembers* narrative, perpetuating many of its predecessor's simplifications and errors. Because of its impressive reputation as the definitive biography, it became required reading for any Beatles historian, influencing every successive work. In 2015, *The Guardian*'s John Harris argued that, since it initiated rock's first wave of "serious literature," readers should forgive Norman's "anti–McCartney bias."[58] MacDonald, while acknowledging *Shout!*'s "hostile portrait" of McCartney, still considered it "the sharpest account of the Beatles' career."[59] In *The Beatles as Musicians*, Walter Everett, another musicologist, cites *Shout!* numerous times and offers interpretations apparently influenced by Norman's conclusions. Norman's contemptuous portrayal of McCartney in *Shout!* also influenced the 100,000 plus readers who initially bought the book, helping cement Beatles historiography's Lennon vs. McCartney division, which began with *Lennon Remembers*.

Shout's legacy in how the Beatles' story has been and continues to be told is a powerful one: It is one of the most important and influential books ever written about the Fab Four. For a historian, *Shout!* serves an excellent example of how a secondary work can exert heavy influence on a subject despite containing significant historiographical and methodological errors. *Shout's* flawed but enduring legacy also underscores just how essential critical evaluation of secondary sources—regardless of their prestigious reputation— is to a greater understanding of any historical topic.

Looking Back: The Emergence of Retrospective Sources

Any chance of the Beatles reuniting died with Lennon, but the public's appetite for the Fab Four continued. In 1982 Hunter Davies re-issued *The Beatles: The Authorized Biography*. The new edition kept the original material intact; the seismic changes in the group's story since its initial publication were addressed by Davies in the book's appendices. Davies personal observations of the Beatles, both before and after the breakup, subtly disagreed with the caricatured depictions provided in *Shout!* "There were so many facets to each of them," Davies reminded readers. "John was the most original … a strange, one off personality, but I always felt Paul was the most naturally gifted. Music flowed into him all the time. George was a combination…. Ringo has no pretense."[60]

While Davies did not attempt to chronicle the group's post–1968 lives in great detail, there was new primary source material in the 1982 re-edition. Six months after Lennon's death, Davies received a phone call from a hurt and defensive McCartney, upset with some of Ono's recent comments—"John said that no one ever hurt him the way Paul hurt him"[61]—in an interview with Norman. Davies and McCartney considered themselves friends, and McCartney engaged in a far more open and revealing conversation with Davies than any he ever had given to the press, before or after. McCartney always has maintained that, despite Davies' occupation as a journalist, he meant it as a private conversation, and criticized Davies several times over the years for transcribing it when they were talking and later publishing it as part of the 1982 edition of the authorized biography.

The revealing nature of McCartney's words (in particular, their demonstration of vulnerability, something very out of character for the musician) support McCartney's claim that he never intended for the conversation to become public. As what McCartney believed to be a private conversation, the phone call offers the most credible account of McCartney's genuine state of mind in the aftermath of Lennon's murder. Davies' transcripts reveal a McCartney questioning the intimacy of his friendship with Lennon—"I realize now we never got to the bottom of each other's souls. We didn't know the truth,"[62] and casting blame back at his old partner—"No one ever goes on about the times John hurt *me*."[63] McCartney railed against Lennon's elevation: since the other man's death, McCartney believed he had been unfairly cast as the villain: "John is now the nice guy and I'm the bastard. It gets repeated all the time."[64] He labeled his former partner as both someone he had initially hero-worshipped and as a "manuevering swine," and revealed his concern about how Beatles history was being written, mentioning *Shout!* in particular: "But people are printing facts about me and John. They're *not* facts. They will go in the records. It will become part of history. It will be there for always. People will believe it all[65] … in history books, I'm the one who broke up the Beatles."[66] McCartney's preoccupation with how history would view him, which he revealed in his conversation with Davies, is a key element to understanding many of his later actions and statements. McCartney's deliberate efforts to revise the *Lennon Remembers* and *Shout!* narratives must be taken into account when determining the agenda behind his statements, interviews and retrospective testimony.

With *Shout!* widely regarded as definitive, other authors for a time opted not to write another Beatles biography. Instead, the period following Norman's work saw the release of numerous memoirs. As memoirs, these accounts qualify as primary sources but are subject to varying authorial agendas, the diminished credibility inherent in retrospective testimony, and fluctuating degrees of accuracy and credibility. Liverpool insiders Pete Best, Allan Williams, and Lennon's friend Pete Shotton, among others, all wrote memoirs detailing their experiences with the Beatles. Shotton's account was fond but not idealized, although McCartney later accused it of granting Lennon credit for ideas conceived by the other Beatles,[67] and *The Beatles Bibliography* argued that it "pulled a few historical punches."[68] Despite this, in *John Lennon: In My Life* Shotton acknowledges some of his friend's less attractive traits, at one point recounting a disturbing, previously unknown account of a drunken, teenaged Lennon insulting a Semitic piano player to the point of tears. Shotton also asserted Lennon's lifelong desperate need for some sort of partner,[69] a quality eventually widely accepted as an aspect of Lennon's personality. As an eyewitness to the early days of the Lennon/Ono relationship (Shotton was living with Lennon at the time) he offered mixed views on Ono. Shotton described her as "the best thing that ever happened to him,"[70] and argued that Ono's entrance into Lennon's life probably saved it, providing his deeply depressed friend with artistic direction and a new purpose. However, his personal evaluation of her was negative, depicting her as controlling, irrational, egotistical and manipulative. While Shotton did not identify Ono as the sole cause behind the split, he did identify her presence in the studio as a key source of tension, and argued that both during and after the breakup Ono sought to isolate Lennon from the other important people in his life. "Yoko's possessiveness and jealousy or insecurity ... proved to be such that she apparently couldn't bear to see John enjoying a close rapport with anyone other than herself."[71] Because of this balance, Shotton's work provided ammunition for both sides on the debate over Ono.

At the time, Shotton's work was overshadowed by another memoir published a year later: *The Love You Make*, written by Epstein's assistant Peter Brown. Throughout the breakup, Brown managed to maintain decent relations with all the ex-Beatles, but this insider account resulted in permanent exile from the band's circle. A bestseller, Brown's work was marketed as the true story, but the work is littered with factual errors. Brown emphasized his insider status in the text, dwelling on the band members' flaws. The work exposed more of the Fab Four narrative's whitewashing by detailing the Beatles sexual exploits and extensive drug use, topics which receive far more attention from Brown than their music.[72]

As a retrospective eyewitness account it enjoys strong credibility in certain aspects. However, in other parts, *The Love You Make* extends into historical fiction, describing word for word scenes for which Brown was not present,[73] including Lennon's thoughts and words amid having a sexual encounter in Spain with Epstein.[74] The work nevertheless provides valuable insight into the group's inner workings, as Brown had dealt extensively with all four Beatles, Epstein and Klein. In Brown's eyes, the catalyst behind the rupture was less emotional or musical than chemical: "If there was one single element that was the most crucial in the breakup of the Beatles, it was John's heroin addiction."[75] Brown's work is valuable due to his presence at several important meetings that proved crucial to the business disagreements preceding the band's split. Later works, including Doggett's essential study of the breakup and its financial and legal aftermath, *You Never Give Me Your Money,* rely on Brown's eyewitness accounts.

In analyzing Beatles historiography, it is important to note that Brown's book, which depicted all the Beatles (as well as Yoko Ono and Linda McCartney) in less than glowing terms resulted in Brown's effective banishment from the band's inner circle; he would never work with or for any of them again. Such a lesson could not have gone unnoticed by other insiders interested in telling their less than complimentary stories. Few historians write versions of history that they know ultimately will lead to their exile. With secondary interpretations now dominating their historiography, all three ex-Beatles, as well as Ono, attempted to influence these works. The primary method to achieve such influence consisted of granting or denying interviews and endorsements.

One of the major complications in chronicling the Beatles' story during the 1980s and beyond was that three of them continued to make and shape that history. The lives of the three remaining ex-Beatles influenced how their story was written and rewritten. Meanwhile, Ono promoted Lennon's *Shout!* era image as a peacemaker and *the* artistic genius behind the Beatles. McCartney, Harrison and Starr's personal lives and post–Beatles musical output were used by some to retroactively determine Beatles history. Their marriages, relationship with the press, or newest albums were used as evidence in Beatles historiography's great debates. The disappointing albums Starr released in the late 1970s and 1980s reinforced perceptions of the drummer's insignificant role, a viewpoint that all other Beatles, as well as Martin, disputed. McCartney's inability to maintain a steady lineup for his post–Beatles band Wings generally was considered proof of McCartney's difficult personality.[76] That none of Harrison's albums scaled the heights of his first solo album, *All Things Must Pass,* led some to underestimate his musical contributions as a Beatle.

Tug of War, McCartney's first album following Lennon's death, was widely viewed as his best work since *Band on the Run*: even *Rolling Stone* regarded it as a "masterpiece."[77] McCartney followed it, however, with two of the most poorly regarded works of his entire career: his album *Pipes of Peace* and *Give My Regards to Broad Street,* a movie written by and starring McCartney which the critics savaged and audiences ignored. For a time following *Tug of War,* critics viewed much of McCartney's musical output as reinforcing Norman's assessment of him: facile, shallow and sentimental, incapable of either taking criticism or writing decent lyrics. At the same time, news stories from some ex-members of Wings described McCartney as cheap, controlling in the studio, and thin-skinned.[78]

McCartney's somewhat distant relationship with the press did not help repair the damage *Lennon Remembers* and *Shout!* had done to his reputation.[79] Wings dissolved shortly after McCartney's 1980 arrest in Japan for marijuana possession. McCartney, a consummate performer, would not tour again for eight years. Harrison also issued an album following Lennon's death and then retreated somewhat from the public eye, raising his son and investing his energy in his movie production company, HandMade Films. Starr remarried and maintained the lifestyle of a worldwide celebrity. Ono, along with *Rolling Stone* editor Jann Wenner and Norman, continued to champion her late husband as an icon of peace and a peerless musician. In 1982, *Rolling Stone* press printed a booklet, *The Ballad of John and Yoko*, celebrating Lennon and Ono's romantic and artistic partnership, with contributions from rock and roll writers such as Christgau and Chet Flippo. The booklet continued *Rolling Stone's* efforts to mythologize Lennon (*The Beatles Bibliography* later labeled its tone "sycophantic"[80]) and trumpet the superiority of his partnership with Ono. It also clearly depicted the other Beatles, and particularly McCartney, as Lennon's moral and artistic inferiors, declaring "John had more energy, more conviction, more emotion, more humor, more ideas and probably more sheer talent" than all the other Beatles.[81]

In contrast, and despite his continuing reputation as a great media relations man, McCartney's relations with reporters were somewhat strained. In the introduction to her famous 1984 interview with the musician, *Playboy* reporter Joan Goodman discusses the pervasive perception of McCartney's superficiality among her colleagues in the press. While his commercial successes and the sentimental quality of some of his songs encouraged this, Goodman argues that at least some of it could be attributed to "the posthumous adoration" of his former songwriting partner. She then acknowledged how Lennon's criticisms, particularly in the early 1970s, damaged McCartney's professional reputation: "Lennon reinforced the public perception of McCartney with often vitriolic and sneering comments on his music."[82]

Goodman went on to describe how her fellow journalists had cautioned her not to take McCartney too seriously, stating she was "warned" by colleagues (none of whom had met McCartney) that he manipulated reporters with charm. They also reinforced their commonplace belief in McCartney's superficiality and contrasted it with Lennon's perceived depth. According to Goodman, some journalists equated liking McCartney with "being relegated to an intellectual Siberia." Despite such warnings, numerous interviews with McCartney over the course of several months prompted Goodman to admit that she liked and respected McCartney. The musician, for his part, offered one of his more revealing interviews in years, including the first public admission of his profound depression following the Beatles breakup. He recounted overpowering feelings of "emptiness" and "uselessness," during which he lied in bed for days at a time drinking. According to McCartney, his new wife, Linda, saved him, pulling him out of his depression by praising his work as a songwriter, urging him to start writing and recording again and supporting his lawsuit to dissolve the band.

McCartney's *Playboy* interviews, done on the set of *Broad Street*, can be viewed as a response to the criticisms lobbed at him in the press and *Shout!*, as well as a way of selling the film, the same way Lennon used *Lennon Remem-*

bers to draw attention to *Plastic Ono Band*. The McCartney in the interviews is very much the antithesis of the one depicted in *Shout!*—candid, weighty and surprisingly vulnerable in his memories of Lennon, describing a onetime comment from his songwriting partner of "I probably like your songs better than mine," about his writing on some songs as the "height of praise I ever got off him."[83]

In addition to the interview's public nature, there are other factors that affect the agenda and accuracy of McCartney's Goodman interview. His statements concerning illegal drugs, in particular, are contradicted by numerous other sources. A father of four, McCartney responded to questions regarding his previous drug use by stating "I've got kids," and then lied when asked about his and the other Beatles' hard drug use.[84] The musician declared that they were unaware of Lennon and Ono's heroin addiction during the recording of *Let It Be*, something which his later statements in *Many Years from Now* and the *Let It Be* tapes themselves disprove. He also denied having ever taken heroin himself, but admitted a decade later in his semi-autobiography to taking the drug once.[85]

McCartney's interview with Goodman, as well as a series of atypically revealing interviews in 1986 with journalist Chris Salewicz, provided Beatles writers with information and quotes that they would recycle endlessly. Like *Lennon Remembers*, that McCartney's *Playboy* interview was intended for public consumption and given with an obvious agenda impacts its source value. In evaluating the interview's overall credibility, it is worth noting that, according to Garraghan, McCartney's false statements regarding his drug use do not invalidate his other statements on separate subjects, particularly as his reason for lying (his children) is identified in the interview itself. The interview contributed to McCartney's efforts to publicly contradict the *Lennon Remembers* and *Shout!* narratives which he believed portrayed him unfairly. However, McCartney's attempts to shift the narrative were hampered by his obvious agenda and by the mythology that continued to surround Lennon. Those fans already inclined to support McCartney found fresh evidence for revising the current narrative: those who supported Lennon accused McCartney of re-writing history.

In 1984, the same year as McCartney's *Playboy* Interview, *Penthouse* released the full transcript of Peter McCabe's extensive St. Regis Hotel interview with Lennon and Ono. While the interview had been conducted in September 1971 and parts of it had been used in McCabe's 1972 account of the breakup, *Apple to the Core*, this was the first time it had been released in its entirety. The St. Regis interview offered Beatles writers a heretofore unseen glimpse back into 1971, the most contentious year of the breakup. Thirteen years later McCabe acknowledged Lennon's turbulent emotional state: "It was obvious from the start that he was still angry at Paul."[86]

McCabe's interview provided a less severe version of the same story Lennon and Ono had told in *Lennon Remembers*. As he had in his earlier *Rolling Stone* interview, Lennon criticized Martin and Taylor for claiming undue credit for the band's successes. He also criticized his fellow Beatles for their treatment of Ono while admitting his own reflexive chauvinism towards women. Reiterating his claim that he and McCartney had stopped writing together very early on, Lennon also dismissed *Sgt. Pepper's Lonely Hearts Club Band*. "The Pepper myth is bigger, but the music on the White Album is far superior, I think."[87] Widely regarded as both the Beatles most iconic album and the work which, at the time, cemented their stature as legitimate artists, *Sgt. Pepper's* had been masterminded by McCartney. However accurate or inaccurate Lennon's evaluation was, the reasons for his repeated public criticisms of *Pepper* have provoked discussion among numerous Beatles authors. Christgau acknowledged Lennon's assessment and the album's increasingly polarizing critical reputation: "Depending on who you ask, *Sgt. Pepper* is either the greatest album of all time or Paul McCartney's folly—cute, contrived, dinky except, for 'A Day in the Life.'"[88] Other Beatles writers maintain that, whatever his musical preferences, Lennon had additional reasons for devaluing the album. In *The Beatles: The Music and the Myth*, Peter Doggett and Patrick Humphries argue that Lennon perceived *Sgt. Pepper's* as McCartney's album from its very inception, inspiring his jealous disdain:

> More than other Beatles' album bar *Abbey Road*, *Pepper* was a Paul McCartney creation. He it was who dreamed up the concept, the title, the idea behind Peter Blake's remarkable cover, the orchestrations, and the device of pretending the LP was the work of another band entirely ... meanwhile, Lennon was deep in a creative trough ... he raised the emotional barriers and took against the Pepper album from the start.[89]

Lennon admitted in 1980 that he had "resented" *Sgt. Pepper's* because of McCartney's dominance on the album.[90]

In devaluing the Lennon/McCartney partnership, Lennon's 1971 interview ultimately reinforced both the *Lennon Remembers* and the *Shout!* narratives. By contradicting Lennon's accounts and promoting his own version of the Beatles' story, it was McCartney's interview with *Playboy* that appeared to be encouraging revisionism: Norman later accused McCartney of rewriting history.[91] With Lennon gone, McCartney theoretically could make any number of claims which Lennon was no longer around to dispute.

The Polarization of John Lennon: From Ray Coleman to Albert Goldman

A widely repeated maxim among historians states that a credible biography of an individual is impossible to write until the subject has been dead at least 50 years. This interval allows for a crucial amount of historical distance. It grants time for a more impartial view of the individual's strengths, flaws, and legacy; in addition, the interpretations of the facts are less likely to be overly influenced by the immediate politics of the time. Time also allows the opportunity for new sources to become available and authors to gain access to archives. The mid to late 1980's saw a number of biographies on Lennon and McCartney. Ultimately all these biographies underline the importance of achieving some measure of historical distance before attempting to analyze a subject.

The largest and most influential work is Ray Coleman's *Lennon: The Definitive Biography*, first published in a single volume in 1984. Written by a journalist who knew Lennon for years, Coleman's biography is extensive and impressive, particularly in its examination of Lennon's early life. It also contains some of Lennon's previously unavailable personal letters and was the first secondary work to attempt to discuss the musician's last few years. Coleman's admiration for his subject is tangible: "Lennon made a profound impact on all people of all generations, more as a philosopher than a rock star."[92] But his personal attachment to Lennon precludes any attempts at impartiality, and in parts the work leans towards hagiography.

Coleman bristles at any criticism, however legitimate or mild, of Lennon or Ono, unquestioningly accepts their statements and either applauds or excuses their actions. A typical example of this is found in the book's introduction, where Coleman downplays the damage caused by Lennon's occasional acts of physical violence by arguing that the injured parties ultimately benefited: "Even to have been attacked, in any way, by John Lennon brought fame of a kind."[93] By idealizing Lennon, Coleman fails at one of the core requirements of legitimate biography: "Accept, as a biographer, who your subject was, for better or for worse. No sweeping of dirt under the rug: but no halo's either."[94] This failure to produce a balanced portrayal of his subject permeates and weakens all of *Lennon: The Definitive Biography*.

In addition to Coleman's "pro–Lennon bias" and "syncophantic"[95] tone, the work suffers from many of the same methodological issues as *Shout!*, including lack of access to sources which only became available after its publication, and absence of any citations or a bibliography. Combined with Coleman's frequent editorializing and sweeping generalizations, this failure to cite sources undermine the reader's trust in the author.

It is not enough to get the facts straight. You must also tell the readers the source of the facts so that they can judge their reliability, even check them if they wish. Readers do not trust a source they do not know and cannot find. If they do not trust your sources, they will not trust your facts; and if they do not trust your facts, they will not trust your argument.[96]

Like *Shout!, Lennon: The Definitive Biography* suffers from a lack of historical distance, as it accompanied the wave of adulation following the musician's death. In addition, the latter half of the book is far too dependent on the testimony of Ono's employee Eliot Mintz. Coleman's overreliance on this single source, regardless of the source's credibility issues, weakens his argument.

Coleman settles both debates in favor of Lennon and against McCartney. This is unsurprising: In *The Beatles Bibliography*, Michael Brocken concisely summarizes the work's view of both men: "John was a genius and Paul was a superficial idiot."[97] On the split, the author casts Lennon's departure as a break for artistic and personal freedom; an action Lennon was forced to take due to other Beatles refusal to accept Ono and by McCartney's usurpation of power following Epstein's death.[98]

The work reinforces the *Lennon Remembers* and *Shout!* narratives by severely diminishing the Lennon/McCartney partnership and minimizing McCartney's contributions to Beatles music. Coleman emphasizes Lennon's one-line contribution to McCartney's song "Hey Jude" but presents "A Day in the Life," widely regarded as the single greatest songwriting collaboration between the two, numerous times as solely Lennon's song.[99] Like Norman, Coleman's analysis of the music is selective, minimal and confined almost solely to lyrics. Like Norman, Coleman interviewed Martin only to ignore his assessment of Lennon and McCartney as musical equals. When Coleman asked which man deserved more credit for the band's genius, Martin declared that assigning artistic superiority was impossible: "'It's like asking what's the most important constituent in a sauce vinaigrette: the oil or the vinegar.'"[100] In spite of Martin's testimony, in early editions, Coleman anoints Lennon as the band's unquestioned artistic force—"where McCartney had great talent, Lennon was a genius"—and also denounces the importance of the men's friendship: "John and Paul never had much in common."[101] By mythologizing Lennon, dismissing the Fab Four version of an equal Lennon/McCartney partnership,[102] downplaying the men's friendship and blaming McCartney for the band's split, Coleman's *Lennon* reinforces every major element of the *Shout!* narrative.

Lennon: The Definitive Biography betrays a lack of objectivity in other ways. In later, revised editions, Coleman applies source analysis to and questions the credibility of numerous eyewitnesses that dispute Lennon and Ono's version of their relationship. However, Coleman does not apply the same standards to witnesses promoting his preferred view. This is most evident in Coleman's denunciation of Fred Seaman, Lennon's personal assistant whose memoir *The Last Days of John Lennon* argues that the couple's final years were unhappy, with both pursuing extra-marital affairs, and Ono planning divorce.[103] Contrary to the "house husband" image the two promoted during *Double Fantasy*, according to Seaman Lennon spent much of this time suffering from depression and writer's block. Coleman's analysis of Seaman is methodologically sound: he argues that Seaman's theft of Lennon's personal diaries in the days following the musician's death demonstrates a lack of honesty and credibility and accuses him of pursuing an anti–Ono agenda because of his position as a disgruntled ex-employee.[104] However, Coleman's preferred, optimistic version of the couple's last few years is heavily reliant on interviews with Mintz, Ono's publicist. In contrast to his evaluation of Seaman's credibility, Coleman recounts Mintz's testimony without question,[105] never discussing how Mintz's position as Ono's current employee and press representative presents an obvious conflict of interest. In applying critical source analysis to *only* those eyewitnesses whose testimony he personally disagrees with, Coleman demonstrates a severe lack of balance.

Contemporaneous biographies on McCartney were nowhere near as extensive. *Yesterday*, written by Chet Flippo, a journalist friend of Lennon's, relied heavily on the Flippo's personal undocumented conversations with Lennon and, like virtually all other Beatles works of its time, did not cite sources within the text or provide a bibliography. Written in a conversational, easy style, it was poorly researched, much of its text lifted, uncredited, from previously published works, and obviously written more to sell copies than to gain a greater understanding of McCartney as an individual or an artist. A superior work is Chris Salewicz's 1986 biography, *McCartney: The Definitive Biography* written after he had conducted a series of atypically revealing interviews with McCartney. Like Flippo, Coleman and Norman, Salewicz failed to document his sources, but demonstrated considerable skill in researching McCartney's childhood and pre–Beatles life. While the work is largely complimentary of McCartney's life and music, Salewicz's work does not approach Coleman's level of hagiography. In a radical statement for a rock and roll journalist at the time, Salewicz argued against the perception of McCartney as shallow, declaring he "was just as much an artist as John Lennon."[106] Salewicz also regarded the condemnation of McCartney following the breakup as unfair, arguing that parts of the press turned the musician into a "sacrificial scapegoat" and "an object of utter derision."[107]

Salewicz's account, though far from being the definitive biography its title claims, is important because it directly challenged the standard narrative of the time, which depicted Lennon as the Beatles' sole genius and cast McCartney in the role of the villain behind the breakup. In 1988, a far more infamous biography, this time of Lennon, also disputed the *Shout!* narrative. Even before it was published, Albert Goldman's *The Lives of John Lennon* was already the most controversial book in Beatles historiography. Prior to its release, it was the subject of a BBC documentary that discussed the validity of its sources and conclusions. Lennon's former and current press champion, *Rolling Stone*, issued a cover story fiercely denouncing Goldman's research, sources, and analysis. In a rare display of unity, both Ono and McCartney urged Lennon's fans not to read the book.

The Lives of John Lennon provides an unfailingly negative view of Lennon, both as musician and human being. Goldman was an English professor, not a journalist, and his biography of Lennon depicts a man struggling with several issues, including megalomania and dyslexia.[108] Goldman portrays Lennon as a bully quick to outbursts of harsh violence against both women and men: a far cry from the late rock star's well cultivated image as a man of peace. In a book riddled with small (and some not so small) factual errors, Goldman accuses Lennon of being both a rapist and a murderer.[109] His relationship with McCartney was strictly professional: the two did not like each other, distrusted each other, and almost never wrote together.[110] As a musician, Lennon had "sold out," and his melodies and lyrics were heavily plagiarized. Harrison and Starr's musical talents (and, to a lesser extent, McCartney's) were derided as well.[111] He also argued that Lennon was a homosexual who engaged in a longstanding affair with Beatles manager, Brian Epstein, whose 1967 death left Lennon lost and vulnerable until Ono appeared and fulfilled Lennon's psychological desire to be dominated by a strong woman.[112]

His depiction of Ono is equally negative and, at times, couched in distressingly pejorative language.[113] Goldman brutally dismisses the romantic image promoted in the couple's final *Playboy* interviews and *Rolling Stone*'s *The Ballad of John and Yoko*. He begins his book by describing Ono's retching in the toilet due to her resurgent heroin addiction and blasts her manipulations of the press, luxurious wealth, lack of maternal instinct and alleged extra-marital affairs.[114] He pins primary blame for the breakup on her, not Klein, and argues that she deliberately kept Julian away from his father by threatening suicide if the two spent too much time together.[115] According to Goldman, the househusband image Lennon and Ono promoted during *Double Fantasy* was mere fiction invented for the press. In contrast, Goldman's sources argue in the years following his second son's birth Lennon retreated into his room at the Dakota, a prisoner of his depression, drugs and Ono's psychological manipulations.[116]

Just as the purpose behind *Lennon Remembers* was to demolish the Beatles' myth, *The Lives of John Lennon* was written to destroy Lennon's posthumous mythologization. Goldman claimed, somewhat disingenuously, that he had embarked on the book as a genuine fan of Lennon[117] before his research left him bitterly disillusioned. However, previous biographies by Goldman on celebrities, including Lenny Bruce and Elvis Presley, also presented their subjects in an unfailingly negative light, demonstrating little impartiality, balance or understanding. Goldman's evident glee in recounting Lennon and Ono's negative qualities did not help the author's claims to impartiality. Decades later, Hertsgaard offered insight into of one of the major weaknesses of *The Lives of John Lennon*: "Goldman seems reflexively driven to interpret any and all evidence in the most sensational manner possible."[118]

In many ways, *The Lives of John Lennon* serves as the mirror opposite of *Shout!*. But where Norman came to praise Lennon, Goldman came to bury him. As in *Shout!* the author indulges in numerous editorial comments and unevenly applied moral standards. Those few individuals to escape Goldman's harsh judgment are all those who agreed to be interviewed.[119] Pete Best receives one of his most complimentary portrayals: despite being "the best drummer in Liverpool," Best was expelled from the group partly because McCartney was jealous of Best's good looks, and Lennon envious of Best's "quiet strength."[120] Goldman's generosity extends to Klein who, in a dramatic reversal of his role in the *Lennon Remembers* narrative, argues that Ono unfairly manipulated Lennon into leaving his management.[121] Goldman also paints a favorable picture of Sam Green, a member of Ono's inner circle. Green claims to have engaged in an affair with Ono and argues that she intended to divorce Lennon.

Goldman's contemptuous portrayal of perhaps the most revered icon in the history of rock and roll was regarded by many journalists and publications as an assault on the institution of rock and roll itself. In the 1988 BBC documentary *John Lennon and Albert Goldman*, rock and roll journalist Bob Spitz argued that his colleagues refused to accept any of Goldman's work as true because of corrupting self-interest. According to Spitz, the position of rock journalist offered considerable benefits: access to exclusive parties, free records and other perks bestowed by musical celebrities and record companies. In exchange, there was an understanding: "They can't afford to write anything negative, or severely negative, about the rock music business: that would be biting the hand that feeds them." As an outsider, Goldman could reveal information his journalist counterparts could not. Spitz praised Goldman's work as one that was "starkly realistic, tells the truth, pulls the veneer off what these rock journalists have been writing for the past 20 years ... it makes them look like fools, it makes them look like liars." He argued that self-interest motivated not only Lennon's media coverage, but eyewitness accounts of him as well. "I know a lot of people who were friendly with John Lennon who were terribly treated by him, but say only wonderful things about him and the reason they do that ... is that they must protect their own history. And their own history is that they are John Lennon's friend."[122]

Newsweek magazine argued at the time that in many ways the furor surrounding Goldman's work was far more revealing than the book's scandalous allegations. Radio stations urged listeners to boycott *The Lives of John Lennon.* Martin dismissed several of its findings, including Lennon's supposed homosexuality and affair with Epstein, and argued that the book never would have been written during Lennon's life.[123] Ono evidently contemplated suicide over its publication,[124] but never sued the author for libel. The most vicious denunciation of the work came, predictably, from *Rolling Stone,* the rock magazine, publisher and most avid supporter of *Lennon Remembers* and *The Ballad of John and Yoko.*

However, *Rolling Stone* was hardly an impartial source, a factor *Newsweek* examined in its story on the controversial book, and which included Wenner's declaration that *The Lives of John Lennon* "offended him ... as a professional, as a friend of Yoko's, and as editor of *Rolling Stone.*" Wenner acknowledged how his close friendship with Ono, including mutual vacations and holidays together "don't make him a neutral party," but asserted "my friendship with Yoko does not undermine the credibility or authenticity of *Rolling Stone.*"[125] However, in his next sentence, Wenner announced a blanket ban in which his magazine never would print "anything mean or nasty" about Lennon because "there is nothing mean or nasty in John's life."[126] *Newsweek* found *Rolling Stone's* "'intensive investigation'" and attempts to summarily discredit the entirety of *The Lives of John Lennon* unconvincing. But they also deemed several of Goldman's assertions, including the accusation of murder and Lennon's supposed affair with Epstein and accusations of murder, as implausible, and based on spurious and unverifiable evidence.[127]

One crucial component that *The Lives of John Lennon* contains, which its ideological opposite *Shout!* lacks, is a bibliography. Unlike Norman, Goldman provided a list of his sources, including some 1,200 interviews done by a team of research assistants over a period of six years. It did not, however, include citations within the text, so that some of the most severe accusations leveled against Lennon—such as the accidental murder of a Hamburg sailor during an attempted mugging and an account of him raping a female fan backstage before a Beatles show—are untraceable and impossible to verify or disprove.

Despite its serious methodological and interpretive errors, *The Lives of John Lennon* did offer a large amount of original research, especially on Ono's family and background, which most Beatles' biographers largely had ignored. Goldman's account of the 1970's, the last decade of Lennon's life, was also far more extensive than in any other Lennon biography, before or since. Where Coleman's biography (which Goldman used extensively in his own work but dismissed as "infatuated with its subject")[128] overly relied on Mintz's[129] interviews, Goldman cited at least 20 different eyewitness interviews for Lennon's "Lost Weekend" and 20 more for Lennon's final years. That these sources provided an unremittingly negative view was the fault of Goldman who, like Norman and Coleman before him, selected the facts and eyewitness accounts that supported his pre-determined thesis but ignored those that contradicted it. Decades later, Spitz, who accessed Goldman's taped interviews, acknowledged this selective use of evidence in *The Lives of John Lennon*.[130] Goldman's attempts to discredit the depiction of Lennon as a secular saint led him to craft an extreme counter-narrative, portraying a man of unquestionable musical brilliance, deep friendships and powerful personal charisma as a largely unremarkable musician and intensely unpleasant individual.

Goldman asserted that, with the publication of *The Lives of John Lennon*, "the jack is out of the box ... there will be a different John Lennon from now on."[131] But his efforts to destroy the *Shout!* narrative were premature, in no small part because *The Lives of John Lennon* told a story that the public, and Lennon's fan in particular, did not want to hear. In his essay on the role popular pressure plays on a narrative's acceptance or rejection, C. Vann Woodward observes: "It was a long time before it was entirely safe for an American historian to point out that George III was a comparatively mild monarch and that British rule of the American colonies was exceptionally liberal."[132] Likewise, it was a long time before the public could accept harsh criticism of the murdered Lennon, a man who, for many, symbolized the 1960s. *Newsweek* acknowledged this: "If John Lennon was a fraud, where does that leave all the values he was thought to embody?"[133] In both cases (the popular mythology constructed around America's origin story and the mythology built up around Lennon) popular opinion rejected the interpretation contrary to the public's preferred version. The role of the intended audience (in the standards of historical methods, the "who" it was written for) should not be ignored: Most prospective buyers of a Lennon biography would have been fans of the musician, and no publisher wanted to invest in a book that lost money.

Ultimately it became clear the public did not want to see Lennon through

Goldman's eyes, and the book proved a financial and critical failure. However, although it was initially dismissed as offensive and illegitimate, elements of Goldman's work (in no small part due to his extensive research) gradually gained some measure of credibility. *The Beatles Bibliography* notes that, while *The Lives of John Lennon* contains "serious problems largely surrounding Goldman's preconceptions, methods and approaches ... on close examination, it does tend to reveal a great deal about John that is based upon very solid research," and argues that it "should not be dismissed out of hand."[134] A decade after McCartney urged people not to read Goldman's book, his semi-autobiography *Many Years from Now* included *The Lives of John Lennon* among its list of sources, along with a caution. Spitz defended Goldman's research while at the same time acknowledging the other man's bias in selecting negative and sensationalistic material.[135] In *You Never Give Me Your Money*, Doggett discusses both the strengths and weaknesses of *The Lives of John Lennon*:

> *The Lives of John Lennon* was lousy with errors of fact and interpretation, speculative in the extreme, ill willed and awash with snobbery. Yet Goldman pinpointed Lennon's almost clinical need for domination by a strong woman; the dark ambiguity of a man of peace being surrounded by violence; the unmistakable decline in his work after he left England in 1971; and the instinctive need to believe in a force greater than himself, which led him from guru to guru, each obsession spilling into disillusionment and creative despair.[136]

The Debate over Lennon's Final Years

For his account of the last few years of Lennon's life, Goldman drew heavily from the recollections of John Green, the Lennons' official tarot card reader. Green had described his interaction with the couple in his 1983 book *Dakota Days: The True Story of John Lennon's Final Years*. In both *Dakota Days* and his interviews with Goldman, Green proclaimed affection for Lennon but argued against the man's idolization. The testimony in *Dakota Days* is presented in a methodologically flawed way: Green recalls word for word conversations with Lennon and Ono on numerous subjects that took place over a number of years. At times his recall incorporates everyone's statements, verbatim, for pages at a time. In the book's introduction, Green attempts to justify this by declaring that he has an excellent memory and because his conversations with Lennon and Ono were particularly memorable.[137] However, this makes it impossible to distinguish Green's paraphrasing from Lennon or Ono's actual words or determine where Green inserts his own thoughts and words. Without verification from Ono or Lennon, almost all of Green's account qualifies as hearsay, defined by Garraghan in *A Guide to Historical Method* as "a second hand statement that can't be proven."[138]

According to Green, working as the Lennon's tarot reader made him privy to their private lives. His depiction refutes the version of their marriage that the couple promoted at the time of 1980's *Double Fantasy* and argues that Lennon's musical silence was not rooted in domestic tranquility but severe writer's block. This inability to write plagued Lennon and in early 1978 sent him into a severe depression that lasted more than a year.[139] Green's Lennon was charismatic, witty and generous but also volatile, deeply jealous, insecure and, on occasion, violent towards his family members. Ono is presented as domineering, superstitious and manipulative, her ego bruised at living in Lennon's shadow.

While his version corresponds with Goldman's view, there is no way to verify or disprove many of the statements Green claims to have heard from Ono and Lennon. Another issue that diminishes the work's credibility is its self-serving agenda, as Green credits himself as the source of seemingly every intelligent business decision that the Lennons made during his time with them. Because of these reasons, any direct quote from *Dakota Days* is inherently suspect unless verified by another, independent source.

Another key figure that emerged during this time that contradicted Lennon's canonized image was his eldest son Julian. In the immediate aftermath of his father's murder, Julian downplayed any feelings of anger over his father's callous treatment of him and his mother, Cynthia. As time passed Julian Lennon began openly criticizing his father's dismissal of him both before and after his departure with Ono, and, by 1988, was unfavorably comparing Lennon's parenting with McCartney's. During the next few decades Julian Lennon declared several times that, during the Beatles period, McCartney had helped fill the fatherhood role that failed to interest his own father, and that he had more memories of playing make-believe and photos of himself with McCartney than he did of him and his father.[140] These comments tended to coincide with time periods of particularly poor relations between Julian Lennon and Ono.

As years passed Julian continued to chafe at the widespread adoration of his father, instead emphasizing the gap between the man's words and his actions. "From my point of view, I felt he was a hypocrite. Dad could talk about peace and love out loud to the world but he could never show it to the people who supposedly meant the most to him: his wife and son."[141] His public criticisms of both his father and Ono continued over the years. He accused Ono of deliberately pursuing his father for her own interests, uncaring that her actions would destroy his family: "She knew exactly what she was doing from day one."[142] He blamed her for refusing to share a fair amount of his father's estate with him, prompting him to sue her (a decision that was settled out of court) and accused her of attempting to erase him and his mother from Beatles history.[143]

This message continued, particularly in *John*, Cynthia Lennon's second memoir of her life with her husband. Connolly notes how the work could be viewed as an attempt to push back against the idealization of Lennon's memory,[144] and this possible agenda must be taken into account when reading it, particularly as so much of it consists of personal, and therefore unverifiable, testimony. Much of the work highlights how Lennon failed to practice his message of peace in his own behavior toward his family. In the foreword, Julian describes his conflict with the widespread perception of his father: "To me he wasn't a musician or peace icon, he was the father I loved and who let me down in so many ways.... I felt rejected and unimportant in his life."[145] Lennon's treatment of Cynthia and Julian was largely ignored throughout the *Lennon Remembers* and much of the *Shout!* narratives, which instead emphasized his attempt to make amends with his efforts to be a better father to his second son Sean. But by the 30th anniversary of Lennon's death, even his staunchest defenders acknowledged his parental failures regarding Julian.

Goldman's book also included extensive interviews with May Pang, the Lennon's former employee who, at Ono's urging, had embarked on an affair with Lennon during the 18 months that consisted of his "Lost Weekend." Pang had written her own account of her relationship with Lennon in 1983, five years before *The Lives of John Lennon*, but several subsequent works on Lennon's post–Beatles life, including Coleman's work, severely downplayed their relationship. In *Lennon: The Definitive Biography*, Mintz argued that Pang's account only embarrassed herself; "May contrived a quasi-fictional scenario in an attempt to give form to a relationship that was not there."[146] As Ono's publicist he told *Good Morning America* that Pang's story was a lie.[147] It was a misleading, inaccurate statement, given the voluminous eyewitness testimony, documentation and physical evidence, including pictures, of Lennon and Pang's romantic relationship. Pang defended her account in her book's epilogue, declaring that other people had distorted her relationship with Lennon, both before and after his death. Like Goldman and Green, Pang argued that her testimony was dismissed because it contradicted the mythology that had emerged following Lennon's death. "The story of our relationship had gotten so distorted that I knew I had to fight back.[148] I wasn't going to add to the myths that John's official 'spokespeople' were inventing."[149] Referencing the sanctification of Lennon, Pang also acknowledged that "by remembering the bad parts as well as the good I am contradicting that legend."[150]

Pang's agenda—to demonstrate that their time together was creative, mostly happy and productive for Lennon rather than the bleak separation he and Ono had portrayed afterward for the press—certainly calls into question but does not summarily negate her version of her relationship with Lennon or Lennon's relationship with Ono. *The Lost Weekend* is balanced in that it discusses both the negative and positive elements of Lennon and Pang's relationship. One of the more disturbing aspects of the public reaction to Pang's memoir was that much of the attention it received was due to her assertion, later verified by separate sources, that Lennon was preparing to reunite with McCartney again in early 1975.[151] This collaboration between the two songwriters was prevented when Lennon instead reunited with Ono. Meanwhile Pang's accounts of Lennon's physical abuse (including his twisting her wrist and strangling her to the point that another person had to intervene)[152] received little attention from the press.

It took decades for Pang's account to become an accepted part of Lennon's post–Beatles biographies. Some continued to severely downplay Lennon's time with Pang (a tactic Lennon used with the press once he reconciled with Ono). In *You Never Give Me Your Money*, Doggett examines the flaws in Lennon and Ono's version of the "Lost Weekend." He describes the couple's efforts to portray it as "a period of emotional and creative bankruptcy" as a "revision of history" which diminishes the work Lennon created during the time period, including the 1974 album *Walls and Bridges*. He also argues that Lennon and Ono's retrospective efforts to minimize accounts of Lennon's happiness and productivity during his "Lost Weekend" reinforces their version of Lennon's subsequent househusband years. Such revisionism, according to Doggett, "prolonged the myth that the most productive relationship of Lennon's life was not with Paul McCartney but with Yoko Ono."[153]

With Green's account, as well as *The Lives of John Lennon* and Pang's *The Lost Weekend,* the truth surrounding Lennon's last years became, in effect, another of the great unresolved debates in Beatles historiography. Ono, along with Mintz, Coleman, Norman and Wenner promoted Lennon's image as a happy househusband and father, content without writing music and liberated from contractual obligations. The opposing story, told by Pang and Goldman as well as former Ono employees such as Seaman and Green, described Lennon as reclusive: suffering the effects of heroin and cocaine use, angry with his inability to write and embittered against those artists of his generation that continued to do so, including Bob Dylan, Paul Simon, and McCartney. According to these sources, Lennon joked about suicide at least once.[154] Ono dismissed the negative accounts as the product of disgruntled ex-employees. However, at least one eyewitness description of Lennon's depression pre-dated his death,[155] and other sources, including Shotton, Julian Lennon,[156] and the producer of *Double Fantasy*, Jack Douglas, provided a picture of the Lennon/Ono marriage that fell far short of the domestic, artistic and sexual ideal the couple had sold so enthusiastically.

What is clear is that both sides were heavily invested in promoting their own version of Lennon's story. Almost no new evidence has emerged indicating which version is more accurate, and any more evidence seems unlikely at this time. It is impossible for both versions to be true: "the principle of contradiction pitilessly denies that an event can be and not be at the same time."[157] Lennon's private diaries, seen by only a few individuals before Ono re-possessed them, are what Bloch and Garraghan would categorize as the most credible of primary sources, since they were never intended for public consumption. Yet their contents only have been recounted by those who strongly dispute Ono's version of the story; no independent appraisal of their content ever has been provided. Both sides have their own agendas in promoting their particular versions of events. Both also have legitimate criticisms regarding the opposition's credibility: Mintz's place as Ono's employee seriously impacts the independence and credibility of his eyewitness accounts; Seaman (Lennon's personal assistant who stole the musician's diaries shortly after his death, supposedly to give them to Lennon's son, Julian) would not be considered by any historian as a particularly trustworthy source.

For a student of history, the debate over Lennon's last years matters because of what it reveals about choosing between contradictory sources and clashing interpretations. It illustrates the role eyewitness agenda plays, as both sides attempt to summarily ignore, discount and discredit opposing sources. It indicates how heavily invested they were in their respective mythologies. It reveals the partisanship of Beatles historiography by demonstrating how some authors apply source analysis only to those eyewitnesses with disparate accounts while unquestioningly accepting the testimony of those whose version they prefer. It offers a classic example of choosing between contradictory sources with opposing viewpoints, and determining which one seems the most likely. In his essay *A Short Guide to Writing about History*, Richard Marius recounts similarly opposing versions of Martin Luther's final moments: In one, the theologian and father of a church prayed to heaven with his last breath; in the other he simply asphyxiated and died without a word. According to Marius, "Both stories were told by people at the time. We can only infer which story is more plausible."[158]

John Lennon: The Life, and the Rejection of the Shout! Narrative

Like all initial narratives written too close in time to the actual event, *Shout!* lacked many primary sources which only become available in later years. This author could have addressed this significant flaw with *Shout!'s* enduring credibility in his revised editions of the book, published in 2002 and 2005. In the years between the original and the expanded editions, Beatles scholars gained access to an enormous amount of new material, including interviews, transcripts, and eye-witness and retrospective accounts. Martin's *Summer of Love*, MacDonald's *Revolution in the Head*, Lewisohn's *The Complete Beatles Recording Sessions*, Dave Sulpy's unauthorized "Get Back" transcripts, *The Beatles Anthology* and McCartney's semi-autobiography *Many Years from Now* were only some of the rich new sources that offered Norman an opportunity to document and reassess his research. It was an opportunity Norman ignored. The original and re-editions of *Shout!* are mostly identical, except for a look at the lives of the post-breakup Beatles, expanded sections on the band's music, and the removal of some of Norman's earlier and most blatant anti–McCartney editorializing.

In the introduction to the 2005 re-edition of *Shout!,* Norman wrote that he regretted his previous declaration that "John was three-quarters of the Beatles." But this erroneous percentage, and Norman's obvious preference for Lennon, won him access in 1981 to Ono, who later provided resources for the author's 2008 biography *John Lennon: The Life.* This access benefited both Ono and Norman; like numerous Beatles writers, including the reviled Goldman, Norman tended to favorably portray those living sources which provided him with access to documents and interviews. At the same time, Norman's research benefitted from access to sources that Ono had previously regarded as off-limits to biographers.[159] Norman, who had met Lennon only twice, interviewed Ono over a period of three years.[160]

The result of this access was *John Lennon: The Life,* one of the first major biographies of Lennon since Goldman's work and one which Norman declared in the epilogue he had hoped Ono would anoint as the official, authorized biography. (Ono refused, describing the work as "mean to John."[161]) If Ono's initial cooperation was unsurprising, McCartney's tentative support was astonishing, given the contempt with which all Norman's previous work had portrayed the musician, and of which McCartney was well aware. Although McCartney refused to meet in person with Norman, he displayed what *Mojo's* Paul Du Noyer described as "a forgiving side," and agreed to answer Norman's questions through e-mail.[162] This agreement, as well as the influence of other factors, resulted in a remarkable shift in fewer than three years regarding Norman's portrayal of McCartney. According to his statements to *The Guardian*, this change was not prompted by the newly available sources and eyewitness accounts which contradicted Norman's original assessment, but by a change in Norman's own personal views.

John Lennon: The Life was, like its predecessor *Shout!*, a critical and financial success. It provided new original research into two important figures in Lennon's life: Lennon's Aunt Mimi and Alfred Lennon, his absentee father. At more than 800 pages, its accounts of Lennon's childhood and particularly the Beatles' time in Hamburg were detailed, well researched and extremely well written. The book's less biased view on McCartney granted it a degree of impartiality that its predecessor so blatantly lacked. For the first time, Norman acknowledged McCartney's essential contributions to some of Lennon's work, such as the revolutionary tape loops McCartney added to "Tomorrow Never Knows."[163] His account of Lennon and McCartney's musical partnership and friendship was far more generous than in any of his previous work. These revisions demonstrate the decline of a major element in the *Shout!* narrative, which, in previous works by Coleman, Goldman and Norman had downplayed the importance of the mens' personal and working relationship. Norman now offered a far different interpretation, introducing McCartney as Lennon's "more-than-collaborator, more-than-partner, more-than-brother."[164] In addition Norman's unevenly applied moral judgments, which had weighted so disproportionately against McCartney in *Shout!*, were largely abandoned.

But despite these very real improvements, the credibility of Norman's new version of Lennon's life was compromised, in no small part by his relationship with and access to Ono. It also suffered from one of the major issues that devalued *Shout!*; at a time when virtually all legitimate Beatles' works included at least a bibliography, Norman's biography lacked one and contained no citations. Again, this made it impossible to entirely separate Norman's opinion from eyewitness accounts, or his editorializing from the information provided by primary sources. While his revised view of McCartney allowed for a more impartial evaluation of the man's talents and character, no such generosity was extended to Harrison. Norman continued to portray Harrison as a mediocre musician and almost unrelentingly bitter individual with a "dour and standoffish"[165] personality only capable of producing great work by imitating Lennon.[166] As in *Shout!*, Starr merited little of Norman's attention.

The work was also guilty of ignoring contradictory or unpleasant evidence. An example of this is found in the author's discussion of "Eleanor Rigby," when he applauds Lennon's public praise for the song—"John never rated Eleanor Rigby as anything other than a masterpiece"[167]—while failing to mention the musician's repeated attempts to falsely claim primary authorship. But the greater sin of omission lies with Norman's coverage of Lennon's "Lost Weekend" and of the man's final years. The author uses only one chapter to cover the whole 18 months of the couple's separation, and provides only Ono's approved version of events. Like Coleman, Norman relies almost exclusively on the testimony of Mintz, Ono's employee, for the chapter, and fails to acknowledge any possible conflict of interest.

In half a page, Norman dismissed all accounts that Lennon was less than content in his role as househusband and doting father. Other writers criticized him for ignoring the opposing narrative and unquestioningly accepting Ono's story: In *The Beatles Bibliography* Michael Brocken argues that the author failed to apply even the most basic source analysis: "[Ono's] account of events is treated almost gospel-like ... needless to say, the account comes across as a public relations exercise."[168] In an interview with *Oomska*, an online music magazine, Doggett pinpointed some of the same credibility issues, noting how *John Lennon: The Life* "completely ignored all the reports about Lennon's unhappiness" during this period. "It was almost as if his chronicle of 1975 to 1980 was written to make Yoko Ono happy ... for this section of the book, Norman threw off any pretentions to being a biographer and seemed to function merely as a PR agent."[169]

Critics largely overlooked these weaknesses and tended to regard *John Lennon: The Life* as a necessary midpoint between Coleman's unstinted adoration of its subject and Goldman's contemptuous dismissal. Most reviews focused on the book's more prurient claims, including its argument that Lennon may have entertained a sexual interest in McCartney. According to Ono, by 1971, Lennon had made remarks to her indicating an interest in pursuing a sexual experience with McCartney, but Lennon "had been deterred by Paul's immovable heterosexuality."[170] By the traditional standards of historical methods, Ono's interpretation of Lennon's comments are hearsay and do not carry as much authority as if they had been made directly by Lennon himself. They were also publicly rejected by McCartney after the book's publication.[171] Previous speculation concerning Lennon's sexuality had centered on the figure of Epstein, but Norman's work was the first to discuss the possibility regarding any such feelings Lennon might have held towards McCartney.[172] As hearsay, Ono's claim about Lennon's sexual interest in McCartney remains impossible to verify or disprove.[173]

From a historiographers perspective, it is interesting to note how Norman's more impartial re-assessment of McCartney resulted in a significant shift in his interpretation of facts and evidence previously analyzed in *Shout!*.

In the 2005 re-edition published only three years before, Norman argued that their mutual friend Ivan Vaughn hesitated to introduce McCartney to Lennon because Vaughn only introduced "great guys"[174] to Lennon, and, in Norman's view, Vaughn obviously felt that McCartney didn't qualify.[175] Now Norman's account had changed dramatically, declaring "Ivan had long since marked Paul down as being of potential value to the Quarrymen."[176] In contrast to his portrayal in *Shout!*, McCartney was no longer described as plotting to oust Sutcliffe from the band in order to take the position of bass guitar. Norman also altered his views on certain McCartney songs, describing "Let It Be" as "an elegiac ballad"[177] in contrast to his previous dismissal of it as "the mollifying phrase of a Liverpool mother to a fractious child."[178]

In his coverage of the two major debates in Beatles historiography, Norman's views changed to better fit with the new evidence and slowly emerging new narrative. In contrast to his assessment in *Shout!*, McCartney was no longer was blamed for the split. Instead, the breakup resulted from a number of decisions made by everyone involved, with the core disagreement over Klein serving as the "fatal" blow.[179] Lennon's declaration of divorce was evidence of the maturity and intensity of Lennon and Ono's bond, as Lennon left what had been his most important relationship, with the Beatles, in order to concentrate on his new life with Ono.[180] These tensions, coupled with the schism over Eastman and Klein, brought about the band's dissolution. This marked a fundamental shift in how many Beatles writers told the group's story for decades and a considerable departure from how Norman previous work had portrayed the breakup.

This shift regarding the group's rupture was mirrored by a similar re-interpretation of McCartney's musical skills. In *Shout!* Norman's evaluation was often dismissive, repeatedly describing McCartney's work as conventional and sentimental and his vocals as inferior to those of Lennon.[181] Now Norman argued a new, appreciative assessment of McCartney's talents which, while applauding him as a "peerless commercial songwriter"[182] still maintained Lennon's place as the band's sole genius.

The contrast between Norman's stance on Beatles historiography's two major debates in *Shout!*, as opposed to his interpretation of them in *John Lennon: The Life,* is a remarkable indication of how far out of favor the *Shout!* narrative had fallen by 2008. Norman always maintained that his conversion on McCartney was prompted by a change in his own personal feelings. However, it is difficult to believe that someone so invested in portraying himself as one of the premier Beatles' authorities could fail to notice that, by the beginning of the 21st century, the narrative had shifted away from the *Shout!* thesis.

Certain aspects of *Shout!* continue to influence Beatles historiography. However, by the beginning of the 21st century major elements of the *Shout!* narrative were no longer unquestioningly accepted as the prevailing Orthodoxy, and *The Beatles Bibliography* condemned its closed-minded and inaccurate doctrine. By this time, Beatles historiography had cycled through three major narratives in 30 years. These included the official Fab Four version which established their mythology in the 1960s; the *Lennon Remembers* narrative, predominating throughout the 1970s, and the *Shout!* narrative, which, in the wake of Lennon's murder, exerted such influence in the 1980s. The credibility of the *Shout!* narrative began to decline when, in the late 1980s, a large number of newly available primary and secondary sources began to contradict many of its conclusions.

The vast majority of sources which emerged between the time of Lennon's murder and the beginning of the 21st century painted a far more nuanced picture of the Beatles, their music, and their breakup than the one Norman provided in *Shout!* Multiple biographies, reference books, eyewitness accounts and memoirs contradicted many of Norman's, Coleman's, and Goldman's conclusions and interpretations. Both the new evidence and the passage of time allowed for historical distance and a more impartial assessment of the Beatles story. This is evidenced by the fact that, 30 years after its publication even Philip Norman, the founder of the heavily influential but inherently flawed *Shout!* narrative, had largely abandoned it.

CHAPTER FOUR

The Lewisohn Narrative

History demands an understanding interpretation.
—March Bloch, *The Historian's Craft*

Rejecting the Prevailing Orthodoxy

The Fab Four and *Lennon Remembers* narratives both ended abruptly, influenced by shocking public events that seared themselves into the public consciousness. In April 1970, the *McCartney* press release ended the Fab Four version of the Beatles story: Lennon's murder 10 years later symbolized the end of the era in which the band members shaped own their story. These clear divisions (pre-and post-breakup, before and after Lennon's death) make it easy to pinpoint the chronology where Beatles historiography's first two narratives begin and end. Identifying the onset of the *Shout!* narrative's decline and the Lewisohn narrative emergence is less clear cut, but some events' influence is undeniable. The publication of Lewisohn's *The Complete Beatles Recording Sessions* in 1988 is one of them: It signifies one of the most important moments in all Beatles scholarship. Twenty-five years later in 2013, the publication of the first part of Lewisohn's three volume biography *The Beatles: All These Years, Volume I —Tune In*, can be viewed as the moment when his interpretation was cemented as the prevailing Orthodoxy.

Within the quarter century between *The Complete Beatles Recording Sessions* and *Tune In*, the answers to the two major debates in Beatles historiography—who was responsible for the group's breakup, and whether Lennon or McCartney deserved the most credit for the band's greatness—changed. Ever since 1970, when the Beatles story had splintered into two camps, McCartney had been identified as the primary instigator of the band's dissolution, while Lennon was crowned its sole or greater genius. By 2010, even Beatles authorities who were widely regarded as pro–Lennon (such as Philip Norman and *Rolling Stone)* no longer identified McCartney as the sole or primary reason behind the rupture. Both the *Lennon Remembers* and *Shout!* narratives argued that Lennon was the band's driving artistic force and sole genius as well as its only experimental, artistic and unconventional thinker. Major parts of the Lewisohn narrative disagreed, citing as proof McCartney's retrospective testimony in addition to newly rediscovered primary sources, especially studio tapes of the Beatles recording sessions. In this revised narrative Lennon and McCartney were more or less equals; *both* men were musical geniuses, and it was the unique combination of their personalities and skills, cooperation and competition, which drove the Beatles artistry. In addition, under the Lewisohn narrative, coverage of Harrison and Starr increased and their critical reputations improved.

Three major factors prompted the gradual departure from the *Shout!* interpretation and transition to the Lewisohn narrative. First among these was the passage of time, which allowed for a greater measure of historical distance and more impartial, less emotionally and politically driven evaluation. Second was the emergence of new sources and retrospective testimony, including previously unavailable primary sources. Third, the late 1980s saw McCartney begin a sustained campaign to revise what he perceived as the errors regarding his role in Beatles history. These three elements changed how the band's story had been told since 1970.

The first factor was the passage of time and resultant historical distance. Historical distance provides a crucial element in evaluating history. First, it allows a wider perspective, providing greater context and understanding regarding events and their consequences. Second, it often reduces the strong emotions associated with an event or individual, allowing more impartial evaluation. Third, as decades and centuries pass, new primary sources almost always surface, offering fresh evidence and interpretations. Fourth, political climates often change with time, meaning that versions of history previously regarded as unpopular or forbidden in previous decades or centuries gain acceptance. All these aspects of historical distance, "the growing clarity that comes with the passage of time,"[1] colored Beatles historiography in the late 1980s, 1990s, and beyond.

As the decades distanced them from the two most traumatic moments in Beatles history, the band's rupture and Lennon's murder, more writers could view both with greater impartiality. This is evidenced by a willingness to acknowledge that Lennon *had* been mythologized, something few would have admitted in the years immediately following his death. By the early 1990s, *Time* was arguing that "Lennon's contributions [to the Beatles] had taken on mythic proportions"[2] since 1980, and that part of this revisionism had come at McCartney's expense. The 30th anniversary of Lennon's murder reflected widespread agreement that the musician had been all but canonized in the media. "For the past three decades the man I've been reading about has grown less and less like the John Lennon I knew and generally more like some character out of Butler's *Life of the Saints*."[3] In addition, more Beatles writers were acknowledging how Lennon's breakup-era statements had damaged McCartney's reputation.

> The painting of Paul McCartney as a goody-two-shoes type ... began, of course, with Lennon's post–Beatle "divorce" scourge of his former partner ... and grew after Lennon's death and martyrdom as "St. John." The characterization of McCartney as a lightweight eventually became entrenched to the point that revelations about his interest and involvement in the avant-garde music scene in the '60's (and his technical contributions to Beatles works such as "Tomorrow Never Knows") were rejected as not only impossible but near hearsay. Surely John Lennon had to be the experimental Beatle—he had to be.[4]

In 1995, Connolly argued that, while privately Lennon and McCartney always admired each other's talents, Lennon's "cruel and mischievous"[5] pronouncements in the early 1970s distorted views of the men's partnership. Lennon's criticisms, combined with his sudden, violent death ensured that "his earlier, harsh statements became frozen in the public consciousness"; consequently, "Lennon became the martyred genius with attitude: McCartney the cute one who wrote 'Silly Love Songs.'" Connolly dismissed this stereotyping as erroneous. "Lennon and McCartney were as different as two sides of the same coin, but they were never less than equals."[6]

Another element that encouraged these revisions was new and previously unavailable primary sources. Lewisohn's access to and publication of such sources is arguably the most pivotal factor that shifted the interpretation away from the *Shout!* narrative. This change fits the overall historiographical pattern: The discovery and interpretation of new primary sources constitutes one of the most common reasons a new narrative replaces an old one. In the 1960s Fritz Fischer's unprecedented access to Germany's World War I archives and the primary sources contained therein inspired a starkly different narrative that challenged the traditional German view of the war's origins. Prior to Fischer, German historians (both those working officially for the state and those only allowed incomplete access to the archives) always denied Germany's sole or primary responsibility for instigating The Great War. Fischer's newly discovered primary sources—particularly those that detailed Kaiser Wilhelm II's 1912 War Council, in which the Kaiser and the German military advocated for immediate war but conceded delay to give the German Navy more time to gain strength—changed many historians' views of World War I's origins.

Like Fischer, Lewisohn was the first researcher to gain access to previously unavailable evidence: Like Fischer, the primary sources Lewisohn revealed contradicted the prevailing Orthodoxy. Lewisohn was granted complete access to the tapes of the Beatles studio recording sessions, from 1962 to 1970. These invaluable primary sources provided hundreds of hours of new, contemporary evidence and yielded Lewisohn's essential reference work *The Complete Beatles Recording Sessions*. Much of this newly discovered evidence negated the musical evaluations of the *Lennon Remembers* and *Shout!* narratives, which had elevated Lennon's contributions to the band at the expense of the other members.

The third major element behind the new revisionism came from McCartney, one of Beatles history's most important and contentious figures. During the 1970s and much of the 1980s, McCartney failed to consistently present his version of the Beatles' story. This lack of post-breakup testimony from one of the group's key figures, along with the mythologization following Lennon's death unbalanced Beatles historiography. McCartney's initial reluctance to discuss the Beatles limited the amount of sources (particularly interviews) from his perspective; The volume of Lennon and Ono's public pronouncements on the breakup outnumbered McCartney's. As early as 1972, McCabe, the first author to attempt to chronicle the reasons behind the band's split, acknowledged McCartney's press silence: "[Paul] "made no attempt to retaliate against the criticism from the underground."[7] MacDonald also addressed the issue in his 1995 musicological evaluation of the Beatles, *Revolution in the Head*: "McCartney, wounded by Lennon's attacks on him at the beginning of the Seventies, could have been excused for indulging in similar self-justifications. It's to his credit that he did not (at least at this stage) seek to promote his own view of their relationship, instead just getting on with his own career."[8]

McCartney's relative silence reportedly resulted from a number of factors. Following the *McCartney* press release, the musician fell into a depression so severe he was incapable of getting out of bed, let alone promoting his side of events to the press. In *Many Years from Now*, McCartney argues that he kept quiet in the 1970s out of "cowardice" for fear of a public war of words with the acerbic Lennon: "He'd do me in."[9] During the 1970s hope for some sort of musical reunification may also have been a factor. In the early 1980s, McCartney felt that any of his testimony that contradicted Lennon's was seen not as an attempt to provide his own side of the story, but rather as an attack on the murdered, martyred Lennon.[10] Real life concerns also played a role. Busy raising four young children,[11] recording and touring solo and with his band Wings, and producing, on average, an album a year, McCartney was too preoccupied throughout much of the 1970s and 1980s to concentrate on, let along challenge, his portrayal in Beatles history. (However, the topic clearly bothered him, as evidenced by his 1981 telephone conversation with Davies.) His 1984 *Playboy* Interview with Joan Goodman and 1986 interviews with Chris Salewicz constituted McCartney's main attempts to counter the prevailing narrative. However, they had little initial impact on some key chroniclers.

Starting in the late 1980s, McCartney began a deliberate, sustained campaign to promote his side. This began with his Paul McCartney World Tour, which spanned more than 100 concerts, the globe, and an entire year, from 1989 to 1990. A total of 2,843,297 people worldwide attended McCartney's shows.[12] Ticket buyers received a free, detailed 98-page booklet which introduced the band and discussed Paul and Linda McCartney's key causes of environmentalism and vegetarianism. Two-thirds of the booklet presented McCartney's reflections on his life and career, arguing his version of the Beatles story, their music, and the Lennon/McCartney partnership. The musician countered the perception of Lennon as the only artistic Beatle, asserting his own powerful *avant-garde* influence on *Sgt. Pepper.* "I'm not trying to say it was all me, but I do think John's *avant-garde* period later was really to give himself a go at what he'd seen me having a go at."[13] He also obliquely referenced and criticized writers such as Norman who argued that Lennon was the only Beatle that mattered. (However, McCartney chose to project the issue of unfair attribution onto Harrison rather than himself). "There are certain people who think [John] was the Beatles. There was nobody else. George just stood there with a plectrum waiting for a solo. Now that is not true. George did a hell of a lot more than sit waiting for a solo. John would be the first to tell you that." In a defensive tone, McCartney proclaimed preeminent authority on his songwriting partnership and friendship with Lennon: "It was me and John sitting there, it was me and him who wrote it all, not all these other people who think they know all about it.... I must know better than them. I was the one in the room with him."[14] The World Tour program provided the template for the decades to come, as McCartney campaigned to counter the *Lennon Remembers* and *Shout!* narratives which he believed had treated him unfairly. The musician followed the tour with an increasing number of interviews that advocated his version of events, eventually culminating in his participation in the retrospective collective history *The Beatles Anthology* and his semi-autobiography *Many Years from Now.*

McCartney promoted three main revisions. First, he disagreed with the prevailing perception among Beatles writers such as Norman, Coleman and

Goldman that his relationship with Lennon had been professional at best and adversarial at worst. McCartney repeatedly emphasized their close friendship, declared numerous times that they had loved each other, and maintained that they had repaired much of their friendship before Lennon died. Second, McCartney argued against the prevailing perception of himself as the square, straight conventional musician and Lennon as the group's only experimental, artistic and radical thinker. McCartney repeatedly referenced how his own immersion in London's 1960s *avant-garde* art scene had pre-dated Lennon's. The musician stressed how he had experimented with *musique concrete*, the underground movement, and tape loops while his songwriting partner spent his days watching television and dropping acid in suburbia. Third, McCartney countered the Orthodoxy of Lennon as the group's sole or greater genius and its only real rocker. The musician repeatedly asserted his equality with Lennon in their songwriting partnership, musical talents, and relationship. McCartney laid out part of his platform in his foreword to *The Complete Beatles Recording Sessions*: "John and I were very equal … since John's death this thing has emerged…. I've become known as the soppy balladeer, and John of course did a lot to encourage that when we were having rows. He really tried to put that about but he knew otherwise."[15] Part of McCartney's efforts to assert his equality with Lennon involved McCartney's own attribution of songwriting credits.

McCartney's efforts to change how the Beatles story was told were not universally popular: Norman accused the musician of re-writing history, and a spokesman for Ono labeled McCartney's attempts as revisionism.[16] His efforts to reverse the entrenched Lennon/McCartney credit to McCartney/Lennon on songs which he had primarily or solely authored appeared grasping and ungracious and provoked popular backlash. However, the combination of McCartney's surge of information about his Beatles past along with Lewisohn's research and the establishment of a degree of historical distance all exerted enormous influence on Beatles historiography after 1988. Some established Beatles writers such as Coleman revised their previous opinions of McCartney's musicianship and the Lennon/McCartney partnership. New writers such as Hertsgaard, Spitz, Jonathan Gould and MacDonald also rejected the interpretations in the *Lennon Remembers* and *Shout!* narratives. These writers argued that the combination of Lennon and McCartney's combined genius, as well as Harrison and Starr's invaluable talents (and Martin's essential production) created the Beatles unmatched catalog. As writers and biographers interpreted old facts in new ways and analyzed new pieces of evidence, the historiography of rock's greatest band shifted under their feet.

The Lewisohn Reference Books

In the mid-to-late 1980s and early 1990s, Beatles researcher Mark Lewisohn authored several reference books that altered the direction of Beatles history. The first work published under Lewisohn's name was 1986's *The Beatles Live!* but he had been involved in writing the band's history since the late 1970s, when he served as a researcher for Norman's 1981 biography, *Shout! The True Story of the Beatles*. It was Lewisohn who had discovered the Beatles' genesis, pinpointing the date of the summer fete when Lennon and McCartney met. Norman publicly complimented Lewisohn's skills as a researcher and inserted a cameo of Lewisohn into *Shout!* Throughout the 1980s and 1990s Lewisohn's research appeared in an increasing number of important works. Over the years Norman, Coleman, Martin, Gould, Hertsgaard, Mac-Donald and at times even McCartney all turned to Lewisohn or his reference works for essential information, sources or facts.

His first book on the group, The *Beatles Live!* is a chronological reference detailing the specifics of all the band's public performances. Like all of Lewisohn's early work, the book is likely to appeal only to someone with a passionate or scholarly interest in the band. Lewisohn emphasized how its status as a catalog of events reinforced its impartiality: "It is not an opinionated biography but a reference work, the result of almost seven years painstaking research."[17] *The Beatles Live!* quickly became an invaluable source for all other Beatles writers, as Lewisohn had compiled and synthesized information from more than 1,000 separate primary sources, particularly newspapers.

It disproved one of the most enduring myths about the Beatles: that they seemingly appeared instantaneously and were elevated to stardom and worldwide fame with ease. Hunter Davies addressed this errant perception years later: "When they first appeared, in London and later in New York, they were assumed to be overnight sensations who had come from nowhere."[18] Lewisohn's research proved that the Beatles were anything but an instant success. Chronicling hundreds of appearances across Liverpool, Europe and eventually the world, Lewisohn's work cataloged the massive effort Lennon, McCartney, Harrison and Starr put into their band and music. Its members endured years of practice, harsh musical apprenticeships, and numerous rejections before attaining fame. During this baptism by fire Lennon and McCartney wrote scores of songs together and apart, honing their craft years before anyone outside of their immediate circle heard any of their work: "The Beatles, as this book amply illustrates, absolutely *slogged* for their success."[19]

This emphasis on the group's efforts to achieve stardom and maintain artistic supremacy had been overlooked in the *Lennon Remembers* and *Shout!*

narratives. As the Lewisohn narrative continued, all four members' hard work gained renown as one of the key reasons for the band's ascendance. In his work *Outliers: The Story of Success* which argues that the key to mastery is 10,000 hours of practice at a particular skill, author Malcolm Gladwell cites the Beatles punishing Hamburg apprenticeship as a primary reason for the band's musical supremacy.[20] In 2014, Davies described "hard work and dedication" as "arguably the most important elements in the creation of the Beatles' music … without those ingredients, their legacy would have been puny."[21]

Lewisohn followed *The Beatles Live!* with one of the most important works in all Beatles historiography, *The Complete Beatles Recording Sessions*. Prior to Lewisohn no one, with the exception of Martin, had been allowed to listen to and transcribe the hundreds of hours of tapes chronicling the Beatles studio recording sessions. Because the tapes were inaccessible to previous writers (the Abbey Road archives being even more inaccessible than the Vatican's) much pre–1988 musical analysis contained a significant amount of speculation. The tapes included every attempt to record every song, from the band's first nervous audition in 1962 to their final moment together in 1970. For seven years Lewisohn cataloged the tapes, transcribing available information such as who had played what instrument, performed a particular guitar solo, suggested an arrangement, or sung harmony on a specific song. In addition to these invaluable primary sources, Lewisohn also interviewed key figures such as the Beatles publicist Derek Taylor, engineer Geoff Emerick, and producer George Martin.

Like *The Beatles Live!*, *The Complete Beatles Recording Sessions* is a reference work intended for scholars and devoted fans rather than casual readers. Although Lewisohn injects authorial opinion on the merits of certain songs, such as "Birthday" and "Strawberry Fields Forever," most of the book catalogs information revealed in the recordings. Hundreds of entries in chronological order list the recording date, song title, vocalists, instruments used and their players. Lewisohn's brief explanation also includes various other important details about the recording.

The evidence revealed in *The Complete Beatles Recording Sessions* authoritatively disproved Norman's assertion (which he later renounced) that Lennon was 75 percent of the Beatles. Instead Lewisohn's research revealed the considerable extent to which the Beatles music was a group effort. While intended as a reference work and lacking an obvious agenda, the primary sources revealed the vital role played by all four Beatles as well as Martin and the band's engineers. It exposed essential contributions (such as orchestration, arrangements, and guitar work) McCartney, Harrison, Starr and Martin all made to Lennon's songs, and elements Lennon added to theirs. Lennon's genius was not downplayed but objectively assessed. Lewisohn praised the musician's vocal performance on "Twist and Shout" as so powerful it "certainly hasn't been equaled since"[22] and described "Strawberry Fields Forever" as "one of the greatest pop songs of all time."[23] However, *The Complete Beatles Recording Sessions* provided a balanced musical evaluation by acknowledging the other band members' contributions in a way that the *Lennon Remembers* and *Shout!* narratives did not. Lewisohn also noted the shifts in artistic supremacy that marked the Lennon/McCartney partnership: "*Rubber Soul* was one of the highlights of John Lennon's career, the sort of peak which Paul McCartney was to achieve a few months later with *Revolver*."[24] He also applauded Harrison's work, which more pro–Lennon writers such as Norman or Christgau had undervalued and overlooked, praising Harrison's song "While My Guitar Gently Weeps" and describing another, "Here Comes The Sun," as "one of the best songs on *Abbey Road*."[25]

McCartney provided an interview in the foreword of *The Complete Beatles Recording Sessions*, a tacit endorsement of its contents and of Lewisohn. The musician used the foreword to assert his version of Beatles history by defending his artistic *avant-garde* credentials and declaring that he and Lennon were equals. The prediction that *The Complete Beatles Recording Sessions* would "become the definitive reference book for Beatles fans everywhere"[26] was quickly confirmed: decades later *The Beatles Bibliography* anointed it as "one of the cornerstones of Beatles scholarship."[27]

The book contained a number of revelations that countered the accepted wisdom. The recordings proved that, contrary to the story told during the breakup, Lennon bore just as much blame as McCartney for not supporting Harrison's efforts as a songwriter. The newly revealed sources displayed Lennon's lack of interest in Harrison's work. Particularly in the band's last few years, Lennon often did not bother coming to the studio when he knew they would be working on one of Harrison's songs.[28] Buttressing his claims to musical experimentation, McCartney was credited with conceiving both the orchestration and piano chords for the Beatles *tour de force* "A Day in the Life."[29] According to Lewisohn the tapes also dismissed Lennon's accusations (made in his 1980 interview with *Playboy*) that McCartney had subconsciously "sabotaged" some of this greatest work.[30]

Like its predecessors *Lennon Remembers* and *Shout!*, *The Complete Beatles Recording Sessions* impacted all subsequent scholarship on the group. Its status as a compilation of facts largely devoid of authorial interpretation or evident bias elevated its reputation, while it contains minor errors, there is no reason to doubt its overall accuracy or methodology. (The only other person to listen to all the tapes, Martin, has never disputed Lewisohn's transcripts). Lewisohn subsequently produced another reference book, *The Beatles Day by Day*, which chronicled events in the Beatles lives in chronological order from 1962 through 1989. Exhaustive and detailed, *The Beatles Day By Day* contains little subjective opinion; when it does surface, Lewisohn clearly separates it from the facts. Drawing heavily from newspapers, contemporary interviews, and other primary sources, Lewisohn provided another essential reference work. However, Lewisohn's interpretations differ from the preceding narratives by identifying Klein as the "prime mover"[31] behind the split and emphasizing the essential nature of the Lennon/McCartney songwriting partnership. While it was published almost simultaneously with *The Lives of John Lennon*, Lewisohn's account of Lennon's final years give no credence to any of Goldman's controversial claims. Ending in 1989, *The Beatles Day by Day* noted that Harrison's star was ascendant at the time: he had recently recorded with The Traveling Wilburys, a supergroup including Bob Dylan, Roy Orbison and Tom Petty, and achieved a recent chart-topping U.S. hit with a re-make of Rudy Clarke's "Got My Mind Set on You."

Lewisohn's most comprehensive work, *The Complete Beatles Chronicle* was published in 1992. The result of 12 years of research, it was anointed "the single most authoritative document" about the group and cemented Lewisohn's position as "the world's leading authority" on the band. McCartney had tacitly endorsed *The Complete Beatles Recording Sessions* by helping write the foreword; now Martin did the same in *The Complete Beatles Chronicle*, praising Lewisohn's methodology and criticizing much of the previous scholarship on the band as "misinformed rubbish."[32] The work was a combination of *The Beatles Live* and *The Complete Beatles Recording Sessions*, with a dash of *The Beatles Day by Day* thrown in for good measure. In it Lewisohn offered more interpretation than in his previous works. Despite his respect for the Beatles music and personalities, the work is not hagiographic: The author does not whitewash or ignore their negative qualities: Lewisohn describes Lennon, McCartney and Harrison's behavior over the ousting of drummer Pete Best as "the most underhand, unfortunate, and unforgivable chapter in the Beatles' rise to monumental power."[33] However, unlike those of Norman, Goldman and Coleman, Lewisohn's moral judgments are both understanding and balanced. In contrast to the official narrative, he argues that the Beatles' disillusion with fame began as early as the end of 1963. "It was already getting beyond a joke. Having to wear elaborate disguises to walk in public; being victims of a fake attempted joke kidnap, their families and homes in a permanent state of siege."[34]

Like Lewisohn's earlier work, *The Complete Beatles Chronicle* is balanced and presents authorial interpretations with impartiality. While reinforcing the transition away from the preceding narratives, it is far from a blanket endorsement of McCartney's version of events. Lewisohn's research disproved one of McCartney's most repeated claims; that the group refused to perform in the United States until it already had a number one hit on the American charts. Documentation uncovered by Lewisohn proved that Epstein had signed the contract for the Beatles Ed Sullivan appearance in November 1963: three months before "I Want to Hold Your Hand" became the band's first number one U.S. hit.[35] Despite this proof, in later interviews the musician continued to repeat his story. Other evidence in *The Complete Beatles Chronicle* also countered some of McCartney's claims. McCartney had at times publicly distanced himself from the band's undisputed critical failure, the *Magical Mystery Tour* film, by presenting it as more of a group concept rather than his pet project. Lewisohn disputed that (as did MacDonald) labeling the film and virtually all the band's projects between 1967 and 1970 as "Paul's baby."[36] While Lewisohn's evidence contradicted the musician on these matters, his sources and interpretation reinforced the central elements of McCartney's revisions, including his close friendship with Lennon, their status as equal talents, and his *avant-garde* credentials.

Unlike many Beatles writers, Lewisohn does not demonstrate a preference for any particular Beatle but devotes equal attention, scholarship and analysis to all four: The often marginalized figures of Harrison and Starr receive as much focus as Lennon and McCartney. Reiterating one of the official narrative's key planks, Lewisohn argued in favor of the band's unity and friendship, declaring that as late as the end of 1967 "the Beatles were a group with an unparalleled bond of loyalty and inner strength."[37] His depiction of Ono is strictly factual, with no editorializing, although he characterizes her entrance into the band's story as detrimental. "[Lennon and Ono's] coming together had an undeniably negative bearing on the functioning of the Beatles as a unit, even if it only accentuated the disharmony which had already taken hold."[38] At the same time, he praises the couple's "admirable fortitude in the face of open hostility" during their peace campaign.[39] While identifying Klein as the main cause of the split, he also refrains from caricaturizing the "Demon King," a common practice in Beatles history.

The Complete Beatles Chronicle marked the end of a remarkable stretch of research that changed the way in which Beatles history was written. From the mid–1980s to the early 1990s Lewisohn produced various reference books that revealed previously unknown facts, many of which challenged the prevailing interpretation. Like the *Lennon Remembers* interview, Lewisohn's research had a seismic, although less abrupt, impact on Beatles historiography. After 1971 all works were forced to address Lennon's de-mythologizing interview; many responded by pivoting away from the Fab Four version. Twenty years later they were faced with another choice. The newly accessed primary sources presented facts that forced Beatles writers to select between two options: either revise the prevailing *Shout!* narrative, or ignore Lewisohn's research.

Reinterpreting Lennon/McCartney: Revolution in the Head

In the wake of Lewisohn's research, new biographies, musicological evaluations of the Beatles catalog, memoirs and other works openly challenged the previous narratives. In 1994 Martin published *Summer of Love,* his second book on his time with the band. The work concentrated on the recording of *Sgt. Pepper's Lonely Hearts Club Band* but also offered general observations of the Beatles personalities and musical skills. In the foreword Martin credited Lewisohn for help with the research but freely acknowledged that much of the book was drawn from "that most unreliable of servants, my memory."[40]

Martin's recollections were consistent with the ones he had provided in countless interviews as well as his 1979 work, *All You Need Is Ears,* and reinforced many of McCartney's claims. Martin repeatedly referenced McCartney's *avant-garde* exploration and musical experimentation in the studio. The Beatles producer described the Lennon-McCartney friendship as "intensely close"[41] and emphasized how much the two men needed each other musically. "Had John never met Paul and vice versa I firmly believe that neither of them would have turned out to be the great songwriters they were. They would have been good, but not blisteringly great."[42] According to Martin both Lennon and McCartney failed to support Harrison's attempts at songwriting. "The electricity that crackled between John and Paul and that led to such great music rather left George out in the cold ... if he needed help from the other two they gave it, but often rather grudgingly."[43] Martin acknowledged his own culpability: "I am sorry to say that I did not help George much with his songwriting either." He also disagreed with the prevailing stereotypes depicting Lennon as the rocker and McCartney as the balladeer.[44]

Martin's evaluation of Lennon and McCartney as musical equals and close friends supported the Lewisohn narrative's basic structure. It did not signify a change in Martin's own views, however: the Beatles' producer had been arguing the same viewpoint since the band's Fab Four days. The shift in Beatles historiography resulting from the passage of time, McCartney's self-promotion, and Lewisohn's research are more evident in other secondary works such as MacDonald's *Revolution in the Head* and Hertsgaard's *A Day in the Life*.

The most important of these is Ian MacDonald's 1994 work *Revolution in the Head*, which drew heavily from evidence revealed in Lewisohn's *The Complete Beatles Recording Sessions*; MacDonald acknowledged the book as "indispensible."[45] MacDonald signifies a change in the qualifications of Beatles authors. Previous biographers such as Norman, Goldman, and Coleman were all journalists or writers without extensive musical training. Therefore, their evaluations of Beatles songs were minimal, amateurish and focused heavily on lyrical analysis but largely ignored melody, chords, countermelody, instrumentation, production and other crucial musical aspects. Musicological evaluations such as Wilfrid Meller's *Twilight of the Gods* already existed, but they focused *solely* on musical analysis and ignored virtually all biographical and contextual information. MacDonald, a musicologist and writer, blended informed musical analysis with research, biographical information and interpretation. *Revolution in the Head* quickly established itself as one of the most essential and influential works in Beatles historiography: Critics praised it, fans bought tens of thousands of copies and the classic rock magazine *Mojo* described it as "the finest piece of fab scholarship ever published."

Like Martin and Lewisohn, MacDonald's conclusions disagreed with the *Lennon Remembers* and *Shout!* narratives. He did not anoint either Lennon or McCartney as the superior genius but instead emphasized the complementarity of their differences: "The two represent a classic clash between truth and beauty."[46] While repeating the accepted wisdom that they rarely wrote together—"their partnership was a fiction"—MacDonald maintained that the men's collaboration and competition drove the band's genius. "Their creative proximity generated the electric atmosphere of fraternal competition which was the secret of the Beatles' extraordinary ability to better themselves."[47] He noted the fluctuations of productivity between them, identifying Lennon's high point during the band's early era and particularly on *A Hard Day's Night*: "McCartney had fallen far behind Lennon in output.... Lennon's album material too had become deeper, more original and more varied ... unless McCartney woke up, he risked losing his equal status in the partnership."[48] Lennon had dated McCartney's creative dominance to 1967's *Sgt. Pepper's Lonely Hearts Club Band*; in *The Complete Beatles Recording Sessions* Lewisohn pinpointed it to 1966's *Revolver*. MacDonald argued it began in autumn 1965 when the primarily McCartney penned A-side "We Can Work It Out" outplayed Lennon's A-side "Day Tripper." "Lennon must have sensed that his era of dominance ... was over. From now on his partner would be in

ascendant not only as a songwriter but also as instrumentalist, arranger, producer and *de facto* musical director of the Beatles."[49] By identifying this shift
in the Lennon/McCartney songwriting partnership, MacDonald rejected one
of the key planks of the *Shout!* thesis, which depicted Lennon as the band's
dominant artistic force for almost the entirety of its existence.[50]

Given Beatles historiography's well-established divisions, MacDonald's
decision not to explicitly declare a preference in the Lennon/McCartney split
provoked speculation about whose side he was on. *The Beatles Bibliography*
labels the work as displaying an "undoubted pro–Paul McCartney bias,"[51] and,
while he devotes more attention to Lennon's songs, MacDonald's work does
demonstrate a preference for McCartney's version of events over Lennon and
Ono's. He sides with McCartney on both of the major disputes over song
authorship, states that the entire melody to "In My Life" clearly bears McCartney's stylistic fingerprints[52] and contests Lennon's claims of having written
70 percent of "Eleanor Rigby" by recounting Shotton's testimony. Like
Lewisohn, he also refutes Lennon's accusation that McCartney sabotaged his
songs and counters that Lennon's poor bass playing on McCartney's "The
Long and Winding Road," while largely unintentional, amounts to the very
sort of sabotage of which Lennon accused the other musician.[53] In the biographical sections he dismisses much of Lennon's version of the band's later
years. MacDonald clearly regards Ono's artistic influence on Lennon as detrimental, argues that their peace campaigns contained "a core of exhibitionist
self-promotion"[54] and condemns their "intellectual scorn for narrative."[55]
However, unlike *Shout!* or *Lennon: The Definitive Biography*, *Revolution in
the Head* contains references, allowing the reader to identify the original
sources and reach their own conclusions. More, unlike Coleman's hagiographic interpretation of Lennon, MacDonald's preference for McCartney's
version of events does not entitle the musician a free pass. MacDonald's view
of some of McCartney's work, such as "Maxwell's Silver Hammer," is scathing,
and he dismisses the emotional power of "Let It Be," one of McCartney's most
beloved songs.

MacDonald's analysis is among the most influential in Beatles historiography in part because it is far more critical than other musicological evaluations. He admitted this was deliberate. "Part of the aim of this book is to
replace gushing hero worship with a detached, posterity-anticipating tally of
what the Beatles did."[56] While identifying them as "far and away the best ever
pop group"[57] MacDonald labels much of their catalog as good-to-great but
finds genius in only approximately 20 songs. He dismisses Beatles' classics
such as McCartney's "Let It Be" and Harrison's "While My Guitar Gently
Weeps" as having overinflated reputations. MacDonald also declares that

Lennon's "I Am the Walrus" was his "final high tide of inspiration" as a Beatle: "He never rose to this stunning level again."[58] This statement reduces Lennon's contributions to *The White Album, Let It Be* and *Abbey Road*. MacDonald's evaluations of Lennon and McCartney's attributes are balanced, but he demonstrates little appreciation for Harrison's songwriting. According to MacDonald Harrison had written only one classic song, his 1969 work "Something." He dismisses Harrison's other most celebrated Beatle's songs "Here Comes the Sun" and "While My Guitar Gently Weeps," which (in an opinion many of his fellow critics find inexplicable) he describes as exuding "a browbeating self-importance which quickly becomes tiresome."[59]

With the possible exception of *The Complete Beatles Recording Sessions* and its offspring *The Complete Beatles Chronicle* no other work was more influential in disputing the primary elements of the *Lennon Remembers* and *Shout!* narratives than *Revolution in the Head*. In addition to rejecting the previous narratives' evaluation of the band's music and its members' musical contributions, MacDonald also disagrees with the Norman-influenced depiction of McCartney as uniformly shallow, snobbish and selfish. He counters accusations of selfishness by describing McCartney's willingness to help record Lennon's "The Ballad of John and Yoko" as "remarkable unqualified support"[60] and mentions McCartney's generosity in caring for Lennon after the latter mistakenly ingested LSD in the studio. Throughout *Shout!* Norman repeatedly labeled McCartney as a pretentious social climber but MacDonald disagreed, and referred to him as a "populist,"[61] a description that an increasing number of Beatles writers, including Coleman and Doggett, were adopting.

MacDonald's interpretation of both the music and the Lennon/McCartney partnership was powerful and exerted widespread influence over later Beatles writers. The book's accessibility and popularity contributed to its popular influence; it appealed to an audience beyond the band's most passionate fans and sold very well. Lewisohn's work was meticulous, documented and impeccably sourced, but it was written primarily as a record of events and consequently was at times dry and pedantic. *Revolution in the Head* presented the facts contained in *The Complete Beatles Recording Sessions* in a more attractive, accessible and interpretive package. It quickly joined *Shout!* near the top of the canon of most influential secondary works on the Beatles, where the two remained in somewhat contradictory co-existence.

Like *Revolution in the Head*, Mark Hertsgaard's biography of the Beatles music *A Day in the Life: The Music and Artistry of the Beatles* (1995) demonstrates the continuing shift away from the previous narratives. Hertsgaard's work combined both musical analysis and biographical context written by a

celebrated journalist and trained musician. Hertsgaard was an admirer of
Lewisohn, and in the book's foreword he accurately cataloged the methodological weaknesses rampant throughout Beatles historiography.

> One simply cannot trust that the "facts" in most books about the Beatles are
> anything more than speculation, heresy or opinion. The daily media reporting
> about the Beatles over the years was often careless or simpleminded. Book
> authors then compounded the confusion by making vast deductive leaps they
> then presented as truth, or by using technically factual evidence in selective
> ways, or by surmising what a given person, usually a Beatle, must have thought
> in a situation and then putting those words in his mouth. Authors rarely both-
> ered to document their conclusions; very few books on the Beatles contain a
> list of often questionable citations in supporting their claims.[62]

Hertsgaard's *A Day in the Life* was the first group biography to document
sources, including endnotes and chapter-by-chapter citations. This documentation, coupled with Hertsgaard's ability to clearly separate his personal
interpretation of events from the facts, reliance on primary sources, (including 400 hours of studio tape) and his impartial, balanced analysis make *A
Day in the Life* the first biography of the Beatles that qualifies as a work of
history.

His musical evaluation of the Beatles catalog and the Lennon/McCartney
partnership reinforced Martin's, Lewisohn's, and MacDonald's interpretation.
While noting that each man displayed evident strengths (Lennon with lyrics,
McCartney with melodies and chords) he argued that both men were equally
necessary to the creation of the music.[63] In a statement unprecedented in the
post-breakup era, he criticized the obsessive urge to parse out songwriting
credit to the very last syllable "to focus on it obsessively is to reduce great art
to a sports event. At some point, keeping score misses the point, which is the
music that the Beatles made as a unit."[64] This supported one of the main
themes of *The Complete Beatles Recording Sessions*, whose evidence had illustrated precisely how much the band's work depended on the alchemy created
by everyone's contributions. He reinforced the point in his discussion of the
Lennon/McCartney dyad.

> As much as fans and critics liked to speculate over who wrote what and who
> was the greater genius, it was the Lennon/McCartney partnership itself that was
> the point. As talented as each man was, it was their coming together, their influ-
> encing and challenging and complementing of one another, that elevated them
> to another dimension, producing music superior to what either man could con-
> sistently create on his own…. Both were fundamentally important: one without
> the other would have been unthinkable in terms of the Beatles success.[65]

Hertsgaard succinctly identified and rejected the "misleading stereotypes" of
the *Lennon Remembers* and *Shout!* narratives: "Paul was cast as the mawkish

lightweight who couldn't write a decent lyric, John as the rebellious artistic and abrasive bad boy." Like *Playboy*'s Goodman, Hertsgaard blamed these gross simplifications on "thickheaded critics" but also attributed part of their existence to Lennon's "less than generous statements about Paul during the bitter post-breakup years of the early 1970s."[66] He concluded by expressing the primary distinction between the Lewisohn interpretation and the *Shout!* narrative. "In the years since Lennnon's murder in 1980, a myth has grown up that John was the all but sole creative force behind the Beatles ... but it was the group, the special dynamic among those four individuals that made the Beatles what they were."[67]

Ever since 1971, arguing whether Lennon or McCartney deserved greater credit for the band's genius had been one of the most popular debates in Beatles history, one waged by journalists, biographers, musicologists and fans. With his declaration that the narrow focus on this question missed the key point of the story, Hertsgaard invited Beatles historiography to progress beyond an obscuring and insoluble debate.

Reinterpreting "Get Back"

In January 1969 the four Beatles (accompanied by Ono) had begun work on a new album, originally titled "Get Back." The idea, coming fast and hard on the heels of the miserable experience of recording "The White Album" was to go back to their roots as club musicians. The Beatles would make an album and visually record the process of creation, which they would release as a film. The music was intended to be raw and honest, stripped of excessive production. The resulting album and film were shelved for more than a year when it became clear that the music needed some level of production and that the film was *too* honest, revealing the intergroup tensions, "capturing their strained relationships and petty bickering."[68] The Beatles were so disillusioned with the material that by the end they changed the project's name from the hopeful "Get Back" to the more fatalistic *Let It Be*. The film was not released until May 1970, weeks after the *McCartney* press release. Given this timing, the movie was viewed from the moment of its release as a portrait of the band in the act of disintegration rather than creation.

The film had a brief re-release in 1981 and then disappeared from the public eye despite constant clamors from fans to release it in a newer format. By the beginning of the 21st century excerpts of it were available online, as were bootlegged copies. But in 1994 when Doug Sulpy and Ray Schweghardt released their analysis of the "Get Back" tapes, *Get Back: The Unauthorized*

Chronicle of the Beatles Let It Be Disaster (1994) the source material from which they drew was hard for the average fan to find. This made it difficult to directly compare Sulpy and Schweghardt's interpretation (the secondary source) with the actual video and audio recordings (the primary sources). Unable to directly quote the transcripts because of copyright reasons,[69] the authors were forced to paraphrase the dialogue and actions contained in scores of hours of recording.

Sulpy's work contains considerable authorial speculation, particularly in areas in which the author attempts to offer context. Much of this involves theorizing on the thoughts, feelings and motivations of the historical subjects. In itself, this is in itself not a methodological error: Because the body of the work involves paraphrasing transcripts, it is easy to distinguish Sulpy's speculation from the primary source material. On the other hand, Sulpy's personal opinions, particularly his negative view of Ono, seem to have colored his theorizing and therefore his contextualizing.

It was around this same time that Lewisohn, MacDonald, Martin and Hertsgaard's works all were contesting the musical Orthodoxy that Lennon was the only Beatle that mattered. Now Sulpy and Schweghardt used similarly untapped primary sources to dispute the prevailing opinion involving the other major debate in Beatles history. Their interpretation of the "Get Back" recordings contradicted the accepted wisdom, dating back to *Lennon Remembers*, that identified McCartney as the primary cause of the tensions leading to the band's split. Sulpy argued that the recordings did not support that view: "The common portrayal of Paul as an excessively bossy, egocentric bully during this period is simply erroneous and unfair."[70]

Throughout *Get Back,* Sulpy's conclusions profoundly reject the *Lennon Remembers* narrative. This is particularly evident in Sulpy's descriptions of Ono. He labels any attempts to downplay the tensions her presence and participation caused as "revisionist"[71] and commonly uses negative terms such as "aggressive" and "domineering" when discussing her behavior. One of her attempts at singing is memorably described as "obnoxious bleating."[72] His depiction of the Lennon/Ono relationship, and its effect on the Beatles as a unit, is also highly critical. According to the tapes everyone involved—from Aspinall to Harrison and Starr to "Get Back's" director Michael-Lindsay Hogg—clearly expressed dissatisfaction with Ono's disruptive presence and urged McCartney to confront Lennon over the issue. (They only did this when Lennon and Ono were absent.) In the tapes, McCartney acknowledges how strained his and Lennon's artistic partnership has become and discusses how difficult Ono's constant presence makes it to compose with Lennon. However, he also argues in favor of accommodation, stating that they should not force Lennon into an either/or choice between Ono and the Beatles.[73] Sulpy also discusses how Ono's inclusion antagonized Harrison, who was already unhappy with his inferior role in the musical hierarchy. "The years of playing second-class Beatle had created a deep, bitter resentment in George Harrison ... in addition, by January 1969, George found yet another person (Ono) ahead of him in the Beatles pecking order."[74] Sulpy concludes that Ono's presence caused significant tensions throughout the Beatles camp, but diverts from the *Lennon Remembers* and *Shout!* narratives by identifying Ono and Lennon as the responsible parties. He states that "the blame for this dysfunctional situation lies as much with John's passivity as Yoko's aggressiveness,"[75] and argues that Lennon and Ono's obsessive relationship, combined with the couple's heroin addiction,[76] crippled any real efforts to solve the band's problems. "Paul could not have stood up to [Ono] for fear of further alienating John. Michael cannot assert himself for fear of alienating *anyone*. George complains, but everyone seems to be used to that by now, and Ringo, as usual, offers no opinion."[77]

Another way in which Sulpy's interpretation diverges from the *Lennon Remembers* narrative is in its depiction of the Lennon-Harrison relationship. During the breakup era and especially at the Beatles trial, both men presented themselves to the press and in court testimony as strong friends with only minor differences. In Klein's 1971 *Playboy* interview, he stressed their camaraderie, mutual respect, and friendship.[78] When Starr followed the majority in accepting Klein and the band split three against one, the belief that no serious conflicts separated Lennon, Harrison and Starr reinforced popular perception that McCartney was the source of all the breakup-era acrimony. Doggett acknowledged this widespread perception years later: "Within the Beatles there was a unified trio, and then there was McCartney—ego driven, spiky, difficult to please and ultimately divisive."[79] After Lennon's death Harrison emphasized his closeness to his old friend and continued to do so for years; it was one of the primary messages he promoted throughout *Anthology*.

In contrast Sulpy determined that during the "Get Back" sessions the Lennon/Harrison relationship was full of conflict. The tapes revealed severe divisions between the two men that went beyond Harrison's obvious resentment of Ono's presence. Sulpy argues that Harrison's proposal that "each member treat everyone else's songs as if they had written them themselves" was "almost certainly directed at John, since Paul can be seen throughout the sessions working enthusiastically on the other's songs."[80] In *Anthology* and elsewhere, Harrison maintained that Lennon was far more open to outside suggestion on his songs than McCartney, but Sulpy's tapes disagree, revealing

Lennon's refusal to listen to Harrison's musical ideas for Lennon's "Don't Let Me Down": "It's interesting to observe that John will entertain any number of musical suggestions from Paul, but does not allow George to present his view as to how the song should be played."[81] Sulpy emphasizes Lennon's disdain for Harrison's songwriting—"John has almost nothing but negative comments to make about 'I Me Mine'"—and their inability to communicate.[82]

Reinforcing this context of tension between Lennon and Harrison, Sulpy's evidence discredits one of the most repeated myths regarding the "Get Back" sessions; that Harrison temporarily left the band because of tensions between himself and McCartney. This belief was based on both a scene from the film in which Harrison bristles at McCartney's attempts to instruct him how to play McCartney's song, and Harrison's own public statements. Beatles writers from Norman to Coleman to Hertsgaard all presented this scene as the motivation for Harrison's departure, and it was used as proof during the *Lennon Remembers* and *Shout!* narratives that McCartney's egocentric, domineering personality caused the breakup. The credibility of the sources providing the story was excellent; over the years various Beatles verified it. Credible sources or not, according to Sulpy it was false. "Despite the fact that all four Beatles have declared that George quit the band because of a musical conflict with Paul, evidence on subsequent tapes strongly suggests otherwise."[83] The tapes proved that, while tensions between Harrison and McCartney certainly existed, the immediate cause of Harrison's departure was a fight (presumably over Ono's presence and Lennon's dismissal of Harrison's work) with Lennon that turned physical. Immediately following the fight, Harrison walked out and quit the band for several days. In Sulpy's interpretation, Harrison was not the only frustrated one: He argues that Lennon, whose heroin use had blunted his productivity, was jealous of both Harrison and McCartney's songwriting output. "John is probably resentful himself, since he sees George contributing a presentable new number every day or two while he himself is unable to write a decent new song."[84]

In several of his post-breakup interviews, Lennon argued that he always supported Harrison, citing as evidence his giving Harrison the song "I'm Happy Just to Dance with You" to sing and providing a few lines in Harrison's "Taxman."[85] "John always maintained that he had encouraged George to write his own songs, and denied that he and Paul kept him in the shadows."[86] The "Get Back" tapes present compelling evidence disputing this, at least during this particular period. After Harrison's departure the three remaining Beatles, along with Ono and Linda Eastman, discussed solutions to the problem caused by Harrison's absence. Eager to get away from the documentary cameras that followed their every move, they held their summit in the lunchroom.

However, they were unaware that the filmmakers had secretly bugged the lunchroom (and the telephones) to record audio. Thanks to this presumption of privacy, the dialogue revealed in the lunchroom sessions provides the most credible evidence in the entire collection of the "Get Back" tapes.

The lunchroom conversation captures Lennon and McCartney acknowledging their inability to treat Harrison as an equal but expressing uncertainty of how to change patterns of behavior developed over a decade. Lennon ignores Starr's repeated suggestions that the four Beatles meet and discuss issues alone (that is, without Ono's presence, as Lennon now had Ono speak for him in Beatles meetings). Lennon reveals his resentment at supporting Harrison and expresses his belief, repeated elsewhere, that he and McCartney were the only two *real* Beatles and that Harrison and Starr were, to a certain extent, replaceable. Lennon reinforces this by arguing that, if Harrison fails to return after a certain interval, they should find a replacement and suggests Eric Clapton. Either placating the Beatles leader or reluctantly following him Starr agrees, but McCartney firmly vetoes this suggestion. Sulpy emphasizes how serious Lennon's idea of replacing Harrison is. "At this point, judging by his tone of voice, he either doesn't care at all if George ever returns, or he's doing an extremely good job of pretending otherwise."[87]

Sulpy's interpretation of the "Get Back" tapes seriously undermines the *Lennon Remembers* and *Shout!* versions of the Beatles breakup. It reveals the stark divisions that existed between Lennon and Harrison and refutes their testimony, given in 1971 at the Beatles trial, that McCartney's refusal to accept Klein was the group's only major conflict. While a pervasively negative view of Ono must be taken into account when reading Sulpy's interpretations, the tapes clearly identify her presence (and Lennon's refusal to confront the animosity her presence caused) as a major source of conflict. Contradicting previous accounts that cast McCartney as the villain, Sulpy argues that the tapes show McCartney attempting to force the other, apathetic band members to either demonstrate some effort or scrap the project. "It's only the moribund behavior of the other Beatles that makes Paul's assertiveness stand out."[88] However, McCartney's lectures only irritated the others further, increased tensions and reinforced their perception of him as controlling and demanding. The sense of disbelief that the group survived the "Get Back" sessions at all, and managed to later create their final masterpiece *Abbey Road*, is palpable. "It is hard to believe the Beatles ever survived" past their first week of the "Get Back" project.[89]

With (illegal) transcripts of the "Get Back" recordings widely available online, it is now possible to check Sulpy's interpretations against the actual tapes and determine the accuracy of his analysis. His obviously negative view of Ono reduces any claim to authorial impartiality concerning her. But Sulpy's paraphrased descriptions of the group's conversations and his chronicling of the sequence of events are accurate. Because the transcripts reveal events as they unfolded, do not contain retrospective testimony, and are uninfluenced by post-breakup agendas, their credibility exceeds other accounts of the "Get Back" sessions.[90] His key argument—that the recordings prove that, while McCartney contributed to the tension, he was not the villain of the "Get Back" disaster—also is reinforced by the tapes. The recordings reveal a splintering band, the result of multiple divisions widening between Lennon and McCartney, Lennon and Harrison, and Harrison and McCartney. This new interpretation, combined with the general consensus by the mid–1990s that (whatever his motivations) McCartney had been correct in viewing Klein as a dishonest and ultimately destructive choice, gradually resulted in a new version of the Beatles breakup. Fifteen years after Sulpy's "unauthorized chronicle" of the "Get Back" sessions appeared even the less than impartial *Rolling Stone* no longer adhered to the *Lennon Remembers* version of the split.

In Their Own Words: The Beatles Anthology

Following Lennon's 1980 death and *Shout!*'s publication the following year, the ex-Beatles began to lose control over the shape of their story. Secondary sources written by journalists, including group and individual biographies, supplied their historiography's predominant voices. All three surviving ex-Beatles expressed their frustrations with this, criticizing the accuracy of these accounts. Both McCartney and Harrison denounced *Shout!*. McCartney accused Norman of "sensationalism"[91] and later dismissed *The Lives of John Lennon* as "a piece of trash."[92] He also disagreed with some of MacDonald's interpretations in *Revolution in the Head*: "I would dip into the book and think 'what's he got to say about this song?' And he'd go 'This is McCartney's answer to'—and I'd go 'No, it wasn't! It was just, I just wrote a song.'"[93] Even Lewisohn, universally recognized as the foremost Beatles authority, did not escape criticism: "George Harrison looked me square in the eye on two separate occasions and said 'You weren't there, so how can you write about us?'"[94]

This frustration is one of the reasons why the three surviving Beatles agreed to participate in the collective, retrospective history *The Beatles Anthology*. Another was money: Harrison reportedly had lost millions of dollars to bad investments, and *Anthology* promised to generate a great deal of wealth for all the surviving Beatles and Ono. Discussion of the project started almost immediately following the breakup, but legal issues and personal conflicts prevented it from gaining any momentum. By the early 1990s, with the lawsuits among the former band members settled and relations among them at the best point since perhaps 1967, the ex-Beatles agreed to the project. The story of the Beatles as told by the members themselves, *Anthology* included both a 1995 video documentary that was broadcast on network television over several nights and a coffee table book including a compilation of interviews published five years later.

Conscious of the accusation that no retrospective history was complete without Lennon's input, the makers of *Anthology* insisted in the books inside cover that Lennon received equal representation along with McCartney, Harrison and Starr. Audio recordings of Lennon's interviews were used in the video section to present his views or memories, and numerous interviews were quilted together in the book to provide Lennon's perspective. That these interviews spanned from the earliest days of Beatlemania to mere days before Lennon's death, and were therefore subject to wildly varying agendas at the time they were given, went unacknowledged. Unlike the other three, Lennon was robbed of any post–1980 retrospective accounts. How his views on certain events, songs or individuals would have changed from his 1980 perspective is impossible to determine. At various points in both the video and the book McCartney, Harrison and Starr's retrospective interviews also were combined with their contemporary ones, but their 1990s view of the group and its history makes up the bulk of their testimony. In the book version the year an interview was given is provided in the text, but no other identification is provided, making it difficult at times to determine from which source the testimony originated. The result, in the *Anthology* book, is a jumble of interviews from over a period of 30 years, given by any of the main actors, each with their own agendas, and spanning every narrative. Because of Lennon's tragic absence, this was the only option available to the makers of *Anthology*.

Anthology, both the TV documentary and book, offers examples of the strengths and weaknesses inherent in authorized versions of history. *Anthology* provides new, albeit retrospective, testimony from all three surviving ex-Beatles as well as key Beatles insiders. *The Authorized Biography* was written before the breakup; *Shout!* was written too soon after it. By the time of *Anthology*, a measure of historical distance allowed for some context in which to view the Beatles achievements and failures. Crucially, the authenticity of the testimony of its key participants is indisputable. Despite their personal and at times clashing agendas, Lennon, McCartney, Harrison and Starr's *Anthology* accounts are among the most valuable sources in Beatles history because, unlike their biographers, they experienced and made history firsthand. "The presumption of adequate knowledge is against those who were not present at events."[95]

However, this same official status that makes *Anthology* an invaluable account of the band's history is also the source of many of its weaknesses. Because *Anthology*'s purpose is to serve as the Beatles' mouthpiece, no dissenting, outside evaluations are allowed. Critical source analysis of the band member's statements and interviews is non-existent. Questioning an ex-Beatle's testimony only occurs when another ex-Beatle or prominent insider contradicts an account. The retrospective quality of the interviews diminishes their accuracy and undoubtedly affected memories. The overall public agenda behind *Anthology* (to regain control of the band's story and shape it for history) lessens its status as a truthful account. And the differing personal agendas of the ex-Beatles are never acknowledged.

Anthology was promoted as the Beatles' story in the band's own words, and the book's cover anointed it "the Beatles Autobiography." Like most official histories, it boasted unprecedented access that others could only envy. *Anthology* secured access to the archives of the individual Beatles as well as extensive interviews with the band's surviving members. Martin, Taylor and Aspinall, all of whom helped create and sustain the band's official mythology, also were interviewed. Lewisohn served as the project's chief researcher, buttressing his well-established claim as the world's greatest Beatles authority. Female voices were noticeably absent: no spouses or girlfriends were interviewed. According to MacDonald, "ex-wives and lovers" were "ruled out by Ono's refusal to take part."[96]

Both the video testimony and the eventual book echoed several key elements of the Fab Four narrative, including the band's overall unity. Like the official narrative, *The Beatles Anthology* noticeably skims over more unpleasant elements. "The Anthology TV series ... skillfully evaded the issues that had divided the group, from the sacking of Pete Best in 1962 to the agonizing corrosion of 1969."[97] While the surviving Beatles express regret at the ugliness of their dissolution, its causes are glossed over, and the split is presented as a *fait accompli* resulting from its member's growing efforts to become adults and establish creative and personal individuality.[98] Any role heavy drug use may have played is downplayed. Klein receives little coverage in the television series. While his destructive impact on the band's unity is minimized by Harrison and Starr in the book,[99] McCartney highlights it: "I'd fallen out with the other three at once over the Klein thing ... so it was three against one."[100]

With four voices offering their personal view of the Beatles story, different memories of events emerged, most often between McCartney and Harrison. Both men's accounts were self-serving: McCartney reiterated the key points he had argued since *The Paul McCartney World Tour* booklet while Harrison repeatedly rejected the view that Lennon/McCartney dominated the band and emphasized the spiritual closeness he achieved with Lennon after their first LSD experience together.[101] Some of their differences (particularly those with little obvious agenda) can be attributed to the malleability of memory, such as when each of the Beatles provided different, somewhat incompatible memories of their meeting with Elvis Presley. Throughout *Anthology*, Harrison repeatedly identifies McCartney's authority as a source of tension[102] while McCartney defends himself.[103]

Always the least divisive and analyzed of all four Beatles, in *Anthology* Starr receives his most comprehensive portrait since Davies *The Beatles: The Authorized Biography*. His story—largely ignored for decades—is one of *Anthology*'s revelations. Starr defends his quasi-controversial replacement of Best by asserting his superiority as a drummer. Starr also reveals his anger at his biological father, who deserted him as a young child.[104] Connolly described *Anthology* as "an eye-opener" about Starr, venturing beyond the *A Hard Day's Night* stereotype of the "lucky Beatle." "He was much more than lucky ... something which leaps off the pages *The Beatles Anthology*."[105] As "the least to blame"[106] for the breakup, Starr's retrospective agenda is less overt than McCartney's or Harrison's, and the Beatles drummer provides one of *Anthology*'s final statements: a poignant declaration whose emphasis on unity reiterates the essential theme of the Fab Four narrative. "There were some really loving, caring moments between four people ... a really amazing closeness. Just four guys who loved each other."[107] The evidence provided in *Anthology* continued the tilt away from the *Shout!* narrative; reinforcing the sources provided in *The Complete Beatles Recording Sessions* which stressed how much the band's music had relied on the contributions of all four members.

Anthology's accuracy and credibility prompted considerable disagreement across Beatles historiography. Norman considered it a "laughably incomplete and doctored account."[108] MacDonald's analysis was kinder: While acknowledging its "party-line tinge," he described it as "an outline of events which most will recognize as accurate."[109] In *You Never Give Me Your Money*, Doggett labeled *Anthology* as "a celebration of the Beatles rather than a truthful self-portrait."[110] As officially sanctioned history, *Anthology*'s weaknesses are evident. However, until its release, few Beatles biographers proved willing to subject their own work to the methodology that results in legitimate history. Condemning *Anthology* while turning a blind eye to the weaknesses in their own research and interpretations underscores one of the least discussed aspects of Beatles historiography: the conflict for control of the narrative between the surviving Beatles (and Ono) and the journalists and biographers who told their story to the world.

Many Years from Now

McCartney had been actively promoting the three main elements of his version of the Beatles story—that he and Lennon were close friends, musical equals, and that his own radical artistic exploration pre-dated Lennon's—since his 1988 World Tour booklet. He followed that by supplying the foreword to Lewisohn's *The Complete Beatles Recording Sessions* and giving numerous interviews that detailed his contributions to the band's catalog and argued against the perception that he was responsible for the breakup. In 1993 he was interviewed by Maureen Cleave, the journalist who had famously profiled all four Beatles almost 30 years before. In their discussion McCartney stressed the intimacy of his relationship with Lennon: "I did love John … and I know he loved me."[111] He reinforced this in the retrospective interviews he provided for *The Beatles Anthology*. These projects and interviews could be considered rough demos for McCartney's finished product, his semi-autobiography *Paul McCartney: Many Years from Now*. Its publication in 1997 marks McCartney's most concentrated and comprehensive push to promote his version of the band's story.

Many Years from Now serves as McCartney's official platform. Partisan and defensive as well as engaging and informative, the book can be viewed as a belated response to Lennon's 1970 *Rolling Stone* interview in which the latter denounced the Lennon/McCartney partnership, blamed McCartney for the breakup, praised Klein, and de-mythologized the Fab Four narrative. Like *Lennon Remembers*, *Many Years from Now* incorporates an obvious agenda and presents the story from only one perspective. McCartney's semi-autobiography therefore suffers from some of the same credibility issues. Like its counterpart, *Many Years from Now* is a public statement, intended to shape public opinion. Both are among the most exhaustive interviews either man gave during their lifetimes. Both rely almost entirely on their subject's eye-witness testimony, although McCartney does include outside verification on certain points, such as his claim to having written most of "Eleanor Rigby" and that he and not Ono helped conceive the idea for the cover of *The White Album*.[112] Where Lennon's testimony occurred in the midst of the breakup (and was compromised by his anger and drug use at the time) almost all of McCartney's interviews in *Many Years from Now* are retrospective. As memoirs, they qualify as a primary source, but lack the immediacy and therefore some of the credibility of more contemporaneous sources. In *Lennon Remembers*, Wenner never challenged Lennon's more outrageous statements. This allowed Lennon's well-known tendency for exaggeration to skew events. McCartney also chose a friendly, non-confrontational chronicler, his old friend and fellow member of the 1960s underground art scene, Barry Miles. Miles's credentials as a member of the *avant-garde* set provided a sympathetic ear and reinforced McCartney's artistic credentials.

Despite these parallels, three main elements distinguish *Many Years from Now* from *Lennon Remembers*. First, unlike Lennon, McCartney was not using heroin either during the breakup period or his interviews (although he still was smoking marijuana, his drug of choice). McCartney's use of cocaine and marijuana during the breakup period undoubtedly influenced his behavior and perceptions at the time. But his consumption of any hard drug always fell far short of Lennon's. Furthermore, neither marijuana nor cocaine appears to have inspired the paranoia in McCartney that heroin prompted in Lennon. Second, unlike the "famously cranky"[113] *Lennon Remembers*, there is no evidence that McCartney gave his interviews in a state of anger. In contrast, most Beatles writers fault McCartney's recollections for obscuring the truth by glossing over the story's negative aspects. Norman frequently criticized McCartney for this tendency in his revised editions of *Shout!*, and MacDonald acknowledged this in *Revolution in the Head*, arguing that "McCartney's recollections of events thirty years later may be tinted by a desire to wish away bad memories of early 1969, when he was isolated in a group he loved and had fought hard for."[114] Finally, while Lennon repeatedly distanced himself from many of his *Lennon Remembers* statements soon after he made them, and later acknowledged lying about the Lennon/McCartney partnership in the interview, McCartney has never denounced *Many Years from Now*.

According to Miles, the book's purpose was to correct many of the myths and misinformation that plagued Beatles history: "Many Years from Now is the book that, at last, sets the record straight."[115] Miles blames the rock and roll press for skewing the band's story while acknowledging how the Beatles themselves often lied to the press.[116] The primary reason for many of these flaws, in Miles's interpretation, is favoritism. "Fans always chose their favorite Beatle and this bias has continued to color even the work of modern popular historians."[117] Miles also discusses how Lennon's tragic death obstructs attempts to determine the truth. "Any attempt at an objective assessment of John Lennon's role in the Beatles inevitably becomes iconoclastic. He has become St. John."[118] After identifying the weaknesses in previous Beatles works, Miles emphasizes *Many Years from Now*'s credibility and research, describing it as the result of "five years of exclusive interviews" over 35 sessions with McCartney and written with "complete access to Paul's archives."[119]

As with all authorized biographies, *Many Years from Now's* official status ensures it provides only approved information; certain topics receive scant attention and others are neglected entirely. Despite its length, which at 500 plus pages dwarfs the 150 pages of *Lennon Remembers*, it omits a number of important events in McCartney's life. These conspicuous absences included any mention of McCartney's 1980 arrest in Japan for marijuana possession or acknowledgement that, at the time of its publication, Linda McCartney had been struggling with breast cancer for two years. It provided little information on McCartney's five-year relationship with Asher beyond rationalizations for his chronic infidelity that argued that the two were not married and that Asher also engaged in additional affairs.[120] It ignored much of McCartney's post–Beatles life. In a scene straight out of a Horatio Alger story, *Many Years from Now* ends with a brief description of McCartney's 1997 knighthood ceremony, emphasizing his remarkable transformation from a working-class boy raised in a Liverpool council house to a multi-millionaire, knight and the best-selling pop musician of all time.

The admitted "center" of *Many Years from Now* is the relationship—personal and professional, collaborative and competitive, affectionate and acrimonious—between McCartney and Lennon. For McCartney, a significant part of this requires insisting that much of the accepted wisdom surrounding him, Lennon, and their relationship is wrong. McCartney denounces their musical stereotypes—"everything remotely experimental or *avant-garde* is always attributed to John"[121]—by arguing that he provided the tape loops for "Tomorrow Never Knows," conceived both the orchestration and the resounding final piano chord for "A Day in the Life" and created a *musique concrete* piece, "Carnival of Light," years before Lennon produced "Revolution 9." He also dismisses the caricature of their personalities. "John and I would never would have stood each other for that length of time had we been just one dimensional."[122]

A major part of McCartney's agenda involves contradicting his characterization in the *Lennon Remembers* and *Shout!* narratives. Arguing that stories of his acrimonious relationship with Sutcliffe are exaggerated, he bluntly rejected Norman's theory that he expelled Sutcliffe from the band to play bass. "Forget it! Nobody wants to play bass, or nobody did in those days ... so I definitely didn't want it."[123] Norman characterized McCartney as a pretentious social-climber who was addicted to adulation. Miles countered by mentioning how McCartney lived simply at the Ashers' for three years during the height of Beatlemania and "stuffed his MBE and gold records under his bed."[124] McCartney indicated he just enjoyed meeting interesting people: "I didn't really think of it as social climbing."[125] He countered the shallow caricature in *Shout!* interpretation of him by arguing that he and Lennon had been best friends since they were teenagers and, that Lennon never would have tolerated a superficial lightweight for a friend or songwriting partner. "I must have been special, because he'd have got rid of me. That's the point about John. He didn't suffer fools lightly."[126] Norman, Coleman and Christgau all had identified Lennon as the only *avant-garde* and musically experimental Beatle, but McCartney exhaustively proved his own immersion in the 1960s *avant-garde* London art scene, emphasizing his interest in Stockhausen, John Cage, and numerous underground movements. McCartney acknowledged that his perfectionist personality exacerbated tensions between himself and the other Beatles: "I could see now how that could get on your nerves," but argued that it was musically necessary. "Looking back on it now, I can say, 'Yes, okay, in the studio I could be overbearing.' Because I wanted to get it right!"[127]

McCartney flatly rejects interpretations casting him as the cause of the split and as Lennon's musical and artistic inferior. He implies that Lennon's psychological issues, along with his jealousy, insecurity and heroin use caused his erratic, destructive behavior. Like Shotton, he argues that Lennon's mental state was extremely fragile by May 1968. The meditation and lack of LSD in India had "brought [John's] deepest problems to the surface, but he was unable to resolve them."[128] As an example of Lennon's shaky mental state, McCartney recounts an Apple business meeting in late May 1968 where Lennon announced he was Jesus Christ, a story verified by numerous other witnesses, including Shotton. He rejects Lennon's accusation, made in *Lennon Remembers*, that the Beatles' reaction to Ono was so hostile it drove the couple into taking heroin: According to McCartney, the two began taking the drug immediately, before the approval or disapproval of the others could have had any impact.[129]

McCartney's portrait of Ono is moderately critical. He clearly resents her presence in the studio: "It is hard to believe that Yoko was unaware of how intrusive her presence was,"[130] her interference in his songwriting partnership with Lennon, and her vocal support of Klein. He identifies her as a motivating factor behind "How Do You Sleep," referencing eyewitness accounts that she and Klein helped write half the song's lyrics and that she abetted Lennon's anger: "If he'd had someone he could confide in, other than Yoko, I think they would have persuaded him to leave it in the vaults for posterity."[131] McCartney also stated that Ono approached him for song lyrics before she ever met Lennon,[132] disputing Ono's claim that she had not known

Beatles music when she and Lennon first encountered each other at one of her art shows.[133]

But McCartney's most pronounced resentment is directed at Klein. (While Ono's control of one-quarter of Apple meant that McCartney's business interests were permanently linked with hers, no such considerations complicated his portrayal of Klein). The musician reinforced the theme he had been arguing since his April 1971 *Life* interview, casting Klein as the Iago figure sowing jealousy and mistrust between McCartney and his fellow band mates. Linda McCartney predictably reinforced this, identifying both Klein and Ono as the reason for souring relations: "They had John so spinning about Paul it was really quite heartbreaking ... he was getting so bitter about Paul."[134] McCartney's answer for *why* Klein was able to provoke such resentment in Lennon argued that many of Lennon's breakup era actions were motivated by jealousy and insecurity. "John could not come to terms with the fact that Paul was now the *de facto* leader of the group ... the problem came because John's productivity fell off dramatically at a time when Paul was building towards his artistic and commercial peak."[135]

In *Many Years from Now* McCartney vociferously defends his refusal to accept Klein as his manager and expresses frustration at the other three's inability, at the time, to question Klein's actions: "They were completely besotted with this guy."[136] The musician declared that his lawsuit to end the group and extract himself from Klein's management was the hardest thing he ever did, but argued it was a necessary safeguard for the band's music and fortune and a corrective for his own acute anxiety and depression.[137] McCartney's depiction of Klein in *Many Years from Now* adds a powerful weight to what has become the almost universal portrayal of Klein as the villain of the Beatles' story. It also reinforces McCartney's own agenda by downplaying the hostility his bandmates felt for him at the time.

On the other great debate in Beatles history, McCartney repeatedly declares that he and Lennon were creative equals. "When it came to songwriting, it was never anything other than an equal partnership."[138] McCartney does this, in part, by identifying songwriting credits, just as Lennon did several times in the 1970s and most extensively in his 1980 *Playboy* Interview. McCartney examines the Beatles catalog song-by-song, parceling out each man's authorship of lyrics, melody and at times musical arrangements or instrumentation. According to Miles, McCartney did this purely from memory and without consulting Lennon's previous interviews.[139] Their attributions were similar, but not identical. McCartney claims significant contributions to what Lennon previously identified as solely "his" songs, with McCartney granting himself approximately 40 percent of the lyrics of "Norwegian

Wood"[140] and 30 percent of "Help!"[141] He also emphasizes how even those songs that were completely solo creations were influenced by the other's editing or approval. "The more you analyze it, the more you get to the feeling that both of us always had, which was one of equality.... It was just that I brought a certain 50% and John brought a certain 50%."[142]

Many Years from Now's flaws are obvious: McCartney's account is self-serving, despite the legitimacy of his grievances regarding much of his depiction in the *Lennon Remembers* and *Shout!* narratives. Miles does not identify which pieces of information came from his access to McCartney's archives. The interviews on which the book relied were conducted approximately 25 years after the Beatles dissolved; the accuracy of McCartney's memory must have been affected. His business relationships with Ono and the other ex-Beatles may have mediated his honesty regarding the breakup period. Where Lennon's tendency towards hyperbole must be taken into account when determining the accuracy of his statements, McCartney's own inclination to downplay the uglier aspects must also be acknowledged when analyzing his retrospective testimony. Finally, Lennon's absence makes McCartney's revisions of Lennon's attribution of songwriting credits impossible to verify or disprove.

Despite these weaknesses, as McCartney's version of events, *Many Years from Now* provides a substantial counterweight. The work is essential to any accurate understanding of the band's story, if only to balance out the pro–Lennon bias of the *Lennon Remembers* and *Shout!* narratives. Although McCartney's obvious agenda impacts his testimony's credibility, any reading of Beatles history that purports to be accurate must acknowledge the *existence* of his perspective and statements. "The writer of a historical narrative must deal with the contradiction. You cannot pretend the contradiction does not exist."[143] Acknowledging the existence of contradictory sources does not automatically imply agreement. However, the standard for balanced work requires writers utilizing eyewitness testimony from equally credible but contrasting primary sources to acknowledge both versions. "There's always the possibility that new evidence from the past will cause historians to reassess the origins of even the most familiar and agreed upon historical events."[144]

McCartney's semi-autobiography prompted mixed reactions in the Beatles community. While the work revealed valuable new information and its main elements aligned with the primary sources revealed by Lewisohn's research, many chafed at the book's defensive tone and overtly self-serving agenda. Davies believed it contained a "little too much self-justifying about Paul's contributions."[145] Doggett concurred. "Here was all the evidence to prove the point, but presented in such a defensive way that it begged criticism from those who felt that he ought to let history run its course and the facts speak for themselves."[146] With the publication of *Many Years from Now*, McCartney produced his strongest piece of evidence that disputed previous versions of Beatles history that he believed treated him unfairly. Combined with the primary sources unearthed by Lewisohn, *The Beatles Anthology*, *Revolution in the Head* and favorable reviews for his 1997 album "Flaming Pie," McCartney's reputation was on the upswing. In January 1998, *The Telegraph* noted how "after decades of critical abuse,"[147] the narrative around him was shifting.

A few months later, McCartney became an object of almost universal public sympathy when Linda McCartney, his wife of 29 years, died of breast cancer (the same disease that had caused his mother's death when he was 14). Over the decades public opinion towards Linda McCartney had gradually improved,[148] encouraged in part by her evident skills as a mother and her enduring and affectionate relationship with her husband. By the time of her death, the McCartney marriage was considered the "gold standard" of rock marriages for its longevity and fidelity. Decades later, *Life* described it as "perhaps the greatest and most acclaimed (justly acclaimed!) marriage in rock 'n' roll history."[149]

For a period following his wife's death McCartney was unable, for the first time in his life, to maintain his emotionally controlled public image. During a 1982 interview, McCartney explained how his reserve with the press was part of his personality. "Someone like me, I cover up what's wrong. I'm just not the kind of character who could admit everything that's wrong."[150] This pain was too great to cover up. Grief visibly aged him. McCartney admitted pursuing professional counseling. He wept constantly, including in interviews, and expressed disbelief that he could go on without his wife. "How am I still here? How am I talking, eating? I just am."[151]

Both Lennon and McCartney lost their mothers as teenagers. But the death of Mary McCartney and its impact on her son's life seemed to resonate less with many Beatles writers who devoted more attention and analysis to Lennon's identical tragedy. Davies acknowledged this perception in *The Beatles Lyrics*: "The characters of John and Paul are forever being contrasted, with Paul typified as the happy, cheerful, optimistic one and John the tortured soul thanks to his troubled background. But Paul had his own traumas, most notably the loss of his mother at a young age."[152] Some Beatles writers opined that because Lennon's grief was more vocal, it was therefore greater: "The emotional wounds appeared to be more painful and enduring for John."[153] In 1993 Cleave described McCartney's life at the time as one that "lacked angst."[154] Now the death of the woman Martin described as not only McCartney's love "but also the best friend he ever had"[155] imbued the musician's image with a *gravitas* it previously lacked.[156]

Resisting the New Narrative

In *The Great War in History*, Jay Winter and Antoine Prost emphasize the necessity of incorporating new sources in historical writing. Both applauded the willingness of post–World War I French researchers to accept new information as it was revealed, even when it undermined their already written theses. The initial French historians of the Great War "retained a deep sense of precariousness of their own conclusions and of the vital necessity of continuing vigilance: Not all documents were published; not all archives were open; and new documentation could transform what historians had previously stated."[157] Their willingness to accept new information and use it to revise their interpretations and conclusions demonstrated their objectivity, one of the essential elements in creating legitimate history.

In the wake of the Lewisohn narrative's new influx of information some Beatles writers displayed, in Winter's terms, "continuing vigilance" regarding the transformation of the band's history. Others did not. The primary sources provided by Lewisohn and Sulpy, retrospective accounts from Martin and McCartney, and new interpretations of the band's music and dynamic by Hertsgaard and MacDonald continued to power the shift away from previous interpretations. *Rolling Stone's* influence and readership waned while new magazines including British rock journals *Q* and *Mojo* emerged as influential and more impartial publications on classic rock and the Beatles. Meanwhile *The Beatles Anthology* introduced younger generations, freed from the breakup-era politics and bitterness, to the group's music and story.

However, not all authorities agreed with the emerging Orthodoxy. In spite of the new evidence, some chose not to revise their previous interpretations. Norman continued to issue re-editions of *Shout!* that ignored many of McCartney's statements in *Many Years from Now* as well as the evidence provided by Lewisohn in *The Complete Beatles Recording Sessions*. In his 1998 book *Grown Up All Wrong*, rock critic Robert Christgau again relayed his verdict on both major debates in Beatles history, declaring that the band broke up because "three of them believed they were geniuses and only one of them was."[158] Ian MacDonald argued that Alan Kozinn's 1995 work *The Beatles: 20th Century Composers*, also pushed a pro-Lennon narrative, citing as evidence the book's cover, which put Lennon out front, McCartney on the back, and eliminated Harrison and Starr. McDonald's reading of the cover's significance may be overblown. However, *The Beatles Bibliography* denounce Kozinn's work as "yet another tired, biased volume."[159]

Following the breakup Harrison and McCartney had at times publicly and legally sparred, but these instances lessened prior to *Anthology* and ceased after Linda McCartney's death. The primary conflict for control of the Beatles story continued to be waged between McCartney and Ono and Beatles writers who sided with one or the other. When relations between the two camps achieved a level of personal détente, such as during *Anthology*, silence was their most generous public offering. According to Norman, Ono "made it clear" to him during a 1995 meeting that "the reconciliation with Paul had been for the sake of business only and that there was still bitterness between them."[160] McCartney's depiction of her in *Many Years from Now* could hardly have thrilled Ono; nor did his continuous requests and occasional attempts to reverse the Lennon/McCartney name credit to McCartney/Lennon on the songs that he had solely or primarily authored. In December 1997 Ono gave an interview to the BBC in which she described Lennon as the group's visionary and McCartney as its organizer, casting him as the inferior Salieri to Lennon's Mozart.[161] The press, which avidly reported any disputes between the two, regarded it as a re-opening of hostilities after their brief *Anthology*-era ceasefire.

Ono responded to McCartney's efforts to revise the *Lennon Remembers* and *Shout!* narratives with two major projects. The first of these was the 30th anniversary edition of the release of *Lennon Remembers*, the 1970 *Rolling Stone* interview that many regarded as Lennon's post–Beatles manifesto. The second was a Rock and Roll Hall of Fame exhibition *Lennon: His Life and Works*, which appeared in 2000. In the 30th anniversary edition of the *Lennon Remembers* re-release, Ono endorsed Lennon's statements, urging people to read the interview and explaining the anger in it. "You need to experience John's words in the context of the times. In 1970 the whole world was against John, starting with his mates."[162] There is no acknowledgement in either the foreword from Ono or the two written by Wenner that the interview contains numerous inaccuracies or exaggerations, and they make no attempt to place Lennon's words in the larger context of the Beatles' breakup beyond providing motivation for his anger. Lennon's later lawsuit against Klein is not mentioned. Neither are Lennon's efforts to distance himself from some of the interview's statements. While labeling the Fab Four version of the story, with some legitimacy, as a "protected, beloved fairy tale," Wenner ignores the obvious agenda and partisanship of *Lennon Remembers*, repeatedly asserting the interview's status as truth. In violation of Bloch's methodology, which declares that testimony given under extreme emotion weakens its credibility, Wenner argues that Lennon's "busting and bitter"[163] anger at the time he gave the interview makes the musician's claims *more* credible. In the numerous reflections by Wenner and Ono on how essential the interview is to understanding Lennon and the Beatles, no contradictory or opposing perspectives are presented or even acknowledged. Thirty years earlier, *Rolling Stone*'s promotion of *Lennon Remembers* as the definitive view of the breakup was understandable if partisan. Continuing to do so in 2000, after an abundance of evidence had disproven many of its claims, was self-serving at best and misleading at worst. "An honest essay takes contrary evidence into account."[164]

By the end of the 20th century McCartney and Ono were exploring additional ways to promote their particular stories. In "Spinning the Historical Record," John Kimsey noted how the two expanded their conflict to "official" academic mediums such as museums and universities.[165] Such institutions serve as gatekeepers, wielding considerable influence over the formation of narratives. In both the United States and Japan Ono sponsored several museum exhibits, a form of popular history automatically imbued in the public eye with historical legitimacy. Although the historiography of public history such as museum exhibits has been neglected; "Professional historians have paid remarkably little attention to presentation and perception of history outside the classroom,"[166] the standards established by the American Historical Association provide a starting point. Like all forms of history, museum displays are subject to historical methods analysis, as choosing or ignoring items, as well as providing commentary on them "implies interpretive judgments about cause and effect, perspective, significance and meaning."[167]

In 2000 Ono and Wenner collaborated on *Lennon: His Life and Work*, a Rock and Roll Hall of Fame exhibit providing Ono's view of her late husband's legacy. Despite its presence at the preeminent American rock and roll museum, the exhibit failed to meet three of the American Historical Association's four key standards. In Kimsey's analysis, he explained how the exhibit's artifacts, their presentations and the accompanying commentary supported several major themes of the *Lennon Remembers* narrative. First, the exhibit "confirms Lennon's status as an icon and martyr," refuses to look at the musician's life and work objectively and portrays him as "a saint or a messiah."[168] This is the exhibit's first flaw. The American Historical Association warns museums against promoting hagiography: "Attempts to impose an uncritical point of view, however widely shared, are inimical to open and rational discussion."[169] Kimsey describes the exhibit as "rewriting the conventional narrative" by indicating that Lennon's solo work surpasses his Beatles songwriting.[170] This is done by celebrating Lennon's artistic and personal partnership with Ono while diminishing the work he created with McCartney in the Beatles. Not only does the exhibit downgrade McCartney from "Lennon's greatest collaborator" to a "relatively marginal figure," it also presents him as Lennon's "inauthentic other."[171] *Lennon: His Life and Work*, depicts McCartney as an impediment to Lennon's artistry and personal growth. Despite Kimsey's note that there is almost universal critical agreement that Lennon's Beatles work is superior to his solo material, the exhibit ignores this view. Its promotion of this one-sided version indicates that *Lennon: His Life and Work* was not subjected to "rigorous peer review,"[172] the first major requirement for any legitimate museum exhibit.

The methods the exhibit uses to elevate Lennon's time with Ono include providing far more artifacts about Lennon's post–Beatles life (54) than his Beatles years, (18) downplaying the latter's importance. Much of Lennon's Beatles work, including the misogynistic "Run for Your Life," is labeled as "inauthentic," absolving Lennon of responsibility for writing the song's lyrics. In contrast the artistry Lennon created while with Ono is applauded for its honesty and depth. The minimal amount of attention devoted to the Beatles contains incomplete and ultimately misleading information. Lennon's contributions to some of McCartney's songs, such as "Drive My Car," are detailed, but the exhibit displays no reciprocity; there is no mention of McCartney's contributions to Lennon's songs, even those on display, including "In My Life" and "Tomorrow Never Knows." "The exhibit identifies 'In My Life' as purely a Lennon composition, which is either somewhat wrong or very wrong."[173] In another glaring omission, McCartney is identified as instigating the breakup in April 1970: There is no admission that Lennon left the band months earlier. Both of these omissions (the failures to acknowledge McCartney's contributions to Lennon's work and Lennon's September 1969 departure from the band) violate the fourth standard for museum exhibits. "When an exhibit addresses a controversial subject, it should acknowledge the existence of competing points of view."[174] Kimsey identifies this error: "The problem lies in the exhibition's failure to acknowledge that it is propagating a particular view—and a controversial one at that."[175]

Lennon: His Life and Work also illustrates the complexities posed by sponsorship, and how sponsorship can influence an exhibit's contents and context. While Ono donated the exhibit's pieces, Kimsey criticizes the museum for not "prominently" revealing her sponsorship or explaining that the display offers only Ono's version of Lennon's life and artistry. Ono and Wenner's involvement is only revealed on the final page of the exhibit's 176 page catalog.[176] This failure to openly reveal Ono as the source behind the exhibit's artifacts violates the third A.H.A. standard: "At the outset of the museum process, museums should identify stakeholders in any exhibit."[177]

Kimsey noted how *Lennon: His Life and Work* was Ono's project, and that its other main contributor was Wenner, a longtime advocate of Lennon and Ono's version of events.[178] The author speculated that Ono promoted the exhibit in an attempt at "damage control"[179] as a response to accounts such as Goldman's *The Lives of John Lennon*, Green's *Dakota Days*, Pang's accounts.[180] Ultimately, he concludes that *Lennon: His Life and Work* fails as an accurate account of public memory, John Lennon, or Beatles history. "The exhibit relies on dubious omissions, questionable emphases, and unexamined binaries such as authenticity/artifice."[181]

The primary methodological weakness of all these works (the revised editions of *Shout!*, the re-issue of *Lennon Remembers*, *Lennon: His Life and Work*) is their failure to acknowledge primary sources providing contradictory evidence and secondary sources with differing interpretations. In *A Short Guide to Writing About History*, Marius stresses how essential such acknowledgement is. "Different historians interpret the same facts in very different ways ... you must take into account views that oppose your own."[182] The introduction of new facts into a historical narrative demands reciprocity. First, it requires verification from those who present the evidence. "Newly discovered evidence has to be compared with what's already known."[183] In turn, once the evidence has been authenticated, its existence *must be acknowledged*. If the newly discovered sources support previous evidence, it strengthens their legitimacy and reinforces the prevailing narrative. If the new sources contradict previous evidence, the two opposing sources are subjected to source analysis. If analysis fails to prove that one source is more credible than the other, it is the writer's responsibility to provide readers both pieces of evidence, allowing them to weigh their relative credibility.

The conflicting interpretations between those writers who incorporated the new information and those who did not widened Beatles historiography's pre-existing split. This is evident in both the 2002 and 2005 revised editions of Norman's *Shout!*, and in the revised edition of MacDonald's *Revolution in the Head*. Both books ranked as essential works in spite of their starkly different interpretations. In later editions of *Revolution in the Head*, MacDonald cited *Many Years from Now* as a primary inspiration for his revisions, described it as "one of the best books on the Beatles" and upgraded his description of the Lennon/McCartney partnership from "fictional" to "professional."[184] As in the original edition, MacDonald granted more credibility to McCartney's version of events. He justifies this by arguing that, by 1980, Lennon had retreated from many of his *Lennon Remembers* era statements and that Lennon had proven himself guilty of "misrepresentation" on songwriting matters with his claims that he authored McCartney's songs "Two of

Us" and "Eleanor Rigby."[185] While conceding McCartney's "freedom to say what he likes in Lennon's absence," and acknowledging that McCartney was "generally as prone to self-justification as Lennon was," MacDonald found McCartney's version "closer to the truth."[186] By acknowledging the differing versions and offering his reasoning for choosing one source over the other, MacDonald's work demonstrates objectivity and source analysis.

Norman takes the opposite approach. He cites *Many Years from Now* as one of the sources utilized in his revised editions of *Shout!* but largely ignores McCartney's version of events as well as much of the evidence produced by Sulpy and Lewisohn. He refuses to acknowledge McCartney's contributions to such songs as "Tomorrow Never Knows" and "Lucy in the Sky with Diamonds." Norman also continues to blame Harrison's departure during the "Get Back" sessions solely on McCartney.[187] In the epilogue, Norman discusses McCartney's efforts to revise the popular perception of him as the conventional tunesmith and Lennon as the experimental artist: "Every interview he gives fulminates against this gross misconception."[188] Meanwhile, he fails to mention how his own admittedly "unfair" portrayal of McCartney solidified and perpetuated this errant view. At this point, Norman makes no attempt to analyze McCartney's account as a counterweight to Lennon's, or, in most cases, to even acknowledge its existence.

The Death of George Harrison

In her 1966 profile of Harrison, Cleave argued that the youngest and most thoughtful Beatle was also its most overlooked member. This tendency to downplay Harrison's role and musical contributions began under the official narrative and extended into every successive version. There are numerous reasons for this. With the brief exception of the period surrounding *Abbey Road* and his magnum opus *All Things Must Pass*, critics never held Harrison's songwriting in the same esteem they did Lennon and McCartney's. The tendency of both the *Lennon Remembers* and *Shout!* narratives to proclaim Lennon as the band's sole genius further marginalized Harrison's contributions: attributing the lion's share of the Beatles brilliance to Lennon left less for McCartney, Harrison and Starr to claim. Harrison gave fewer interviews than Lennon during the breakup period and retreated from the public eye after his band mate was killed. Unlike McCartney, Harrison rarely toured after the Beatles disbanded. Many of Harrison's interviews reinforced the impression that he disdained discussing the Beatles era. His autobiography *I Me Mine* devoted little attention to that period of his life, and Harrison never produced a major work of self-justification the way Lennon did with *Lennon Remembers* and McCartney did in *Many Years from Now.*

Harrison's role was also marginalized in much Beatles scholarship, in part because both major debates revolved around Lennon and McCartney. Musicological evaluations such as Meller's *Twilight of the Gods* either omitted Harrison's songwriting or, as in MacDonald's *Revolution in the Head,* found most of it wanting. In the original edition of *Shout!* virtually every description of Harrison, either as a person or a musician, was negative, and Norman's marginal attention to how songs were crafted in the studio meant that many of Harrison's musical contributions, guitar solos, and suggestions went unrecognized. *Many Years from Now's* focus on the Lennon/McCartney relationship sidelined the other two Beatles: Doggett described Harrison as "the person with the strongest claim to feeling diminished"[189] by McCartney's book. In his latter memoir, *Summer of Love,* Martin both apologized for and defended his tendency to overlook Harrison's songwriting: "Being a very pragmatic person, I tended to go with the folks who were delivering the goods."[190]

This trend began to reverse, to an extent, under the Lewisohn narrative. *The Complete Beatles Recording Sessions* proved that Harrison had made essential contributions to some of the Beatles finest works. The tapes demonstrate that songs which had been written either by Lennon, McCartney or both still bear Harrison's vital musical input. In his 2003 article examining Harrison's role, David Simons argues that bootlegs and *The Beatles Anthology* also contributed, supporting the idea that Harrison "had more to do with the making of the Beatles legacy than we've been led to believe."[191] *Anthology* was the first group biography since Davies' *The Beatles: The Authorized Biography* to grant Harrison (and Starr) equal attention with Lennon and McCartney, and Harrison's *Anthology* video interviews provide a wry, necessary counterpoint to McCartney's version of events. Harrison's 1971 Concert for Bangladesh spurred numerous imitations, most famously Live Aid in 1985, and his reputation as a lead guitarist continued to grow. MacDonald described him as "a role model for student lead guitarists."[192] Simons detailed Harrison's musical contributions to the Beatles, including "adding simple guitar counterpoint ... echoing melody lines ... and crafting guitar hooks from scratch.... Harrison crafted intros, fills and lead lines that were nearly as hooky as the songs themselves."[193] McCartney offered a specific (and heretofore unknown) example in *Living in the Material World,* Martin Scorsee's 2011 documentary of Harrison. McCartney credited Harrison with creating the guitar riff on McCartney's classic song "And I Love Her," declaring that the riff "made the song."[194] Such examples gradually increased awareness of Harrison's overlooked but indelible and transformative imprint on Beatles music.

In 1999, in a horrific echo of Lennon's assassination, a deranged man broke into Harrison's house during the middle of the night and attacked him with a knife, puncturing his lung. Harrison survived thanks to the intervention of his wife, Olivia, who beat the assailant over the head with a poker until police arrived. The intruder, Michael Abram, later testified he was convinced that the Beatles were witches and that God instructed him to kill Harrison, who Abram believed had possessed him. (Abram was found not guilty by reason of insanity, although he was committed to psychiatric care.)[195] Two years earlier Harrison had discovered a cancerous tumor in his neck which received treatment, but his health waned after the attack, and Harrison died of cancer in late November 2001. The musician's death made worldwide news; it was the first event since the September 11, 2001, terrorist attacks to pre-empt television coverage of the "War on Terror." Headlines across the globe mourned the man his obituaries named the "quiet," "reluctant" "spiritual" "thoughtful" and occasionally "bitter" Beatle. Virtually all these remembrances noted both Harrison's philanthropic efforts and his astonishing growth as a songwriter.

Most writers celebrated Harrison's life and career and acknowledged his essential role. "His contribution to the overall sound of the Beatles music was, as their lead guitarist, massive."[196] Yet both in obituaries at the time and in later retrospectives of his life, he still ranked behind the "two larger than life figures"[197] of Lennon and McCartney. In 2001, Paul Du Noyer described Harrison's role: "He was a fine and versatile guitar player, but Harrison was inevitably overshadowed by the songwriting brilliance of Lennon and McCartney. Nor could he match them for sheer force of personality."[198] *The Guardian* agreed: "Off to the side in the Beatles, you could always feel George Harrison sensing his exclusion from the hot center where the geniuses held court."[199] Where Harrison's joining the band was viewed as a pivotal point, even his biographies acknowledged that "the big cosmic moment"[200] of Beatles history remained Lennon's first meeting with McCartney.

Harrison's musical reputation improved during the Lewisohn narrative and continued to do so after his death. The amount of attention Beatles writers paid him increased, as the new post–Lewisohn group biographies such as Spitz's *The Beatles: The Biography* and Gould's *Can't Buy Me Love* noted Harrison's contributions. Biographies of the man provided a more nuanced portrait, as writers attempted to reconcile the duality of Harrison's spiritual pursuits and ideals, which contrasted with his occasional less-than ideal behavior. In *Living in the Material World*, Starr acknowledged Harrison's contradictory character: "George had two very incredible personalities. He had the big bag of love, bag of beads personality, and the bag of anger. He was very black and white."[201]

New musical evaluations such as *All the Songs* were far more favorable to Harrison's songwriting than previous interpretations. (Where MacDonald found one of Harrison's signature works, "While My Guitar Gently Weeps," "tiresome," *All the Songs* regarded it as "magnificent" and argued "it made it possible for George to establish his status as a writer on par with John and Paul.")[202] This necessary effort to expand Beatles historiography beyond its narrow Lennon/McCartney focus continued with *Tune In*'s publication. In the book Lewisohn acknowledged that Harrison's role in crafting Beatles music had been unfairly overlooked during the official era and beyond: "In the natural scheme of things, whenever they brought a song to the group, everyone would chip in with suggestions, George in particular contributing solos and other ideas, and this would continue—but he'd receive no credit or reward for it."[203] At the same time, Lewisohn explained why, despite the increased attention, the Beatles' lead guitarist (and drummer) remained somewhat peripheral figures. "George and Ringo were essential to the Beatles but John and Paul drove the bus and wrote the catalog, and theirs is an especially fascinating tale ... their determination, their egos, and their creative rivalry made them the greatest songwriters of the age."[204]

The Post-Anthology Group Biographies

Prompted by the original information revealed in *The Beatles Anthology* and previously undiscovered sources, including Lewisohn's research, new Beatles biographies emerged in the first decade of the 21st century. In 2005, rock and roll journalist Bob Spitz published his mammoth *The Beatles: The Biography*, which was followed the next year by Jonathan Gould's part biography, part musicological analysis, part cultural history *Can't Buy Me Love*. With the exception of Hertsgaard's 1995 work *A Day in the Life*[205] they were the first new, major biographies to appear since 1981's *Shout!* Their publication demonstrates a growing effort to challenge *Shout's* definitive status.

Spitz's ambition was to re-interpret and re-evaluate, to research and write about the Beatles story as if there had never been a book about them before. Gould's was to explore the Beatles story and examine their music in the context of their times. While Spitz's work contained far more original research, Gould's ultimately proved more popular and credible among knowledgeable readers. One of the reasons Spitz's work failed to receive acclaim in the Beatles community was its timing. Published in 2005, *The Beatles: The Biography* was the first group biography of the Internet age. The few years that separated the book edition of *Anthology* from Spitz's work witnessed the exponential growth and popularity of the Internet. Beatles discussions and debates moved from fan conventions and magazines to internet forums and websites. Millions of fans, in addition to journalists and professional book reviewers, now scrutinized every new work. Any errors were quickly exposed but not so quickly forgiven. After *Daytrippin,'* (a Beatles magazine and website) documented a large number of inaccuracies in Spitz's work, ranging from minor (Spitz claimed "Run for Your Life" was one of the last songs recorded for *Rubber Soul,* when it was the first) to lazy (numerous incorrectly captioned pictures) the reputation of *The Beatles: The Biography* never recovered among devoted fans.[206]

Despite this, Spitz's biography sold well and received good reviews from newspapers such as *The Washington Post* and *The New York Times.* Spitz promoted the book by emphasizing its original research and the cooperation of key figures, including McCartney and Harrison.[207] Spitz spent six years on research and writing, and declared that he had interviewed 650 people, some of whom previous biographers had overlooked. Another resource Spitz utilized was the taped interviews Goldman used in *The Lives of John Lennon.* These interviews appear to have shaped Spitz's pervasively negative view of both Ono and the Lennon/Ono relationship. Almost every reference to Ono is critical; Spitz refers to Ono's "unspeakable presence" in the studio, criticizes Lennon's "zombielike regard"[208] for her, and emphasizes the couple's unhealthy drug use.

The credibility of Spitz's work is weakened by one of the same methodological errors seen in *Shout!* Like Norman's work, *The Beatles: The Biography* lacks citations. Coupled with Spitz's tendency for editorializing and inserting his own opinion into the thoughts of historical figures, this makes it impossible for the reader to separate verified facts, unverified testimony, and personal interpretation. His bias against Ono and his editorializing are evident in his dramatic rendition of Ono's thoughts regarding McCartney in 1968 and 1969. "No matter how Yoko might deny it, Paul remained her lone nemesis, her obstacle to claiming complete control of John. She would destroy him. She had to."[209]

Authorial interpretation in itself is not a methodological error: Historians from Bloch to Gaddis all acknowledge that interpretation is a necessary element in historical writing. However, legitimate history clearly distinguishes between proven facts, or "the outside of an event," with authorial interpretation, or "the inside of the event." Gaddis labels the "outside of the event" as "everything belonging to it which can be described in terms of bodies and their movements." As Bloch notes, "no valid objection will ever be raised to the fact that Caesar defeated Pompey."[210] He then identifies the inside of the event, that "which can only be described in terms of thought."[211] The outside of events are widely regarded as fact. It is the inside of events—the biographer's account of Caesar's *thoughts* as he triumphs over Pompey—that are subjective, and must be clearly distinguishable either from their source material or as authorial interpretation, rather than imposed as the historical subject's thoughts.

As a musician and a writer, Spitz's musical analysis of the group's catalog is written with authority and depth and, like MacDonald, owes a significant debt to Lewisohn's scholarship. His evaluation of the band's music and the Lennon/McCartney partnership reinforced the emerging interpretation that both men were equally essential in creating the band's genius. However, Spitz flatly rejects other elements of McCartney's version of the band's story. *The Beatles: The Biography* presents perhaps the most negative evaluation of the men's friendship since Goldman's *The Lives of John Lennon*. According to Spitz, Lennon's jealousy and McCartney's manipulative personality began to erode their close friendship shortly after Julia Lennon's death. "Even then, there was great jealousy there. He was all too aware of Paul's talent and wanted to be as good and grand himself.... He wasn't about the let somebody like Paul McCartney pull his strings."[212] McCartney's willingness in 1962 to trade in the Beatles trademark leather stage outfits for more commercially appealing suits is identified as the first irreparable schism between the two.[213] The conflicts resulting from their contradictory personalities only widened: by the time of 1967's *Sgt. Pepper's Lonely Hearts Club Band* "all intimacy had disappeared from their relationship."[214] In contrast to *Shout!*, Spitz clearly identifies Ono's presence and Lennon's obsession with her as undermining the band, and his portrayal of Klein is unrelentingly critical. However, he condemns McCartney's behavior as well and argues that, by the time of *Abbey Road*, relations between McCartney, Harrison and Lennon had degenerated to the point where the latter two could not bear to be in the same room with "clever," "manipulative," "controlling Paul."[215]

One of the *The Beatles: The Biography's* key strengths is Spitz's refusal to engage in favoritism; the work strives to maintain the author's balance despite his tendency towards presenting the most negative interpretation on "the inside of the event" as possible. By declining to champion a particular Beatle, Spitz's work demonstrates writers' emerging tendency to present more balanced interpretations of the group's story.

Spitz's work was followed the next year by Gould's *Can't Buy Me Love*. Initially overshadowed by *The Beatles: The Biography*, Gould's work quickly gained a reputation as one of the group's best biographies: In its review *The Guardian* anointed it "an essential addition to Beatles literature."[216] Researched and written over a period of 20 years, *Can't Buy Me Love* approaches the band's story from new angles. The work is part biography, part musicological analysis and part social history. *Shout!* and *The Beatles: The Biography* had both mentioned various social and cultural movements of the Beatles era, but Gould's analysis was far more in depth, discussing everything from mod fashion trends to Kennedy's assassination to the Profumo Affair in comprehensive detail . As a project two decades in the making,[217] *Can't Buy Me Love* is one of the most beautifully written books in Beatles historiography. It also provides the most thorough, detailed analysis of placing the band in the context of its time and offers some of the most informed and detailed musicological analysis of their catalog.

Gould's work was far more interpretive than Spitz's. Drawing heavily from already available primary and secondary sources, *Can't Buy Me Love* provides virtually no new interviews but does include chapter endnotes detailing source material. By citing sources, Gould distinguishes authorial opinion and interpretation from proven fact. Like Spitz, Gould refuses to champion a favorite Beatle and devotes more attention to and demonstrates greater respect for Harrison and Starr's personalities and musicianship than either man received in *Shout!*.[218] Like Lewisohn, Hertsgaard, Spitz, and MacDonald, Gould's musicological analysis disputes the *Lennon Remembers* and *Shout!* descriptions of Lennon as the band's sole genius. Instead, his evaluation emphasizes how both Lennon and McCartney complemented each other as songwriters and contributed to each other's work.

> (John) often got stuck for a line or a chord, and he had particular difficulty coming up with middles and endings. Paul was adept at hearing the musical possibilities suggested by John's bits, and he was often able to suggest a chord, a line, a transition, a counter melody or, on several memorable occasions, an entire section that meshed with Lennon's work. McCartney's problem was the opposite of Lennon's. Chords and melodies flowed out of him so easily that his facility as a musician often outstripped his facility as lyricist. John's role had always been to get Paul to focus more intently on the language and sense of his songs, and to temper his self-acknowledged tendency toward the trite and sentimental.[219]

Both *The Beatles: The Biography* and *Can't Buy Me Love* are the products of writers and musicians. This demonstrates a significant shift in the qualifications of those biographers who analyzed the band's music, providing the element of authorial expertise which Startt identified as a component of source analysis. Their informed appraisal allows for more comprehensive evaluation and, according to historical methods, grants their musicological analysis more credibility. Gould's stance on Beatles historiography's other great debate attributed the split to a number of reasons but refrained from pinning blame on any one individual or event. Both Ono and Klein are identified as contributors, widening divisions that emerged following Epstein's death, but Gould refrains from demonizing either figure. Where Spitz downplayed the Lennon-McCartney friendship, Gould regarded it as the origin of the Beatles story and the core of their artistry.[220]

The key differences between Spitz's *The Beatles: The Biography* and Gould's *Can't Buy Me Love* result from their contrasting views on the "inside of the events," Spitz's numerous factual errors, and Gould's use of documentation. This documentation allows the reader to identify and analyze source material and differentiate between authorial opinion and evidence. It also allows the reader to analyze what type of sources the author used to draw conclusions, and ask vital questions. Does the author overly rely on a single source to present a one-sided view of an event or individual? Did contemporaneous testimony receive more credibility than retrospective accounts? Did the work differentiate between different sources' credibility, or accept information unquestioningly? Did the author relate hearsay or unverified testimony as fact? By documenting his sources, Gould provided readers with the information to answer these questions.

Despite their differences in authorial interpretation, both disputed the accepted wisdom of the two previous narratives. While acknowledging that McCartney's behavior and actions contributed to the tensions leading to the breakup, neither author identified him as the sole or primary cause. In addition, both clearly concurred with McCartney's repeated declaration that he and Lennon were equally essential in crafting the Beatles catalog. Academic explorations of the Beatles written during the same time period, including *The Cambridge Companion to the Beatles* (2009) and *Reading the Beatles: Cultural Studies, Literary Criticism, and the Fab Four* (2006) largely agreed with Spitz's and Gould's conclusions. All these works, as well as Norman's considerable revisions in his 2008 biography of Lennon, demonstrate continued momentum away from the previous Orthodoxy.

Revising the story of the Beatles Breakup: You Never Give Me Your Money *and* Rolling Stone

One of the most influential books in all Beatles historiography, Peter Doggett's *You Never Give Me Your Money* (2009) details the band's breakup and its legal, financial, artistic and personal aftermath. The book's owes its importance in part to its concentration on one of the group's most debated but least studied eras: its dissolution. Doggett's book was the first major work to attempt to explain the band's split since Peter McCabe and Robert Schoenfeld's 1972 effort, *Apple to the Core*. While Doggett cites *Apple to the Core* in his bibliography, *You Never Give Me Your Money* is by far the superior account.

The only significant methodological flaw in *You Never Give Me Your Money* is Doggett's occasional tendency to relay unverified testimony as fact without acknowledging its unverified status.[221] (Doggett is not alone in committing this error: this tendency is widespread throughout Beatles history.) In every other respect his account ranks among the best researched, well documented, most impartial, and essential works in Beatles historiography. Doggett's impartiality is crucial. Chronicling the most divisive period in Beatles history—the breakup—the author refuses to choose between Lennon or McCartney. Moral judgments are distributed equally. No Beatle is elevated at the expense of another. Facts are not ignored or selected in order to fit a pre-determined thesis. Both the sources he provides on Ono and his interpretation of her are balanced, and Klein is not vilified. Doggett also emphasizes the credibility of contemporaneous interviews over retrospective and at times revisionist accounts. While the relations between Lennon and McCartney (and later, McCartney and Ono) predominate throughout the book, Harrison and Starr's lives also receive considerable research, attention and analysis. The author provides chapter endnotes in which he cites his sources; therefore Doggett's interpretations are distinguished clearly from the evidence he provides. And unlike most Beatles writers he applies source analysis, noting both authorial agenda and eyewitness state of mind when discussing interviews such as *Lennon Remembers*.

One of the great strengths of *You Never Give Me Your Money* is Doggett's analysis of the Beatles' personalities: They are presented with far greater depth than some previous works, which reduced each man to little more than their *A Hard Day's Night* caricatures. Because most of the subject matter Doggett covers (including numerous lawsuits, public spats, and financial disputes) involves arguments among the Fab Four and Ono, much of the book is negative. More than any other Beatles biography, *You Never Give Me Your Money* reveals how the weight of the Beatles legacy and the band's split burdened its members financially, musically, and emotionally for the rest of their lives. However, Doggett's moral judgments are balanced, a requirement sorely lacking in much of Beatles history. Starr, so often simplified as "the amiable mediocrity"[222] of the band, receives both thoughtful research and analysis. Starr's emotional struggles with the Beatles breakup, his divorce, music and alcoholism are chronicled with an informed and understanding interpretation. Harrison's musical talents are not ignored and the man's lifelong efforts to attain greater spirituality are recounted with respect and honesty. Doggett notes both the maturity of the man's statements during the breakup-era press wars—"Harrison retained a sense of objectivity ... he was now the group's wisest spokesman"[223]—and the instances when he fell short of his own ideals: "Friends reported he often showed signs of obsession with perceived slights from the Beatles era."[224] While Doggett does not shy from discussing Lennon's unstable personality, his account differs from Goldman's in that he refuses to gloat over Lennon's struggles. McCartney attracts both Doggett's criticism and defense. The author describes the musician's refusal to attend the 1988 induction of the Beatles into the Rock and Roll Hall of Fame as "the action of a petulant child" and labels some of his efforts to revise Beatles history as "graceless." At the same time, Doggett acknowledges the legitimacy of McCartney's grievances. "For too long he had been caricatured as the 'straight' Beatle (not least by Lennon). The evidence supported him; he had been the instigator of the Beatles' forays into experimental music and the early champion of the psychedelic underground."[225]

Doggett's evidence and interpretations provide a view of Lennon considerably at odds with his *Shout!* era image. *You Never Give Me Your Money* continues the gradual trend to attempt to understand the link between Lennon's mental state and his words and actions. During the Lewisohn narrative, authorial acknowledgement of Lennon's alleged psychological issues increased. Writers began using terms such as "emotional instability," "bi-polar muse" and "depressive" to describe his mindset. In his memoirs, Emerick notes Lennon's volatile mood swings and describes him during the first White Album session as "almost psychotic."[226] Bramwell, a longtime witness to both Lennon's public and private life, was blunt. "George, Ringo and especially Paul were normal lads, but there is no doubt that John was different. He was a genius but nuts."[227] When comparing Lennon and McCartney in *Tune In's*, introduction, Lewisohn describes McCartney as "mentally strong"[228] but pointedly does not apply the same term to Lennon. Harrison acknowledged the issue in *Anthology*: "I think we didn't really realize the extent to which John was screwed up," and argues it was not until 1970/71 that "I realized he was even more screwed up than I thought."[229] MacDonald agreed with Shotton and McCartney's descriptions of Lennon's precarious mental state following his LSD use. In his revised edition of *Revolution in the Head*, the author declared that by spring 1968 "Lennon was a mental wreck struggling to stitch himself back together."[230] Doggett concurred, describing Lennon at the time of his 1968 "Jesus Christ" announcement as "teetering between insanity and eccentricity"[231] and maintained that, throughout 1971, "there was a sense that Lennon's emotions were running out of control."[232]

Doggett's analysis of the breakup utilizes Sulpy and Schwegardt's analysis of the "Get Back" transcripts, and corresponds with many of the conclusions reached by Hertsgaard, Gould, MacDonald and Spitz. *You Never Give Me Your Money* identifies numerous reasons for the band's split. Musical and ideological differences, monetary disputes, the strains caused by Ono, Eastman and Klein, and drug use, among other causes, are all identified. Using Brown's accounts of numerous business meetings, the "Get Back" transcripts, and hundreds of public and private interviews, Doggett argues that, while Klein was a key factor, there is plenty of responsibility for the split to go around. Doggett acknowledges that McCartney's public statements officially revealed the break and made it almost impossible to achieve any reconciliation, but maintains that he did not want the dissolution and was only finalizing what had already been set in motion.[233] Lennon's September 1969 announcement that he was leaving the group and his, Klein, and Harrison's refusal to allow McCartney out of the contract forced, to a certain extent, the other man's hand.[234]

Doggett's research, sources and analysis established a new standard, and many Beatles writers accepted his major conclusions on the breakup as the new Orthodoxy. The most telling evidence of this is Mikal Gilmore's 2009 *Rolling Stone* cover story, "Why the Beatles Broke Up." Ever since December 1970, when Lennon sat down for his de-mythologizing interview with Wenner, *Rolling Stone* had promoted *Lennon Remembers* as *the* definitive version of the band's split. The magazine's 2000 re-release of the interview, coupled with Wenner's endorsement, demonstrates the publication's continuing support. However, only nine months after Doggett's work disproved the *Lennon Remembers* version of the breakup, *Rolling Stone* also denounced the previous Orthodoxy.

A major part of *Lennon Remembers* involved Lennon casting himself and Ono as the story's victims, but Gilmore disagreed. While arguing that no one was blameless, he condemned Lennon and Harrison's behavior, declaring "they treated McCartney shamefully in 1969 and unforgivably in 1970." Harrison and Lennon had complained repeatedly about McCartney's domination both in the studio and at Apple, particularly after Epstein's death, and McCartney's perfectionist and controlling tendencies were repeatedly identified as primary factors in the breakup. While acknowledging the legitimacy of their grievances, Gilmore balanced them out by also noting that neither Lennon nor Harrison ever offered any alternative vision for the band's post–Epstein future. As irritating as both men found McCartney's direction, the band might have split years earlier without it, and some of their final albums (*Magical Mystery Tour, The White Album, Let It Be* and *Abbey Road*) might never have been made.

More importantly, for the first time *Rolling Stone* identified Lennon and not McCartney as the driving force behind the rupture. "[Lennon's] caprices and rages had destroyed the band." According to Gilmore, Lennon's actions (hiring Klein, bringing Ono into the studio, giving producer Phil Spector the *Let It Be* tapes without informing McCartney) were deliberate attempts by Lennon to re-assert his position as the band's leader, actions which backfired when McCartney announced the split and instigated the lawsuit. "McCartney had simply been forced into an impossible situation by John Lennon, George Harrison, and Allen Klein." However, Gilmore and Doggett disagreed on two key points. The first concerned Lennon's intentions. Doggett argued that the Beatles broke up for numerous reasons, with the crucial division occurring between McCartney and the other three over Klein. According to Gilmore, Lennon never intended a permanent break. Instead Lennon, and to a lesser extent Harrison "'sabotaged'" the group from 1968 onward as a way to re-assert power over McCartney: their actions were an "attempt to shift the balance of power ... but they overplayed their hand."[235]

Despite these differences of interpretation both Doggett's and Gilmore's conclusions contradicted the *Lennon Remembers* and *Shout!* narratives by refusing to identify McCartney as the primary cause of the rupture. While they agreed on one debate topic, they split on the other. Doggett clearly regarded both Lennon and McCartney as equals, praising McCartney's "melodic gift" and arguing that Lennon's death left his former partner fighting "for the recognition that, rightfully, should already have been his."[236] Gilmore disagreed, declaring that Lennon's status as the Beatles "true genius" was "inarguable."[237] (This statement is methodologically flawed in that, by declaring his opinion "inarguable," Gilmore refuses to acknowledge the informed analyses of numerous musicians and musical experts including Alan Moore, Ian MacDonald, Mark Hertsgaard, Jonathan Gould, Wilfrid Mellers, William Mann, Ned Rorem, Bob Spitz, George Martin and Howard Goodall, among others, all of whom argue in favor of McCartney's genius).

Rolling Stone's refusal to overtly promote *Lennon Remembers* as the definitive version of the Beatles dissolution is a significant indication of the narrative's decline. Almost 40 years after *Lennon Remembers* de-mythologized the Fab Four story and promoted Lennon's version as the truth of music history's most famous breakup, the evidence and interpretations produced by Spitz, Lewisohn, Hertsgaard, Gould, Sulpy, Doggett and Gilmore established a new Orthodoxy.

The Influence of Favoritism on Memoirs

During this same period, several Beatles "insiders"—including their assistant Tony Bramwell, pressman Tony Barrow, and engineers Geoff Emerick and Ken Scott—provided memoirs of their time with the band. These sources demonstrate how personal preference influences the credibility and accuracy of memoirs, and how essential balance, or examining varying perspectives on an event or individual, is in establishing an accurate narrative.

A childhood friend of Harrison and McCartney, Bramwell was a key employee and friend, hired early on by Epstein. He accompanied the Beatles from Liverpool to London and witnessed many of the band's historic moments. In 2005 Bramwell published *Magical Mystery Tours*, an engaging but biased and self-serving memoir. Many of Bramwell's recollections contrast with the more critical account of the Beatles' personalities provided by Brown, another of Epstein's assistants, in *The Love You Make*. The major flaw concerning the accuracy of Bramwell's account is his omission of unpleasant facts that might reflect poorly on his friends, particularly Harrison and McCartney. He depicts Harrison's first wife, Pattie Boyd, as the sole cause of the couple's eventual split—"It's a shame she was such a flirt"—while failing to mention the damage caused by Harrison's numerous and occasionally flagrant infidelities.[238] Testimony provided during the official narrative, including *A Cellarful of Noise* and *The Beatles: The Authorized Biography* identified McCartney as the Beatle with whom Epstein had the most difficult relationship (and numerous other sources, including Brown, reinforce this). However, Bramwell declares that McCartney "never criticized Brian."[239] He also absolves both Harrison and McCartney for their disagreements during the *Let It Be* film by arguing that the tensions between them were caused by the irritant of Ono's presence.[240]

McCartney in particular receives Bramwell's praise and virtually none of his criticism. The author agrees with all McCartney's key points, arguing that the Lennon/McCartney partnership was one of musical equals,[241] that McCartney's *avant-garde* explorations pre-dated Lennon's, and that the two were very close friends until Ono's unreasonable demands forced them apart. Bramwell also obliquely criticizes Harrison and Starr for "blindly following John's lead"[242] in choosing Klein. The reason for Bramwell's one-sided portrait of McCartney is up for speculation. In addition to their friendship, Bramwell may have been motivated by efforts to maintain his position as a key insider. Brown's negative portrait had led to his exile from the Beatles circle. Bramwell, (who, if his portrayal of Ono is any indication, clearly does not maintain decent relations with her) may not have wished to alienate the financially and musically powerful McCartney with a more critical appraisal.

In contrast, Bramwell offers a scathing depiction of Ono. *Mojo* magazine noted the book's condemnation of her in its review: "The recent trend has been to regard Yoko as benign if a bit dotty.... But in Tony Bramwell's view she is everything the cynics suspected—a pseudo-artist, haughty and manipulative, who brought out the very worst in John Lennon."[243] Bramwell argues that, after failing to gain financial patronage from Epstein and McCartney, Ono pursued Lennon for more than a year prior to their official relationship,[244] that she introduced Lennon to heroin in an attempt to distance him from his friends; "She could not cope with the fact that John could love three other guys,"[245] and that her campaign for peace was hypocritical, given her imperious treatment of Apple employees and her wasteful spending on luxuries. He identifies her as the motivating factor pushing Lennon towards the breakup. His portrayal of Klein is almost as negative, describing him as "fat and grubby" and a "fraudster."[246] As in Brown's work, Epstein receives thorough attention from Bramwell, who depicts the Beatles manager with affection. However, he also notes Epstein's managerial mistakes, mood swings, insecurity and self-destructive tendencies.

Bramwell's work was followed the next year by the memoir of another "insider," Beatles P.R. man Tony Barrow. Less entertaining than Bramwell's (and less detailed, as Barrow was never as close to the Fab Four as Bramwell was) Barrow's *John, Paul George, Ringo and Me* nonetheless provides a balance to *Magical Mystery Tours,* if only by preferring a different Beatle. Where Bramwell's memoirs clearly favor McCartney, Barrow identifies Lennon as the Beatle to whom he was closest[247] and recalls Harrison with great affection and respect. The personal preferences Beatles insiders, from Brown to Bramwell to Barrow, display in their memoirs is one of the key factors any reader must account for when analyzing their credibility as sources. Accepting any one memoir as the definitive account lacks balance.

Another account that generated controversy thanks to its partisanship and minor factual errors were the memoirs of Geoff Emerick. Emerick had worked as the band's studio engineer on *Revolver* and all subsequent albums, with the exception of *Let It Be.* Credited with a number of technological breakthroughs during these sessions, Emerick was awarded two Grammys for his work with the Beatles. Martin acknowledged Emerick's contributions to the band's sound in both his books, *All You Need Is Ears* and *Summer of Love* and Lewisohn interviewed him for *The Complete Beatles Recording Sessions.* Like Martin, Emerick is considered a key eyewitness to and participant in helping craft the Beatles' sound in the studio.

In *Here, There and Everywhere,* Emerick agrees with many of Martin's descriptions and characterizations. Like Martin, he disagrees with the "four stereotypes"[248] of the Beatles characters popularized by *A Hard Day's Night.* Also like Martin, Emerick argues that Lennon clearly regarded Harrison as inferior, treating him "like a kid brother or even as a subordinate,"[249] and that

McCartney "actually seemed a bit embarrassed by Harrison's musical limi-tations."[250]Reinforcing two of McCartney's key platforms he identifies Lennon and McCartney's relationship as one between two peers each "equal in terms of talent and songwriting ability,"[251] and argues that their friendship was very close.[252] He also defends McCartney's efforts to take control of the band after Epstein's death, declaring that "between his drug use and unfocused mind," Lennon was incapable of keeping the Beatles together or providing them direction. "[Paul] kept the greatest band in the world going at a time when they could have easily crumpled. I reckon he deserves a lot of credit for that."[253]

Even though many of his observations agree with Martin's, Emerick's book provides (with the exception of *Lennon Remembers*) perhaps the most negative portrait of the Beatles producer. Emerick accuses Martin of ushering the engineers out of the studio when the producer knew he was going to be interviewed: "George always wanted the limelight to shine on him alone."[254] He also declares that Martin "never displayed the kind of leadership skills"[255] working with the Beatles required and states that, by the recording of *Abbey Road*, Lennon and Harrison "couldn't care less what George Martin thought."[256] Although Emerick maintains that Martin "seemed to have the closest relation-ship with Paul,"[257] an assessment with which Martin concurs in his memoirs, Emerick recounts a rare harsh disagreement between the two while recording *The White Album*. Martin had obliquely referenced this previously, but Emer-ick's account was far more detailed. When Martin offered a mild criticism of McCartney's vocals, McCartney's response—"Why don't you fucking come down here and sing it yourself?"[258]—convinced Emerick to quit the tense *White Album* sessions; he agreed to engineer *Abbey Road* after McCartney personally asked him to return. Emerick stresses how toxic the band was by this time, "No one wanted to be assigned to their sessions, despite the prestige,"[259] and disagrees with Martin's more optimistic account of the final state of the band's inter-personal relations. "By the end it's fair to say that the four Beatles hated one another, for a variety of reasons."[260]

Harrison is another figure that receives the brunt of Emerick's criticism. In *Summer of Love*, Martin declared that Emerick loved Harrison's music,[261] but *Here, There and Everywhere* provides the opposite impression. Emerick repeatedly criticizes Harrison's musicianship and songwriting and declares that everyone in the studio dreaded working on Harrison's songs.[262] His view of Harrison's personality is also critical. While acknowledging that Harrison could be "kind and generous" to other employees at EMI, with Emerick he was always "dour and humorless."[263] In addition, Emerick's work perpetuates the overall tendency to focus on Lennon and McCartney and minimize Harrison and Starr's contributions. He describes the lead guitarist and drummer as the band's "bottom tier" and declares "I always felt that the artist was John Lennon and Paul McCartney, not the Beatles."[264]

Emerick's characterization of Harrison provoked a public rebuttal from another Beatles engineer, Ken Scott. Their exchange illustrates one of the most important lessons in Beatles historiography, how personal preferences and friendships influence memories and memoirs, and therefore history. Where Emerick made no secret of his preference for and closer relationship with McCartney (noting in his book how McCartney served as the best man at his wedding) Scott was far closer to Harrison. Scott publicly described *Here, There and Everywhere* as a "'disappointment,'" criticized several factual inaccuracies, and argued that, prior to writing the book, Emerick had quizzed his fellow Beatles engineers for information to compensate for his own poor memory. Scott accused Emerick of only liking McCartney and condemned his portrayal of Harrison.[265] Emerick responded by arguing that Scott had seen an uncorrected proof of his manuscript and denied accusations of a "relentless tirade" against Harrison, arguing that he praised the man's musicianship various times and that his view of Harrison's personality was a matter of memory and opinion. Scott's rejoinder was honest and telling as well as a demonstration of how much personal opinion infused the memories of everyone involved: "I am biased. I was and still am very fond of George. To see him described the way he is on numerous pages makes me mad."[266]

Years later, in *From Abbey Road to Ziggy Stardust*, his own memoirs, Scott again rejected the harsh portrayal of Harrison: "George was one of the nicest and certainly one of the funniest people I have ever met in this business … to portray him as sour or negative or untalented as some have is so far from anything that I ever saw during my time with him."[267] Emerick's eyewitness account of how the Beatles worked in the studio differed from Scott's, particularly in their evaluation of Harrison's personality and musical skills.[268] Their testimonial differences illustrate the impact personal friendships have on how history is written. In *The Historian's Craft*, Bloch noted the ways friendship can influence eyewitness testimony. During his discussion of Marbot's fictitious heroism, Bloch noted how Pelet, one of Marbot's friends, had recounted Marbot's tale prior to the publication of Marbot's own memoirs. For Bloch, this demonstrated how friendships can tilt and/or result in borrowed and therefore inauthentic testimony. "As for Pelet, he did indeed write before Marbot; but he was his friend and, doubtless, he had often heard him recall his fictitious feats of valor."[269]

Given the abundance of Beatles memoirs, interviews, and biographies, it is virtually impossible to determine to what extent eyewitness recollection has been retrospectively influenced by other accounts. Various insiders, as well as reporters, also maintained closer friendships with or favored a specific Beatle, a factor which often lends a partisan element to their recollections and interpretations. These factors of favoritism and borrowed testimony in memoirs emphasize how essential balance (achieved by acknowledging contrary points of view) and source analysis (or determining the eyewitnesses credibility) is in producing an accurate historical account. Ultimately, the reader of any Beatles memoir should first ask one basic question: "Good historians ask themselves: 'Should I trust what this person is telling me?'"[270]

Cementing the Lewisohn Orthodoxy: Tune In

Fifty years after the name "the Beatles" first appeared in newspapers outside of Liverpool, Lennon, McCartney, Harrison and Starr's status as historical figures was unquestioned. The subject of hundreds of books and countless articles, the four men and the music they created together were regarded as an essential element to understanding the 20th century. "One of the strange things about the Beatles phenomenon is that the further we get from them, the bigger they become."[271] Countless "End of the Century" retrospectives and "Best of" lists crowned them rock and roll's undisputed greatest band. *Time* declared that Lennon's introduction to McCartney was one of the pivotal first meetings of the 20th century.[272] Even the most prestigious historical institutions in the world agreed that the Beatles belonged to the ages. Mere decades after Lennon and McCartney scribbled out their lyrics on the backs of envelopes and postcards, Davies donated some of these scraps of paper to the British Museum. They are now displayed in the same room with the most treasured documents in Britain's history, a few feet away from Tennyson, Shakespeare and the Magna Carta.

However, this universal agreement that the Beatles were important historical figures had not translated into accurate historical examination of their story. Beatles historiography had been dominated first by the band's members and later by journalists and musicologists, few of whom demonstrated the basic elements of objectivity and impartiality or met the required standards of documentation, verification and source analysis that create legitimate history. This was the paradox at the core of Beatles historiography. The story of one of the most important cultural forces of the 20th century had been repeatedly packaged and sold to millions of people as "'definitive'" and "'true'" in spite of the fact that many of these works failed to qualify as history.

In addition to Lewisohn's reference works, by the first decades of the

21st century Beatles writers such as Hertsgaard, Gould, and Doggett all produced works that contained the methodology that creates enduring history. However, a truly definitive biography of the Beatles still did not exist. Davies' authorized account suffered from its status as an official history; Norman's from his lack of documentation and admitted bias. Gould's work was highly interpretive and lacked original research; Spitz's suffered from factual errors and a failure to distinguish between his thoughts and the thoughts of the historical subjects. Although McCartney and Ono's efforts to promote their own particular versions of the Beatles story continued to complicate matters, by 2013, enough time had passed since the band's split and the tragedy of Lennon's death to provide a legitimate history of pop's greatest band.

In that year Lewisohn, widely acknowledged as the undisputed Beatles authority, published *Tune In*, the first volume of his three-part Beatles biography. There was universal agreement on its status as a work of history: Even those who disagreed with Lewisohn's interpretations did not dispute his methodology or research. "*Tune In* will be remembered as the turning point between journalism on the band and proper history."[273] In interviews, Lewisohn stressed his independence and objectivity, arguing that he did not already have a predetermined thesis. "I have no preconceived notions.... I am willing to have my own views challenged." He also detailed his research methods, emphasizing his preference for contemporary documentation, particularly those sources without public agendas, such as legal documents and private letters. In addition, Lewisohn defended *Tune In's* necessity by asserting that *Shout!* no longer could be viewed as the definitive biography. Lewisohn claimed that initially he had supported the book's interpretation, but now regarded Norman's work as "out of date ... that book has had thirty years in the sunshine, but it is in no way the definitive book.[274] Lewisohn criticized previous Beatles scholarship in another interview, maintaining that their story "had never been told properly,"[275] a claim he reiterated in the book's introduction.

Tune In demonstrates how proper application of historical methods separates history from myth. Perhaps the most consistent error in Beatles historiography is writers' tendency to accept the words of primary sources, particularly testimony provided in interviews, without subjecting the claims to cross-examination or source analysis. Lewisohn identified the problem and vowed not to repeat it: "I cannot swallow everything I am told, or everything that I read. I have to question it."[276] As a result of this critical source analysis *Tune In*, which covers the Beatles story until the end of 1962, debunks various myths that had been accepted wisdom for decades. One longstanding myth involves the replacement of Beatles drummer Pete Best by Starr in 1962.

Over the decades rumors persisted that Best was ousted not because of a lack of drumming ability, but because McCartney resented competing with the equally handsome Best for the attention of the band's female fans. Despite repeated dismissals of the story by various Beatles both before and after the breakup, numerous biographers from Norman and Goldman to Spitz all identified McCartney's jealousy as a key factor in Starr's replacement of Best.

However, Lewisohn rejects the theory, identifying its origin as a rumor among Best's female fans[277] and exhaustively proving that Best was replaced for two reasons. First, the drummer was always exiled from the key inner friendship among Lennon, McCartney and Harrison; while smart, he lacked their quick wit. In addition, Lewisohn provided numerous documents[278] as well as contemporary and retrospective interviews proving that Best was replaced in large part because his drumming was inferior to Starr's. Sources, including key Beatles insider Aspinall, also argued that it was *Harrison,* and not McCartney, who had been the prime force pushing for Best's replacement.[279] These conclusions debunked other misconceptions as well. Authors had used McCartney's ousting of Best as evidence of his selfish and manipulative personality, a conclusion that now required reassessment. The perception that Best had been Starr's equal or superior as a drummer, and that Best was unfairly rejected for non-musical reasons, helped undermine Starr's musical reputation for decades. In addition, Lewisohn argues that Harrison's role as the instigator behind bringing Starr into the band had significant consequences; it helped create a unique relationship between the two men. "Ringo's relationship with George was always vastly different to what he had with Paul or John. He felt he *owed* George."[280] In *The Historian's Craft*, Bloch cautions that "one fraud begets another." Lewisohn's research demonstrates the opposite: by disproving one myth, the author exposes others.

Lewisohn subjected even the most dramatic stories in Beatles history to cross-examination. In his 1968 edition of *The Beatles: The Authorized Biography*, Davies provided the origin of one of the most famous stories regarding John Lennon's tumultuous childhood, one used by numerous writers to explain both the man's music and his conflicted psychology. John Lennon's parents had separated after his birth and his father Alfred Lennon, a sailor, disappeared from his son's life, failing to contact John for decades. In Davies' interviews with Alfred Lennon (who was attempting at the time to re-establish ties with his now famous and wealthy son) Alfred claimed he had not abandoned John, but that he had taken his six-year-old son to Blackpool with the intention of taking the boy to New Zealand to live with him. According to Alfred, John's mother Julia found them before they could sail and demanded John back. In *The Beatles: The Authorized Biography*, Alfred Lennon recounted how he then told John to choose which parent he wanted to stay with. After initially choosing Alfred, John Lennon ran after his departing mother, ultimately choosing Julia. Alfred then disappeared from his son's life for approximately 20 years, something he explained in *The Authorized Biography*. "That was the last I saw of him or heard of him till I was told he'd become a Beatle."[281]

Davies' expressed his doubts concerning Alfred Lennon's credibility in his 1982 revised biography,[282] but this story quickly became an essential element of any recounting of Lennon's life. Beatles historiography frequently presented it as the most famous example of Lennon's unstable parenting situation, which continued to affect him psychologically for the rest of his life. Biographers from Norman to Coleman to Goldman emphasized the event's importance to Lennon's psyche. It seeped into popular culture: the 2010 movie *Nowhere Boy*, about Lennon's adolescence, uses Mimi Smith's dramatic recounting of the event as the film's climax. Even though no other witness except Alfred described the event (Julia Lennon was dead by the time of Alfred's account) and John Lennon never recounted it prior to hearing Alfred's story, (qualifying his later recollections as borrowed testimony) all later accounts of Lennon's life relayed it as fact.

Tune In disputes this version of events with a separate, independent eyewitness account. Lewisohn's research uncovered Bill Hall, an eyewitness who argued that the traumatic choice between mother and father that Alfred forced six-year old-John to make never happened. Hall, a friend of Alfred Lennon's who served as a fellow member of the merchant navy with him on the *Queen Mary*, lived in the house in Blackpool where the supposed incident took place and was at the house when it occurred. Hall disputes Alfred's story by arguing that Alfred had no concrete plans to take John with him permanently, was not planning to go to New Zealand at the time, and could not have taken John regardless because they were "only on leave."[283] After Julia Lennon arrived, "there was definitely no tug of love" scene; John Lennon went home with Julia while Alfred went back to sea satisfied that his son would be looked after "properly."[284]

Faced with these conflicting accounts, both of which lack independent verification, the credibility of each source needs to be examined in order to determine which version is most probable. Both sources are retrospective, although Alfred's recollection occurred closer in time to the actual event and is therefore slightly more credible in that regard. However, as Davies noted, Alfred Lennon's interviews in *The Beatles: The Authorized Biography* display a self-serving, fanciful and exaggerated quality which, by Garraghan's standards, lessens their credibility. Under these circumstances, eyewitness agenda provides the best means of analysis. In this instance, Alfred Lennon's agenda

at the time he originally told the story is obvious. Alfred had been an absent
father for most of his son's life and was attempting in 1966 to excuse that failure in the eyes of his son and the world. He only attempted to re-establish
contact once his son was wealthy and famous and Alfred, working a number
of menial jobs, needed money, declaring he would not object to help "if John
happened to offer it."[285] Arguing that he intended to take John with him to
New Zealand and that John ultimately refused him by choosing his mother
painted a more sympathetic portrait of Alfred. Eventually Alfred's story did
help re-establish some contact between him and his son, facilitated by Davies.
Hall's agenda, however, is far less evident. Simply put, Alfred Lennon had far
more motive to lie to Davies in 1966 than Bill Hall did to Lewisohn in 2013;
this indicates that Hall's version is more credible. "When two sources disagree
and there's no other means of evaluation, take the source which best accords
with common sense."[286]

　　Lewisohn's use of historical methodology reinforces *Tune In*'s status as
a work of history. In addition to the new conclusions regarding Best and
Alfred Lennon, numerous other commonly held myths—about the poor
stature of Parlophone,[287] the record label that signed the Beatles, and why
Martin offered them a contract at all after being previously rejected[288]—fall
apart under Lewisohn's research and cross examination. The scope of the
work (the extended edition of *Tune In*, which covers the band's story until
the end of 1962 is 1,728 pages) enhances the study's comprehensive nature.
(In many ways *Tune In* is a six-part biography, covering all four Beatles as
well as the crucial figures of Epstein and Martin). The work contains extensive
original research, utilizing new interviews and previously undiscovered documents. Unlike most biographers, Lewisohn secured interviews with Aspinall,
the most trusted of all Beatles insiders. Documentation is one of *Tune In*'s
strengths: the work includes citations within the text and extensive endnotes,
detailing the origin of hundreds of sources. Authorial interpretation is minimal: the outside of events are clearly distinguished from the inside of events.
Moral judgments are infrequent and balanced. *Tune In* demonstrates the
objectivity essential to writing history. When two equally credible but conflicting versions of the same story exist, Lewisohn provides both and allows
the reader to evaluate them.[289]

　　Unlike most Beatles biographies *Tune In* does not neglect Harrison and
Starr and Lewisohn's biographical coverage of the two men is one the book's
great strengths. Lewisohn identified how, by neglecting Starr, many Beatles
writers had weakened their own work. "It's really rather shocking that he's
been given such a short shrift for fifty years in other books on the Beatles."[290]
Tune In provides one of the first major biographies ever on the band's drum-

mer. While well written, Lewisohn's status as a researcher rather than a journalist means his descriptions at times pale beside Norman and Gould's more
eloquent prose. However, in *A Guide to Historical Method*, Garraghan cautions against equating style with methodology: "Literary quality, however
desirable in itself, belongs to the accidentals, not to the essentials of history."[291]

By 2010 *Rolling Stone*, the primary advocate of the *Lennon Remembers*
narrative, and Philip Norman, the founder of the *Shout!* narrative, had shifted
their partisan views on both of Beatles history's key debates. As the first truly
definitive biography of the band, *Tune In* concretized these revisions, and
solidified a methodologically superior Orthodoxy. Parts of Lewisohn's interpretation harkened back to the major elements of the Fab Four narrative,
including the band's unity, the equality of the Lennon/McCartney partnership
and their close friendship.[292] Because *Tune In* ends in 1962, the book does
not cover the contentious debate over the band's breakup. But Lewisohn's
introduction leaves no doubt regarding his conclusions on the core relationship that, through every narrative, remains at the center of the Beatles story.
"And so Lennon-McCartney stood shoulder to shoulder as equals, connected
at every level, their considerable talents harmonized, their personalities
unchecked, their goal in focus. They were a union, stronger than the sum of
their parts, and everything was possible."[293] Ever since the collapse of the official narrative, the popular trend was to pit Lennon and McCartney against
one another as competitors and ignore the depth of their collaboration, a
pattern that resulted in highly partisan and at times inaccurate history. With
Tune In, Lewisohn rejected this approach.

Post-Lewisohn Beatles Historiography

How will the story of the Beatles be told fifty years from now? Inevitable events will impact subsequent narratives. Within the next quarter-century, all the remaining key figures—McCartney, Starr, Martin (who passed away in 2016), and Ono—will be gone. Personal efforts by these historical figures to shape their history will end. Beatles history will finally achieve the ultimate measure of historical distance, but at the expense of the loss of invaluable, and irreplaceable, primary sources. The trend by journalists to provide favorable portrayals in exchange for personal access will end. Or perhaps it will only shift, with writers offering rose-colored versions in exchange for access to private, and therefore inaccessible, archives. Presumably, the children of the key figures, some of whom are famous in their own right, will continue to promote and shape their parent's legacy. Despite these complications, the passage of time will ultimately allow for more impartial evaluation of the individual Beatles, their music, and their story.

When completed, Lewisohn's three-volume group biography will cement itself as the cornerstone of Beatles research. Due to his methodological example, bibliographies and citations will become required elements for any Beatles work that wants to be viewed as legitimate. Lewisohn's impartial interpretation will also have an impact. While authorial favoritism (preferring one Beatle over another) will continue, extreme examples of partisanship will diminish. More insidiously, authorial bias may simply be conveyed with greater subtlety.

As the definitive work, Lewisohn's interpretations will provide the prevailing Orthodoxy; a history of the band that any subsequent researcher will find difficult to unseat. One consequence of this definitive version of the band's overall story is that it will ultimately lead to greater topic diversification. Studies of smaller topics, rather than the over-arching nature of the band's saga, will increase. The amount of attention writers devote to Harrison and Starr will increase as well. Lewisohn's conclusions on the great debates will hopefully offer an opportunity for writers and fans to advance past the partisan obsession over these topics that have, at times, paralyzed Beatles historiography and obscured historical truth. Those Beatles writers who dispute Lewisohn's interpretations will be faced with two choices. In order to establish a counter-narrative, they can either use Lewisohn's sources and interpret them in different ways, or discover new, equally credible sources which contradict Lewisohn's.

What role the internet will play is uncharted, if fascinating, territory, but we can glimpse parts of the future in present-day patterns. The internet contains vast amounts of previously difficult-to-find primary and secondary sources, which influence the research and interpretations of both Beatles scholars and fans. This wealth of information ensures that all works on the band are already subjected to an informal form of fan-supplied source analysis, albeit one without the clarity provided by the established historical methods standards. In an age in which information is limitless and instantaneous, secondary works which gloss over negative aspects, provide only one-side of a multi-sided account, are blatantly biased or omit key facts find their credibility seriously questioned by informed readers in popular forums, blogs, and on book reviews. This fan-driven scholarship both feeds off of and contributes to the band's overall historiography.

Where will this bottom-up historiography lead? Will younger generations continue to avidly discuss details concerning the lives and music of their grandmother's favorite band, or will this scholarship erode with the passing of the Beatles own generation? Once the band's most obvious fan base (and market) is gone, will their media coverage and popularity decrease? At the same time, academic interest in the band is increasing. These two factors may transform Beatles historiography from a vibrant popular topic into one where the Beatles themselves exist as popular culture icons but serious scholarship occurs only in smaller, more academic circles. Lewisohn could propel this momentum. If his work establishes a crushing and unassailable Orthodoxy (and if the Beatles market disappears over time) writers may venture to other topics, convinced that, in Beatles historiography at least, there are no more worlds to conquer.

The Lessons of Beatles Historiography

Historians, as Gaddis notes in *The Landscape of History*, "relish revisionism and distrust Orthodoxy, not least because were we to do otherwise

we might put ourselves out of business." Certainly the historiography of the
Beatles—how their story has been told—is rife with revisionism. By the publication of *Tune In*, fifty years had passed since that first triumphant year,
1963, in which the Beatles achieved nationwide fame across Britain and began
making history. In the years following, they had created a catalog of music
that was, by almost universal assent, unmatched in the history of popular
music. They also helped manufacture one of the most powerful mythologies
of the 1960s and were regarded by millions as the oracle of their generation.
The band splintered publicly in the late 1960s and early 1970s; after Lennon
and McCartney's once united voices split, Beatles history split with them.
Both men (as well as Ono, after Lennon's death) spent the rest of their lives
promoting their own, at times conflicting, versions of the band's story and
of the Lennon/McCartney songwriting partnership. This self-promotion
demonstrates the extent to which both sides provided and at times shaped
information with an eye toward how history would perceive them. Numerous
journalists and biographers, musicologists and the memoirs of countless Beatles insiders chose sides in the Lennon-McCartney division that now dominated Beatles historiography. Because of this few works demonstrated the
objectivity essential to producing legitimate history.

     This division as well as Lennon's murder resulted in narratives domi-
nated by two of the most influential sources in Beatles history, one primary
(the *Lennon Remembers* interview) and one secondary (Philip Norman's biography of the group, *Shout!*). These sources are heavily flawed, according to
standard historical methods and source analysis. So are the narratives they
helped create, which presented unbalanced, inaccurate and biased versions
of Beatles history. As decades passed some measure of historical distance,
the discovery of previously unused primary sources, and new retrospective
testimony shifted Beatles historiography away from these interpretations
until a new methodologically sound Orthodoxy emerged.

     What can we learn from how the Beatles story has been told over time?
Some of its lessons are universal. Others reveal the unique challenges and
concerns that exist in analyzing modern historical topics, where most primary
sources are not diplomatic cables or diary entries but interviews, speeches
and other words largely intended for public consumption. The arc of Beatles
historiography reminds us that revisionism is not a weakness, but an essential
element to gaining greater understanding. Initial impressions, even simplified
and inaccurate ones, are difficult to dislodge. The political climate of the time
both in which events occur and in which they are written influences how
they are told. Those people who are in the midst of making history are not
above twisting facts and influencing others to ensure that posterity views

them favorably. We see how emotion is an unavoidable element both for those who make history and those who chronicle it. For students of modern history the story of the Beatles highlights the pivotal role the not always impartial press plays in shaping popular perception and influencing historical narratives. Friendship and personal preference and the way they influence memory are evident in the interviews and memoirs of some Beatles insiders. Fame, wealth and access and their effect on how history is told cannot be ignored, particularly in the modern era. Numerous secondary works throughout Beatles historiography show the corrosive effect explicit bias has on interpretation. Partisanship results in poor works of history. And while methodological issues such as documentation rarely excite readers, citing sources remains one of the essential elements to producing legitimate history. So is distinguishing between verified facts, unverified testimony, and authorial speculation.

The story of the Beatles is a fascinating one. It evokes Campbellian myth, Shakespearean drama, and elements of Greek tragedy along with sex, drugs and rock and roll. Over the last half century the Beatles and many others have attempted to tell their story countless times and in wildly differing ways. They have created and destroyed mythologies and, in a few cases, produced works of enduring history. The historiography of the Beatles—the story of how their story has been and is still being told—is also fascinating. It provides crucial insight into how modern narratives are shaped and discarded and how emotion and personal opinion influence primary and secondary sources. It demonstrates how being either granted or denied access to historical figures informs the interpretations of their biographers. It reveals the conflicts over control of the narrative between those who *make* history and those who *write* it. It explores how the world's most famous men and women deliberately pursue efforts to ensure and direct their legacy and their historiography. It shows how essential historical distance, proper methodology and objectivity are to producing accurate accounts of events. The story of the Beatles underlines how vital the use of historical method is to gaining a greater understanding of the truth. It reminds us how history is always, at its core, a human story; one involving "beings who are, by nature, capable of pursuing conscious ends" but also one that "demands an understanding interpretation." Both as history and historiography, the Beatles story illustrates the struggles of those men and women who, as legends in their own lifetimes, carry that weight of history upon their backs.

Chapter Notes

Introduction

1. Mark Bloch, *The Historian's Craft* (New York: Alfred A. Knopf, 1953), 88.

2. John Lewis Gaddis, *The Landscape of History: How Historians Map the Past* (New York: Oxford University Press, 2002), 136.

3. McCartney's mother, Mary, died suddenly from complications caused by breast cancer when he was 14, and Lennon's mother, Julia, was struck and killed by a car when he was 17. Agreement in Beatles historiography is universal: for both McCartney and Lennon, the loss of their mother was the defining event of their lives.

4. Philip Norman, *John Lennon: The Life* (New York: Ecco, 2008), 537.

5. Jonathan Gould, *Can't Buy Me Love: The Beatles, Britain and America* (New York: Harmony, 2007), 462.

6. Mark Lewisohn, *The Complete Beatles Recording Sessions: The Official Story of the Abbey Road Years: 1962–1970* (London: Octopus, 1988), 134.

7. Mark Hertsgaard, *A Day in the Life: The Music and Artistry of the Beatles* (New York: Delacorte, 1995), 232.

8. Barry Miles, *Paul McCartney: Many Years from Now* (New York: Henry Holt, 1997), 449.

9. A significant number of primary and secondary sources in Beatles historiography contain profanities, obscenities, and, at times, derogatory and discriminatory language. After careful consideration, I have chosen to allow these sources to remain uncensored and present them in their original form.

Chapter One

1. Philip Norman begins his extremely popular and influential 1981 group biography, *Shout! The True Story of the Beatles*, by describing this exact scene.

2. Mark Lewisohn, *The Beatles Live!* (New York: Henry Holt, 1986), 9.

3. *Ibid.*, Foreword.

4. Hertsgaard, *A Day in the Life*, 326.

5. Gilbert J. Garraghan, *A Guide to Historical Method* (Westport, CT: Greenwood, 1946), 35.

6. Mark Bloch, *The Historian's Craft* (New York: Alfred A. Knopf, 1953), 97.

7. Garraghan, *A Guide to Historical Method*, 269.

8. Larry Kane, *Ticket to Ride: Inside the Beatles 1964 Tour that Changed the World* (Philadelphia: Running, 2003), 77.

9. Pete Shotton and Nicholas Schaffner, *John Lennon: In My Life* (New York: Stein and Day, 1983), 95–96.

10. All public paternity suits brought against McCartney were eventually resolved by the use of blood testing, which proved McCartney was not the biological father.

11. Jann Wenner, *Lennon Remembers* (London: Verso, 2000), 61.

12. Peter Doggett, *You Never Give Me Your Money: The Beatles After the Breakup* (New York: HarperCollins, 2009), 42.

13. Michael Braun, *Love Me Do: The Beatles' Progress* (New York: Penguin, 1964), 11.

14. Beatles Press Conference, Sydney, Australia, June 11, 1964, The Beatles Interview Database, Jay Spangler, ed., http://www.beatlesinterviews.org/db1964.0611.beatles.html (accessed December 27, 2014).

15. Lewisohn, *The Beatles Live!*, 9.

16. Christopher Porterfield, "Pop Music, The Messengers," *Time,* September 22, 1967, 68.

17. Hunter Davies, *The Beatles: The Authorized Biography* (New York: McGraw Hill, 1968), 191.

18. Dibbs Mather, Interview with the Beatles, Doncaster, England, December 10, 1963, The Beatles Interview Database, http://www.beatlesinterviews.org/db1962. 1028.beatles.html (accessed January 4, 2015).

19. Ray Connolly, *The Ray Connolly Beatles Archive* (London: Plumray, 2011), Kindle e-book, 104.

20. "The Beatles" of course, is a generalization, as each individual member had different views on touring, fans, and fame. Evidence indicates that Harrison tired of touring first, followed by Lennon and then Starr. McCartney finally agreed to stop touring after the group's disastrous 1966 Asian and American tours. Conventional wisdom depicts McCartney as the Beatle fans found to be the most approachable, followed by Starr, Lennon, and Harrison. Harrison, a self-admitted introvert, was also the first to tire of the demands of fame. Likewise, the extent of their drug and sexual habits differed, with Lennon using the most and the heaviest drugs, followed by Harrison, Starr and McCartney. Partly due to his status as the last unmarried Beatle, McCartney is reputed to have had the largest number of sexual encounters prior to his 1969 marriage, followed by Harrison, Lennon and Starr.

21. Shotton and Schaffner, *John Lennon: In My Life,* 104.

22. The Beatles, *The Beatles Anthology* (San Francisco: Chronicle, 2000), 354.

23. George Martin with William Pearson, *Summer of Love: The Making of Sgt. Pepper* (London: Macmillan, 1994), 165.

24. George Martin, Foreword to *The Complete Beatles Chronicle,* by Mark Lewisohn (New York: Harmony, 1992).

25. Tony Barrow, *John, Paul, George, Ringo and Me: The Real Beatles Story* (New York: Thunder's Mouth, 2005), 137.

26. Peter McCabe and Robert Schonfeld, *Apple to the Core: The Unmaking of the Beatles* (London: Martin, Brian and O'Keefe, 1972), 59.

27. Davies, *The Beatles: The Authorized Biography,* 1968, 210.

28. Hertsgaard, *A Day in the Life: The Music and Artistry of the Beatles,* 87.

29. In *The Beatles Anthology,* Harrison touchingly argues that it was their unity as a group that allowed them to go on, and expressed sympathy for Elvis, who had an entourage and a backing group, but no real equals on which to rely.

30. The Beatles, *The Beatles Anthology,* 354.

31. Beatles interview with Frank Hall, RTE, Dublin, Ireland, November 7, 1963, The Beatles Interview Database, http://www.beatlesinterviews.org/db1963.1107.beatles.html (accessed February 3, 2015).

32. "George Interviews George," *The Beatles Book,* November 1964, The Beatles Interview Database, http://www.beatlesinterviews.org/db1964.1100.beatles.html (accessed January 27, 2015).

33. Beatles Press Conference, Tokyo Hilton, May 30, 1966, The Beatles Interview Database, http://www.beatlesinterviews.org/db1964.0611.beatles.html (accessed January 14, 2015).

34. Christopher Porterfield, "Pop Music: The Messengers," *Time,* September 22, 1967, 67.

35. Norrie Drummond, "Beatle Paul's New Life," *New Musical Express,* September 1967, The Beatles Interview Database, http://www.beatlesinterviews.org/db1967.0909.beatles.html (accessed March 2, 2015).

36. Shotton and Schaffner, *John Lennon: In My Life,* 105.

37. Hertsgaard, *A Day in the Life,* 145.

38. The most frequent and serious exception to this "Follow the Leader" mentality appears to be McCartney, described by Shotton as "the most independent member of the group" (Shotton and Schaffner, *John Lennon: In My Life,* 99). McCartney refused to take LSD until eighteen months after Lennon and Harrison had taken it, despite serious sustained pressure from both men to join them in using the drug. McCartney declined to join Lennon, Harrison and Starr in moving to the suburbs, something which evidently astonished Lennon. "(John), at least, would never have dreamed of living more than a few minutes away from the other three" (*ibid.*). In

1967, Lennon pursued a scheme to buy an uninhabited Greek island and set up a permanent Beatles settlement there. In his semi-autobiography McCartney's friend, Marianne Faithful, declared that McCartney viewed the idea as "a nightmare; the last thing Paul wanted to do was live on some fucking island" (Miles, *Many Years from Now*, 377), and while the Beatles bought the island, the scheme eventually died out. McCartney was also the only member of the group who refused to follow Lennon's demand, after he had left his first wife Cynthia for Yoko Ono, that no one should contact or speak to Cynthia. Cynthia Lennon, *John*, 228.

39. Ray Connolly, *The Ray Connolly Beatles Archive.*, Kindle e-book, 129.

40. David Vetter, "Allen Klein: A Candid Conversation with the Embattled Manager of the Beatles," *Playboy*, November 1971, 90.

41. Mark Lewisohn, *Tune In: The Beatles, All These Years, Volume I* (New York: Crown Archetype, 2013), 690.

42. Shotton and Schaffner, *John Lennon: In My Life*, 105.

43. Hunter Davies, *The John Lennon Letters* (New York: Little Brown, 2012), 119.

44. Martin and Pearson, *Summer of Love,* 122.

45. Cynthia Lennon, *John* (New York: Crown, 2005), 33.

46. The Beatles, *The Beatles Anthology*, 180.

47. Howard Smith, interview with George Harrison, WABC New York, May 1970, The Beatles Interview Database, http://www. beatlesinterviews.org/db1970.04gh.beatles. html (accessed February 18, 2015).

48. Geoff Emerick and Howard Massey, *Here, There and Everywhere: My Life Recording the Music of the Beatles* (New York: Gotham, 2006), 43.

49. Michael Brocken and Melissa Davis, *The Beatles Bibliography: A New Guide to the Literature* (Manitou Springs, CO: Beatles Works, 2012), 265.

50. The Beatles, *The Beatles Anthology*, 316.

51. Interview with George Harrison, *Beatles Book Monthly*, October 1966, The Beatles Interview Database, http://www. beatlesinterviews.org/db1966.10gh.beatles. html (accessed January 11, 2015).

52. Another possibility is that Harrison, well known for his very dry humor, was being sarcastic in the written interview.

53. William J. Dowlding, *Beatlesongs* (New York: Simon and Schuster, 1989), 112.

54. Ray Connolly, *The Ray Connolly Beatles Archive*, Kindle e-book, 53.

55. The Beatles, *The Beatles Anthology*, 316.

56. Hunter Davies, *The Beatles: The Authorized Biography*, rev. ed. (New York: W.W. Norton, 1996), 291.

57. Interview with Paul McCartney, Thomas Thompson, "The New Far Out Beatles," *Hit Parader*, May 1967, The Beatles Interview Database, http://www.beatles interviews.org/db1967.05HP.beatles.html (accessed January 29, 2015).

58. Davies, *The Beatles: The Authorized Biography*, 1968, 370.

59. Hildegard Anderson and Elizabeth Hoover, *Remembering John Lennon 25 Years Later* (New York: Life, 2006), 7.

60. Ray Connolly, *The Ray Connolly Beatles Archives*, Kindle e-book, 14.

61. *Ibid.*

62. McCartney's innate musical talent is acknowledged by a number of informed eyewitnesses, including Beatles producer George Martin (Martin and Pearson, *Summer of Love*, 98) and engineers Ken Scott and Geoff Emerick, as well as their official biographer, Hunter Davies.

63. Davies, *The Beatles: The Authorized Biography*, 1982, 372.

64. Joan Goodman, "Paul and Linda McCartney's Whole Story," *Playboy*, December 1984, The Beatles Interview Database, http://www.beatlesinterviews.org/db1984. pmpb.beatles.html (accessed February 5, 2015).

65. Jim Irvin, "Sir George Martin: The Mojo Interview," *Mojo*, March 2007, 59.

66. Paul Grien, Interview with George Martin, "Martin/McCartney 'Tug' Team Scores," *Billboard*, February 26, 1983, 5.

67. Shotton and Schaffner, *John Lennon: In My Life*, 105.

68. Joan Goodman, "Paul and Linda McCartney's Whole Story," *Playboy*, December 1984.

69. Ray Coleman, *Lennon: The Definitive*

Biography (New York: McGraw Hill, 1985), 384.

70. For an in-depth examination of the reasons for Martin's credibility as a source, see Chapter Two.

71. Martin and Pearson, *Summer of Love*, 70.

72. The Beatles, *The Beatles Anthology*, 191.

73. Robert Christgau and John Piccarella, "Portrait of the Artist as a Rock and Roll Star," in *The Ballad of John and York* (New York: Rolling Stone, 1982), 240–260, 244.

74. Wilfrid Mellers, *Twilight of the Gods: The Music of the Beatles* (New York: Viking, 1973), 32.

75. Ian MacDonald, *Revolution in the Head: The Beatles Music and the Sixties* (New York: Henry Holt, 1994), 12.

76. Ray Connolly, *The Ray Connolly Beatles Archive*, Kindle e-book, 69.

77. Wenner, *Lennon Remembers*, 26.

78. In his 1980 *Playboy* interview, Lennon admitted to lying in *Lennon Remembers* about when he and McCartney had stopped writing together.

79. Lewisohn, *Tune In*, 704.

80. Monty Lister, Interview with the Beatles, Radio Clatterbridge, October 10, 1962, The Complete Beatles Interview Database, http://www.beatlesinterviews.org/db1962.1028.beatles.html (accessed January 14, 2015).

81. David Sheff, *All We Are Saying: The Playboy Interviews with John Lennon and Yoko Ono* (New York: Penguin, 1981), 137.

82. Beatles Interview by Phil Tate, *Non Stop Pop*, BBC, July 30, 1963, The Beatles Interview Database, http://www.beatlesinterviews.org/db1963.0730.beatles.html (accessed January 3, 2015).

83. Robert Christgau, "Portrait of the Artist as a Rock and Roll Star," in *The Ballad of John and Yoko*, 253.

84. Beatles Press Conference, Tokyo Japan, 1966, The Beatles Interview Database, http://www.beatlesinterviews.org/db1966.0630.beatles.html (accessed January 14, 2015).

85. Beatles Press Conference, Edgewater Inn, Seattle, August 25, 1966, The Beatles Interview Database, http://www.beatlesinterviews.org/db1966.0825.beatles.html (accessed January 5, 2015).

86. John Lennon and Paul McCartney, Interview with Joe Garagiola, *The Tonight Show*, NBC, May 14, 1968, The Beatles Interview Database, http://www.beatlesinterviews.org/db1968.05ts.beatles.html (accessed January 29, 2015).

87. According to *All the Songs*, the last song Lennon and McCartney seriously collaborated on was "I've Got a Feeling," recorded in January 1969, eleven months before Lennon's interview. Jean-Michael Guesdon and Phillipe Margotin, *All the Songs*, 630.

88. Alan Smith, "Beatles Music Straightforward on New Album," *New Musical Express*, May 3, 1969, The Beatles Interview Database, http://www.beatlesinterviews.org/db1969.0503.beatles.html (accessed January 29, 2015).

89. Kenneth Womack and Todd F. Davis, "Mythology, Remythology and Demythology: The Beatles on Film," in *Reading the Beatles: Cultural Studies, Literary Criticism and the Fab Four*, edited by Kenneth Womack and Todd F. Davis, 97–110. Albany: State University of New York Press, 2006, 102.

90. Richard Lester, "Look At My Direction: Richard Lester, the Director," *A Hard Day's Night*, special ed. DVD, directed by Richard Lester, Miramax Films, 2000.

91. *Ibid.*

92. Womack and Davis, "Mythology, Remythology and Demythology," in *Reading the Beatles*, 100.

93. Miles, *Paul McCartney: Many Years from Now*, 197.

94. The most notable exception to this was Joe Orton's "Up Against It," a script which Orton submitted to the Beatles involving war, polyandry and the political assassination of a female prime minister by one of the main characters.

95. Nick Logan, "An Interview with Ringo," *Hit Parader*, March 13, 1969, published October 1969, The Beatles Interview Database, http://www.beatlesinterviews.org/db1969.10rs.beatles.html (accessed January 29, 2015).

96. Brant Mewborn, "Ringo Starr in the Afternoon," *Rolling Stone* April 30, 1981, http://www.rollingstone.com/music/features/ringo-in-the-afternoon-19810430 (accessed May 5, 2015).

97. Richard Corliss, "That Old Feeling:

Meet the Beatles," *Time*, February 7, 2004, http://content.time.com/time/arts/article/ 0,8599,588789,00.html (accessed June 4, 2015).

98. Gerhard Weinberg, "Hitler's Image of the United States," *The American Historical Review* 69, no. 4 (July 1964): 1012.

99. There was good reason for this: practicing homosexuality in England in 1964 was illegal.

100. Brian Epstein, *A Cellarful of Noise* (New York: Doubleday, 1964), 66.

101. *Ibid.*, 86.

102. *Ibid.*, 85.

103. *Ibid.*

104. *Ibid.*, 88–89.

105. *Ibid.*, 119.

106. Michael Braun, *Love Me Do: The Beatles' Progress* (New York: Penguin, 1964), 91.

107. *Ibid.*, 111.

108. *Ibid.*, 136.

109. *Ibid.*, 50.

110. *Ibid.*, 82.

111. Maureen Cleave, interview with Ringo Starr, *London Evening Standard*, exact date unknown, 1966.

112. Maureen Cleave, interview with George Harrison, *London Evening Standard*, exact date unknown, 1966.

113. Maureen Cleave, interview with Paul McCartney, *London Evening Standard*, exact date unknown, 1966.

114. *Ibid.*

115. *Ibid.*

116. Maureen Cleave, "How Does a Beatle Live? John Lennon Lives Like This," *London Evening Standard*, March 4, 1966.

117. Barrow, *John, Paul George, Ringo and Me*, 202.

118. According to Rodriguez, *Datebook's* editor, Art Unger, wrongly anticipated that McCartney's comments, not Lennon's, would provoke widespread publicity. "Unger had in fact expected Paul's comment to incite a reaction, influencing his decision to run the most popular Beatle's photo on the cover. He was as astonished as anyone in an era of heightened civil-rights sensitivities, that Paul's remark was ignored while John's touched a raw nerve." Robert Rodriguez, *Revolver*, 171.

119. This "courting" usually consisted of

granting American historians special access to government controlled archives in nations such as Germany. Not coincidentally, in the case of Germany, these archives contained sources that overwhelmingly supported Germany's version of the war's origins.

120. Wenner, *Lennon Remembers*, 61.

121. Bob Spitz, *The Beatles: The Biography* (New York: Little Brown, 2005), 861.

122. *Ibid.*

123. "Albert Goldman v. Hunter Davies," BBC 1989, YouTube, https://www.youtube.com/watch?v=hiltVC3uAh8 (access date November 22, 2014).

124. Davies, *The Beatles: The Authorized Biography*, 1996, iv.

125. *Ibid.*, 13.

126. Hunter Davies, "Why I Didn't Tell the Whole Truth About the Beatles," *New Statesman*, October 25, 2012, http://www.newstatesman.com/culture/culture/2012/10/why-i-didnt-tell-whole-truth-about-beatles (accessed May 4, 2015).

127. Miles, *Paul McCartney: Many Years from Now*, 303.

128. Davies, *The Beatles: The Authorized Biography*, 1996, lx.

129. *Ibid.*

130. Davies, *The Beatles: The Authorized Biography*, 1968, 336.

131. *Ibid.*, 349.

132. *Ibid.*, 231.

133. *Ibid.*, 230.

134. *Ibid.*

135. *Ibid.*, 337.

136. *Ibid.*, 306.

137. *Ibid.*, 306.

138. *Ibid.*, 309.

139. *Ibid.*, 301.

140. *Ibid.*, lix.

141. *Ibid.*, lxiii.

142. James Kaplan, *Paul McCartney: The Legend Rocks On*, edited by Stephen Koepp (New York: Life, 2012), 58.

143. Doggett, *You Never Give Me Your Money*, 23.

144. Davies, *The Beatles: The Authorized Biography*, 1968, 318.

145. Epstein, *A Cellarful of Noise*, 85.

146. Davies, *The Beatles: The Authorized Biography*, 1968, 15.

147. *Ibid.*, 301.

148. *Ibid.*, 36.

149. *Ibid.*, 301.

150. Sheff, *The Playboy Interviews with John Lennon and Yoko Ono*, 137.

151. David Marshall Kopp, "Linking Differences in Self-Directed Learning Competency to Dyadic Conflict: An Instrumental Case study of the Leadership Dyad of John Lennon and Paul McCartney," *Twenty-First Century Approaches in Self Directed Learning* (Huey B. Long, 2003), 56–74, 72.

152. *Ibid.*

153. Ray Connolly, *The Ray Connolly Beatles Archive*, Kindle e-book, 25.

154. Spitz, *The Beatles: The Biography*, 784.

155. Tony Bramwell, *Magical Mystery Tours: My Life with the Beatles* (New York: Thomas Dunne, 2005), 171.

156. Ray Coleman, *Lennon: The Definitive Biography,* rev. ed. (New York: HarperCollins, 1992), 18.

157. John Lewis Gaddis, *The Landscape of History*, 47.

158. Richard Marius, *A Short Guide to Writing About History*, 2d ed. (New York: HarperCollins College, 1995), 59.

159. Stacey Schiff, "Rehabilitating Cleopatra," *Smithsonian*, December 2010, Smithsonian.com, http://www.smithsonianmag.com/history/rehabilitating-cleopatra-70613486/?no-ist (accessed February 12, 2015).

160. *Sixty Minutes*, "The 2 Mrs. Lennons," Interview of Cynthia Lennon and Yoko Ono by Mike Wallace, CBS, October 2, 1988.

161. Joshua Wolf Shenk, *Powers of Two: Finding the Essence of Innovation in Creative Pairs* (Boston: Houghton Mifflin, 2014), 220.

162. Wenner, *Lennon Remembers*, 14.

163. Gould, *Can't Buy Me Love*, 512.

164. Wenner, *Lennon Remembers*, 44.

165. Ray Connolly, *The Ray Connolly Beatles Archive*, Kindle e-book, 41.

166. Norman, *John Lennon: The Life*, 570.

167. *Sixty Minutes*, "The 2 Mrs. Lennons" Interview of Cynthia Lennon and Yoko Ono by Mike Wallace, CBS, October 2, 1988.

168. Coleman, *Lennon: The Definitive Biography*, 1985, 363.

169. Pete Hamill, "Long Night's Journey Into Day: A Conversation with John Lennon,"

Rolling Stone, June 5, 1975, The Beatles Interview Database, http://www.beatlesinterviews.org/db1975.0605.beatles.html (accessed February 18, 2015).

170. Robert Christgau, "Symbolic Comrades," *Village Voice*, January 20, 1981.

171. Norman, *John Lennon: The Life*, 552.

172. Hertsgaard, *A Day in the Life*, 240.

173. Gould, *Can't Buy Me Love*, 482.

174. Shenk, *Powers of Two*, 220.

175. Emerick and Massey, *Here, There and Everywhere,* 223.

176. *Ibid.*, 235.

177. *Ibid.*, 243.

178. Bramwell, *Magical Mystery Tours*, 305.

179. Doggett, *You Never Give Me Your Money*, 46.

180. Sheff, *All We Are Saying,* 74.

181. Coleman, *Lennon: The Definitive Biography*, 1992, 563.

182. Ray Coleman, *Lennon: The Definitive Biography* (London: Pan, 2000), 22.

183. Ray Connolly, *The Ray Connolly Beatles Archive*, Kindle e-book, 99.

184. Sheff, *All We Are Saying*, 85.

185. Ray Connolly, "Has Yoko Whitewashed John's Image?" *Daily Mail*, December 8, 2000.

186. Ian MacDonald, *Revolution in the Head: The Beatles Records and the Sixties* (New York: Henry Holt, 1994), 276.

187. *Ibid.*, 277.

188. *Ibid.*, 190.

189. Ian MacDonald, *Revolution in the Head: The Beatles Records and the Sixties*, 3d ed. (Chicago: Review, 2005), 239.

190. *Ibid.*, 375.

191. The Beatles, *The Beatles Anthology*, 349.

192. *Ibid.*, 310.

193. Shotton and Schaffner, *John Lennon: In My Life*, 171.

194. *Ibid.*, 171–172.

195. Bramwell, *Magical Mystery Tours*, 291.

196. Lennon himself discussed the double standard of this argument in his 1980 *Playboy* interview: "Nobody ever said anything about Paul having a spell on me, or me having one on Paul. They never said that

was abnormal—and in those days! … Why didn't they ever say 'How come these guys don't split up? I mean, what's going *on* backstage? *What is this Paul and John business?* How can they be together so long?" Sheff, *All We Are Saying*, 43–44.

197. Gaddis, *The Landscape of History*, 10.

198. Garraghan, *A Guide to Historical Method*, 39.

199. Julie Goldman, "The Two Women Who Broke Up the Beatles," *McCall's*, July 1971, 73.

200. Tony Scherman, *Paul* (New York: Life, 2014), 79.

201. Ray Connolly, "The Story of Paul and Linda," *Daily Mail*, April 25–28, 1998.

202. Denis Barker, "From The Archive: 13 March 1969," *Guardian*, March 13, 2013, http://www.theguardian.com/theguardian/2013/mar/13/beatles-paul-mccartney-linda-wedding (accessed July 1, 2015).

203. Alex Tresniowski, "Paul's Lovely Linda," *People*, May 4, 1998, 12.

204. Zoe Heller, "Moll of Kintyre," *Vanity Fair*, October 1992, 37.

205. Julie Goldman, "The Two Women Who Broke Up the Beatles," *McCall's*, July 1971, 77.

206. Peter Brown and Steven Gaines, *The Love You Make: An Insider's Story of the Beatles* (New York: Signet, 1984), 367.

207. Philip Norman, *Shout! The True Story of the Beatles* (New York: Simon and Schuster, 1981), 339.

208. McCabe and Schonfeld, *Apple to the Core*, 112.

209. Howard Sounes, *Fab: An Intimate Life of Paul McCartney* (New York: DaCapo, 2010), 175.

210. According to an unsubstantiated account by a female fan, or "Apple Scruff," watching through the window, during one particularly contentious 1969 business meeting Lennon drew back his arm to hit a then-pregnant Linda McCartney, stopping only when Paul McCartney physically placed himself between the two. Several histories of the group (including MacDonald's *Revolution in the Head*) have presented this account as fact; however, its unconfirmed status should be acknowledged by those authors who recount the story. While Lennon's

life includes a self-admitted pattern of behavior that includes occasional acts of physical violence, including against women (Cynthia Lennon as well as Lennon's girlfriends Thelma Pickles and May Pang all describe being physically hurt by Lennon) it should be noted that no other witness, including either Linda or Paul McCartney, ever mentioned the incident. While in certain cases unverified testimony from a single source can be regarded as fact (Garraghan, *A Guide to Historical Method*, 244) the questionable identity of the source means this is not one of those circumstances.

211. Sheff, *All We Are Saying*, 123.

212. Miles, *Paul McCartney: Many Years from Now*, 105.

213. Davies, *The Beatles: The Authorized Biography*, 1968, 314.

214. Rob Sheffield, *Talking to Girls about Duran Duran: One Young Man's Quest for True Love and a Cooler Haircut* (New York: Dutton, 2010), 158.

215. McCabe and Schonfeld, *Apple to the Core*, 148.

216. David Vetter, "A Candid Conversation with the Embattled Manager of the Beatles," 98.

217. *Ibid.*, 100.

218. John Lennon, *The John Lennon Letters*, edited by Hunter Davies (New York: Little, Brown, 2012), 209.

219. McCabe and Schonfeld, *Apple to the Core*, 114.

220. Wenner, *Lennon Remembers*, 129.

221. *Ibid.*, 123.

222. Dorothy Bacon, "The Case of the Missing Beatle: Paul Is Still with Us," *Life*, November 7, 1969, 11.

223. The Beatles, *The Beatles Anthology*, 352.

224. McCabe and Schonfeld, *Apple to the Core*, 111.

225. Norman, *Shout! The True Story of the Beatles*, 1981, 339.

226. Bramwell, *Magical Mystery Tours*, 298.

227. *Ibid.*, 302.

228. *Ibid.*, 264.

229. *Ibid.*, 305.

230. *Ibid.*

231. Ray Connolly, "Allen Klein: Monster

of Rock," *The Daily Mail*, July 5, 2009, http://www.dailymail.co.uk/tvshowbiz/article-1197709/Monster-rock-Allen-Klein-swindled-The-Stones-broke-The-Beatles-rock-n-rolls-ruthless-Svengali.html (accessed January 3, 2015).

232. Spitz, *The Beatles: The Biography*, 817.

233. Gaddis, *The Landscape of History*, 140.

234. Doggett, *You Never Give Me Your Money*, 65–66.

235. David Vetter, "Allen Klein: A Candid Conversation with the Embattled Manager of the Beatles," 90.

236. McCabe and Schonfeld, *Apple to the Core*, 196.

237. The Beatles, *The Beatles Anthology*, 324.

238. Ray Connolly, *The Ray Connolly Archives*, Kindle e-book, 54.

239. Howard Smith Interview with George Harrison, WABC New York, May 1970, The Beatles Interview Database, http://www.beatlesinterviews.org/db1970.04gh.beatles.html (accessed February 18, 2015).

240. Two notable exceptions are Albert Goldman's *The Lives of John Lennon* and Fred Goodman's *Allen Klein: The Man Who Bailed Out the Beatles, Made the Stones, and Transformed Rock and Roll*. Goldman's portrait of Klein in *The Lives of John Lennon* is complimentary, presumably due to Klein's agreement to be interviewed. Goodman was approached by the Klein family to write a new biography, and they opened their archives to him. Goodman insists there was no *quid pro quo* involved; however, his interpretation of some of Klein's questionable legal and financial decisions, as well as the man's role in the breakup, include a number of significant omissions and present a rather one-sided pro-Klein version of events.

241. Paul Gambaccini "Paul McCartney in His Own Words," *Rolling Stone*, January 31, 1974, http://www.rollingstone.com/music/features/the-rolling-stone-interview-paul-mccartney-19740131 (accessed June 3, 2015).

242. There are varying reports on what Stones' frontman Mick Jagger told members of the Beatles about Klein. According to McCartney, Jagger sent him a letter –"Don't go near him" — warning him not to trust

Klein, but when McCartney summoned Jagger to a meeting with the rest of the Beatles to convey the message, Jagger demurred, only telling Lennon, Harrison and Starr "He's alright if you like that sort of thing" (Miles, *Many Years from Now*, 545). Bramwell argues that Jagger wanted the Beatles to sign with Klein and instructed Klein how to approach them: "Mick had told Klein to focus on John" (Bramwell, *Magical Mystery Tours*, 313). In John McMillan's *Beatles vs. Stones*, Jagger's girlfriend at the time, Marianne Faithful, also argues that Jagger encouraged Lennon to take Klein as his manager in a deliberate effort to distract Klein away from the Stones. "'Mick's strategy in dealing with Allen Klein was fairly diabolical. He would fob Klein off on the Beatles. Mick called up John Lennon and told him, 'you know who you should get to manage you, man? Allen Klein.' ... once Mick had distracted Klein's attention by giving him bigger fish to fry, Mick could begin unraveling the Stones' ties to him'" (McMillan, *Beatles vs. Stones*, 201).

243. John McMillan, *Beatles vs. Stones* (New York: Simon and Schuster, 2013), 202.

244. Lewisohn, *The Complete Beatles Recording Sessions*, 308.

245. Brocken and Davis, *The Beatles Bibliography*, 313.

246. Wenner, *Lennon Remembers*, 19.

247. *Ibid.*, 120.

248. Fred Goodman, *Allen Klein: The Man Who Bailed Out the Beatles, Made the Stones, and Transformed Rock and Roll* (Boston: Houghton Mifflin, 2015), 129.

249. Gould, *Can't Buy Me Love*, 546.

250. McMillan, *Beatles vs. Stones*, 210.

251. Ono's support of Klein was crucial in Lennon's decision: In *Anthology* McCartney declares that Lennon told him he chose Klein because "he was the only one Yoko liked" (*Anthology*, 324). Her preference could be due to Klein's promise to use Apple's money to sponsor her art exhibits (*ibid.*, 326).

252. Norman, *John Lennon: The Life*, 591.

253. Wenner, *Lennon Remembers*, 123.

254. The irony is that Lee Eastman was also a self-made man, a poor son of immigrants who worked his way through Harvard to become a successful lawyer.

255. The Beatles, *The Beatles Anthology*, 324.

256. May Pang and Henry Edwards, *John Lennon: The Lost Weekend* (New York: Spi, 1992), 277.

257. David Vetter, "Allen Klein: A Candid Conversation with the Embattled Manager of the Beatles," 94.

258. Shenk, *Powers of Two*, 224.

259. Lennon and McCartney's 1971 trial testimony disagrees on the subject of unanimity. McCartney argues that Klein's appointment as Beatles manager over his objections violated a previously unbroken precedent of unanimous voting: "On the way in which the four of us had sorted out our differences in the past, I deny that it had been on a three-to-one basis. If one disagreed, we discussed the problem until we reached agreement or let the matter drop. I know of no decision taken on a three-to-one basis" (Keith Badman, *The Beatles After the Breakup*, 30). Lennon argued that the three-to-one vote had been employed prior to Klein's arrival. Lennon's statements are contradicted by Norrie Drummond's 1967 *Melody Maker* interview with McCartney, which notes the band's insistence on unanimity: "If they are asked to do something as a group and any one of them doesn't want to take part, then the scheme is dropped," and by Harrison's May 1998 testimony to the London High Court regarding the Star Club Tapes. "We had a democratic thing going between us. Everyone had to agree with everything that was done, whether it was a concert in Liverpool or to go to Hamburg" (*ibid.*, 591).

260. Beatles historians have attributed this to McCartney's distrust of Klein, which the Eastmans informed and nurtured, and McCartney's preference that the Eastmans serve as the new Beatles managers. Over the years, McCartney has emphasized that it was his distrust of Klein's legal and financial dealings, more than his desire to see his in-laws appointed as the Beatles financial managers, which prompted him to dislike Klein. Whether this is an attempt by McCartney to rewrite the past in order to appear reasonable or was, in fact, the truth at the time is open to interpretation. However, as a result of this evidence, any analysis of the personal relationship between Klein and McCartney has been unfortunately neglected. While Klein's *Playboy* interview regarding his inability to connect with McCartney— "I don't know if we could ever have been good friends. I'm not sure that's possible with McCartney" (Vetter, 91) — must be interpreted in the context of his agenda to blame McCartney's unreasonable attitude for the breakup, it also fits other, separate descriptions of McCartney as the most independent and self-contained Beatle. Shotton described McCartney as the Beatle who was "the hardest to really get to know as a close friend: the one Beatle who played his cards close to the chest" (Shotton and Schaffner, *John Lennon: In My Life*, 104). Other sources reinforce this description of McCartney's guarded character. Peter Brown mentioned it: "Paul, it should be noted, was the first Beatle to show any distance or privacy from the others" (Brown, *The Love You Make*, 203). Hunter Davies described McCartney in similar terms in the authorized biography: "Paul is the easiest to get to know for an outsider, but in the end he is the hardest one to get to know. There's a feeling that he is holding things back" (Davies, *The Beatles: The Authorized Biography*, 318). The reasons for McCartney's reserve, and the impact it had on his relations with the other band members, are up for debate. MacDonald argues that this veneer was the result of McCartney's upbringing and that it left him oblivious at times to the feelings of the other Beatles: "The others' beef was that his middle-class reflex of adopting a diplomatic face served to repress his emotions, leaving him with little idea of how *they* felt" (MacDonald, *Revolution in the Head*, 281). McCartney himself offered a far different reason, stating that it was after his mother's death when he was 14 that he "learnt to put a shell around me" (*Anthology*, 19).

261. David Vetter, "Allen Klein: A Candid Conversation with the Embattled Manager of the Beatles," 95.

262. Miles, *Paul McCartney: Many Years from Now*, 544.

263. Goodman, *Allen Klein*, 192.

264. Glyn Johns, *Sound Man: A Life Recording Hits with the Rolling Stones, the*

Who, Led Zepplin, the Eagles, Eric Clapton, the Faces... (New York: Blue Rider, 2014), 141–142.

265. Paul Du Noyer, "Paul McCartney: The 2003 Interview for The Word," http://www.pauldunoyer.com/pages/journalism/journalism_item.asp?journalismID=179 (accessed January 5, 2015).

266. Doggett, *You Never Give Me Your Money*, 99.

267. One possible explanation for this is that Klein, who claimed in his November 1971 *Playboy* interview that "John had written most of the stuff" (Vetter, 98) under the Lennon/McCartney credit, genuinely believed that Lennon had written material that actually had been written by McCartney. If Klein was not merely attempting to flatter Lennon, but convinced that McCartney's contributions to the group were drastically outweighed by Lennon's, his treatment of McCartney makes more sense. Another possible reason is that Klein may have believed McCartney had no way to legally extract himself from the 1967 contract that bound the musician to the band for 10 years, and therefore poor relations between himself and McCartney did not matter. According to statements given by McCartney and Brown, Klein laughed when McCartney threatened to sue in order to extract himself from Klein's management, indicating that Klein did not take McCartney's threats (or the possibility that he might lose the lawsuit) seriously.

268. Gaddis, *The Landscape of History*, 59.

269. Alan Smith, "Beatles Are on the Brink of Splitting," *New Musical Express*, December 13, 1969, The Beatles Interview Database, http://www.beatlesinterviews.org/db1969.1213.beatles.html (accessed February 3, 2015).

270. David Wigg, "Scene and Heard: Interview with Ringo Starr," BBC Radio One, Jan. 21, 1969, The Beatles Interview Database, http://www.beatlesinterviews.org/db1969.0121.beatles.html (accessed February 3, 2015).

271. Ray Connolly, *The Ray Connolly Archives*, Kindle e-book, 69.

272. Ray Connolly, "The Day the Beatles Died," *Evening Standard*, November 27, 1969.

273. Alan Smith, "Beatles Are on the Brink of Splitting," *New Musical Express*, December 13, 1969, The Complete Beatles Interview Database, http://www.beatlesinterviews.org/db1969.1213.beatles.html (accessed February 3, 2015).

274. Miles, *Paul McCartney: Many Years from Now*, 563.

275. *Ibid.*, 564.

276. Paul McCartney, *McCartney* Press Release, April 9, 1970, The Beatles Interview Database, http://www.beatlesinterviews.org/db1970.0417.beatles.html (accessed February 3, 2015).

277. Lewisohn, *The Complete Beatles Chronicle*, 341.

278. Hedley Donovan, ed., "Music Review," *Time*, April 20, 1970, 57.

279. Kitty Empire, "A History of Rock Music: Paul McCartney Leaves the Beatles," *Guardian*, June 11, 2011, http://www.theguardian.com/music/2011/jun/12/paul-mccartney-leaves-beatles (accessed January 15, 2015).

280. Gaddis, *The Landscape of History*, 165.

281. *Ibid.*, 83–84.

Chapter Two

1. Paul McCartney, *McCartney* Press Release, April 9, 1970, The Beatles Interview Database, http://www.beatlesinterviews.org/db1970.0417.beatles.html (accessed February 3, 2015).

2. Doggett, *You Never Give Me Your Money*, 129.

3. Kitty Empire, "A History of Rock Music: Paul McCartney Leaves the Beatles," *Guardian*, June 11, 2011, http://www.theguardian.com/music/2011/jun/12/paul-mccartney-leaves-beatles (accessed January 15, 2015).

4. Greil Marcus, interview with Simon Reynolds, *Los Angeles Review of Books: Myths and Depths*, April 27, 2012.

5. Miles, *Paul McCartney: Many Years from Now*, 570.

6. However, McCartney gave this version of events publicly several times when Harrison was still alive and capable of refuting McCartney's statements, but Harrison never did.

7. Doggett, *You Never Give Me Your Money*, 154.

8. Wenner, *Lennon Remembers*, 8–10.

9. *Ibid.*, 35.

10. *Ibid.*, viiii.

11. Brocken and Davis, *The Beatles Bibliography*, 475.

12. Wenner, *Lennon Remembers*, 26.

13. *Ibid.*, 23–24.

14. *Ibid.*, 36.

15. *Ibid.*, 64.

16. *Ibid.*, 16.

17. Jon Wiener, *Come Together: John Lennon in His Time* (Chicago: University of Illinois Press, 1991), 4.

18. Brocken and Davis, *The Beatles Bibliography*, 475.

19. Wenner, *Lennon Remembers*, x.

20. *Ibid.*, 105.

21. *Ibid.*, 102.

22. Doggett, *You Never Give Me Your Money*, 153.

23. Bloch, *The Historian's Craft*, 140.

24. Brocken and Davis, *The Beatles Bibliography*, 475.

25. Jeremy Harding, "The Dream Is Over: Lennon in Search of Himself," *Guardian*, December 26, 2012, http://www.theguardian.com/music/2000/dec/21/thebeatles.johnlennon (accessed January 15, 2015).

26. Bloch, *The Historian's Craft*, 101.

27. Hertsgaard, *A Day in the Life*, 411.

28. Wenner, *Lennon Remembers*, 82.

29. Ray Coleman's 1985 edition of *Lennon: The Definitive Biography* provides one of the most glaring examples of this, and the work serves as a cautionary example of the methodological errors created by blindly accepting any testimony from a primary source. Coleman relates Lennon and Ono's version of events without question or verification, and uses *Lennon Remembers* and other breakup-era sources to present a one-sided history, something which Michael Brocken noted in *The Beatles Bibliography*: "He clearly does not have much time for Paul McCartney and so tries to convince the reader that John Lennon *was* the Beatles. Anything that went wrong was Paul's fault, while anything that was a success was down to John. Coleman uses any number of John Lennon's post–Beatles quotes to back up his arguments. But in 1971, John Lennon was very bitter and talked a load of rubbish after the Beatles split up, therefore quotes of him slagging off Paul, Magical Mystery Tour, Apple, etc. need to be carefully contextualized" (Brocken and Davis, *The Beatles Bibliography*, 115).

30. Another factor, which impacts *Lennon Remembers* but is not specific to it, is Lennon's tendency to exaggerate. Garraghan describes "an unconscious habit of exaggeration" as something that affects the accuracy of a witness (Garraghan, *A Guide to Historical Method*, 71). By these standards, Lennon's well documented and widely acknowledged tendency for hyperbole in both public and private statements must be taken into account when evaluating the accuracy of his testimony on specific issues and his overall credibility as a source when providing statements that cannot be verified or disproved by other sources.

31. James Startt, *Historical Methods in Mass Communication* (Northpoint, AL: Vision, 2003), 179.

32. *Ibid.*, 142.

33. Wenner, *Lennon Remembers*, xiv.

34. Ray Connolly, a reporter who knew and liked both Lennon and McCartney and was particularly close to Lennon, believes that cultural differences also played a role. Connolly argues that Wenner, an American, failed to comprehend the very English irony in many of Lennon's statements, or acknowledge Lennon's well known and documented tendency towards hyperbole. Connolly describes *Lennon Remembers* as an interview where Lennon's "tendency to exaggerate and go on a rant went unchallenged," and that Wenner failed to understand when the musician was being "straight faced, British 'tongue in cheek'" (Connolly, *The Ray Connolly Beatles Archive*, 250). In *Revolution in the Head*, MacDonald also acknowledges the contrast between understated English irony and the more telegraphed American style, which can lead to misinterpretations on both sides.

35. Bloch, *The Historian's Craft*, 111–112.

36. Doggett, *You Never Give Me Your Money*, 150.

37. Bloch, *The Historian's Craft*, 101.

38. Howard Massey, "Interview with George Martin," *Musician*, February 1999.

39. Pang and Edwards, *The Lost Weekend*, 252–253.

40. Pete Hamil, "Long Night's Journey Into Day: A Conversation with John Lennon," *Rolling Stone*, June 5, 1975, The Beatles Interview Database, http://www.beatlesinterviews.org/db1975.0605.beatles.html (accessed February 18, 2015).

41. John Lennon and George Harrison, Interview with KHJ 930-AM, December 21, 1974, https://www.youtube.com/watch?v=ffRqVXr9zwo (accessed March 2, 2015).

42. Sheff, *All We Are Saying*, 137.

43. *Ibid.*, 117.

44. Lennon's letter to Wenner protesting the interview's publication as a book was harsh and blunt: "I gave you an interview which was to run *one time only*, with *all rights* belonging to me. You saw fit to publish a book of my work without my consent—in fact, against my wishes—having told you many times on the phone, and *in writing* that I did *not want a book, an album, or anything else* made from it" (Draper, *The Uncensored History of Rolling Stone*, 142).

45. Wenner, *Lennon Remembers*, x.

46. Robert Draper, *Rolling Stone Magazine: The Uncensored History* (New York: Doubleday, 1990), 318.

47. *Ibid.*, 141.

48. Wenner, *Lennon Remembers*, xiv.

49. *Ibid.*

50. John Kimsey, "The Beatles for Sale and for Keeps," in *The Cambridge Companion to the Beatles*, edited by Kenneth Womack (Cambridge: Cambridge University Press, 2009), 241.

51. Brocken and Davis, *The Beatles Bibliography*, 489.

52. Startt, *Historical Methods in Mass Communication*, 19.

53. Tim Riley, *Lennon: The Man, the Myth, the Music—The Definitive Life* (New York: Hyperion, 2011), 509.

54. Bloch, *The Historian's Craft*, 64.

55. Connolly, *The Ray Connolly Beatles Archives*, Kindle e-book, 250.

56. Weiner, *Come Together*, 113.

57. Michael Frontani, "The Solo Years," in *The Cambridge Companion to the Beatles*, 153–182, 164.

58. McMillan, *Beatles vs. Stones*, 180.

59. Wenner, *Lennon Remembers*, 53.

60. Tom Doyle, *Man on the Run: Paul McCartney in the 1970s* (Edinburgh: Polygon, 2013), 61.

61. Keir Keightley's "Reconsidering Rock," found in *The Cambridge Companion to Rock and Pop*, provides an examination of the ideological conflict caused by rock's countercultural message being produced commercially for mass consumption.

62. Simon Frith, "Star Profiles," in *The Cambridge Companion to Pop and Rock*, edited by Simon Frith. (Cambridge: Cambridge University Press, 2001), 89.

63. Wenner, *Lennon Remembers*, 6–8.

64. C. Vann Woodward, "On Believing What One Reads: the Dangers of Popular Revisionism," in *The Historian as Detective: Essays on Evidence*, edited by R. Winks. (New York: Harper and Row, 1969), 24–38, 25.

65. C. Vann Woodward's definition of the "public's business" is as follows: "If as an individual, I decide that I dislike most people who speak with a particular accent, such an irrational fancy is my business: but if, as a teacher, I decide to bar from my class those same people, my fancy has become the public's business." Woodward, "On Believing What One Reads," 25.

66. MacDonald, *Revolution in the Head*, 2005, 375.

67. C. Vann Woodward, "On Believing What One Reads: The Dangers of Popular Revisionism," in *The Historian as Detective: Essays on Evidence*, 27.

68. Michael Frontani, "The Solo Years," in *The Cambridge Companion to the Beatles*, 162.

69. *Ibid.*

70. Paul Levinson, "A Vote for McCartney," *Village Voice*, October 21, 1971.

71. Wiener, *Come Together*, 39.

72. Norman, *Shout! The True Story of the Beatles*, 1981, 388.

73. Keir Keightly, "Reconsidering Rock," *The Cambridge Companion to Pop and Rock*, 110.

74. Mark Lewisohn, *The Beatles Day by Day: A Chronology, 1962–1989* (New York: Harmony, 1990), 141.

75. John Lennon, Interview by B.P. Fallon, *Melody Maker*, March 1969.

76. George Harrison, interview by

Howard Smith, WABC-FM, New York, May 1, 1970, broadcast May 3, 1970, The Beatles Interview Database. http://www.beatles interviews.org/db1970.04gh.beatles.html (accessed February 18, 2015).

77. *Ibid.*

78. Lewisohn, *The Beatles Day by Day*, 141.

79. Epstein, *A Cellarful of Noise*, 50.

80. Beatles Press Conference, Sydney Australia, June 11, 1964, The Beatles Interview Database, http://www.beatlesinter views.org/db1964.0611.beatles.html (accessed December 27, 2014).

81. Starr also described the incident where, upset over attempts by the other three to delay the release of his *McCartney* album, McCartney had physically intimidated him and thrown him out of his house.

82. McCabe and Schonfeld, *Apple to the Core*, 167.

83. The importance of the recorded disagreement between McCartney and Harrison during the *Let It Be* sessions has been overinflated by many works in Beatles historiography. This is due, in part, to Harrison's identifying it, in his trial testimony, as the reason for his departure from the sessions. Harrison repeatedly claimed that this disagreement, and general tensions between himself and McCartney over McCartney's domineering role, were the reason for his temporarily quitting the band. However, the *Let It Be* transcripts prove that the immediate reason behind Harrison's departure was a physical fight with Lennon. Harrison never acknowledged, either in his trial testimony or even in *Anthology*, that this conflict with Lennon instigated his departure.

84. McCabe and Schonfeld, *Apple to the Core*, 168.

85. *Ibid.*

86. Wenner, *Lennon Remembers*, 64.

87. Richard Williams, *Melody Maker*, April 18, 1970.

88. Connolly, *The Ray Connolly Beatles Archive*, Kindle e-book, 131.

89. Doggett, *You Never Give Me Your Money*, 163.

90. McCabe and Schonfeld, *Apple to the Core*, 184.

91. *Ibid.*, 187.

92. *Ibid.*, 189.

93. Many fans (although not all) eventually forgave McCartney his perceived role in breaking up the band, and McCartney's sustained commercial success serves as an indication of his mainstream popularity.

94. Doyle, *Man on the Run*, 39.

95. David Vetter, "Allen Klein: A Candid Conversation with the Embattled Manager of the Beatles," 89.

96. *Ibid.*, 98.

97. *Ibid.*, 90.

98. *Ibid.*, 92.

99. *Ibid.*, 104.

100. *Ibid.*, 95.

101. McCabe and Schonfeld, *Apple to the Core*, 152.

102. *Ibid.*, 98.

103. *Ibid.*, 100.

104. *Ibid.*, 151.

105. McCabe and Schoenfeld, "John and Yoko," *Penthouse*, October 1984, The Beatles Interview Database, http://www.beatles interviews.org/db1971.0905.beatles.html (accessed March 1, 2015).

106. Lennon, *The John Lennon Letters*, 214.

107. Wenner, *Lennon Remembers*, 32.

108. *Ibid.*, 76.

109. Connolly, *The Ray Connolly Beatles Archives*, Kindle e-book, 16.

110. Miles, *Paul McCartney, Many Years from Now*, x.

111. John Kimsey, "The Beatles For Sale and For Keeps," in *The Cambridge Companion to the Beatles*, 241.

112. These numbers are compiled from various sources, including *The Beatles Day by Day, The Beatles After the Breakup, Eight Arms to Hold You: The Solo Beatles Compendium, The Beatles Off the Record* and The Beatles Interview Database.

113. Ray Connolly, *The Ray Connolly Beatles Archives*, Kindle e-book, 250.

114. Norman, *John Lennon: The Life*, 589.

115. Paul Gambaccini, "Paul McCartney: The Rolling Stone Interview," *Rolling Stone*, July 12, 1979, http://www.rollingstone.com/music/news/paul-mccartney-the-rolling-stone-interview-19740131 (accessed June 3, 2015).

116. Pang and Edwards, *The Lost Weekend*, 93.

117. *Ibid.*, 253.

118. MacDonald, *Revolution in the Head*, 1994, 214.

119. Pang and Edwards, *The Lost Weekend*, 93.

120. Richard Merryman, "Paul McCartney: The Ex-Beatle Tells His Story," *Life*, April 16, 1971, The Beatles Interview Database, http://www.beatlesinterviews.org/db 1971.04pm.beatles.html (accessed March 1, 2015).

121. *Ibid.*

122. Chris Salewicz, *McCartney: The Definitive Biography* (New York: St. Martin's, 1986), 236.

123. McCartney would not admit this publicly until 1984.

124. Miles, *Paul McCartney: Many Years from Now*, 570.

125. McCabe and Schoenfeld, *Apple to the Core*, 174.

126. Chris Charlesworth, "Interview with Paul McCartney," *Melody Maker*, November 1971, The Beatles Interview Database, http://www.beatlesinterviews.org/db1971.11jp.beatles.html (accessed February 14, 2015).

127. *Ibid.*

128. John Lennon, "John Raps Paul," *Melody Maker*, December 4, 1971, The Beatles Interview Database, http://www.beatles interviews.org/db1971.11jp.beatles.html (accessed February 14, 2015).

129. Weiner, *Come Together*, 163.

130. Ben Gerson, Review of *Imagine*, Rolling Stone, October 28, 1971, http://www. rollingstone.com/music/albumreviews/ imagine-19711028 (accessed December 11, 2014).

131. *Ibid.*

132. John Lennon interview by Howard Smith, St. Regis Hotel, New York, September 9, 1971.

133. Tom Zito, "Peace, Love and Yoko," *Washington Post*, October 9, 1971.

134. Joshua Wolf Shenk, "Inside the Lennon/McCartney Connection," Slate.com, September 14, 2010, http://www.slate.com/ articles/life/creative_pairs/features/2010/two_ of_us/inside_the_lennonmccartney_ connection_part_1.html (accessed November 30, 2014).

135. Jack Breschard and Patrick Snyder Scumpy, "Sometime in L.A., Lennon Plays it as it Lays," *Crawdaddy*, March 1974, 54

136. "Too Many People" and "How Do You Sleep?" were not the only songs McCartney and Lennon wrote in this period that were directed at each other. McCartney responded to "How Do You Sleep?" with "Dear Friend," on his 1971 album *Wild Life*. Lyrical references to McCartney's songs such as "Yesterday" and "Getting Better" in Lennon's conciliatory 1973 song "I Know (I Know)" indicate the song might have been intended for McCartney. According to Alice Cooper, a friend of Lennon's during his "Lost Weekend," Lennon wrote "Instant Karma" about McCartney (Alice Cooper, Interview by Kim Mitchell, May 24, 2011). McCartney also indicated in a February 1985 *Playgirl* interview with Diane du Dubovay that Lennon said that the apologetic "Jealous Guy," from the *Imagine* album, was for him, but the claim is impossible to verify, and Lennon indicated elsewhere that the song was written for Ono. In *Come Together*, Wiener speculates that "Jealous Guy" may have been intended for both Ono and McCartney.

137. "John and Yoko Reply to Simon and Gill," Letters to the editor, *Melody Maker*, December 31, 1971.

138. Connolly, *The Ray Connolly Beatles Archives*, Kindle e-book., 127.

139. Lennon, *The John Lennon Letters*, 221.

140. Jack Breschard and Patrick Snyder Scumpy, "Sometime in L.A., Lennon Plays It as It Lays," *Crawdaddy*, March 1974, 54

141. Sheff, *All We Are Saying*, 178.

142. Robert Christgau, "Living without the Beatles," *Village Voice*, September 1971.

143. Ben Gerson, "Review of Imagine," *Rolling Stone*, October 28, 1971, http://www. rollingstone.com/music/albumreviews/ imagine-19711028 (accessed December 11, 2014).

144. Doggett, *You Never Give Me Your Money*, 170.

145. Miles, *Paul McCartney: Many Years from Now*, 584.

146. Ray Connolly, "I Remember the Real John Lennon, Not the One Airbrushed by History," *Telegraph*, December 4, 2010.

147. Lennon, *The John Lennon Letters*, 223.

148. Although parts of the Lennon and Ono interview with McCabe, known as part of their St. Regis interviews, made it into *Apple to the Core*, the full transcript wasn't available until 1984, when *Penthouse* published it.

149. *Apple to the Core* does include substantial transcripts from the trial, but does little to verify either side's competing claims.

150. McCabe and Schonfeld, *Apple to the Core*, 180.

151. *Ibid.*, 139.

152. *Ibid.*, 62.

153. *Ibid.*, 112.

154. *Ibid.*, 98.

155. Miles, *Paul McCartney: Many Years from Now*, 596.

156. Wenner, *Lennon Remembers*, 82.

157. Lennon, *The John Lennon Letters*, 214.

158. John Lennon, interview by Alan Smith, "Lennon/McCartney Songalong: Who Wrote What," *Hit Parader*, February 1972.

159. Sheff, *All We Are Saying*, 118.

160. Miles, *Paul McCartney: Many Years from Now*, 284.

161. Bloch, *The Historian's Craft*, 118.

162. Hertsgaard, *A Day in the Life*, 112.

163. *The Beatles: The Authorized Biography*, published in 1968 prior to the breakup (and with the pre-approval of all four Beatles) also repeatedly refers to McCartney as the primary author of "Eleanor Rigby." *The Beatles* attributes the song to McCartney, although Martin goes on to claim that the track demonstrates how the two men impacted each other's styles, arguing that McCartney would not have attempted to write "Eleanor Rigby" without Lennon's emphasis on the importance of lyrics (Davies, *The Beatles*, 285).

164. George Martin, interview by Jim Irvin, "Sir George Martin: The Mojo Interview," *Mojo*, March 2007, 59.

165. Miles, *Paul McCartney: Many Years from Now*, 232.

166. Shotton and Schaffner, *John Lennon: In My Life*, 123.

167. *Ibid.*

168. Sheff, *All We Are Saying*, 119.

169. Kenneth Womack, *Long and Winding Roads: The Evolving Artistry of the Beatles* (New York: Continuum, 2007), 184.

170. Gould, *Can't Buy Me Love: The Beatles, Britain and America*, 351.

171. Ray Connolly, *The Ray Connolly Beatles Archive*, Kindle e-book, 93.

172. Wenner, *Lennon Remembers*, 120.

173. Vetter, "Allen Klein: A Candid Conversation with the Embattled Manager of the Beatles," 98.

174. Startt, *Historical Methods in Mass Communication*, 174.

175. Even so, McCartney notably disputes Martin's interpretation of at least two of his songs, "Yesterday" and "When I'm 64," in Ray Coleman's *McCartney: Yesterday and Today* (Coleman, *McCartney*, 21).

176. Mark Binelli, "Paul McCartney: Now I'm Sixty-Three," *Independent*, October 22, 2005.

177. Paul Gambaccini, "The Rolling Stone Interview: Paul McCartney," *Rolling Stone*, January 31, 1974, http://www.rollingstone.com/music/news/paul-mccartney-the-rolling-stone-interview-19740131 (accessed June 3, 2015).

178. George Martin and Jeremy Hornsby, *All You Need Is Ears* (New York: St. Martin's, 1979), 31–32.

179. George Martin, interview by Jim Irvin, "Sir George Martin: The Mojo Interview," *Mojo*, March 2007, 57.

180. *Ibid.*, 259.

181. Cal Fussman, [qm]George Martin,[qm] *Esquire* 139, no. 1 (January 2003): 72, Academic Search Premier, EBSCOhost (accessed July 14, 2015).

182. Martin and Hornsby, *All You Need Is Ears*, 137.

183. George Martin, interview by Eliot Mintz, "The Lost Lennon Tapes," Westwood One, September 24, 1990.

184. Connolly, *The Ray Connolly Beatles Archive*, Kindle e-book, 274.

185. Wilfrid Mellers, *Twilight of the Gods: The Music of the Beatles* (New York: Viking, 1973), 32.

186. *Ibid.*, 153.

187. *Ibid.*, 182.

188. David Vetter, "Allen Klein: A Candid Conversation with the Embattled Manager of the Beatles," 106.

189. Jack Breschard and Patrick Snyder Scumpy, "Sometime in L.A., Lennon Plays it as it Lays," *Crawdaddy*, March 1974, 52.

190. Peter McCabe, "John and Yoko," *Penthouse*, Sept. 5, 1971, published October 1984, The Beatles Interview Database, http://www.beatlesinterviews.org/db19 71.0905.beatles.html (accessed March 1, 2015).

191. Keith Badman, *The Beatles: After the Breakup,1970–2000: A-Day-by-Day Diary* (London: Omnibus, 1999), 95.

192. Norman, *John Lennon: The Life*, 709.

193. Albert Goldman, *The Lives of John Lennon* (New York: William Morrow, 1988), 447.

194. Goodman, *Allen Klein*, 234.

195. *Ibid.*, 202.

196. Jack Breschard and Patrick Snyder Scumpy, "Sometime in L.A., Lennon Plays it as it Lays," *Crawdaddy*, March 1974, 52.

197. Derek Taylor, interview by Peter Doggett for *Record Collector*, August 1988.

198. *Ibid.*, 65.

199. Michael Bonner, "Paul McCartney: The Story of John and I," *Uncut*, October 2015, 46.

200. Norman, *John Lennon: The Life*, 591.

201. *Ibid.*, 590.

202. Riley, *Lennon*, 483.

203. *Ibid.*, 579.

204. Weiner, *Come Together*, 249.

205. *Ibid.*

206. Goldman, *The Lives of John Lennon*, 457.

207. According to Pang, Lennon deliberately chose to present a less confrontational and more likable image to the press during this period. Pang, *The Lost Weekend*, 88.

208. Alice Cooper, interview by Kim Mitchell, "Live and Uncut," Classic Rock Q107, May 24, 2011.

209. Pete Hamill, "Long Night's Journey Into Day: A Conversation with John Lennon," *Rolling Stone*, June 5, 1975, http://www.beatlesinterviews.org/db1975.0605.beatles.html (accessed February 18, 2015).

210. Paul Gambaccini, "Paul McCartney: The Rolling Stone Interview," *Rolling Stone*, Jan. 31, 1974, http://www.rollingstone.com/music/news/paul-mccartney-the-rolling-stone-interview-19740131 (accessed June 3, 2015).

211. Jack Breschard and Patrick Snyder Scumpy, "Sometime in L.A., Lennon Plays it as it Lays," *Crawdaddy*, March 1974, 47.

212. Lennon and McCartney saw each other numerous times during and immediately after Lennon's "Lost Weekend," and at one point in 1974 casually performed together, jamming with a group of fellow musicians in an L.A. studio, known as "A Toot and a Snore in '74."

213. Pete Hamill, "Long Night's Journey Into Day: A Conversation with John Lennon," *Rolling Stone*, June 5, 1975, http://www.beatlesinterviews.org/db1975.0605.beatles.html (accessed February 18, 2015).

214. Doggett, *You Never Give Me Your Money*, 266.

215. John Green, *Dakota Days: The True Story of John Lennon's Final Years* (New York: St. Martin's, 1983), 237.

216. Norman, *John Lennon: The Life*, 771.

217. Doyle, *Man on the Run*, 183.

218. The Beatles, *The Beatles Anthology*, 180.

219. Sheff, *All We Are Saying*, 126.

220. John Lennon's Word Association List, http://gothamist.com/2011/12/17/john_lennons_word_association_list.php (accessed June 5, 2015).

221. Pang and Edwards, *John Lennon: The Lost Weekend*, 277.

222. Miles, *Paul McCartney: Many Years from Now*, 584.

223. Ray Connolly, *The Ray Connolly Beatles Archives*, Kindle e-book, 250.

224. Philip Norman, *Shout! The Beatles in Their Generation* (New York: Simon and Schuster, 2005), 467.

225. Lennon, *The John Lennon Letters*, 375.

226. Sheff, *All We Are Saying*, 81.

227. *Ibid.*, 122.

228. Jack Douglas interview in *Beatlefan*, Issue 116, January/February 1999.

229. Lennon declared that he had written two songs: "Eleanor Rigby" and "Two of Us," that had been written primarily by McCartney. Lennon also claimed to have written most of the melody of "In My Life," crediting McCartney with only a small section of it. McCartney disputes this by arguing that he wrote the entire melody.

230. Michael Frontani, "The Solo Years,"

in *The Cambridge Companion to the Beatles*, 154.

231. Sheff, *All We Are Saying*, 157.

232. Jonathan Cott, *Days That I'll Remember: Spending Time with John Lennon and Yoko Ono* (New York: Doubleday, 2013), 198.

233. *Ibid.*

234. Robert Hilburn, *Cornflakes with John Lennon and Other Tales From a Rock and Roll Life* (New York: Rodale, 2010), 3.

235. Cott, *Days That I'll Remember*, 180.

236. John Lennon, interview by Dave Sholin, RKO, December 8, 1980.

237. Mark Lewisohn, *The Beatles Day by Day*, 193.

238. Robert Christgau, "John Lennon: 1940–1980," *Village Voice*, December 22, 1980.

239. Riley, *Lennon: The Man, The Myth, The Music*, 646.

240. Norman, *Shout!*, 2002, xviii.

241. Robert Draper, *Rolling Stone Magazine: The Uncensored History* (New York: Doubleday, 1990), 318.

242. *Ibid.*, 319.

243. Ray Connolly, "Unimaginable," *Daily Mail*, December 3, 2005.

244. Doggett, *You Never Give Me Your Money*, 279.

245. Ray Connolly, "I Remember the Real John Lennon, Not the One Airbrushed by History," *Telegraph*, December 4, 2010.

246. Michael Frontani, "The Solo Years," in *The Cambridge Companion to the Beatles*, 177.

247. Anthony DeCurtis, "Crossing the Line: The Beatles in My Life," in *Read the Beatles: Classic and New Writing on the Beatles, Their Legacy, and Why They Still Matter*, 306.

248. Abi Frost, "She Loves You, Yeah Yeah Yeah: John Lennon Memorial Issue," *New River Blues*, December 1980.

249. Robert Christgau, "Symbolic Comrades," *Village Voice*, January 20, 1981.

250. *Ibid.*

251. Christagu, "John Lennon: 1940–1980," *Village Voice*, December 22, 1980.

252. C. Vann Woodward, "On Believing What One Reads: the Dangers of Popular Revisionism," 35.

253. Gould, *Can't Buy Me Love*, 605.

254. Mark Saber Phillips, *On Historical Distance* (New Haven, CT: Yale University Press, 2013), 2.

Chapter Three

1. Gaddis, *The Landscape of History*, 136.

2. *Ibid.*, 85.

3. *Ibid.*, 79.

4. Randolph Hohan, "The Love They Take and Make," review of *Shout! The True Story of the Beatles*, by Philip Norman, April 5, 1981, http://www.nytimes.com/1981/04/05/books/the-love-they-take-and-make.html, (accessed October 20, 2014).

5. James Perone, "Shout! The Beatles in Their Generation," *Library Journal*, Vol. 130, no. 2, 2005, 576.

6. Norman, *Shout!*, Prologue.

7. John Harris, "The Best Books on the Beatles," *The Guardian*, Thursday, September 26, 2012, http://www.theguardian.com/books/2012/sep/26/beatles-best-books (accessed June 14, 2015).

8. Jay Cocks, "The Last Day in the Life," *Time*, December 22, 1980, http://content.time.com/time/magazine/article/0,9171,924600,00.html (accessed June 3, 2014).

9. Sheff, *All We Are Saying*, 116.

10. *Ibid.*, 162.

11. Brocken and Davis, *The Beatles Bibliography*, 349.

12. Peter Doggett, interview by John Carville, *Oomska*, October 10, 2010, www.oomska.co.uk/peter-doggett-interview/ (accessed September 12, 2014).

13. Phillips, *On Historical Distance*, xi

14. *Ibid.*, 2

15. Norman, *Shout!*, Prologue.

16. Jay Winter and Antoine Prost, *The Great War in History: Debates and Controversies, 1914 to the Present* (Cambridge: Cambridge University Press, 2005), 14.

17. Norman, *Shout!*, xiv.

18. John Harris, "The Best Books on the Beatles," *The Guardian*, September 26, 2012, http://www.theguardian.com/books/2012/sep/26/beatles-best-books (accessed June 14, 2015).

19. Norman, *Shout!*, 305.

20. Brocken and Davis, *The Beatles Bibliography*, 348.

21. Bloch, *The Historian's Craft*, 64.
22. Norman, *Shout! The True Story of the Beatles*, 340.
23. *Ibid.*, 340.
24. *Ibid.*, 385.
25. Gaddis, *The Landscape of History*, 114.
26. Startt, *Historical Methods in Mass Communication*, 153.
27. Garraghan, *A Guide to Historical Method*, 47.
28. Mark T. Gilderhus, *History and Historians: A Historiographical Introduction*, 6th ed. (Upper Saddle River, NJ: Pearson Prentice Hall, 2007), 47.
29. Norman, *Shout!*, xxviii.
30. Gaddis, *The Landscape of History*, 116.
31. Norman, *Shout!*, 484.
32. Philip Norman, "Sweet George," *Sunday Times*, December 2, 2001.
33. Norman, *Shout!*, xxviii.
34. Norman, *John Lennon: The Life*, 820.
35. John Harris, "Paul McCartney's Olympic Gig Will Crown a Decade of Continued Success," *Guardian*, June 14 2012, http://www.theguardian.com/music/2012/jun/14/paul-mccartney-olympic-gig (accessed January 2, 2015).
36. Alan Kozinn, "Author Who Annoyed McCartney Will Write His Biography," *New York Times*, April 16, 2013, http://artsbeat.blogs.nytimes.com/2013/04/16/author-who-annoyed-mccartney-will-write-his-biography/?_php=true&_type=blogs&_r=0 (accessed November 3, 2014).
37. Gaddis, *The Landscape of History*, 142.
38. Bloch, *The Historian's Craft*, 141.
39. Startt, *Historical Methods in Mass Communication*, 22.
40. Gaddis, *The Landscape of History*, 86.
41. *Ibid.*
42. Norman, *Shout!*, 1981, 100.
43. Miles, *Paul McCartney: Many Years from Now*, 74.
44. Norman, *Shout!*, 1981, 291.
45. Startt, *Historical Methods in Mass Communication*, 179.
46. Bloch, *The Historian's Craft*, 140.
47. Gaddis, *The Landscape of History*, 123.
48. Norman, *Shout!*, 1981, 258.

49. *Ibid.*, 243.
50. *Ibid.*, 335.
51. It is worth noting that many of the terms Norman uses to describe McCartney: "pretty," "pretty-faced," "sentimental" and "cloying," among others, are in heavily gender coded language. In his essay "Reconsidering Rock," Keir Keightley addresses the use of such terms by the rock and roll press: "An important part of rock's taste war against the mass mainstream is conducted in gendered terms, so that 'soft,' 'sentimental,' or 'pretty' become synonyms for insignificance, terms of dismissal, while 'hard,' 'tough' or 'muscular' become descriptions of high praise for popular music" (Keightly, *The Cambridge Companion to Pop and Rock*, 117). Richard Corliss agrees, and argues that this "feminine" association contributed to undervaluing McCartney's Beatles contributions. "Paul composed the group's top-selling single, 'Hey Jude,' its most widely covered tune, 'Yesterday' and much of its, most enduring music. He was the Beatles most versatile singer ... Yet Paul always shivered in John's shadow. Partly it was his looks. He was cute, coquettish—almost the girl of the group—so how could he be smart? He was the favorite of the girls at early Beatles concerts, but he was not a guy's guy. No way could he satisfy the male coterie of rock critics" ("That Old Feeling" *Time*, February 7, 2004).
52. *Ibid.*, 184.
53. Norman, *Shout!*, 2005, 548.
54. Philip Norman, interview by Allan Gregg, TVO, Friday, February 27, 2009, http://feeds.tvo.org/podcasts/video/AllanGreggInConversation (accessed June 14, 2015).
55. Norman, *Shout!*, 1981, 258.
56. Martin and Hornsby, *All You Need Is Ears*, 259.
57. Norman's assessment of Harrison's musical skills had not improved by 2005, the most recent edition of *Shout!* "George was not great; just an average guitarist who got incredibly lucky" (Norman, *Shout!*, 521).
58. John Harris, "Musicians and Writers Choose Their Favorite Book About Music," *Guardian*, June 26, 2015.
59. MacDonald, *Revolution in the Head*, 359.

60. Hunter Davies, *The Beatles: The Authorized Biography* (New York: W.W. Norton, 1982), lxi.

61. Yoko Ono, interview by Philip Norman, "Life after John," *Sunday Times,* May 25, 1981.

62. Hunter Davies, *The Beatles: The Authorized Biography* (New York: W.W. Norton, 1996), 372.

63. *Ibid.*, 368.

64. *Ibid.*, 372.

65. *Ibid.*

66. *Ibid.*, 373.

67. Miles, *Paul McCartney: Many Years from Now*, 283.

68. Brocken and Davis, *The Beatles Bibliography*, 420.

69. Shotton and Schaffner, *John Lennon: In My Life*, 52.

70. *Ibid.*, 171.

71. *Ibid.*, 171–172.

72. It was the first work to reveal Harrison's affair with Maureen Starkey, Starr's first wife, which was later verified in numerous other memoirs.

73. Brown and Gaines, *The Love You Make*, 85.

74. There is no way of knowing whether such an encounter between Lennon and Epstein actually occurred. Lennon confirmed the encounter to Hunter Davies, Pete Shotton, and Allen Klein, but Epstein's assistants Alistair Taylor and Tony Bramwell staunchly deny it.

75. Brown and Gaines, *The Love You Make*, 277.

76. Lewisohn, *The Beatles Day by Day*, 141.

77. Stephen Holden, "Review: Tug of War," *Rolling Stone*, May 27, 1982, http://www.rollingstone.com/music/albumreviews/tug-of-war-19820527 (accessed October 3, 2014).

78. Peter Carlin, *Paul McCartney: A Life* (New York: Simon and Schuster 2009), 264.

79. According to Lewisohn, McCartney's relations with Britain's *The New Musical Express* were particularly poor. When discussing McCartney's 1986 album *Press to Play*, Lewisohn declared that "*The New Musical Express ...* had loathed Paul for almost a decade. (A feeling which was mutual)" (Lewisohn, *The Beatles Day by Day!,* 141).

80. Brocken and Davis, *The Beatles Bibliography*, 124.

81. Robert Christgau and John Picarella, "Portrait of the Artist as a Rock and Roll Star," in *The Ballad of John and Yoko*, edited by Jonathan Cott and Christine Doudna (New York: Rolling Stone, 1982), 242.

82. Joan Goodman, "Paul and Linda McCartney's Whole Story," *Playboy*, December 1984, The Beatles Interview Database, http://www.beatlesinterviews.org/db1984.pmpb.beatles.html (accessed February 5, 2015).

83. *Ibid.*

84. *Ibid.*

85. Miles, *Paul McCartney: Many Years from Now*, 253.

86. McCabe and Schoenfeld, "John and Yoko," *Penthouse*, October 1984.

87. *Ibid.*

88. Robert Christgau and John Picarella, "Portrait of the Artist as a Rock and Roll Star," in *The Ballad of John and Yoko*, 252.

89. Peter Doggett and Patrick Humphries, *The Beatles: The Music and the Myth* (London: Omnibus, 2010), 58.

90. Sheff, *All We Are Saying*, 157.

91. George Harrison/Philip Norman Interview, 1988, https://www.youtube.com/watch?v=a0rMOznjnK0 (accessed December 4, 2014).

92. Ray Coleman, *Lennon: The Definitive Biography*, 2000, 12.

93. Ray Coleman, *Lennon: The Definitive Biography* (New York: HarperCollins, 1992), x.

94. Gaddis, *The Landscape of History*, 124.

95. Brocken and Davis, *The Beatles Bibliography*, 115.

96. Kate Turabian, *A Manual for Writers of Research Papers, Theses and Dissertations: Chicago Style For Students and Researchers*, 7th ed. Revised by Wayne C. Booth, Gregory G. Colomb, Joseph M. Williams (Chicago: University of Chicago Press, 2007), 134.

97. Brocken and Davis, *The Beatles Bibliography*, 115.

98. Coleman, *Lennon*, 1992, 363.

99. Coleman, *Lennon: The Definitive Biography*, 1985, 434.

100. *Ibid.*, 363.

101. *Ibid.*, 384.

102. By the time of his 1995 biography of McCartney, *McCartney: Yesterday and Today*, Coleman had amended his views, describing McCartney repeatedly as a genius and deriding those critics who "taunted him for his alleged superficiality" (Coleman, *McCartney*, x) without acknowledging that he had been one of them. The revised 2000 edition of *Lennon: The Definitive Biography* deletes Coleman's pronouncement of Lennon as the band's sole genius. Whether this shift was caused by the decline in the *Shout!* narrative's popularity, McCartney's agreement to grant Coleman extensive interviews for *Yesterday and Today*, a change in Coleman's own personal views, or his tendency to effusively praise his biographical subjects is not clear.

103. Frederick Seaman, *The Last Days of John Lennon: A Personal Memoir* (New York: Birch Lane, 1992), 177.

104. Ray Coleman, *Lennon: The Definitive Biography* (New York: Harper Perennial, 1992), 36.

105. *Ibid.*, 491.

106. Chris Salewicz, *McCartney: The Definitive Biography* (New York St. Martin's, 1986), 120.

107. *Ibid.*, 228.

108. Goldman, *The Lives of John Lennon*, 43.

109. *Ibid.*, 107.

110. *Ibid.*, 249.

111. *Ibid.*, 324.

112. *Ibid.*, 140.

113. At one point, Goldman describes Ono's physical appearance as "simian" (Goldman, *The Lives of John Lennon*, 316).

114. David Gates, "Lennon: The Battle Over His Memory," *Newsweek*, Oct. 17, 1988, 65–66.

115. Goldman, *The Lives of John Lennon*, 384.

116. *Ibid.*, 574.

117. David Gates, "Lennon," 64.

118. Hertsgaard, *A Day in the Life*, 326.

119. As with *Shout!*, none of the surviving Beatles agreed to be interviewed. Goldman did not ask Harrison or Starr. McCartney refused, at least in part, because he had intensely disliked Goldman's previous negative biography of Elvis, one of McCartney's boyhood heroes (Gates, "Lennon," 65).

120. *Ibid.*, 127.

121. *Ibid.*, 447.

122. John Lennon and Albert Goldman: The Making of a Bestseller," BBC4, 1988, https://www.youtube.com/watch?v=m19El1wEssg (accessed February 5, 2015).

123. Paul McCartney and George Martin, Interview by David Frost, *Today Show*, September 1988, https://www.youtube.com/watch?v=eIDwOAkfA1M (accessed July 6, 2015).

124. Norman, *Shout! The True Story of the Beatles* (New York: Sidgwick and Jackson, 2002), 428.

125. Gates, *Lennon*, 64.

126. *Ibid.*, 67.

127. *Ibid.*

128. Goldman, *The Lives of John Lennon*, 701.

129. Gates, "Lennon," 67.

130. Spitz, *The Beatles: The Biography* , 863

131. Gates, "Lennon," 73.

132. C. Vann Woodward, "On Believing What One Reads: The Dangers of Popular Revisionism," in *The Historian as Detective: Essays on Evidence*, 24–38.

133. Gates, "Lennon," 67.

134. Brocken and Davis, *The Beatles Bibliography*, 191.

135. Spitz, *The Beatles: The Biography*, 863.

136. Doggett, *You Never Give Me Your Money*, 297.

137. John Green, *Dakota Days: The True Story of John Lennon's Final Years* (New York: St. Martin's, 1983), x.

138. Garraghan, *A Guide to Historical Methods*, 59.

139. *Ibid.*, 70.

140. Julian Lennon, interview by Charles Gibson, *Good Morning America*, March 15, 1999.

141. Elizabeth Grice, "Dad Was a Hypocrite," *Telegraph*, May 23, 1998.

142. Dini Petty, Interview with Julian Lennon, March 18, 1999, https://www.youtube.com/watch?v=F815coz2A3s (accessed March 12, 2015).

143. Julian Lennon, interview by Charles

Gibson, *Good Morning America*, March 15, 1999.

144. Connolly, *The Ray Connolly Beatles Archive*, Kindle e-book, 233.

145. Julian Lennon, Foreword to *John*, by Cynthia Lennon (New York: Crown, 2005).

146. Coleman, *Lennon: The Definitive Biography*, 1985, 491.

147. Pang and Edwards, *The Lost Weekend*, 337.

148. *Ibid.*, 335.

149. *Ibid.*, 336.

150. *Ibid.*, 334.

151. *Ibid.*, 286.

152. *Ibid.*, 201

153. Doggett, *You Never Give Me Your Money*, 235.

154. *Ibid.*, 259.

155. Laurence Shames, "John Lennon: Where Are You?," *Esquire*, November 1980, 40.

156. Cynthia Lennon, *John*, 267.

157. Bloch, *The Historian's Craft*, 113.

158. Marius, *A Short Guide to Writing About History*, 35.

159. As stated in "The Dangers of Popular Revisionism" (Woodward, 36), one of the ways to control the past is by controlling access to the archives.

160. Norman, *John Lennon: The Life*, 819.

161. *Ibid.*, 820.

162. Philip Norman, interview by Paul Du Noyer, May 27, 2010, www.pauldunoyer.com.

163. Evidence supporting McCartney's claim to have originated the tape loops on "Tomorrow Never Knows" dates to a June 1966 interview he did with Alan Smith from *Hit Parader*. "We've got this track with electronic effects I worked out myself … we did it because I, for one, am sick of doing sounds that people can claim to have heard before," and is verified by Emerick and Martin.

164. Norman, *John Lennon: The Life*, 103.

165. *Ibid.*, 424.

166. *Ibid.*, 576.

167. *Ibid.*, 435.

168. Brocken and Davis, *The Beatles Bibliography*, 351.

169. Peter Doggett, Interview by John Carville, *Oomska*, Oct. 10, 2010.

170. Norman, *John Lennon: The Life*, 659.

171. Paul McCartney, interview by Howard Stern, "Paul McCartney on Lennon's Sexuality," November 15, 2012. https://www.youtube.com/watch?v=P-q0rVzl6vU (accessed May 11, 2015).

172. Norman had hinted at the topic in the afterword of his 2002 edition of *Shout!*, evidently prior to Ono's statements: "It almost suggests that, beneath the schoolboy friendship and complementary musical brilliance, lay some streak of homosexual adoration that John himself never realized" (Norman, *Shout!*, 411).

173. There is also testimony, again reliant entirely on hearsay, that Ono was sexually attracted to McCartney. According to John Green, her tarot reader, Ono confided in him that she was attracted to McCartney and initially pursued Lennon in an attempt to get McCartney's attention (Green, *Dakota Days*, 232).

174. Norman, *Shout!, The True Story of the Beatles*, 42.

175. This was an egregious misreading of Vaughn's own description of McCartney in Davies: "I knew this was a great fellow. I only ever brought along great fellows to meet John" (Davies, *The Beatles*, 22).

176. Norman, *John Lennon: The Life*, 103.

177. *Ibid.*, 643.

178. Norman, *Shout!*, 2002, 393.

179. Norman, *John Lennon: The Life*, 591

180. *Ibid.*, 624.

181. Norman, *Shout*, 1981, 360.

182. *Ibid.*, 416.

Chapter Four

1. Phillips, *On Historical Distance*, 2.

2. Cathy Booth, "Paul at Fifty: Paul McCartney," *Time*, June 8, 1992, http://content.time.com/time/magazine/article/0,9171,975715,00.html.

3. Ray Connolly, "I Remember the Real John Lennon, Not the One Airbrushed by History," *Telegraph*, December 4, 2010.

4. Michael Brocken and Melissa Davis, *The Beatles Bibliography: A New Guide to the Literature, Supplement 2013* (Manitou Springs, CO: Beatles Works, 2014), 86.

5. Ray Connolly, "Paul McCartney on

the Beatles: Anthology Part II," *Daily Mail,* November 30, 1995.

6. *Ibid.*

7. McCabe and Schonfeld, *Apple to the Core,* 202.

8. MacDonald, *Revolution in the Head,* 375.

9. Miles, *Paul McCartney: Many Years from Now,* 587.

10. *Ibid.,* x-xi.

11. Unlike most rock stars the McCartneys did not employ a nanny and by all accounts both parents were highly involved in the time-consuming day-to-day raising of their children.

12. The Paul McCartney World Tour, PaulMcCartney.com, http://www.paulmc-cartney.com/live/tour-archives/the-paul-mccartney-world-tour (accessed March 5, 2015).

13. Paul Du Noyer, *The Paul McCartney World Tour Booklet: 1989–1990* (New York: EMAP Metro, 1989), 51.

14. *Ibid.,* 85.

15. Lewisohn, *The Complete Beatles Recording Sessions,* 11.

16. John Kimsey, "Spinning the Historical Record," in *Reading the Beatles,* 197.

17. Lewisohn, *The Beatles Live!,* 9.

18. Hunter Davies, *The Beatles Lyrics: The Story Behind the Music, Including the Handwritten Drafts of More Than 100 Classic Beatles Songs* (New York: Little Brown, 2014), 16.

19. Lewisohn, *The Beatles Live!,* 9.

20. Malcolm Gladwell, *Outliers: The Story of Success* (New York: Little Brown, 2008), 50.

21. Davies, *The Beatles Lyrics,* 16.

22. Lewisohn, *The Beatles Live,* 11.

23. *Ibid.,* 87.

24. *Ibid.,* 69.

25. *Ibid.,* 178.

26. *Ibid.,* 4.

27. Brocken and Davis, *The Beatles Bibliography,* 289.

28. Lewisohn, *The Beatles Live,* 159.

29. *Ibid.,* 96.

30. *Ibid.,* 133.

31. Mark Lewisohn, *The Beatles Day by Day: A Chronology 1962–1989* (New York: Harmony, 1990), 112.

32. George Martin, Foreword to *The Complete Beatles Chronicle,* by Mark Lewisohn.

33. Lewison, *The Complete Beatles Chronicle,* 58.

34. *Ibid.,* 93.

35. *Ibid.,* 94.

36. *Ibid.,* 239.

37. *Ibid.*

38. *Ibid.,* 276.

39. *Ibid.,* 317.

40. Martin and Pearson, *Summer of Love,* xi.

41. *Ibid.,* 110.

42. *Ibid.,* 97.

43. *Ibid.,* 123–124.

44. *Ibid.,* 137.

45. MacDonald, *Revolution in the Head,* 2005, xii.

46. MacDonald, *Revolution in the Head,* 1994, 11.

47. *Ibid.,* 12.

48. *Ibid.,* 123.

49. *Ibid.,* 138.

50. Precisely when McCartney usurped Lennon's place as the band's dominant creative force is the subject of heated disagreement, in part because various authors tie the issue to the debate over who was the greater/sole genius. Authors such as Norman and Mikal Gilmore, both of whom argue that McCartney was not a genius, claim that McCartney did not surpass Lennon until the band's final albums, *Let It Be* and *Abbey Road.* Those authors, such as MacDonald and Lewisohn, who regard McCartney and Lennon as equal geniuses mark McCartney's creative dominance as occurring years earlier, most commonly in the period surrounding 1966's *Revolver.* Rodriguez also supports this chronology: "1966 marked the point where things began to shift. Paul's creative renaissance came just as John's point of engagement started to wane … *Revolver* marked the exact midpoint in the shift between dominance of the two top-tier Beatles" (Rodriguez, *Revolver,* 15).

51. Brocken and Davis, *The Beatles Bibliography,* 300.

52. MacDonald, *Revolution in the Head,* 1994., 137.

53. *Ibid.,* 272.

54. *Ibid.,* 277.

55. *Ibid.,* 33.

56. MacDonald, *Revolution in the Head,* 2005, xxi.

57. *Ibid.*, 1.

58. *Ibid.*, 269.

59. MacDonald, *Revolution in the Head*, 1994, 242.

60. *Ibid.*, 277.

61. *Ibid.*, 109.

62. Hertsgaard, *A Day in the Life: The Music and Artistry of the Beatles,* xi.

63. *Ibid.*, 111.

64. *Ibid.*, 77.

65. *Ibid.*, 114.

66. *Ibid.*

67. *Ibid.*, 146.

68. Davies, *The Beatles Lyrics*, 321.

69. However, by 2015 illegal transcripts of parts of the "Get Back" sessions were widely available on the internet.

70. Doug Sulpy and Ray Schweghardt, *Get Back: The Unauthorized Chronicle of the Beatles "Let It Be" Disaster* (New York: St. Martin's, 1994), 2.

71. *Ibid.*, 1–2.

72. *Ibid.*, 225.

73. *Ibid.*, 182–183.

74. *Ibid.*, 1.

75. *Ibid.*, 61.

76. While Lennon publicly denied in *Lennon Remembers* that he and Ono had ever injected heroin (Wenner, *Lennon Remembers*, 14) the "Get Back" tapes strongly argue otherwise. Sulpy recounts an instance where Lennon and Ono joke that the act of injecting heroin is one of the ways they get physical exercise (Sulpy, *Get Back*, 199).

77. *Ibid.*, 61.

78. Vetter, "Allen Klein: A Candid Conversation with the Embattled Manager of the Beatles," 98.

79. Doggett, *You Never Give Me Your Money*, 159.

80. Sulpy and Schweghardt, *Get Back*, 47–48.

81. *Ibid.*, 64.

82. Ibid, 169.

83. *Ibid.*, 169–170.

84. *Ibid.*

85. Sheff, *All We Are Saying*, 140–141.

86. Davies, *The Beatles Lyrics*, 68.

87. *Ibid.*, 170.

88. Sulpy and Schweghardt, *Get Back*, 2.

89. Several essays in *The Cambridge Companion to the Beatles* dispute this interpretation. In his article "On Their Way Home: The Beatles in 1969 and '70" Steve Hamelman argues that members of the film crew described the sessions as "lively" and "fun" (131). In "The Beatles for Sale and for Keeps," John Kimsey says the *Let It Be* film was edited by its director, Michael Lindsay Hogg, to look like it contained more conflict than it did. (242).

90. Startt, *Historical Methods in Mass Communication*, 179.

91. Paul McCartney, interview by Roger Scott, Capital Radio, December 1983.

92. Coleman, *Lennon: The Definitive Biography*, 1992, 31.

93. Paul McCartney, interview by Chris Dalhlen, *Pitchfork* Interviews, May 21, 2007, http://pitchfork.com/features/interviews/6612-sir-paul-mccartney/ (accessed March 3, 2014).

94. Mark Lewisohn, "Q&A With Mark Lewisohn," October 3, 2013, www.tunein book.com, (accessed March 13, 2015).

95. Garraghan, *A Guide to Historical Method*, 71.

96. MacDonald, *Revolution in the Head*, 2005, 380.

97. Doggett, *You Never Give Me Your Money*, 318.

98. The Beatles, *The Beatles Anthology*, 352.

99. *Ibid.*, 324.

100. *Ibid.*, 349.

101. *Ibid.*, 180.

102. *Ibid.*, 317.

103. *Ibid.*, 340.

104. *Ibid.*, 33.

105. Ray Connolly, "Hospitals, Gangs, Drums, and Ringo," *The Daily Mail*, Sept. 4, 2000.

106. The Beatles, *The Beatles Anthology*, 351

107. *Ibid.*, 356.

108. Norman, *Shout!* 2005, 525.

109. MacDonald, *Revolution in the Head*, 2005, 380.

110. Doggett, *You Never Give Me Your Money*, 318.

111. Maureen Cleave, "The Gospel According to Paul," *London Evening Standard*, August 26, 1993.

112. Miles, *Paul McCartney: Many Years from Now*, 501.

113. McMillan, *Beatles vs. Stones*, 220.

114. MacDonald, *Revolution in the Head*, 2005, 352.

115. Miles, *Paul McCartney: Many Years from Now*, Introduction.

116. According to McCartney this was a game that all four Beatles played to escape the tedium of endless, inane interviews. Whichever band member got the press to repeat the biggest lie won (Miles, *Many Years from Now*, xii).

117. Miles, *Paul McCartney: Many Years from Now*, x.

118. *Ibid.*

119. *Ibid.*, Introduction.

120. According to Miles, while McCartney retained final editing control, these two subjects—Linda McCartney's cancer and McCartney's relationship with Asher—were the only two topics where McCartney requested edits (http://barrymiles.co.uk/all-books/paul-mccartney-many-years-from-now/).

121. Miles, *Paul McCartney: Many Years from Now*, x.

122. *Ibid.*, xi.

123. *Ibid.*, 75.

124. *Ibid.*, 114.

125. *Ibid.*, 123.

126. *Ibid.*, 151.

127. *Ibid.*, 579.

128. *Ibid.*, 462.

129. *Ibid.*, 463.

130. *Ibid.*, 531.

131. *Ibid.*, 586.

132. *Ibid.*, 272.

133. Anthony Bozza and Shawn Dawl, *Rolling Stone Raves: What Your Rock & Roll Favorites Favor* (New York: Harper Perennial, 1999), 300.

134. Miles, *Paul McCartney: Many Years from Now*, 549.

135. *Ibid.*, 563.

136. *Ibid.*, 548.

137. *Ibid.*, 570.

138. *Ibid.*, 596.

139. *Ibid.*, xi.

140. *Ibid.*, 271.

141. *Ibid.*, 199.

142. *Ibid.*, 177.

143. Marius, *A Short Guide to Writing About History*, 59.

144. Gaddis, *The Landscape of History*, 103.

145. Hunter Davies, *The Beatles: The Authorized Biography* (New York: W.W. Norton, 2000), 406.

146. Doggett, *You Never Give Me Your Money*, 326.

147. Neil McCormick, "Must It Be Lennon or McCartney?," *The Telegraph*, January 10, 1998.

148. In his 2002 edition of *Shout!*, Norman disagrees; he argues that the public and press mourning for her was mainly an echo of England's hysterical grief for Princess Diana's death a short time earlier and had little to do with Linda herself. "An appetite still remained for a blond haired female martyr and Linda McCartney perfectly fit that bill" (Norman, *Shout!*, 496).

149. Tony Scherman, *Paul* (New York: Life, 2014), 79.

150. Ray Bonici, "Paul McCartney Flying on Clipped Wings," *Music Express*, April/May 1982, The Beatles Interview Database, http://www.beatlesinterviews.org/db1982.0400.beatles.html (accessed February 18, 2015).

151. Rebecca Hardy, "My Love for Linda," *Daily Mail*, October 17, 1998.

152. Davies, *The Beatles Lyrics*, 48.

153. Hertsgaard, *A Day in the Life*, 13.

154. Maureen Cleave, "The Gospel According to Paul," *London Evening Standard*, August 26, 1993.

155. Chris Taylor, "'Lovely Linda' Remembered," *Time*, April 20, 1998, http://content.time.com/time/nation/article/0,8599,10974,00.html (accessed May 12, 2015).

156. For some, this *gravitas* quickly evaporated upon McCartney's second marriage, to former model and land-mine activist Heather Mills. Their short-lived marriage produced one daughter, Beatrice, while their separation and contentious divorce produced reams of tabloid fodder. By the time their divorce was finalized, Mills had lost much of her credibility (Justice Hugh Bennett, the presiding judge over the McCartneys' divorce proceedings, described her as a "fantasist"). To date, her portrayal in Beatles historiography has been minimal and negative. Many sources argue that she pursued McCartney for his wealth and that McCartney, still grieving for his first wife, married her on the re-

bound: "Sir Paul was a sitting duck" (James Kaplan, *Paul McCartney: The Legend Rocks On*, 107). However, her accusations against McCartney, combined with her age (she was decades younger than McCartney when they married) dented his previously excellent reputation as a devoted father and family man.

157. Winter and Prost, *The Great War in History*, 13.

158. Robert Christgau, *Grown Up All Wrong: 75 Great Rock and Pop Artists from Vaudeville to Techno* (Cambridge, MA: Harvard University Press, 1998), 125.

159. Brocken and Davis, *The Beatles Bibliography*, 265.

160. Norman, *Shout!* 2002, 476.

161. Neil McCormick, "Must It Be Lennon or McCartney?," *Telegraph*, Jan. 10, 1998.

162. Wenner, *Lennon Remembers*, viii.

163. *Ibid.*, x.

164. Marius, *A Short Guide to Writing About History*, 26

165. John Kimsey, "Spinning the Historical Record," in *Reading the Beatles: Cultural Studies, Literary Criticism and the Fab Four*, edited by Kenneth Womack and Todd F. Davis (New York: State University of New York Press, 2006), 198.

166. Stephen Brier, Foreword to *Presenting the Past: Essays on History and the Public*, edited by Susan Porter Benson, Stephen Brier and Roy Rosensweig (Philadelphia: Temple University Press, 1986), xvi.

167. American Historical Association, Standards for Museum Exhibits Dealing with Historical Subjects, www.historians.org (accessed February 12, 2015).

168. John Kimsey, "Spinning the Historical Record," 198.

169. American Historical Association (accessed February 12, 2015).

170. John Kimsey, "Spinning the Historical Record," 198.

171. *Ibid.*, 212.

172. American Historical Association (accessed February 12, 2015).

173. John Kimsey, "Spinning the Historical Record," in *Reading the Beatles*, 207.

174. American Historical Association (accessed February 12, 2015).

175. John Kimsey, "Spinning the Historical Record," 205.

176. *Ibid.*, 245.

177. American Historical Association (accessed February 12, 2015).

178. John Kimsey, "Spinning the Historical Record," 203.

179. *Ibid.*, 205.

180. A 1999 interview (issue 116) in *Beatlefan* magazine with Jack Douglas, the producer of *Double Fantasy*, Lennon and Ono's last album, was also highly critical of Ono. Douglas argued that the couple appeared unhappy and rarely collaborated in the studio, defended Lennon's assistant Fred Seaman, and criticized Eliot Mintz (arguing that Lennon personally disliked Mintz, contradicting claims by Norman, Ono and Coleman that the two were good friends). Douglas claimed Ono refused to pay him his contractually guaranteed royalties for *Double Fantasy*, forcing him to launch a lawsuit in which he won a $3 million settlement. Douglas also indicates that Ono deliberately obstructed efforts by Lennon and McCartney to communicate with one another during this period. In terms of source analysis, Douglas's negative statements, while providing a balance to Ono's version of events, must be evaluated in the context of his lawsuit with Ono and the collapse of their professional relationship.

181. *Ibid.*, 212.

182. Marius, *A Short Guide to Writing About History*, 26.

183. Gaddis, *The Landscape of History*, 45.

184. MacDonald, *Revolution in the Head*, 2005, 473.

185. *Ibid.*, 13

186. MacDonald, *Revolution in the Head*, 2005, xii.

187. Norman, *Shout!* 2002, 410.

188. *Ibid.*, 504.

189. Doggett, *You Never Give Me Your Money*, 326.

190. Martin and Pearson, *Summer of Love*, 124.

191. David Simons, "The Unsung Beatle: George Harrison's Behind the Scenes Contributions to the World's Greatest Band," *Acoustic Guitar*, February 2003, 55.

192. MacDonald, *Revolution in the Head*, 2005, 383.

193. David Simons, "The Unsung Beatle:

George Harrison's Behind the Scenes Contributions to the World's Greatest Band," 56.

194. *George Harrison: Living in the Material World*, DVD, Directed by Oliver Stone (New York: Grove Street Pictures, 2011).

195. Steven Morris, "The Night George Harrison Thought He Was Dying," *The Guardian*, November 14, 2000, http://www.theguardian.com/uk/2000/nov/15/stevenmorris (accessed March 12, 2015).

196. Ray Connolly, "George: The Reluctant Beatle, 1943–2001," *The Daily Mail*, December 1, 2001.

197. Marilyn Fu, *Remembering George Harrison: 10 Years Later,* edited by Robert Sullivan (New York: Life, 2011), 8.

198. Paul Du Noyer, "George Harrison, An Obituary," *Blender,* Feburary/March 2002, www.pauldunoyer.com

199. Greil Marcus, "A Virtuoso Would Have Destroyed the Beatles," *The Guardian*, December 2, 2001.

200. Marilyn Fu, *Remembering George Harrison: 10 Years Later,* 13.

201. *George Harrison: Living in the Material World*, DVD.

202. Jean-Michael Guesdon and Phillipe Margotin, *All the Songs: The Story Behind Every Beatles Release* (New York: Black Dog and Leventhal, 2013), 630.

203. Lewisohn, *Tune In*, 705.

204. *Ibid.*, 4.

205. Hertsgaard described *A Day in the Life* as a biography of the band's music, not its members, and it does not follow the typical format of most Beatles biographies.

206. "New Beatles Bio Is Riddled with Errors," by Trina Yannicos and Shelley Germeaux, 2005, http://www.beatlesnews.com/news/the-beatles/200510280101/new-beatles-bio-is-riddled-with-errors.html (accessed June 1, 2015).

207. David Bauder, "Author Bob Spitz Obsesses over the Beatles," *Washington Post*, November 6, 2005.

208. Spitz, *The Beatles: The Biography*, 784.

209. *Ibid.*, 820.

210. Bloch, *The Historian's Craft*, 103.

211. Gaddis, *The Landscape of History*, 79.

212. Spitz, *The Beatles: The Biography*, 153.

213. The debate over the Beatles trading in their leather stage outfits for suits dates back to *Lennon Remembers*. In the interview, Lennon argues that the group "sold out" when, at Epstein's request, it adopted the new suits (Wenner, *Lennon Remembers*, 20). According to Lennon, he had protested the switch while McCartney supported it: Lennon used the example as evidence of McCartney's preoccupation with commercialism, as opposed to his own focus on authenticity. Multiple other sources including McCartney, Harrison, Shotton, Barrow, Bramwell and contemporary interviews with Lennon all dispute Lennon's claim that he protested and did not want to wear the suits. By the publication of *Tune In*, Lennon's claim that the suits had caused an open division within the group and particularly between himself and McCartney was largely dismissed as retrospective revisionism.

214. *Ibid.*, 671.

215. Hertsgaard preemptively disputed this statement in 1995, 10 years before Sptiz's biography was published. "To hear most Beatles books tell it, John and Paul could barely stand to be in the same room at this point" (the photo shoot of the *Abbey Road* album cover) "but in fact the two of them slipped back to Paul's house together to pass the time" (Hertsgaard, *A Day in the Life*, 295).

216. John Savage, "Beatles for Sale: Book Review, *Can't Buy Me Love*," *The Guardian*, December 15, 2007.

217. Gould, *Can't Buy Me Love*, dust jacket.

218. *Ibid.*, 573.

219. *Ibid.*, 513.

220. *Ibid.*, 536–537.

221. *Ibid.*, 49.

222. MacDonald, *Revolution in the Head*, 2d edition, 383.

223. Doggett, *You Never Give Me Your Money*, 133.

224. *Ibid.*, 289.

225. *Ibid.*, 292.

226. Emerick and Massey, *Here, There and Everywhere*, 232.

227. Bramwell, *Magical Mystery Tours*, 392.

228. Lewisohn, *Tune In*, 8.

229. *The Beatles Anthology*, 180.

230. MacDonald, *Revolution in the Head*, 2005, 193.

231. Doggett, *You Never Give Me Your Money*, 38.

232. *Ibid.*, 170.

233. One of the ways Doggett reinforces this claim is by acknowledging how traumatic the aftermath was for McCartney, declaring "His account of the spring and summer of 1970 reads like a textbook description of clinical depression" (Doggett, *You Never Give Me Your Money*, 135). In contrast, the *Lennon Remembers* narrative focused on Lennon's vocal pain and accepted McCartney's façade to the extent that, in 1975 *Rolling Stone* argued that "when it was finally over … it often seemed that John was the only one whose heart was truly broken" (Hamill, "Long Night's Journey Into Day," *Rolling Stone*, June 5, 1975).

234. Doggett, *You Never Give Me Your Money*, 153.

235. Mikal Gilmore, Why the Beatles Broke Up," *Rolling Stone*, September 3, 2009, http://www.rollingstone.com/music/news/why-the-beatles-broke-up-20090903 (accessed March 23, 2014).

236. Doggett, *You Never Give Me Your Money*, 12.

237. Mikal Gilmore, "Why the Beatles Broke Up: The Story Behind Our Cover," *Rolling Stone*, August 18, 2009, http://www.rollingstone.com/music/news/why-the-beatles-broke-up-the-story-behind-our-cover-20090818 (accessed March 23, 2014).

238. Bramwell, *Magical Mystery Tours*, 117.

239. *Ibid.*, 119.

240. *Ibid.*, 306–307.

241. *Ibid.*, 107.

242. *Ibid.*, 317.

243. Robson, Book Review, "Tony Bramwell: Magical Mystery Tours," December 2, 2011. www.Pauldunoyer.com (accessed January 12, 2015).

244. Bramwell, *Magical Mystery Tours*, 172.

245. *Ibid.*, 303.

246. *Ibid.*, 313.

247. Barrow, *John, Paul, George, Ringo and Me*, 68.

248. Emerick and Massey, *Here, There and Everywhere*, 87.

249. *Ibid.*, 11.

250. *Ibid.*, 102.

251. *Ibid.*, 324.

252. *Ibid.*, 100.

253. *Ibid.*, 212.

254. *Ibid.*, 109.

255. *Ibid.*, 65.

256. *Ibid.*, 304.

257. *Ibid.*, 7.

258. *Ibid.*, 255.

259. *Ibid.*, 276.

260. *Ibid.*, 324.

261. Martin and Pearson, *Summer of Love*, 126.

262. Emerick and Massey, *Here, There and Everywhere*, 83.

263. *Ibid.*, 101.

264. *Ibid.*, 102.

265. "Major Controversy Surrounding Geoff Emerick's New Book," April 1, 2006, http://newsgroups.derkeiler.com/Archive/Rec/rec.music.beatles/2006–04/msg00061.html (accessed March 12, 2015).

266. Mike Kovacich, "Geoff Emerick and Ken Scott Differences of Opinion on Some Events," March 1, 2007, http://www.maccacentral.com/news/2100/ (accessed March 12, 2015).

267. Ken Scott and Bobby Owsinski, *Abbey Road to Ziggy Stardust: Off the Record with the Beatles, Bowie, Elton and So Much More* (Los Angeles: Alfred Music, 2012), 66.

268. Robert Rodriguez also disputes Emerick's opinion of Harrison's musical skills in general and his account of why McCartney and not Harrison played the guitar solo on "Taxman" in particular. Emerick's eyewitness account argues that Harrison's inability to play the solo, despite repeated efforts, prompted Martin's request that McCartney do it. But according to Rodriguez, interviews with McCartney and Harrison do not mention Harrison attempting the solo at all. They argue that McCartney had an idea for the solo and asked to try it, Harrison agreed, and was (understandably) pleased with the result, widely regarded as one of the greatest guitar solos ever produced by any of the Beatles (Rodriguez, *Revolver*, 128).

269. Bloch, *The Historian's Craft*, 111–112.

270. Startt, *Historical Methods in Mass Communication*, 174.

271. Davies, *The Beatles Lyrics*, 1.

272. Richard Corliss and James Poniewozik, "Fateful Meetings," *Time: 80th Anniversary Edition*, March 30, 2003, 17.

273. Shenk, *Power of Two*, 257.

274. Mark Lewisohn, interview by Deidre Kelly, "Setting the Record Straight: Interview with Beatles Biography Mark Lewisohn, Critics at Large," July 30, 2014, http://www.criticsatlarge.ca/2014/07/setting-record-straight-interview-with.html (accessed March 17, 2015).

275. Mark Lewisohn, interview, London Beatles Day, October 20, 2013, https://www.youtube.com/watch?v=80crClQWHig (accessed March 17, 2015).

276. *Ibid.*

277. Lewisohn, *Tune In*, 679–680.

278. *Ibid.*, 651.

279. *Ibid.*, 663.

280. *Ibid.*, 690.

281. Davies, *The Beatles: The Authorized Biography*, 1968, 9.

282. Davies, *The Beatles: The Authorized Biography*, 1982, Foreword.

283. Lewisohn, *Tune In*, 41.

284. *Ibid.*, 42.

285. *Ibid.*, 247.

286. Garraghan, *A Guide to Historical Method*, 39.

287. *Ibid.*, 614.

288. *Ibid.*, 616.

289. *Ibid.*, 512–513.

290. Mark Lewisohn, interview by Deidre Kelly, "Setting the Record Straight: Interview with Beatles Biography Mark Lewisohn, Critics at Large," July 30, 2014, http://www.criticsatlarge.ca/2014/07/setting-record-straight-interview-with.html (accessed March 17, 2015).

291. Garraghan, *A Guide to Historical Method*, 42.

292. Lewisohn, *Tune In*, 656.

293. *Ibid.*, 17.

Bibliography

Works on History

For those interested in a nuts-and-bolts instruction of historical methods and source analysis, Garraghan's *A Guide to Historical Method* is essential. Startt's *Historical Methods in Mass Communication* offers a more modern, popular media-centric guide, necessary when dealing with a topic such as the Beatles. On Historiography, Gaddis's *The Landscape of History* offers new insight as well as instruction and analysis, while Bloch's *The Historian's Craft* remains one of the most important books ever written on subject.

Benson, Susan Porter, Stephen Brier and Roy Rosensweig, eds. *Presenting the Past: Essays on History and the Public.* Philadelphia: Temple University Press, 1986.

Bloch, Marc. *The Historian's Craft.* Trans. Peter Putnam. New York: Alfred A. Knopf, 1953.

Brands, H.W. *The Man Who Saved the Union: Ulysses S. Grant in War and Peace.* New York: Doubleday, 2012.

Breisach, Ernst. *Historiography: Ancient, Medieval and Modern.* Chicago: University of Chicago Press, 1983.

Gaddis, John Lewis. *The Landscape of History: How Historians Map the Past.* New York: Oxford, 2002.

Garraghan, Gilbert J. *A Guide to Historical Method.* Westport, CT: Greenwood, 1946.

Gilderhus, Mark T. *History and Historians: A Historiographical Introduction.* 6th ed. Upper Saddle River, NJ: Pearson Prentice Hall, 2007.

Kammen, Michael G. *Mystic Chords of Memory: The Transformation of Tradition in American Culture.* New York: Alfred A. Knopf, 1991.

Marius, Richard. *A Short Guide to Writing About History.* 2d ed. HarperCollins College, 1995.

Phillips, Mark Saber. *On Historical Distance.* New Haven, CT: Yale University Press, 2013.

Schiff, Stacey. "Rehabilitating Cleopatra." *Smithsonian*, December 2010. http://www.smithsonianmag.com/history/rehabilitating-cleopatra-70613486/?no-ist (accessed February 12, 2015).

Startt, James D., and William David Sloan. *Historical Methods in Mass Communication.* Rev. ed. Northport, AL: Vision, 2003.

Turabian, Kate L. *A Manual for Writers of Research Papers, Theses and Dissertations: Chicago Style for Students and Researchers.* 7th ed. Edited by Wayne C. Booth, Gregory G. Colomb, Joseph M. Williams. Chicago: University of Chicago Press, 2007.

Weinberg, Gerhard. "Hitler's Image of the United States." *The American Historical Review* 69, no. 4 (July 1964): 1006–1021.

Winter, Jay, and Antoine Prost. *The Great War in History: Debates and Controversies, 1914 to the Present.* Cambridge: Cambridge University Press, 2005.

Woodward, C. Vann. "On Believing What One Reads: The Dangers of Popular Revisionism." In *The Historian as Detective: Essays on Evidence*, edited by R. Winks. 24–38. New York: Harper and Row, 1969.

Works on the Beatles

Hundreds of books have been published on the Beatles. This work does not discuss all of them: Attempting to analyze every book would make a coherent historiographical analysis impossible. Those books which received historical analysis were selected for two reasons. The first was their overall influence. No discussion of Beatles historiography would be complete without *The Beatles: The Authorized Biography, Lennon Remembers* or *Revolution in the Head*. The second factor was the ability to use them as examples in applying historical methods or examining historiography. *Shout!* and *The Lives of John Lennon* provided an excellent opportunity to explore the issue of authorial bias in secondary works; *Magical Mystery Tours* offered the chance to discuss the issue of favoritism in memoirs; and *The Complete Beatles Recording Sessions* illustrated how the discovery of new primary sources often leads to the revision of existing narratives. Some of the most important works are listed numerous times in different editions. These revised and expanded versions of the same book offered an excellent window into how authors reinterpreted and revised their views (or failed to do so) from narrative to narrative as Beatles historiography shifted over the decades.

Anderson, Hildegard, and Elizabeth Hoover. *Life: Remembering John Lennon 25 Years Later*. Ed. Robert Anders. New York: Life, 2006.

Aronowitz, Al. *Bob Dylan and the Beatles: Volume One of the Blacklisted Journalist*. Bloomington, IN: 1stBooks, 2003.

Badman, Keith. *The Beatles: After the Breakup, 1970–2000: A-Day-by-Day Diary*. London: Omnibus, 1999.

_____. *The Beatles Off the Record*. London: Omnibus, 2008.

Barrow, Tony. *John, Paul, George, Ringo and Me*. New York: Thunder's Mouth, 2005.

Beatles, The. *The Beatles Anthology*. San Francisco: Chronicle, 2000.

Bozza, Anthony, and Shawn Dawl. *Rolling Stone Raves: What Your Rock & Roll Favorites Favor*. New York: Harper Perennial, 1999.

Bramwell, Tony, and Rosemary Kingsland. *Magical Mystery Tours: My Life with the Beatles*. New York: St. Martin's, 2005.

Braun, Michael. *Love Me Do: The Beatles' Progress*. New York: Penguin, 1964.

Brocken, Michael, and Melissa David. *The Beatles Bibliography: A New Guide to the Literature*. Manitou Springs, CO: Beatles Works, 2012.

_____. *The Beatles Bibliography: A New Guide to the Literature, Supplement 2013*. Manitou Springs, CO: Beatles Works, 2014.

Brown, Peter, and Stephen Gaines. *The Love You Make: An Insider's Story of the Beatles*. New York: Signet, 1984.

Carlin, Peter Ames. *Paul McCartney: A Life*. New York: Simon and Schuster, 2009.

Christgau, Robert. *Grown Up All Wrong: 75 Great Rock and Pop Artists from Vaudeville to Techno*. Cambridge, MA: Harvard University Press, 1998.

Coleman, Ray. *Lennon: The Definitive Biography*. New York: McGraw-Hill, 1985.

_____. *Lennon: The Definitive Biography*. New York: HarperCollins, 1992.

_____. *Lennon: The Definitive Biography*. London: Pan, 2000.

_____. *McCartney: Yesterday and Today*. London: Dove, 1996.

Connolly, Ray. *The Ray Connolly Beatles Archive*. United Kingdom: Plumray, 2011. Kindle edition.

Cott, Jonathan. *Days That I'll Remember: Spending Time With John Lennon and Yoko Ono*. New York: Doubleday, 2013.

Davies, Hunter. *The Beatles: The Authorized Biography*. New York: McGraw-Hill, 1968.

_____. *The Beatles: The Authorized Biography*. Rev. ed. New York: W.W. Norton, 1982.

_____. *The Beatles: The Authorized Biography*. Rev. ed. New York: W.W. Norton, 1996.

_____. *The Beatles: The Authorized Biography*. New York: W.W. Norton, 2000.

_____. *The Beatles Lyrics: The Story Behind the Music, Including the Handwritten Drafts of More Than 100 Classic Beatles Songs*. New York: Little, Brown, 2014.

DiLello, Richard. *The Longest Cocktail Party: An Insider's Diary of the Beatles*. Chicago: Playboy, 1972.

Doggett, Peter. *You Never Give Me Your Money: The Beatles After the Breakup*. New York: HarperCollins, 2009.

Doggett, Peter, and Patrick Humphries. *The Beatles: The Music and the Myth.* London: Omnibus, 2010.

Dowlding, William J. *Beatlesongs.* New York: Simon & Schuster, 1989.

Doyle, Tom. *Man on the Run: Paul McCartney in the 1970s.* Edinburgh: Polygon, 2013.

Draper, Robert. *The Uncensored History of Rolling Stone.* New York: Doubleday, 1990.

Du Noyer, Paul. *The Paul McCartney World Tour Booklet: 1989-1990.* New York: EMAP Metro, 1989.

Emerick, Geoff, and Howard Massey. *Here, There and Everywhere: My Life Recording the Music of the Beatles.* New York: Gotham, 2006.

Epstein, Brian. *A Cellarful of Noise.* New York: Doubleday, 1964.

Everett, Walter. *The Beatles as Musicians: Revolver Through Anthology.* Oxford: Oxford University Press, 1999.

_____. *The Beatles as Musicians: The Quarry Men Through Rubber Soul.* Oxford: Oxford University Press, 2001.

Flippo, Chet. *Yesterday: The Unauthorized Biography of Paul McCartney.* New York: Doubleday, 1988.

Frith, Simon, Will Straw and John Steet, eds. *The Cambridge Companion to Pop and Rock.* Cambridge: Cambridge University Press, 2001.

Fu, Marilyn. *Remembering George Harrison: 10 Years Later.* Ed. Robert Sullivan. New York: Life, 2011.

George Harrison: Living in the Material World. DVD. Directed by Oliver Stone. New York: Grove Street Pictures, 2011.

Gladwell, Malcolm. *Outliers: The Story of Success.* New York: Little, Brown, 2008.

Goldman, Albert. *The Lives of John Lennon.* New York: William Morrow, 1988.

Goodman, Fred. *Allen Klein: The Man Who Bailed Out the Beatles, Made the Stones, and Transformed Rock and Roll.* Boston: Houghton Mifflin, 2015.

Gould, Jonathan. *Can't Buy Me Love: The Beatles, Britain and America.* New York: Harmony, 2007.

Green, John. *Dakota Days: The True Story of John Lennon's Final Years.* New York: St. Martin's, 1983.

Harrison, George. *I, Me, Mine.* New York: Simon & Schuster, 1980.

Harrison, Olivia. *George Harrison: Living in the Material World.* New York: Abrams, 2011.

Hertsgaard, Mark. *A Day in the Life: The Music and Artistry of the Beatles.* New York: Delacort, 1995.

Hilburn, Robert. *Cornflakes with John Lennon and Other Tales from a Rock and Roll Life.* New York: Rodale, 2010.

Johns, Glyn. *Sound Man: A Life Recording Hits with the Rolling Stones, the Who, Led Zeppelin, the Eagles, Eric Clapton, the Faces...* New York: Blue Rider, 2014.

Kane, Larry. *Ticket to Ride: Inside the Beatles 1964 Tour that Changed the World.* Philadelphia: Running, 2003.

Kaplan, James. *Paul McCartney: The Legend Rocks On.* Ed. Stephen Koepp. New York: Life, 2012.

Lennon, Cynthia. *John.* New York: Crown, 2005.

Lennon, John. *The John Lennon Letters.* Ed. Hunter Davies. New York: Little, Brown, 2012.

Lewisohn, Mark. *The Beatles: All These Years, Volume I: Tune In.* New York: Crown Archetype, 2013.

_____. *The Beatles Day by Day: A Chronology, 1962-1989.* New York: Harmony, 1990.

_____. *The Beatles Live! The Ultimate Reference Book.* New York: Henry Holt, 1986.

_____. *The Complete Beatles Chronicle.* New York: Harmony, 1992.

_____. *The Complete Beatles Recording Sessions: The Official Story of the Abbey Road Years, 1962-1970.* London: Octopus, 1988.

MacDonald, Ian. *Revolution in the Head: The Beatles' Records and the Sixties.* New York: Henry Holt, 1994.

_____. *Revolution in the Head: The Beatles' Records and the Sixties.* 3d. ed. Chicago: Chicago Review, 2005.

Madinger, Chip. *Eight Arms to Hold You: The Solo Beatles Compendium.* Chesterfield: 44.1, 2000.

Margotin, Phillipe, and Jean-Michael Guesdon. *All the Songs: The Story Behind Every Beatles Release.* New York: Black Dog and Leventhal, 2013.

Martin, George, with Jeremy Hornsby. *All*

You Need Is Ears: The Inside Story of the Genius Who Created the Beatles. New York: St. Martin's, 1979.

Martin, George, and William Pearson. *Summer of Love: The Making of Sgt. Pepper.* London: Macmillian, 1994.

McCabe, Peter, and Robert Schonfeld. *Apple to the Core: The Unmaking of the Beatles.* London: Martin, Brian and O'Keefe, 1972.

McKinney, Devin. *Magic Circles: The Beatles in Dream and History.* Cambridge, MA: Harvard University Press, 2003.

McMillan, John. *Beatles vs. Stones.* New York: Simon & Schuster, 2013.

Mellers, Wilfrid. *Twilight of the Gods: The Music of the Beatles.* New York: Viking, 1973.

Miles, Barry. *In the Sixties.* London: Jonathan Cape, 2002.

_____. *Paul McCartney: Many Years from Now.* New York: Henry Holt, 1997.

Norman, Philip. *John Lennon: The Life.* New York: Ecco, 2008.

_____. *Shout! The Beatles in Their Generation.* Rev. ed. New York: Simon & Schuster, 2005.

_____. *Shout! The True Story of the Beatles.* New York: Simon & Schuster, 1981.

_____. *Shout! The True Story of the Beatles.* Rev. ed. New York: Sidgwick and Jackson, 2003.

O'Dell, Chris, and Katherine Ketcham. *Miss O'Dell: My Long Days and Hard Nights with the Beatles, the Stones, Bob Dylan, Eric Clapton and the Women They Loved.* New York: Touchstone, 2009.

Pang, May, and Henry Edwards. *John Lennon: The Lost Weekend.* New York: Spi, 1992.

Peel, Ian. *The Unknown Paul McCartney: McCartney and the Avant-Garde.* London: Reynolds and Hearn, 2002.

Produced by George Martin. DVD. Directed by Francis Hanley and Martin R. Smith. London: Grounded, 2012.

Reeve, Andru. *Turn Me On, Dead Man: The Beatles and the "Paul-Is-Dead" Hoax.* Bloomington, IN: SubRosa, 2004.

Riley, Tim. *Lennon: The Man, the Myth, the Music: The Definitive Life.* New York: Hyperion, 2011.

_____. *Tell Me Why: The Beatles, Album by Album, Song by Song, the Sixties and After.* New York: Alfred A. Knopf, 1988.

Rodriguez, Robert. *Revolver: How the Beatles Re-imagined Rock and Roll.* Milwaukee: Backbeat, 2012.

Rolling Stone. *The Ballad of John and Yoko.* New York: Rolling Stone, 1982.

Rosen, Robert. *Nowhere Man: The Final Days of John Lennon.* New York: Quick American Archives, 2002.

Salewicz, Chris. *McCartney: The Definitive Biography.* New York: St. Martin's, 1986.

Sawyer, June Skinners, ed. *Read the Beatles: Classic and New Writings on the Beatles, Their Legacy, and Why They Still Matter.* New York: Penguin, 2006.

Scott, Ken, and Bobby Owsinski. *Abbey Road to Ziggy Stardust: Off the Record with the Beatles, Bowie, Elton and So Much More.* Los Angeles: Alfred Music, 2012.

Seaman, Frederick. *The Last Days of John Lennon: A Personal Memoir.* New York: Carol, 1991.

Sheff, David. *All We Are Saying: The Playboy Interviews with John and Yoko.* Ed. G. Barry Golson. New York: Penguin, 1981.

Sheffield, Rob. *Talking to Girls About Duran Duran: One Young Man's Quest for True Love and a Cooler Haircut.* New York: Dutton, 2010.

Shenk, Joshua Wolf. *Powers of Two: Finding the Essence of Innovation in Creative Pairs.* Boston: Houghton Mifflin, 2014.

Shotton, Pete, and Nicholas Schaffner. *John Lennon: In My Life.* New York: Stein and Day, 1983.

Sounes, Howard. *Fab: An Intimate Life of Paul McCartney.* New York: DaCapo, 2010.

Spitz, Bob. *The Beatles: The Biography.* New York: Little, Brown, 2005.

Starr, Michael Seth. *Ringo: With a Little Help.* Milwaukee: Backbeat, 2015.

Sulpy, Doug, and Ray Schweghardt. *Get Back: The Unauthorized Chronicle of the Beatles "Let It Be" Disaster.* New York: St. Martin's, 1994.

Thomson, Graeme. *George Harrison: Behind the Locked Door.* New York: Omnibus, 2015.

Wenner, Jann. *Lennon Remembers.* New ed. London: Verso, 2000.

Wiener, Jon. *Come Together: John Lennon in His Time.* Chicago: University of Illinois Press, 1991.

Womack, Kenneth. *Long and Winding Roads: The Evolving Artistry of the Beatles.* New York: Continuum, 2007.

_____, ed. *The Cambridge Companion to the Beatles.* New York: Cambridge University Press, 2009.

Womack, Kenneth, and Todd F. Davis, eds. *Reading the Beatles: Cultural Studies, Literary Criticism and the Fab Four.* Albany: State University of New York Press, 2006.

Newspaper and Magazine Articles

While it is not required to fully cite newspaper articles, that methodology would be unhelpful regarding this particular historiographical subject. An enormous amount of Beatles historiography is presented in newspapers, magazines and popular media. Most interviews were conducted by members of the press. Some of the most influential sources in Beatles history, such as *Lennon Remembers*, were initially published as magazine articles. Furthermore, both the popular media and rock and roll press exerted enormous influence over how each narrative was shaped: The Beatles may be the first historical subject whose historiography was dominated by the media, rather than the church, government, or historians. As such, the numerous inaccuracies and biases that exist throughout Beatles historiography serve as a cautionary tale for anyone inclined to accept media coverage at face value. Under these circumstances, source analysis and documentation are essential. Readers do not trust a source they cannot find. All newspaper articles, including ones accessed online, are included in the chapter notes. Print and online magazine articles are listed below:

Bacon, Dorothy. "The Case of the Missing Beatle: Paul Is Still with Us." *Life*, November 7, 1969.

Bonner, Michael. "Paul McCartney: The Story of John and I." *Uncut*, October 2015.

Booth, Cathy. "Paul at Fifty: Paul McCartney." *Time*, June 8, 1992.

Breschard, Jack, and Patrick Snyder Scumpy. "Sometime in L.A. Lennon Plays It as It Lays." *Crawdaddy*, March 1974.

Cocks, Jay. "The Last Day in the Life." *Time*, December 22, 1980. http://content.time.com/time/magazine/article/0,9171,924600,00.html (accessed June 3, 2014).

Corliss, Richard. "Like Yesterday: America Meets the Beatles." *Time*, February 7, 2014. http://content.time.com/time/arts/article/0,8599,588789,00.html (accessed June 4, 2014).

Corliss, Richard, and James Poniewozik. "Fateful Meetings." *Time: 80th Anniversary Edition*, March 30, 2003.

Donovan, Hedley. "Music Review: Hello, Goodbye, Hello." *Time*, April 20, 1970.

Doggett, Peter. Interview by John Carville. *Oomska*, October 10, 2010. www.oomska.co.uk/peter-doggett-interview/ (accessed September 12, 2014).

Du Noyer, Paul. "George Harrison: An Obituary." *Blender*, Feburary/March 2002.

Gambaccini, Paul. "Paul McCartney in His Own Words." *Rolling Stone*, January 31, 1974. http://www.rollingstone.com/music/features/the-rolling-stone-interview-paul-mccartney-19740131 (accessed June 3, 2015).

Gates, David. "Lennon: The Battle Over His Memory." *Newsweek*, Oct. 17, 1988.

Gerson, Ben. Review of *Imagine*. *Rolling Stone*, October 28, 1971. http://www.rollingstone.com/music/albumreviews/imagine-19711028 (accessed December 11, 2014).

Gilmore, Mikal. "Why The Beatles Broke Up." *Rolling Stone*, September 3, 2009. http://www.rollingstone.com/music/news/why-the-beatles-broke-up-20090903 (accessed March 23, 2014).

_____. "Why The Beatles Broke Up: The Story Behind Our Cover." *Rolling Stone*, August 18, 2009. http://www.rollingstone.com/music/news/why-the-beatles-broke-up-the-story-behind-our-cover-20090818 (accessed March 23, 2014).

Goldman, Julie. "The Two Women Who Broke Up the Beatles." *McCall's*, July 1971.

Grien, Paul. Interview with George Martin. "Martin/McCartney 'Tug' Team Scores." *Billboard*, February 26, 1983.

Heller, Zoe. "Moll of Kintyre." *Vanity Fair*, October 1992.

Holden, Stephen. "Review: Tug of War." *Rolling Stone*, May 27, 1982. http://www.

rollingstone.com/music/albumreviews/ tug-of-war-19820527 (accessed October 3, 2014).

Irvin, Jim. "Sir George Martin: The Mojo Interview" *Mojo,* March 2007.

Kopp, David Marshall. "Linking Differences in Self-Directed Learning Competency to Dyadic Conflict: An Instrumental Case Study of the Leadership Dyad of John Lennon and Paul McCartney." In *Twenty-First Century Approaches in Self Directed Learning* (Huey B. Long, 2003), 56–74.

Massey, Howard. "Interview with George Martin." *Musician,* February 1999.

Marcus, Greil. "Interview with Simon Reynolds." *Los Angeles Review of Books: Myths and Depths,* April 27, 2012.

McCartney, Paul. Interview by Chris Dalhlen. *Pitchfork Interviews,* May 21, 2007. http://pitchfork.com/features/interviews/6612-sir-paul-mccartney/ (accessed March 3, 2014).

Mewborn, Brant. "Ringo Starr in the Afternoon." *Rolling Stone* April 30, 1981. http://www.rollingstone.com/music/features/ringo-in-the-afternoon-19810430 (accessed May 4, 2015).

Moldana, Michael. "His Majesty's Ears: An Interview with George Martin." *Guitar Player,* December 1998.

Perone, James. "Shout! The Beatles in Their Generation." *Library Journal* vol. 130, no. 2 (2005).

Shames, Laurence. "John Lennon, Where Are You?" *Esquire,* November 1980.

Shenk, Joshua Wolf. "Inside the Lennon/ McCartney Connection." Slatewww, September 14, 2010. http://www.slate.com/articles/life/creative_pairs/features/2010/two_of_us/inside_the_lennonmccartney_connection_part_1.html (accessed November 30, 2014).

Simons, David. "The Unsung Beatle: George Harrison's Behind the Scenes Contributions to the World's Greatest Band." *Acoustic Guitar,* February 2003.

Taylor, Chris. "'Lovely Linda' Remembered." *Time,* April 20, 1998. http://content.time.com/time/nation/article/0,8599,10974,00.html (accessed May 12, 2015).

Tresniowski, Alex. "Paul's Lovely Linda." *People,* May 4, 1998.

Vetter, David. "A Candid Conversation with the Embattled Manager of the Beatles." *Playboy,* November 1971.

Internet Sources (Chronological)

The Beatles, and everything to do with them, are exhaustively discussed on countless websites and forums. Many of the same topics that are debated in books and magazines (Lennon vs. McCartney? Who is responsible for the breakup? What is their greatest album?) are avidly debated by fans. An enormous and impressive amount of fan-driven scholarship exists on these websites. In addition, Beatles fans have a very low tolerance for factual errors in professional publications. Some of the debates center on the band's historiography, debating the merits of various biographies, memoirs and reference books. What impact this fan-driven interpretation of Beatles history, propelled by the internet, has on the band's historiography will be fascinating and informative to watch as it unfolds.

www.youtube.com offers a range of Beatles-related videos, including performances, interviews and press conferences. Sources cited from this website include the following, listed in chronological order of creation:

John Lennon/George Harrison, interview with KHJ, 930 AM, December 21, 1974. https://www.youtube.com/watch?v=ffRqVXr9zwo (accessed March 2, 2015).

George Harrison/Philip Norman Interview, 1988. https://www.youtube.com/watch?v=a0rMOznjnK0 (accessed December 4, 2014).

"John Lennon and Albert Goldman: The Making of a Bestseller," BBC4, 1988. https://www.youtube.com/watch?v=m19Ell1wEssg (accessed February 5, 2015).

Paul McCartney and George Martin, Interview by David Frost, *Today Show,* September 1988. https://www.youtube.com/watch?v=eIDwOAkfA1M (accessed July 6, 2015).

"Albert Goldman v. Hunter Davies," BBC 1989. https://www.youtube.com/watch?v=hiltVC3uAh8 (accessed November 22, 2014).

Dini Petty, interview with Julian Lennon, March 18, 1999. https://www.youtube.com/watch?v=F815coz2A3s (accessed March 12, 2015).

Paul McCartney, interview by Howard Stern, "Paul McCartney on Lennon's Sexuality," November 15, 2012. https://www.youtube.com/watch?v=P-q0rVz16vU (accessed May 11, 2015).

Mark Lewisohn, interview, London Beatles Day, October 20, 2013. https://www.youtube.com/watch?v=80crClQWHig (accessed March 17, 2015).

The Beatles Interview Database, www.beatlesinterviews.org, offers transcripts of dozens of Beatles interviews and press conferences, from 1962 to 1984. Sources cited from this website include the following, listed in chronological order:

Monty Lister, interview with the Beatles. Radio Clatterbridge, October 10, 1962. http://www.beatlesinterviews.org/db1962.1028.beatles.html (accessed January 14, 2015).

Beatles interview by Phil Tate. *Non Stop Pop*, BBC, July 30, 1963. http://www.beatlesinterviews.org/db1963.0730.beatles.html (accessed January 3, 2015).

Beatles interview with Frank Hall. RTE, Dublin, Ireland, November 7, 1963. http://www.beatlesinterviews.org/db1963.1107.beatles.html (accessed February 3, 2015).

Beatles, interview by Frank Hall. Doncaster, England, December 10, 1963. http://www.beatlesinterviews.org/db1963.1210.beatles.html (accessed January 4, 2015).

Beatles Press Conference. Sydney, Australia, June 11, 1964. http://www.beatlesinterviews.org/db1964.0611.beatles.html (accessed December 27, 2014).

"George Interviews George." *The Beatles Book*, November 1964. http://www.beatlesinterviews.org/db1964.1100.beatles.html (accessed January 27, 2015).

Beatles Press Conference. Tokyo Hilton, June 30, 1966. http://www.beatlesinterviews.org/db1966.0629.beatles.html (accessed January 14, 2015).

Beatles Press Conference. Tokyo, Japan, June 30, 1966. http://www.beatlesinterviews.org/db1966.0630.beatles.html (accessed January 14, 2015).

Beatles Press Conference. Edgewater Inn, Seattle, August 25, 1966. http://www.beatlesinterviews.org/db1966.0825.beatles.html (accessed January 5, 2015).

Interview with George Harrison. *Beatles Book Monthly*, October 1966. http://www.beatlesinterviews.org/db1966.10gh.beatles.html (accessed January 11, 2015).

Interview with Paul McCartney, Thomas Thompson. "The New Far Out Beatles," *Hit Parader*, May 1967. http://www.beatlesinterviews.org/db1967.05HP.beatles.html (accessed January 29, 2015).

Norrie Drummond. "Beatle Paul's New Life." *New Musical Express*, September 1967. http://www.beatlesinterviews.org/db1967.0909.beatles.html (accessed March 2, 2015).

John Lennon and Paul McCartney. Interview by Joe Garagiola, *The Tonight Show*, NBC, May 14, 1968. http://www.beatlesinterviews.org/db1968.05ts.beatles.html (accessed January 29, 2015).

David Wigg, "Scene and Heard: Interview with Ringo Starr." BBC Radio One, Jan 21, 1969. http://www.beatlesinterviews.org/db1969.0121.beatles.html (accessed February 3, 2015).

Nick Logan, "An Interview with Ringo." *Hit Parader*, March 13, 1969, published October 1969. http://www.beatlesinterviews.org/db1969.10rs.beatles.html (accessed January 29, 2015).

Alan Smith, "Beatles Music Straightforward on New Album." *New Musical Express*, May 3, 1969. http://www.beatlesinterviews.org/db1969.0503.beatles.html (accessed January 29, 2015).

Alan Smith, "Beatles Are on the Brink of Splitting." *New Musical Express*, December 13, 1969. http://www.beatlesinterviews.org/db1969.1213.beatles.html (accessed February 3, 2015).

Paul McCartney. *McCartney* Press Release, April 9, 1970. http://www.beatlesinterviews.org/db1970.0417.beatles.html (accessed February 3, 2015).

Howard Smith. Interview with George Harrison, WABC New York, May 1, 1970. http://www.beatlesinterviews.org/db1970.04gh.beatles.html (accessed February 18, 2015).

Richard Merryman. "Paul McCartney: The Ex-Beatle Tells His Story," *Life*, April 16,

1971. http://www.beatlesinterviews.org/db1971.04pm.beatles.html (accessed March 1, 2015).

Chris Charlesworth. "Interview with Paul McCartney," *Melody Maker*, November 1971. http://www.beatlesinterviews.org/db1971.11jp.beatles.html (accessed February 14, 2015).

John Lennon. "John Raps Paul," *Melody Maker*, December 4, 1971. http://www.beatlesinterviews.org/db1971.11jp.beatles.html (accessed February 14, 2015).

Pete Hamill. "Long Night's Journey Into Day: A Conversation with John Lennon," *Rolling Stone*, June 5, 1975. http://www.beatlesinterviews.org/db1975.0605.beatles.html (accessed February 18, 2015).

Ray Bonici. "Paul McCartney Flying on Clipped Wings," *Music Express*, April/May 1982. http://www.beatlesinterviews.org/db1982.0400.beatles.html (accessed February 18, 2015).

McCabe and Schoenfeld. "John and Yoko," *Penthouse*, October 1984. http://www.beatlesinterviews.org/db1971.0905.beatles.html (accessed March 1, 2015).

Joan Goodman. "Paul and Linda McCartney's Whole Story," *Playboy*, December 1984. http://www.beatlesinterviews.org/db1984.pmpb.beatles.html (accessed February 5, 2015).

Additional Internet Sources

American Historical Association, Standards for Museum Exhibits Dealing with Historical Subjects. www.historians.org (accessed February 12, 2015).

Lewisohn, Mark. "Q&A with Mark Lewisohn." October 3, 2013. www.tuneinbook.com, (accessed March 13, 2015).

Norman, Philip. Interview by Allan Gregg. TVO, February 27, 2009. http://feeds.tvo.org/podcasts/video/AllanGreggInConversation (accessed June 14, 2015).

The Paul McCartney World Tour. PaulMcCartney.com. http://www.paulmccartney.com/live/tour-archives/the-paul-mc-cartney-world-tour (accessed March 5, 2015).

"Tony Bramwell: Magical Mystery Tours." Book Review, December 2, 2011. www.Pauldunoyer.com (accessed January 12, 2015).

Yannicos, Trina, and Shelley Germeaux. "New Beatles Bio Is Riddled with Errors." 2005. http://www.beatlesnews.com/news/the-beatles/200510280101/new-beatles-bio-is-riddled-with-errors.html (accessed June 1, 2015).

Index